FRM 一级习题与解析

（上）

融跃教育 FRM 研究院　编著

立信会计出版社
LIXIN ACCOUNTING PUBLISHING HOUSE

图书在版编目(CIP)数据

FRM 一级习题与解析 / 融跃教育 FRM 研究院编著. —
上海：立信会计出版社，2020.5
ISBN 978-7-5429-6476-2

Ⅰ.①F… Ⅱ.①融… Ⅲ.①金融风险—风险管理—资格考试—题解 Ⅳ.①F830.9-44

中国版本图书馆 CIP 数据核字(2020)第 077147 号

策划编辑　方士华　孙　勇
责任编辑　方士华　孙　勇

FRM 一级习题与解析(全两册)
FRM Yiji Xiti Yu Jiexi

出版发行	立信会计出版社		
地　　址	上海市中山西路 2230 号	邮政编码	200235
电　　话	(021)64411389	传　　真	(021)64411325
网　　址	www.lixinaph.com	电子邮箱	lixinaph2019@126.com
网上书店	http://lixin.jd.com		http://lxkjcbs.tmall.com
经　　销	各地新华书店		

印　　刷	河南美图印刷有限公司		
开　　本	787 毫米×1092 毫米	1/16	
印　　张	24.75		
字　　数	602 千字		
版　　次	2020 年 5 月第 1 版		
印　　次	2020 年 5 月第 1 次		
书　　号	ISBN 978-7-5429-6476-2/F		
定　　价	159.00 元		

F 序
OREWORD

本书是 FRM 一级考试的精讲阶段习题集，由融跃教育 FRM 研究院精心编纂而成，主要是为了帮助同学们在学习精讲阶段后进行相应的课后练习。同学们每学完一个单元之后，可以做本书的相关练习题进行巩固；也可以在第一轮复习时将本习题集同步做完。

本书内容分成 4 个部分 18 个单元，题量超过 1 100 题。其中，第一部分是风险管理基础，一共 4 个单元 187 题；第二部分是数量分析，一共 4 个单元 214 题；第三部分是金融市场和产品，一共 5 个单元 309 题；第四部分是估值和风险模型，一共 5 个单元 397 题。

由于 FRM 的考纲在不同部分有一定的重叠，为了避免缺漏，我们对少量经典题目在不同部分做了复现的处理；另外，对于 FRM 考纲中未涉及、但是仍可能考到的基础知识（例如，现代资产组合理论、计算器的使用、债券的基础定价等）我们也在相应章节安排了一定数量的习题帮助同学们巩固基础知识。

通过本书掌握知识点，后续再通过融跃教育的押题习题集适应考试内容和风格，相信同学们将获得更多的学习优势，并信心满满地走入考场。

最后，感谢同学们选择融跃教育，预祝同学们在 FRM 考试中取得好成绩！

融跃教育 FRM 研究院

2020 年 1 月

目 录
CONTENTS

第一部分 风险管理基础

第二部分 数量分析

第三部分 金融市场和产品

第四部分 估值和风险模型

第一部分

风险管理基础

第 1 单元

风险管理基础知识

1. Which of the following risks is best described as a financial risk? (　　)
   A) credit risk
   B) business risk
   C) strategy risk
   D) operational risk

2. What is funding liquidity? It is a risk (　　).
   A) resulting from a large position size in an asset relative to the trading volume
   B) that a firm will decide to terminate a business
   C) that an institution may fail to raise cash necessary to make debt payments
   D) that a counterparty to a financial transaction may default

3. Liquidity risk is most associated with (　　).
   A) the probability of default
   B) a widening bid-ask spread
   C) a poorly functioning market
   D) volatility of asset price

4. When a financial institution is planning to exit a position at a fair price, it may incur losses because it is hard to find a counterparty in the market in a short time. What is the most possible type of risk? (　　)
   A) market risk
   B) liquidity risk
   C) operational risk
   D) credit event risk

5. An investment manager is given the task of beating a benchmark. Hence the risk should be measured in terms of (　　).
   A) loss relative to the initial investment

B) loss relative to the expected portfolio value
C) loss relative to the benchmark
D) loss attributed to the benchmark

6. An example of a non-financial risk is (   ).
A) credit risk
B) market risk
C) liquidity risk
D) settlement risk

7. Which of the following can be best used to describe the volatility of total returns? (   )
A) relative risk
B) absolute risk
C) directional risk
D) non-directional risk

8. For individual investors, risk management is most concerned with (   ).
A) avoid risk exposures
B) hedging risk exposures
C) maximizing utility while bearing a tolerable level of risk
D) maximizing utility while avoiding exposure to undesirable risks

9. In an investment bank, James used an equation that is proved to be mis-specified on some important coefficients. The risk of losses in this situation is (   ).
A) measurement risk
B) forecasting risk
C) model risk
D) sovereign risk

10. An asset may have price volatility due to its characteristics. We can expect volatility by different models. However, there can be unexpected volatility. We can view the unexpected volatility as (   ).
A) asset price instability
B) a businesssurprise
C) price risk
D) biased expectations

11. Many risks can be categorized as operation risks. In the following risks, all are

operational risks except (　　).

A) risk from competitors that may develop a better product/service

B) risk of business operation inefficiency and ineffectiveness

C) risk from inability of information technology to function in a changing operational environment due to obsolescence

D) risk of incompetent leadership in the management team

12. If a counterparty fails to deliver its obligation, we call this kind of risk as (　　).

A) delivery risk

B) settlement risk

C) liquidity risk

D) people risk

13. Jeffery Bautista is investing in a bond issued by a developing country, hoping for higher yield. However, his risk manager reminds him that there can be more risks than domestic investing. Jeffery admits that the developing country may fail to repay its debt. We call this kind of risk (　　).

A) settlement risk

B) repayment risk

C) recovery rate risk

D) sovereign risk

14. Whether to hedge or which specific risk factors should be hedged are usually determined by the help from board of directors. Which of the following statements is incorrect about the role of the board? (　　)

A) The board does not need to consider time horizon when determining its risk management goals for management to achieve.

B) The board should clarify whether it is accounting or economic profits that are to be hedged.

C) The board must ensure that its goads are expressed clear and actionable.

D) The board needs to help set and communicate the firm's risk appetite in a quantitative and/or qualitative manner.

15. There are many risk management tools can be utilized, such as VaR, exposure limits, stop-loss limits, etc. How many of the following statements are CORRECT? (　　)

Ⅰ. Value-at-risk (VAR) is an ex-post measure of risk.

Ⅱ. Notional limits can be aggregated across assets.

Ⅲ. An exposure limit is a predictive risk management measure.

Ⅳ. A stop-loss limit eliminates a position after a cumulative loss threshold is exceeded.

A) 1

B) 2

C) 3

D) 4

16. If a company has a one-day 5% Value at Risk of $1 million, this means (　　).

Ⅰ. 5% of the time the firm is expected to lose at least $1 million in one day

Ⅱ. 95% of the time the firm is expected to lose no more than $1 million in one day

Ⅲ. 95% of the time the firm is expected to lose at least $1 million in one day

Ⅳ. 5% of the time the firm is expected to lose no more than $1 million in one day

A) Ⅰ, Ⅱ

B) Ⅰ, Ⅳ

C) Ⅱ, Ⅲ

D) Ⅱ, Ⅳ

17. Which of the following may be controlled by an investor? (　　)

A) risk exposure

B) total returns

C) average returns

D) risk-adjusted returns

18. Financial institutions can use exchange-trade instruments or over-the-counter (OTC) instruments for risk management. Which characteristic is related to exchange-traded instruments? (　　)

A) Either of the counterparties in the transaction has counterparty risk.

B) Cover only certain underlying assets and are standardized.

C) Are privately traded between a bank and a firm.

D) Can be customized to meet the firm's risk management demand.

19. Jon Fisher is evaluating the advantages and disadvantages of hedging risk exposures. In a presentation to the board, his makes the following statements. Which of the following statements does not mention an advantage of hedging? (　　)

A) Hedging may decrease the variability of the firm's earnings due to the difference between accounting earnings and cash flows.

B) Hedging by derivatives may be cheaper than insurance policies.

C) Hedging may allow management to control its financial performance to meet the requirements of the board of directors.

D) Hedging may result in operational improvements within a firm.

20. Douglas Moody is discussing with his colleagues about the differences between static and dynamic hedging strategies. During the discussion, Douglas makes 4 statements. How many of his statements are correct regarding these two hedging strategies? (　　)

Ⅰ. A static hedging strategy assumes that the attributes of the underlying risky position will not change with time.

Ⅱ. A static hedging strategy is a complex process in which the risky investment position is initially determined and an appropriate hedging vehicle is used to match that position as close as possible and for as long as required.

Ⅲ. More time and monitoring efforts are required for a dynamic hedging strategy compared to a static hedging strategy.

Ⅳ. A dynamic hedging strategy is a less complex than a static hedging strategy, because of simpler modeling required.

A) 1

B) 2

C) 3

D) 4

21. Which of the following is a process of risk management? (　　)

A) minimizing risk

B) maximizing returns

C) avoid risk

D) defining and measuring risksbeing taken

22. What is risk governance? It (　　).

A) aligns risk management activities with the goals of the overall enterprise

B) defines the qualitative assessment and evaluation of potential sources of risk in an organization

C) delegates responsibility for risk management to all levels of the organization's hierarchy

D) provides return oversight and guidance to match returns with enterprise goals

23. Mason Mclean plans to make presentation on the role and responsibilities of audit committee. In his ppt, he writes several statements regarding the audit committee. Which of the following statements is incorrect? (　　)

A) It has traditionally been in charge of the accuracy of the firm's financial statements and its regulatory reporting requirements.

B) It must ensure that the firm has taken all steps to avoid the risk of financial statements being materially misstated due to unknown errors and/or fraud.

C) It monitors the underlying systems in place regarding financial reporting, regulatory compliance, internal controls, and risk management.

D) It discusses and approves the remuneration of key management personnel.

24. Lorraine Gentry is a board director of a local bank. In a seminar about risk management, he learns that it's quite important to introduce a risk advisory director in the board. Although he agrees with the concept, but he is still a little bit confused about the duty of the risk advisory director, especially about what kind of information should the risk advisory director review and analyze. What kind of information is recommended to be reviewed by the risk advisory director? (　　)

A) Any audit reports from internal audits, but no need of external audits.

B) The firm's financial statements, but no need of the firm's disclosures.

C) The firm's risk appetite and how it impacts on business strategy.

D) Competitors' risk management practices, but no need of the industry.

25. Regarding the best practices in corporate governance, the board of directors should most likely (　　).

Ⅰ. act on behalf of the interests of the debtholders.

Ⅱ. remain independent from management.

A) Both Ⅰ and Ⅱ

B) Ⅰ only

C) Ⅱ only

D) Neither Ⅰ nor Ⅱ

26. The factors a risk management framework should address include all of the following except (　　).

A) people and systems

B) communications

C) policies and processes

D) names of responsible individuals

27. Which of the following is not a responsibility of a firm's risk management committee? (　　)

A) Implementing risk procedures and processes.

B) Approving the governing body's proposed risk policies.

C) Deliberating the governing body's risk policies at the operational level.

D) Providing top decision-makers with a forum for considering risk management issues.

28. Which of the following activities are most likely applied by senior management? (　　)

A) Approves business plans and targets, sets risk tolerance and ensures performance of the firm.

B) Handles trades, reconciles front- and back-office positions, and prepares and decomposes daily P&L.

C) Develops policies of valuation and finance, ensures integrity of P & L, and manages business planning process.

D) Manages risk exposure, ensures timely, accurate, and complete deal capture, and signs off on official P&L.

29. Which of the following is the correct sequence of events for risk governance and management that focuses on the entire enterprise? Establishing (　　).

A) risk tolerance, then risk budgeting, and then risk exposures

B) risk budgeting, then risk tolerance, and then risk exposures

C) risk exposures, then risk tolerance, and then risk budgeting

D) risk budgeting, then risk exposures, and then risk tolerance

30. Lino Barnes and Guadalupe Morris are discussing about the relationship between a firm's risk appetite and its business strategy. Which of the following statements is true? (　　)

A) Focus on the downside risks of only risky business strategies.

B) The risk management team provides input to business strategy planning meetings.

C) Business activities that beyond risk appetite should be maintained.

D) A firm's risk appetite shows the willingness of the firm to minimize risk.

31. Which of the following best describes activities that are supported by a risk management infrastructure? (　　)

A) risk tolerance, budgeting, and reporting

B) risk tolerance, measurement, and monitoring

C) risk identification, reporting, and budgeting

D) risk identification, measurement, and monitoring

32. Effective risk governance in an enterprise provides guidance on all of the following except (　　).

A) unacceptable risks

B) worst losses that may be tolerated

C) specific methods to mitigate risk for each subsidiary in the enterprise

D) acceptable risks

33. Once an enterprise's risk tolerance is determined, the role of risk management is to ( ).

A) analyze risk drivers

B) measure risk scales

C) align risk exposures with risk appetite

D) identify the extent to which the enterprise is willing to fail in meeting its objectives

34. Which of the following is the biggest factor that could affect a company's ability to tolerate risk? ( )

A) a stable market environment

B) the beliefs of the individual board members

C) a capable management team

D) the ability to dynamically respond to adverse events

35. Which of the following is included in risk budgeting? ( )

Ⅰ. determining the target return

Ⅱ. quantifying tolerable risk by specific metrics

Ⅲ. allocating a portfolio by some risk characteristics of the investments

Ⅳ. implementing models to predict risks

A) Ⅱ, Ⅲ

B) Ⅰ, Ⅳ

C) Ⅱ, Ⅳ

D) Ⅰ, Ⅱ, Ⅲ

36. Michael Woods is the CRO of Snyder Investment Inc. Now he is implementing the enterprise risk management (ERM) program for his firm, starting from analyzing the main components of a strong ERM framework. Which of the following is true about the ERM component of portfolio management? ( )

A) Quantifies risk exposures for use in risk analysis, measurement, and reporting.

B) Reduces or transfers out risks that are either undesirable risks or are desirable but considered concentrated.

C) Provide an overview of the firm's risks if these risks are viewed as individual components of the aggregate risks facing the firm.

D) Communicates a firm's internal risk management process to external stakeholders, including shareholders, creditors, regulators, and the public.

37. A benefit of risk budgeting is that it ( ).

A) makes risk target clear qualitatively

B) considers risk tradeoffs

C) establishes a firm's risk tolerance

D) reduces uncertainty facing the firm

38. Which of the following statements most accurately describe enterprise risk management (ERM)? ERM ( ).

A) decisions are made on an overall basis

B) separately manages individual risks within an organization

C) focuses on monitoring risks from all sources for the purpose of increasing the organization's long-term value

D) takes an integrated approach to the total return process

39. An entity choosing to accept a risk exposure may ( ).

A) quit the risk-related business

B) buy insurance

C) enter into a derivative contract

D) establish a reserve fund to cover losses

40. Which of the following consideration for ERM implementation is INCORRET? ( )

A) developing ERM quickly

B) quantifying operational and strategic risks

C) determining interrelationships between various risks

D) integrating ERM into an organization's culture

41. The chief risk officer (CRO) is usually responsible for developing and implementing an enterprise risk management (ERM) strategy. Which of the following statements is correct regarding the role and responsibilities of the CRO? ( )

A) The CRO develops a framework of management policies, including approving the overall risk appetite of the firm.

B) The CRO typically get reports from the heads of different risks, such as credit, market, operational, and insurance risks.

C) The CRO is a mid-level management responsible for assisting with ERM.

D) Setting a CRO role is the most effective way to establishing risk oversight.

42. The choice of risk-modification method is based on ( ).

A) minimizing risk at the lowest cost

B) maximizing returns at the lowest cost

C) weighing cost versus benefits in light of the entity's return objective

D) weighing costs versus benefits in light of the entity's risk tolerance

43. Risk management is important because it may increase firm value by decreasing the costs of bankruptcy and financial distress. Which of the following strategies are examples of that? ( )

Ⅰ. Reducing the potential costs of financial distress and bankruptcy.

Ⅱ. Reducing the weighted average cost of capital.

Ⅲ. Improving management incentives.

Ⅳ. Reducing information asymmetries.

A) Ⅰ only

B) Ⅰ and Ⅱ only

C) Ⅰ and Ⅲ only

D) Ⅰ, Ⅱ, and Ⅳ only

44. Banks may take too little or too much risk compared to its optimal level, both can decrease value. Which of the following is an example of taking on too little risk? ( )

A) A bank generated superior returns for consecutive 3 years.

B) A bank failed to capitalize on enough profitable opportunities in the past 3 years.

C) A distressed bank brings losses for counterparties.

D) A bank invests in consumer loans for a higher interest rate.

45. Risk management should be designed to reduce the probability of financial distress. Risk management ( ).

A) can increases firm value in all situations

B) can be easily done by investors themselves

C) can increase firm value because financial distress has measurable costs

D) cannot reduce the weighted average cost of capital

46. Regarding a bank's plan to determine their optimal level of risk exposure, which of the following statements is most likely incorrect? ( )

A) A bank should always aim the highest credit rating possible.

B) Aiming for low credit rating (e.g., BBB) may lose customers, because the customers believe that the bank is taking excessive risk.

C) Aiming for a high credit rating (e.g., AAA) may constrain the bank's risk-taking ability.

D) Earning a AAA rating would bring more investment opportunity.

47. In which of the following situations can risk management add value for a bank?

( )

A) Requiring all business units to ignore the perspective of the entire bank when making decisions regarding risks.

B) Avoiding taking on incremental risk that would otherwise result in excessive total risk and a significant decrease in the bank's value.

C) Accepting a very low cost of having incremental risk above the optimal level.

D) Incremental changes in risk taken do not result in much change in the value of a bank.

48. Which of the following will bad to a decrease of a firm's value? ( )

Ⅰ. To decrease the probability of default, debt holders prevent equity holders from investing in positive NPV projects.

Ⅱ. Paying a favorable coupon to debtholders reduce the value created for equity holders.

A) Both Ⅰ and Ⅱ

B) Ⅰ only

C) Ⅱ only

D) Neither Ⅰ nor Ⅱ

49. Based on the risk assessment of the CRO, Bank United's CEO decided to make a large investment in a levered portfolio of CDOs. The CRO had estimated that the portfolio had a 1% chance of losing $1 billion or more over one year, a loss that would make the bank insolvent. At the end of the first year the portfolio has lost $2 billion and the bank was closed by regulators. Which of the following statements is correct? ( )

A) The outcome demonstrates a risk management failure because the bank did not eliminate the possibility of financial distress.

B) The outcome demonstrates a risk management failure because the fact that an extremely unlikely outcome occurred means that the probability of the outcome was poorly estimated.

C) The outcome demonstrates a risk management failure because the CRO failed to go to regulators to stop the shutdown.

D) Based on the information provided, one cannot determine whether it was a risk management failure.

50. Which of the following statements is/are true about the potential impact of a bank's risk culture on its risk profile and performance? ( )

Ⅰ. Companies where managers were perceived as honest and trustworthy were more profitable and were given higher valuations.

Ⅱ. Shareholder governance improvements would change a firm's culture from focusing on end results to focusing on employee integrity and customer service.

A) Ⅰ only

B) Neither Ⅰ nor Ⅱ

C) Ⅱ only

D) Both Ⅰ and Ⅱ

第 2 单元

金融风险案例

51. Joseph Jett, the head of the government bond trading desk at Kidder Peabody, misreported trades, and reported substantial profits. Regarding this case, which of the following statements is incorrect? (　　)

A) The trades caused a loss of confidence in the management of Kidder Peabody.

B) After Kidder Peabody realized that no individual trading strategy could produce such substantial profits, Jett's profits were questioned.

C) Kidder Peabody suffered $350 million realized losses fromthe events.

D) This case demonstrated that it is important to investigate large profits from unknown trading strategies.

52. John Rusnak, a currency trader for Allied Irish Bank (AIB), hides $691 million losses from management between 1997 and 2002. Which of the following means did he use? (　　)

Ⅰ. Threatening back-office stuffs not to check for confirmationsfor imaginary trades.

Ⅱ. Reporting substantial fake gains from small currency arbitrage positions.

A) Ⅰ only

B) Ⅱ only

C) Both Ⅰ and Ⅱ

D) Neither Ⅰ nor Ⅱ

53. The collapse of Barings Bank may be caused by which of the following factors? (　　)

A) a maturity mismatch between the hedging instrument and the assets being hedged

B) german financial reporting requirements

C) giving a trader authority in the settlement process

D) basis risk

54. The collapse of Barings Bank could have been avoided with (　　).

A) more robust reporting and control systems

B) improvement of pricing models to reduce model risk
C) matching maturity between the hedging instrument and the risk being hedged
D) less leverage

55. Which of the following reasons does not demonstrate the deficiency of the information systems at Barings Bank? ( )
A) The inconsistency of Leeson's trading strategy and profits was undetected by the management.
B) Accounting information on gains and losses was incomplete.
C) Financial reporting quality was not properly audited by management.
D) Accurate financial reporting was limited due to technological reasons.

56. Which of the following is associated with Nicholas Leeson? ( )
A) Sumitomo bank
B) Allied Irish Bank
C) LTCM
D) Nikkei stock index futures

57. Nick Leeson engaged in aggressive speculative trading in the Barings Bank collapse, which of the following is not a reason? ( )
A) His authority to control settlement operations helped him hide trading losses.
B) Barings' risk management models were not well developed.
C) Risk management oversight was absent in Barings Bank.
D) He was trying to recoup previous trading losses on options strategy.

58. In the case of Baring scollapse, which of the following statement shows an example of operational risk? ( )
A) The Japanese firms' default.
B) Large position of the company's assets was in illiquid derivative products.
C) Management's inability to supervise trader's actions.
D) The Nikkei collapsed after an earthquake.

59. Which of the following statement indicate Metallgesellschaft's mismanagement in its long-term fixed contract strategy? ( )
Ⅰ. Refund customers who agreed to cancel their long-term obligation.
Ⅱ. Quit the arrangement too early while the positive legs of the contracts could have beensold at a profit or used for additional financing.
A) Ⅰ only
B) Ⅱ only

C) Both Ⅰ and Ⅱ
D) Neither Ⅰ nor Ⅱ

60. Metallgesellschaft could have employed which of the following strategies to solve the liquidity crisis result from their stack-and-roll hedge strategy? (　　)
Ⅰ. Requiring periodic cash settlements from customers.
Ⅱ. Selling calls.
Ⅲ. Selling puts.
Ⅳ. Buying puts.
A) Ⅰ only
B) Ⅳ only
C) Ⅰ and Ⅳ only
D) Ⅰ and Ⅲ

61. In 1997, several different factors resulted in the equity derivative losses at the Union Bank of Switzerland (UBS). Which one shown below is the most unique factor that did not impact its competitors? (　　)
Ⅰ. The change of British tax law and large position in Japanese bank warrants.
Ⅱ. Inaccurate valuation of long-dated options on equity baskets and incorrect modeling of other options.
A) Ⅰ only
B) Ⅱ only
C) Both Ⅰ and Ⅱ
D) Neither Ⅰ nor Ⅱ

62. Model risk is relevant in the Long-Term Capital Management case. Which of the following are examples of model risk? (　　)
Ⅰ. Underestimating correlations among asset classes during economic crises.
Ⅱ. Ignoring autocorrelation of economic shocks.
Ⅲ. Financial reporting standards.
Ⅳ. Poor management oversight.
A) Ⅰ, Ⅱ, and Ⅲ only
B) Ⅰ, Ⅱ, Ⅲ, and Ⅳ
C) Ⅰ and Ⅱ only
D) Ⅳ only

63. Which of the following statements is false regarding Long-Term Capital Management (LTCM) case? (　　)
A) Because of the large size of their positions, LTCM could only liquidate their

assetsby selling at large discounts.

B) LTCM obtained financing through repurchase agreements at very favorable terms.

C) LTCM increased funding risk by requiring their investors to invest for three years.

D) The amount of gross positions in swaps was very large, but due to offsetting positions, the amount of net risk was in theory very small.

64. Banker's Trust used derivative trades for corporate clients. These tradeshelp them achieve a high-probability, small reduction in funding costs while can also result in a low-probability, large loss. Unfortunately, the derivative trades resulted in significant losses for its clients. This case demonstrated that it's crucial to (　　).

A) incorporate liquidity risk into valuation models

B) compute collateral more accurately when borrowing bonds

C) make investigation on unknown trading strategies when large profits arise

D) match trades with a client's needs and provide price quotes that are not influenced by the front office

65. Which of the following statements illustrated the high degree of operational risk in the Sumitomo case? (　　)

Ⅰ. Model risk.

Ⅱ. Absence of informed supervisors to approve large trades.

Ⅲ. The trader can execute highly levered positions, due to high degree of autonomy,

Ⅳ. The trader's ability to keep two sets of trading books and manipulate profit and losses.

A) Ⅰ only

B) Ⅰ and Ⅳ only

C) Ⅱ, Ⅲ, and Ⅳ

D) Ⅱ and Ⅲ only

66. Which of the following does not affect the role of operational risk management in preventing large trading losses? (　　)

A) marked-to-market losses

B) the breadth of authority and power given to traders

C) the degree of supervision and oversight by management

D) multiple approvals from senior management regard to large trades

67. A rolling long hedge strategy uses long futures contracts to hedge a pre-existing short

position. Which of the following situations may increase the cost of this strategy? ( )

Ⅰ. A market shift from normal backwardation to contango.

Ⅱ. A market shift from contango to normal backwardation.

Ⅲ. Futures prices rising above the spot price.

Ⅳ. Futures prices falling below the spot price.

A) Ⅰ and Ⅲ

B) Ⅱ and Ⅳ

C) Ⅱ and Ⅲ

D) Ⅰ and Ⅳ

68. Rising mortgage delinquencies and falling housing prices resulted in the financial crisis, which in turn led to a worldwide liquidity crisis. This is because institutions had ( ).

A) not massively used leverage trading

B) maintained substantial equity capital

C) generated large maturity mismatches between assets and liabilities

D) become more independent from each other

69. Suppose that two investors, investor A and investor B, each have an original investment position of $100. with $20 of equity capital and $80 of borrowing (i. e., their leverage ratio 5) Suppose that the investment assets of investor A experience a 10% decline in asset value, from $100 to $90, while investor A's leverage ratio remains at 5. Investor B experiences no decline in asset value; however, investor B experiences a decline in the permitted leverage ratio from 5 to 2. Which of the investors would be forced to sell more assets to maintain their leverage ratio? ( )

A) Investor A.

B) Investor B.

C) Both investors would be forced to sell the same amount of assets.

D) Neither investor would be forced to sell assets.

70. Which of the following statements is correct as regard to the key factors that led to the housing bubble in 2007—2008? ( )

A) A decrease in demand for U. S. securities by foreign governments put upward pressure on interest rates.

B) Cheap credit caused the excess money rush to the purchases of real estate, which pushed housing price upward.

C) An increase in lending standards and lack of cheap credit led banks to offer credit at high interest rates.

D) The Federal Reserve tried to maintain low interest rates to avoid inflation after the bursting of the internet bubble.

71. Regarding the 2007—2009 liquidity and credit crunch, which of the following statements is accurate? (　　)

A) Because of the forced sale of assets due to declining asset values, a loss spiral generates a lower new position value than a margin spiral.

B) The counterparty who receives cash flows is a CDS arrangement is the credit protection buyer.

C) A liquidity backstop is a temporary halt in funding liquidity to structured investment vehicles (SⅣs) in order to minimize credit losses.

D) The narrower the bid-ask spread, the better the market liquidity.

72. The following statements are about liquidity definitions. Which describes the market liquidity risk? (　　)

A) The risk that depositors will withdraw funds from banks, or that investors will redeem their shares.

B) The risk that arises when the value of the collateral asset declines, margin requirementmight increase, requiring additional equity capital.

C) The loss that would occur when selling an asset and then immediately buying it back.

D) The risk that investors may not be able to raise fund through short-term debt to finance the purchase of an asset.

73. The following statements are about liquidity definitions. Which describes the funding liquidity risk? (　　)

A) The loss that would occur when selling an asset and then immediately buying it back.

B) The length of time for an asset to regain its price after the price has fallen temporarily.

C) The amount of an asset a trader can buy or sell at the current market bid/ask.

D) The risk that investors may not be able to raise fund through short-term debt to finance the purchase of an asset.

74. Which of the following statements is correct regarding funding liquidity and market liquidity? (　　)

A) Using a purchased asset as collateral to borrow money against it is associated with market liquidity.

B) An increase in margin has the same effect as a decline in a source of funding.

C) In a margin spiral, a trader is forced to sell the assets in order to maintain the leverage ratio (i. e. , constant margins).

D) A loss spiral is positively related to market liquidity.

75. When losses in the asset-backed security (ABS) asset pool occur, which of the following ABS tranches will firstly absorb the losses? (　　)

A) Super-senior tranche

B) Senior tranche

C) Equity tranche

D) Mezzanine tranche

76. Using equity to raise money to finance investments purchase and the forced sale of assets due to a decline in their value while maintaining a constant leverage ratio, respectively, refer to raising money to finance forced sale of assets (　　).

A) Funding liquidity and Margin spiral

B) Market liquidity and Loss spiral

C) Market liquidity and Margin spiral

D) Funding liquidity and Loss spiral

77. Which of the following process is most likely to be associated with the creation of collateralized debt obligations (CDOs)? (　　)

A) creating an undiversified portfolio from a small sample of debt securities

B) selling the equity tranche to investors that require investment grade debt instruments

C) slicing the cash flows from a pooled portfolio into a number of investable tranches

D) the CDO issuer retaining the most senior tranches, thus making the issuer motivated to monitor the loan

78. There were two main panic periods in the financial crisis, which includes (　　).

Ⅰ. Runs on asset backed commercial paper (ABCP) since August 2007.

Ⅱ. Filing of bankruptcy by Lehman Brothers since September 2008.

A) Ⅰ only

B) Ⅱ only

C) Neither Ⅰ nor Ⅱ

D) Both Ⅰ and Ⅱ

79. The following measures were used in developed countries to stabilize the markets in the period of 2007—2008 financial crises: interest rate change, liquidity support,

recapitalization, liability guarantees, and asset purchases. Which one of these measures was most effective before the Lehman Brothers failure? (　　)

A) interest rate change

B) asset purchases

C) liability guarantees

D) liquidity support

80. Which of the following extents led up to previous major banking crises in developed countries? (　　)

A) decline in public debt

B) significant increase in credit supply

C) significant decrease in housing prices

D) decline in private debt

81. Which of the following statements best describes the influence of the financial crisis on firms and the economy? (　　)

Ⅰ. Supply of credit by syndicated lenders decreased.

Ⅱ. Borrowing from regulated banks increased.

A) Ⅰ only

B) Ⅱ only

C) Both Ⅰ and Ⅱ

D) Neither Ⅰ nor Ⅱ

82. Lehman Brothers failure caused which of the consequences on the global financial markets? The failure (　　).

A) caused a run on money market mutual funds

B) resulted in banks spending more cash

C) brought the financial crisis to an end

D) increased confidence in the rest of the financial institutions who survived

83. Regarding the importance of effectively communicating the results of the risk management process, the following statements are correct except which? (　　)

A) The purpose of risk management is to allow senior managers of the firm to make the best decisions to maximize firm stock price.

B) If the results cannot be effectively communicated to the appropriate decision makers, the risk management efforts are of no use.

C) The risk management process may be harmful if it is not well communicated, thus make the senior managers get a false sense of safety from the information that is provided.

D) Effective communication requires timely communication and accurate communication that has not been distorted by intermediaries.

84. Which of the following statements are examples of ignoring or not adequately using data? (　　)

Ⅰ. assuming constant correlations among different assets during financial crises.

Ⅱ. accepting the assumption that AAA-rated assets have very low risk.

A) Ⅰ only

B) Ⅱ only

C) Neither Ⅰ nor Ⅱ

D) Both Ⅰ and Ⅱ

85. Which of the following occurrences is not an example of risk mismeasurement? When risk managers (　　).

A) use subjectivity when measuring extreme and rare events

B) do not understand the distribution of a single risk

C) consider both known and unknown risks

D) do not understand the relationships of the distributions among different positions

86. All of the following actions could result in failing to manage risk exposure except (　　).

A) not measuring unknown risks correctly

B) not monitoring risk adequately

C) not applying appropriate risk metrics

D) not communicating risks to decision makers

87. The role of risk management involves performingall of the following tasks expect which? (　　)

A) Evaluate all risks faced by the firm.

B) Make sure the firm takes greater than the necessary amount of risk because it should try to achieved higher returns.

C) Monitor and manage all risks.

D) Communicate all risks to risk-taking decision makers.

88. Firms may fail to correctly monitor and manage risk on an ongoing basis. Which of the following statements might NOT be a reason for this problem? (　　)

A) No adequate risk culture that encourages effective risk management.

B) No adequate incentive structure.

C) Risk profiles of portfolios stay constant over time.

D) Some securities have complex relationships with variables such as exchange rates.

89. Predatory trading happens when (   ).

A) borrower misrepresents the mortgage application

B) a large position held by a player in the market is in trouble and the other firms attempt to push the price down further in order to trigger a stop loss and fill the trade at advantageous price

C) a borrower becomes worse off after a loan than before

D) a firm with small loss in a given market can influence the activity in that market

第 3 单元

资产组合管理

90. Usually, investors construct portfolios to (　　).

A) eliminate risk

B) decrease risk

C) transfer risk

D) avoid risk

91. Why do investors lay emphasis on the composition of a portfolio? (　　)

A) To avoid extreme events.

B) To reduce risk.

C) To decrease downside risk.

D) To increase return.

92. Which of the following statements is true about the formation of portfolios? (　　)

A) Portfolios only influence returns.

B) Portfolios only influence risk.

C) Portfolios influence returns but not influence risk.

D) Portfolios influence risk more than returns.

93. An analyst obtains the following information of three portfolios.

Portfolio	Fixed Income	Equity	Alternative Assets
1	10%	65%	25%
2	65%	25%	10%
3	20%	65%	15%

Which of the portfolios is most likely appropriate for an investor with a low degree of risk aversion? (　　)

A) Portfolio 1

B) Portfolio 2

C) Portfolio 3

D) Can't judge by the information

94. An investor purchased 200 shares of a stock for \$30 per share at the beginning of the month. At the end of the month, the investor sold all of the shares for \$32 per share and received a \$105 dividend payment, the holding period return is (　　).

A) 12%

B) 11.4%

C) 8.42%

D) 9.1%

95. An analyst has a mutual fund with the following information:

Year	Return
2×12	15%
2×13	-15%
2×14	-1%

Calculate the fund's holding period return over the three-year period. (　　)

A) 3.23%

B) -3.23%

C) 4%

D) -4%

96. An investor has a fund with the following information

Year	Return (%)
2×10	20
2×11	-15
2×12	10

Calculate the fund's annual geometric mean return. (　　)

A) 3.91%

B) 2.012%

C) 2.38%

D) -4.1%

97. An investor has made annual deposits to a portfolio for each of the last three years. Which of the following return calculating methods is most appropriate to evaluate the annualized returns of the portfolio? (　　)

A) Arithmetic mean return
B) Geometric mean return
C) Weighted mean return
D) Harmonic mean return

98. Regarding to capital market theory, which of the following statements is least likely to affect the variance of an equally weighted portfolio? ( )
A) correlation between assets
B) standard deviation of the asset
C) covariance between assets
D) return of the asset

99. An investor has a portfolio with the following information:

Security	Security Weight	Expected Standard Deviation
1	20%	20%
2	80%	15%

The correlation of returns between the two securities is 0.50, calculate the portfolio's expected standard deviation. ( )
A) 10.2%
B) 11.5%
C) 14.42%
D) 2.08%

100. An investor has a portfolio with the following information.

Security	Security Weight	Expected Standard Deviation
1	20%	20%
2	80%	15%

The covariance of returns between the two securities is 0.015, calculate the expected standard deviation of the portfolio. ( )
A) 2.6%
B) 7.4%
C) 14.42%
D) 13%

The following information relates to the next two questions.
An investor has a portfolio with the following information:

Security	Security Weight	Expected Standard Deviation
1	20%	20%
2	80%	15%

101. The standard deviation of the portfolio is 14.42%, calculate the correlation between the two securities. (　　)

A) 1.0

B) 0.2

C) −0.5

D) 0.5

102. The standard deviation of the portfolio is 14.42%, calculate the covariance between the two securities. (　　)

A) 0.06

B) 0.25

C) 1.00

D) 0.015

103. An investor has a portfolio with the following information:

Asset Class	Geometric Return
Equities	9.0%
Corporate Bonds	6.0%
Treasury bills	3.0%
Inflation	2.0%

Calculate the real rate of return for equities. (　　)

A) 5.5%

B) 5.9%

C) 6.9%

D) 11.18%

104. Risk aversion means the relation between risk and return is (　　).

A) positive

B) neutral

C) negative

D) independent

105. Regarding to the mean-variance portfolio theory, capital allocation line is the combination of the risk-free asset and a portfolio of all (   ).

A) risk-free asset

B) feasible investments

C) equity assets

D) risky asset

106. Investors with different levels of risk tolerance will have optimal portfolios that are (   ).

A) above the capital allocation line

B) below the capital allocation line

C) on the capital allocation line

D) none of the above is true

The following information relates to the next three questions.

A portfolio manager creates the following portfolio:

Security	Expected Annual Return	Expected Standard Deviation
1	15%	25%
2	10%	25%

107. The portfolio of the two securities has an expected return of 12.5%, calculate the weight of security 1 in the portfolio. (   )

A) 35%

B) 50%

C) 25%

D) 100%

108. The correlation of returns between the two securities is 0.5, calculate the expected standard deviation of an equal-weighted portfolio. (   )

A) 11.14%

B) 12.60%

C) 12.87%

D) 21.65%

109. The two securities are uncorrelated, calculate the expected standard deviation of an equal-weighted portfolio. (   )

A) 15.00%

B) 14.20%

C) 20.15%

D) 17.68%

110. During a market downturn, the correlation between assets in a two-asset portfolio tend to increase. Keep the weight of each asset constant, the volatility of the portfolio will ( ).

A) decrease

B) increase

C) remain the same

D) none of the above is true

111. Efficient frontier is the set of all attainable risky assets with the ( ).

A) highest expected return for a given level of risk

B) highest amount of risk for a given level of return

C) highest expected return relative to the risk-free rate

D) lowest expected return for a given level of risk

112. The portfolio on the minimum-variance frontier with the lowest standard deviation is ( ).

A) the global minimum-variance portfolio

B) the optimal risky portfolio

C) unattainable

D) the risk-free asset

113. The portfolios that dominates all sets of portfolios below the global minimum-variance portfolio is the ( ).

A) security market line

B) optimal risky portfolios

C) efficient frontier

D) the risk-free asset

114. The capital market line combines the risk-free asset and the ( ).

A) optimal risky portfolio

B) risky assets

C) global minimum-variance portfolio

D) none of the above is true

115. The reason that the portfolios on capital allocation line have higher rates of return than the optimal risky portfolio is the investor's ability to ( ).

A) buy risky assets

B) sell risky assets

C) lend at the risk-free rate

D) borrow at the risk-free rate

116. Regarding to the mean-variance theory, the optimal portfolio is determined by investor's ( ).

A) risky asset

B) risk-free rate

C) lending rate

D) risk preference

117. The line connecting risk-free asset and any risky asset is the ( ).

A) security market line

B) capital market line

C) security characteristic line

D) capital allocation line

118. The risk adjusted return of the portfolio investing in both risk free asset and risky asset is higher than the portfolio investing in only one asset type, because the correlation between the risk-free asset and the risky asset is ( ).

A) 0

B) 1

C) −1

D) 0.5

119. With respect to capital market theory, an investor's optimal portfolio is the combination of a risk-free asset and a risky asset with the highest ( ).

A) indifference curve

B) expected return

C) security market line

D) volatility

120. Investors with highest risk aversion tend to invest the majority of their wealth in ( ).

A) risk-free assets

B) risky assets

C) the optimal risky portfolio

D) global minimum-variance portfolio

121. The capital market line (CML) depicts the risk and return of portfolio

combinations consisting of the risk-free asset and ( ).

A) the market portfolio

B) any risky portfolio

C) equity portfolio

D) global minimum-variance portfolio

122. Regarding the market portfolio in capital market theory, which of the following statements is true? The market portfolio consists of all ( ).

A) risk free asset

B) equity portfolio

C) investable assets

D) risky assets

123. Based on capital market theory, the optimal risky portfolio ( ).

A) has the highest risk

B) is the market portfolio

C) has the highest return

D) includes risk-free asset

124. The portfolios above the CML is considered ( ).

A) efficient

B) inefficient

C) achievable

D) unachievable

125. The return of a portfolio on the capital market line is higher than the return of market portfolio, because the portfolio is a(n) ( ).

A) borrowing portfolio

B) lending portfolio

C) achievable portfolio

D) unachievable portfolio

126. The return of a portfolio on the capital market line is lower than the return of market portfolio, because the portfolio is a(n) ( ).

A) borrowing portfolio

B) lending portfolio

C) achievable portfolio

D) unachievable portfolio

127. Which kind of risk could be avoided by forming a diversified portfoliois? ( )
A) total risk
B) nonsystematic risk
C) systematic risk
D) market risk

128. Which of the following risks belongs to nonsystematic risk? ( )
A) A decline in inflation rates.
B) The resignation of a CEO in a certain company.
C) An increase in the reference rates.
D) An increase in interest rates.

129. Regarding to the pricing of risk in security market line, which of the following statements is true? ( )
A) All risk is priced.
B) Only credit risk is priced.
C) Only nonsystematic risk is priced.
D) Only systematic risk is priced.

130. The sum of an asset's nonsystematic variance and systematic variance of returns is the asset's ( ).
A) correlation
B) beta
C) total variance
D) standard deviation

131. The intercept term of the market model based on return-generating models is the asset's estimated ( ).
A) correlation
B) beta
C) alpha
D) standard variance

132. The slope term of the market model based on return-generating models is the asset's estimated ( ).
A) correlation
B) beta
C) alpha
D) standard variance

133. Return-generating models are used to estimate the portfolio's ( ).
A) correlation
B) covariance

C) variance

D) expected return

The following information relates to the next three questions.

An analyst gathers the following information:

Security	Expected Annual Return	Expected Standard Deviation	Correlation between Security and the Market
Security I	12%	20%	0. 7
Security 2	12%	15%	0. 5
Security 3	15%	12%	0. 9
Market	8%	18%	1. 0

134. Select the security with the highest total risk? (　　)

A) Security 1

B) Security 2

C) Security 3

D) None of the above is true

135. Select the security with the highest beta measure? (　　)

A) Security 1

B) Security 2

C) Security 3

D) None of the above is true

136. Select the security with the least amount of market risk? (　　)

A) Security 1

B) Security 2

C) Security 3

D) None of the above is true

137. What is the average beta of all assets in the market based on capital market theory? (　　)

A) less than 1. 0

B) greater than 1. 0

C) equal to 1. 0

D) equal to 0

138. The slope of the security characteristic line refers to an asset's ( ).

A) correlation

B) excess return

C) beta

D) alpha

139. The line based on the capital asset pricing model is the ( ).

A) security characteristic line

B) capital market line

C) security market line

D) capital allocation line

140. Individual assets priced correctly will be plotted on ( ) based on capital market theory.

A) security market line

B) capital market line

C) security characteristic line

D) capital allocation line

141. What is the primary determinant of expected return of an individual asset based on the capital asset pricing model? ( )

A) unsystematic risk

B) beta

C) standard deviation

D) correlation

142. Which of the following values of beta for an asset is most likely to have an expected return for the asset that is less than the risk-free rate based on the capital asset pricing model? ( )

A) 0.7

B) 0.0

C) −0.2

D) 1

143. Which of the following statements about the market risk premium is true? The market risk premium ( ).

A) equal to the market return

B) less than the excess market return

C) greater than the excess market return
D) equal to the excess market return

The following information relates to the next four questions.
An analyst gathers the following information:

Security	Expected Standard Deviation	Beta
Security 1	20%	1.20
Security 2	10%	1.5
Security 3	15%	0.5

144. The expected market risk premium is 6% and the risk-free rate is 3%, calculate the expected return for Security 1. ( )
A) 9.3%
B) 13.0%
C) 11.5%
D) 10.2%

145. The expected return for Security 2 is equal to 12% and the risk-free rate is 3%, calculate the expected return for the market. ( )
A) 6.0%
B) 9.0%
C) 12.5%
D) 12%

146. The expected market risk premium is 6%, select the security with the highest expected return. ( )
A) Security 1
B) Security 2
C) Security 3
D) None of the above is true

147. An increase in the expected market return will have the greatest influence on the expected return of ( ).
A) Security 1
B) Security 2
C) Security 3
D) None of the above is true

148. Which of the following performance measures has the same results with the CAPM?

(　　)

A) Information Ratio

B) Jensen's alpha

C) Sharpe ratio

D) M-squared

149. An analyst considers to measure the performance of a diversified portfolio. Which of the following performance measures is most appropriate? (　　)

A) Information Ratio

B) Treynor Ratio

C) Sharpe ratio

D) M-squared

150. An analyst considers to measure the performance of an undiversified portfolio. Which of the following performance measures is most appropriate ? (　　)

A) Sharpe ratio

B) Treynor ratio

C) Jensen's alpha

D) Information Ratio

151. The return of an asset is estimated to be higher than the expected return generated by the capital asset pricing model. The asset is (　　).

A) underpriced

B) overpriced

C) properly priced

D) none of the above is true

152. Homogeneity assumption indicates all investors have the same economic expectations of future cash flows for all assets. According to homogeneity assumption, investors will invest in (　　).

A) risk-free asset

B) undiversified portfolio

C) the Standard and Poor's 500 Index

D) the same optimal risky portfolio

153. Which of the following assumptions leads to the existence of the market portfolio based on capital market theory? All investors (　　).

A) are price takers

B) are price discoverers

C) have homogeneous expectations

D) have heterogeneousexpectations

154. An analyst uses a line todepict the relationship between the excess returns of a manager's portfolio and the excess returns of the market. The intercept of the line is Jensen's (　　).

A) beta

B) alpha

C) vega

D) gamma

155. If a portfolio manager seeks to maximize risk-adjusted returns, he needs to invest more in securities with (　　).

A) higher values of Jensen's alpha

B) values of Jensen's alpha equal to 0

C) lower values of Jensen's alpha

D) negative values of Jensen's alpha

156. If a portfolio manager seeks to maximize risk-adjusted returns, he need to invest less in securities with (　　).

A) higher values of Jensen's alpha

B) values of Jensen's alpha equal to 0

C) negative values of Jensen's alpha

D) positive values of Jensen's alpha

157. Which of the following statements is false based on the characteristics of the APT and the CAPM? (　　)

A) Investors who are more risk-seeking will invest less in market portfolio and more in the risk-free asset based on APT.

B) Investors who are more risk-seeking will invest more in market portfolio and less in the risk-free asset based on CAPM.

C) Both models assume unsystematic risks can be diversified.

D) The APT includes more factors than the CAPM.

158. A portfolio with a factor sensitivity of one to a particular factor and zero to all other factors. The risk-free rate is 2.5%, risk premium of the particular factor is 8%. What is the fund's return based on APT? (　　)

A) 10.5%

B) 8.0%

C) 2.5%

D) 11.0%

159. The factor risk premium on factor i in the APT model means ( ).

A) sensitivity of the portfolio to market risk premium

B) expected return on a portfolio with i factors

C) expected risk premium required for factor i

D) expected return required for factor i

160. Which of the following is an assumption of the arbitrage pricing theory (APT)? ( )

A) No arbitrage opportunities exist.

B) Arbitrage opportunities exist.

C) The market contains enough stocks so that systematic risk can be diversified away.

D) Returns on assets can be described by a one factor model.

161. Which of the following statements is true based on the characteristics of the APT and the CAPM? ( )

A) APT contains less factors than CAPM.

B) CAPMis more flexible than APT in its application.

C) APT has more assumptions than CAPM.

D) CAPM is a special case of the APT.

162. Which of the following is true about arbitrage pricing theory (APT)? ( )

A) Investors have quadratic utility functions.

B) Security returns are normally distributed.

C) There are no arbitrage opportunities.

D) APT contains only one factor.

163. The T-bill rate is 3.0%, calculate the expected returns for the two funds based on the information in the table. ( )

Beta estimates for two funds for a three-factor model			
	Factor 1	Factor 2	Factor 3
Factor risk premiums	5%	10%	8%
Betas for $fund_1$	0.6	0.5	1.8
Betas for $fund_2$	0.4	1.5	0.9

	E(fund1)	E(fund2)
A)	22.4%	24.2%
B)	15.0%	16.1%
C)	25.4%	27.2%
D)	32.6%	21.2%

164. Which of the following is not true about arbitrage pricing theory (APT)? (　　)

A) Asset returns are explained by multi-factor model.

B) APT is more flexible than CAPM in its application.

C) The market contains enough stocks so that unsystematic risk can be diversified away.

D) APT is often considered as a special case of the CAPM.

165. Calculate the expected return on the Growth Fund based on a three-factor arbitrage pricing theory (APT) model. (　　)

- The factor risk premiums to factors 1, 2 and 3 are 6%, 10% and 5%, respectively.
- The fund has sensitivities to the factors 1, 2, and 3 of 1.5, 1.2 and 1.0, respectively. The risk-free rate is 2.5%.

A) 30.0%.

B) 26.0%.

C) 28.5%.

D) 32.0%.

166. An arbitrage pricing theory (APT) model has the following information.

- The risk-free rate is 3.0%.
- Factor risk premiums are:
  Factor1: 6%　　Factor2: 5%
  Factor3: 10%　　Factor4: 8%
- The Value Fund has the following sensitivities to the factors.
  Sensitivity to Factor1 is 0.8.
  Sensitivity to Factor2 is 1.
  Sensitivity to Factor3 is 1.5.
  Sensitivity to Factor4 is 1.2.

Calculate the expected return on the Value Fund. (　　)

A) 12.8%

B) 10.2%

C) 37.4%

D) 34.4%

第 4 单元

数据管理和道德

167. Which one of the Basel Committee's principles for effective risk data aggregation and reporting most likely recommends that risk management reports should include risk data, risk analysis, interpretation of risk, and qualitative explanations of risks? (　　)

A) Accuracy and Integrity

B) Completeness

C) Comprehensiveness

D) Clarity and Usefulness

168. Which of the following principles are included in the Basel Committee Principles for effective risk data aggregation capabilities? (　　)

A) competence, diligence, and accuracy and integrity.

B) competence, diligence, and completeness.

C) competence, and diligence and timeliness.

D) accuracy and integrity, completeness, timeliness, and adaptability.

169. Which of the following practices is not consistent with the Basel Committee's principles for effective risk data aggregation and reporting? (　　)

A) Banks should include information on metadata in data architecture.

B) Banks should put capital and human resources into data aggregation and reporting system throughout business cycle.

C) It is risk managers' and business managers' responsibility to accurately enter relevant data into the data infrastructure and manage it.

D) Data must be classified using a single data model.

170. Which of the following statements is not a benefit of effective risk data aggregation? (　　)

A) Increase efficiency, and ultimately increase profitability.

B) Resolvability will be improved during times of bank stress or failure.

C) The bank is more capable of making strategic decisions.
D) It is easier to look at problems faced by the bank if risks are dealt individually rather than as a whole.

171. Which of the following practices is not consistent with the Basel Committee's principles for effective risk data aggregation and reporting? (　　)
A) A bank should ensure its compliance with key principles proposed by the Basel Committee.
B) Time frames should be considered to implement data aggregation process.
C) Data aggregation and risk reporting decisions should be based on a bank's geographical location and legal structure.
D) Data aggregation and risk reporting capabilities should be validated independently.

172. Charlie, FRM, has been managing a portfolio for his clients. His stated strategy is to use a screening process to identify and invest in growth stocks, which are stocks of companies that have high earning growth rates. Because recently Charlie begins to believe that the economy is going to be volatilein the near future, he decides to change his strategy to value stock investment, which involves identifying and investing in companies that have low price-earningsmultiples. Charlie will violate the GARP Code of Conduct if he makes the change in his investment strategy without (　　).
A) acquiring written permission from his clients beforehe makes the change
B) promptly informinghis clients of the strategy change
C) notifying his supervisor in advance of the change
D) getting prompt written acknowledgment of the change from his clients after the change was made

173. Susan, FRM, has a high net worth elderly client. The client is recently looking for various charities to divest her fortune. Susan happens to sit on the Board of a local charitable foundation. Which of the following actions is most appropriate for Susanto do? (　　)
A) She can discuss her client's situation with the charitable foundation as long as she reveals her client's information and intentions to other local charities.
B) She should persuade the client herself to make a larger contribution.
C) She must not discuss anything related to her client' information and intentions with the charitable foundation without the client's permission.
D) She can inform the charitable foundation of her client's intentions, so that they can solicit the client, because it is the client's wish to divest assets to charities.

174. Lynn, FRM, and Isabelle, FRM, are ready to conduct regression analysis on historical returns of equity and bond market. They first plot a scattergram of the data and examine the residuals. Lynn says that the scattergram illustrates whether the relationship is positive or negative. Isabelle says that the residual of a sample regression may not equal the residual of a population regression. With respect to their statement, ( ).

A) Lynn is wrong and Isabelle is correct

B) Isabelle is wrong and Lynn is correct

C) Both Lynn and Isabelle are correct

D) Both Lynn and Isabelle are wrong

175. Robinson, FRM works as an investment advisorfor a firm whose clients mostly consist of high net worth individuals. Robinson personally holds the shares of GymCo, a company that produce sports facilities. He has done a thorough research on GymCo and believes the company is financially strong although significantly undervalued currently. According to the GARP Code of Conduct, Robinson may ( ).

A) recommend GymCo to a client for who it is suitable without disclosure of ownership of the stock

B) recommend GymCo to a client, but must also disclose to his client about his own investment in the stock

C) not recommend GymCo to a client unless he has acquired written consent from his employer

D) not recommend GymCo to a client unless he has already liquidated his personal holdings in the stock

176. ABC, an investment-banking firm, is the principal underwriter for XYZ's upcoming debenture issue. Lee, FRM, works as an analyst with ABC. He recently learned from a friend who works in XYZ's Drug R&D Department that a serious side effect was discovered in adrug of a major product line. In fact, the problem is so serious that many customers have canceled their orders with XYZ. Lee checked the debenture's prospectus and found that the problem is not mentioned. The prospectus has already been distributed. In order to comply with the GARP Code of Conduct, Lee's best course of action is to ( ).

A) report her discovery to the Division of Corporation Finance of the Securitiesand Exchange Commission (SEC).

B) notify potential debenture buyers of the problem on a fair and equitable basis.

C) inform no one because this is material nonpublic information.

D) report the discovery to his immediate supervisor at ABC.

177. According to Preservation of Confidentiality in the GARP Code of Conduct," confidential information" refers to the information that an analyst acquires from ( ).

A) both current clients and former clients
B) both former clients and prospective clients
C) current clients, former clients, and prospective clients
D) both current clients and prospective clients

178. Which of the followings must be disclosed to clients when making investment recommendations? ( )

A) The analyst's farther owns significant shares of the security.
B) The analyst's firm is a market maker in the recommended stock.
C) An employee of the firm also sits on the board of directors of the recommended company.
D) All of the above.

179. William, FRM, works as a financial risk analyst for Emerging Investment; he is preparing a buy recommendation on ABC Corporation. Lambert would have to disclose which of the followings in order to comply with the GARP Code of Conduct? ( )

A) He is the material beneficial owner of ABC Corporation through a family trust.
B) Emerging Investment is a market maker for ABC's stock in OTC market.
C) His wife has a material ownership in ABC Corporation' stock.
D) All of the above.

180. When the investment banking department receives material nonpublic information on a publicly traded company, which of the following is considered the most appropriate action to take in order to comply with the GARP Code of Conduct? ( )

A) Restrict proprietary trading in the securities of companies associated with material nonpublic information.
B) Allow analyst tomake buy or sell recommendation on this information only after ten business days since receipt of this information.
C) Contact the firms involved and request that they make this information public before making trading recommendations tothe clients.
D) Make sure that material nonpublic information is disseminated only within the firm's investment banking, brokerage, and research departments.

181. Jack, FRM, is the manager of a hedge fund. He has been accumulating large

position of Kreg Industry's stock while simultaneously shorting put options on the stock for the past year. Jack did not notify his clients of the recent trades because they are clear in mind what the fund's general strategy is to generate returns. Which of the following statements is most likely correct? (　　)

A) Jack did not violate the Code.

B) Jack violated the Code by not having a reasonable and adequate basis before trading.

C) Jack violated the Code by failing to notify the clients of the transactions beforehand.

D) Jack violated the Code by manipulating the prices of stock and options.

182. John, FRM, works as an analyst for Red Investment Managers (RIM). Recently, ElectroCo, an electronic device company has invited John to visit its facilities. ElectroCo offers to pay for John's accommodations in a suite at a luxury hotel and arranges John to travel to its three facilities located in Tokyo, Hong Kong, and London by the firm's private jet. ElectroCoalso offers two tickets to a formal high-society dinner in Hong Kong. John refuses to use ElectroCo'sprivate jet nor allow the firm to pay for his accommodations but accepts the tickets to the dinner, after disclosing the arrangement to his employer. John considers that he would be able to market RIM's mutual funds to other guests at the dinner. Has John violated the GARP Code of Conduct? (　　)

A) Yes.

B) No, since he only accepted a gift of nominal value and he declined to accept the luxury accommodations and the use of ElectroCo's privatejet.

C) No, since he only accepted the gift after fully disclosing in writing to his employer.

D) No, since the gift he acceptedis to benefit his employer's interests.

183. Bob, FRM, works as an analyst for a U. S brokerage firm. He wrote a research report recently on public utility companies in South American and included the following statement: "Based on the fact that the South American utilities sector's new service orders has been growing rapidly, we expect that most companies in the sector will also see a significant growth in profits. We also believe the trend will continue for the next 2 to 3 years." The report then described the major risks of investing in this market, including the political and exchange rate instability associated with South American countries. Which of the following statements is correct? (　　)

A) Bob violated the Code by failing to provide details on the operations of South American utilities.

B) Bob violated the Code by recommending an investment which would be unsuitable for some of its clients.

C) Bob violated the Code by failing to distinguish between fact and opinions.

D) Bob has not violated the Code.

184. A violation of the GARP Code of Conduct would result in which of the following consequences? (　　)

Ⅰ. Suspension of the GARP Membership.

Ⅱ. Deprivation of the right to work as a risk management professional.

Ⅲ. Removal of the GARP Member's right to use the FRM designation.

Ⅳ. Required to take part in ethical trading.

A) Ⅲ and Ⅳ only

B) Ⅱ and Ⅳ only

C) Ⅰ and Ⅲ only

D) Ⅰ and Ⅱ only

第二部分

数量分析

第 5 单元

概率与统计

1. The joint probability distribution of random variables X and Y is given by $f(x, y) = k \times x \times y$ for $x = 1, 2, 3$, $y = 1, 2, 3$, and k is a positive constant. What is the probability that $X + Y$ will exceed 5? (　　)

   A) 1/9

   B) 1/4

   C) 1/36

   D) Cannot be determined

2. Vic has rolled a three on a single die four times in a row. Assuming it is a fair die, What probability of his rolling another three on the next roll? (　　)

   A) 0.200

   B) 0.167

   C) 0.001

   D) 0.500

3. Dependent random variables that their joint probability is (　　).

   A) equal to zero

   B) not equal to the product of their individual probabilities

   C) equal to the product of their individual probabilities

   D) greater than the product of their individual probabilities

4. Which of the following involves conditional expectations? (　　)

   A) calculating the conditional variance

   B) determining the expected joint probability

   C) estimation the skewness

   D) refining a forecast because of the occurrence of some other event

5. Given the following table about employees of a company based on whether they eat vegetable or not eat vegetable and whether they suffer from any allergies, what is

the probability both suffering from allergies and not suffering from allergies? (　)

	Suffer from Allergies	Don't Suffer from Allergies	Total
Eat vegetable	10	15	25
Not eat	25	10	35
Total	35	25	60

A) 0.45
B) 0.24
C) 0.00
D) 1.00

6. What is the probability of obtaining heads three times, if a fair coin is tossed three times? (　)
A) 1
B) 1/2
C) 1/8
D) 3/4

7. Which of the following is not least likely, If X and Y are independent events? (　)
A) $P(X \text{ or } Y) = P(X) + P(Y)$.
B) X and Y cannot occur together.
C) $P(X \text{ or } Y) = (P(X)) \times (P(Y))$.
D) $P(X \mid Y) = P(X)$.

8. If the probability of both a new Amazon' warehouse and a new School being built next month is 48%, and the probability of a new School being built is 75%, what is the probability of a new warehouse being built if a new School is built? (　)
A) 0.69
B) 0.72
C) 0.64
D) 0.80

9. Which is accurate about a joint probability of A and B? (　)
A) greater than or equal to the probability of A or B
B) less than or equal to the conditional probability of A given B

C) greater than or equal to the conditional probability of A given B
D) less than the probability of A and the probability of B

10. Apple says that whether its earnings increase depends on whether to increase customer from the Chinese market. We can know from this information (　　).
A) P (both customer increase and earnings increase) = P(customer increase).
B) P (earnings increase | customer increase) is not equal to P(earnings increase).
C) P (customer increase | earnings increase) is not equal to P(earnings increase).
D) P (customer increase or earnings increase) = P (both customer and earnings increase).

11. In a High School, the probabilities that two students will earn an A+ on an exam are 0.35, and 0.1 respectively. If each student's performance is independent of that of the other students. The probability that the two students will earn an A+ is closest to (　　).
A) 0.450
B) 0.035
C) 0.075
D) 0.015

12. A rating agency announced the bond default probability in the next year. The A-rated bond, a BBB-rated bond, and a CCC-rated bond where the probabilities of default over the next years are 5 percent, 11 percent, and 40 percent. If the individual default probabilities are independent. What is the probability that all these bonds will default in the next year? (　　)
A) 46.00%
B) 0.220%
C) 0.14%
D) 1.44%

13. If the outcome of Event A is not affected by event B, then events A and B are said to be (　　).
A) collectively exhaustive
B) statistically independent
C) mutually exclusive
D) conditionally dependent

14. $P(A) = 0.60$ and $P(B) = 0.30$. Let A and B be two mutually exclusive events. Which of the following is most accurate? (　　)

A) $P(A \text{ and } B) = 0.18$

B) $P(B \mid A) = 0.30$

C) $P(A \text{ and } B) = 0$

D) $P(A \text{ or } B) = 0.72$

15. Which of the following description about probability is most accurate? (　　)

A) An event is a set of one or more possible values of a random variable.

B) A conditional probability is the probability that two or more events will happen concurrently.

C) An outcome is the calculated probability of an event.

D) Out of a sample of 100 widgets, 19 were found to be defective, 21 were perfect, and 60 were Ok. The probability of picking a perfect widget at random is 29%.

16. If two fair coins are flipped and three fair six-sided dice are rolled, all at the same time, what is the probability of ending up with first ishead and second is back (on the coins) and three ones (on the dice)? (　　)

A) 0.01157

B) 0.001157

C) 0.0089

D) 0.00463

17. An analyst gathered the following information about the return distributions for two portfolios during the same period:

Portfolio	Skewness	Kurtosis
A	−1.6	1.9
B	0.8	3.2

The analyst states that the distribution for Portfolio A is more peaked than a normal distribution and that the distribution for Portfolio B has a long tail on the left side of the distribution. Which of the following is correct? (　　)

A) The analyst's assessment is correct.

B) The analyst's assessment is correct for Portfolio A and incorrect for Portfolio B.

C) The analyst's assessment is not correct for Portfolio A but is correct for Portfolio B.

D) The analyst's assessment is incorrect for both portfolios.

18. Which one of the following statements about the correlation coefficient is false? (　　)

A) It always ranges from −1 to +1.

B) A correlation coefficient of zero means that two random variables are independent.

C) It is a measure of linear relationship between two random variables.

D) It can be calculated by scaling the covariance between two random variables.

19. Suppose that A and B are random variables, each follows a standard normal distribution, and the covariance between A and B is 0.35. What is the variance of (3A+2B)? (　　)

A) 14.47

B) 17.20

C) 9.20

D) 15.10

20. Given that x and y are random variables and a, b, c, and d are constants, which one of the following definitions is wrong? (　　)

A) $E(ax + by + c) = aE(x) + bE(y) + c$, if x and y are correlated.

B) $V(ax + by + c) = V(ax + by) + c$, if x and y are correlated.

C) $\mathrm{Cov}(ax + by, cx + dy) = acV(x) + bdV(y) + (ad + bc)\mathrm{Cov}(x, y)$, if x and y are correlated.

D) $V(x - y) = V(x + y) = V(x) + V(y)$, if x and y are uncorrelated.

21. Which of the following statements about the normal distribution is not accurate? (　　)

A) Kurtosis equals 3.

B) Skewness equals 1.

C) The entire distribution can be characterized by two moments, mean and variance.

D) The normal density function has the following expression:

$$f(x) = \frac{1}{\sqrt{2\pi\sigma^2}}\exp\left[-\frac{1}{2\sigma^2}(x-\mu)^2\right]$$

22. The skew of a lognormal distribution is always (　　).

A) positive

B) negative

C) 0

D) 3

23. X and Y are discrete random variables. The probability that $P(X = 4)$ is 0.30 and that the $P(Y = 4)$ is 0.25. What is the probability of observing that $P(X = 4 \text{ and } Y = 4)$? (　　)

A) 0.075
B) 0.25
C) 0.5
D) cannot answer with the information provided

24. Tesla, Inc., has determined three possible economic scenarios and has projected return for two new Tesla electric car (model 3 and model 2) for their company under each scenario. James's economist estimated the probability of each scenario as shown in the table below. Given the information, what is the expected return on Model 2? (　　)

Scenario	Probability	Model 2	Model 3
A	35%	20%	19%
B	20%	12%	8%
C	45%	35%	35%

A) 25.15%
B) 12.97%
C) 35.55%
D) 9.75%

25. When the tails of a distribution are fatter than the normal distribution, we say that the distribution is (　　).
A) leptokurtic
B) symmetrical
C) platykurtic
D) skewed

26. A distribution has positive excess kurtosis. Which of the following is true? (　　)
A) It is more peaked than a normal distribution.
B) It is more skewed than a normal distribution.
C) It is less peaked than a normal distribution.
D) It has thinner tails than a normal distribution.

27. The following stocks constitute this combination, and the weight of each stock is shown below.

Stock	Market Value	Return Expected Annual
A	$2,500	18%
B	$3,500	14%
C	$4,000	9%

The investor's expected total rate of return (increase in market value) after four years is closest to (　　).

A) 13.0%

B) 44.5%

C) 136.0%

D) 63.04%

28. The variance of the sum of two independent random variables is equal to the sum variances (　　).

A) plus zero

B) minus a positive covariance term

C) plus a positive covariance term

D) plus a non-zero covariance term

29. Use the following probability distribution to calculate the standard deviation for the portfolio. (　　)

State of the Economy	Probability	Return on Portfolio
Good	0.40	25%
Poor	0.60	8%

A) 6.3%

B) 8.33%

C) 1.04%

D) 0.6%

30. A venture company in this year have a 30% chance increase revenue and a 70% chance decrease revenue. If the company increase revenue, your returns will be 40% and if the company decrease revenue, your returns will be −10%. What is your expected return? (　　)

A) 17%

B) 5%

C) 12%

D) 18%

31. A stock trader researches a stock for 11 years observe the following annual returns on the stock for the last ten years: [11%, 11%, 5%, −4%, 6%, 5%, −18%, 11%, −1%, 5%, 5%]. Which measure of central tendency has the highest value? (　　)

A) the mode

B) the median

C) the medianand mode

D) the mean

32. An analyst is currently considering a portfolio consisting of two stocks. The first stock, HM Co., has an expected return of 22% and a standard deviation of 8%. The second stock, Uniqlo, Inc., has an expected return of 25% and a standard deviation of 12%. The correlation of returns between the two securities is 0.35. If the analyst forms a portfolio with 40% in HM and 60% in Uniqlo, What is the portfolio's expected return? (　　)

A) 17.6%

B) 15.3%

C) 23.8%

D) 12.2%

33. Consider the case when the Y variable is in U.S. dollars, and the X variable is in U.S. dollars. The 'units' of the covariance between Y and X are (　　).

A) a range of values from −1 to +1

B) U.S. dollars

C) squared U.S. dollars

D) the square root of U.S. dollars

34. Jack John holds a large position in the common stock of Alibaba, Inc. Jack is about to announce a new CRO, after an extensive executive search and Recommended by other employees. There are three candidates for the CRO position, and each candidate is viewed differently by the shareholder. Jack estimates the following probabilities for the rate of return on Alibaba's stock in the year following the announcement:

Candidate	Probability of Being Chosen	Rate of Return if Chosen
A	40%	20%
B	25%	15%
C	35%	12%

Under Jack's estimates, the expected rate of return on Alibaba's stock following the announcement of the new CRO is closest to (　　).

A) 15.95%

B) −2.64%

C) 9.12%
D) 6.75%

35. About Left-skewed distributions which following is true (　　).
A) A longer tail to the right of the distribution.
B) Greater mass to the left of the expected value.
C) Mean<Median<Mode.
D) Mode<Median<Mean.

36. Assume that sample performance data indicates that a hedge fund manager performed well in the market in each of the last five years. If only the previous five years of data is included in the sample, what would the frequentist approach predict as the probability that this manager will perform well in the market again next year? (　　)
A) 0%
B) 50%
C) 75%
D) 100%

37. The correlation coefficient for two dependent random variables is equal to (　　).
A) the covariance between the random variables divided by the product of the variances
B) the product of the standard deviations for the two random variables divided by the covariance
C) the covariance between the random variables divided by the product of the standard deviations
D) the absolute value of the difference between the means of the two variables divided by the product of the variances

38. Which of the following statements about the correlation coefficient is most accurate? (　　)
A) between $-\infty$ and $+1$
B) boundless
C) bounded between -1 and ∞
D) bounded between -1 and $+1$

39. The characteristic function of the product of independent random variables is equal to the (　　).
A) square root of the product of the individual characteristic functions
B) sum of the individual characteristic functions

C) product of the individual characteristic functions

D) exponential root of the product of the individual characteristic functions

40. A scatter plot is a collection of points on a graph where each point represents the values of two variables (i. e. , an X/Y pair). The pattern of data points will illustrate a correlation between these two variables that is between (　　).

A) −1 to 0

B) −0. 7 to +0. 7

C) −1 to +1

D) 0 to +1

41. Aninvest analyst is looking at historical returns for two portfolios, Portfolio 1 and Portfolio 2. Portfolio 2's returns are much more volatile than Portfolio 1. The variance of returns for Portfolio 1 is 0. 012, and the variance of returns of Portfolio 2 is 0. 308. The correlation between the returns of the two Portfolios is 0. 79, and the covariance is 0. 048. If the variance of Portfolio 1 increased to 0. 036 while the variance of Portfolio 2 decreased to 0. 148 and the covariance remains the same, the correlation between the two bonds will (　　).

A) the values given are not plausible

B) remain the same

C) decrease

D) increase

42. In order to have a positive correlation between two variables, which of the following is most likely? (　　)

A) The covariance of one of the standard deviations must be negative.

B) The covariance can never be negative.

C) Both the covariance and least one of the standard deviations must be negative.

D) The covariance must be positive.

43. Tim Batter, FRM, is a risk analyst with a large hedge fund firm. Currently, Tim is considering the risk and return parameters associated with Plex, a small movie firm. After in-depth analysis of the firm and the economic outlook, Tim estimates the following return probabilities on the chart:

Probability(Pi)	Return(Ri)
0. 4	−8%
0. 5	18%
0. 1	35%

Palm's goal is to quantify the risk/ return relationship for Plex.

Given the returns and probability estimates above, which of the following is true about the expected return for Plex? (　　)

A) 53%

B) 15.5%

C) 11%

D) 9.3%

44. Which type of distribution produces the lowest probability for a variable to exceed a specified extreme value that is greater than the mean, assuming the distributions all have the same mean and variance? (　　)

A) a leptokurtic distribution with kurtosis of 4

B) a leptokurtic distribution with kurtosis of 8

C) a normal distribution

D) a platykurtic distribution

45. The random variable X with density function $f(x) = 1/(b - a)$ for $a < x < b$, and 0 otherwise, is said to have a uniform distribution over (a, b). Calculate its mean. (　　)

A) $(a + b)/2$

B) $(a - b)/2$

C) $(a + b)/4$

D) $(a - b)/4$

46. Assume that a random variable follows a normal distribution with a mean of 80 and a standard deviation of 24. What percentage of this distribution is not between 32 and 116? (　　)

A) 4.56%

B) 8.96%

C) 13.36%

D) 18.15%

47. Which of the following statements best characterizes the relationship between the normal and lognormal distributions? (　　)

A) The lognormal distribution is the logarithm of the normal distribution.

B) If the natural log of the random variable X is lognormally distributed, then X is normally distributed.

C) If X is lognormally distributed, then the natural log of X is normally distributed.

D) The two distributions have nothing to do with one another.

48. Consider a stock with an initial price of \$100. Its price one year from now is given by $S = 100 \times \exp(r)$, where the rate of return r is normally distributed with a mean of 0.1 and a standard deviation of 0.2. With 95% confidence, after rounding, S will be between ( ).

A) \$67.57 and \$147.99

B) \$70.80 and \$149.20

C) \$74.68 and \$163.56

D) \$102.18 and \$119.53

49. For a lognormal variable X, we know that $\ln(X)$ has a normal distribution with amean of zero and a standard deviation of 0.5. What are the expected value and the variance of X? ( )

A) 1.025 and 0.187

B) 1.126 and 0.217

C) 1.133 and 0.365

D) 1.203 and 0.399

50. Which of the following statements is the most accurate about the relationship between a normal distribution and a Student's t distribution that have the same mean and standard deviation? ( )

A) They have the same skewness and the same kurtosis.

B) The Student's t distribution has larger skewness and larger kurtosis.

C) The kurtosis of a Student's t distribution converges to that of the normal distribution as the number of degrees of freedom increases.

D) The normal distribution is a good approximation for the Student's t distribution when the number of degrees of freedom is small.

51. On a multiple-choice exam with four choices for each of six questions, what is the probability that a student gets fewer than two questions correct simply by guessing? ( )

A) 0.46%

B) 23.73%

C) 35.60%

D) 53.39%

52. When you use the normal distribution to approximate the Poisson distribution, assuming you have n independent trials, each with a probability of success of p, which following is true? ( )

A) When the mean of the Poisson distribution is very small

B) When the variance of the Poisson distribution is very small

C) When the number of observations is very large and the success rate is close to 1

D) When the number of observations is very large and the success rate is close to 0

53. A company chief riskofficer thinks the annual portfolio returns is approximately normal with an expected value of \$150 million and a standard deviation of \$30 million. Which of the following is closest to the probability that the value of the portfolio one year from today will be between \$120 million and \$210 million? (　　)

A) 42.65%

B) 74.39%

C) 81.85%

D) 58.15%

54. Which one of the following distributions is described entirely by the degrees of freedom? (　　)

A) Student's t-distribution

B) Normal distribution

C) Binomial distribution

D) Lognormal distribution

55. Regarding a binomially distributed random variable, the variance of the number of successes, X, where n equals the number of trials and p equals the probability of success, is most likely equal to (　　).

A) $P(1-p)$

B) $Np(1-p)$

C) P

D) Np

56. Haidilao receives an average of 2 clients per minutes. The probability that they will receive ten clients in a 6-minutes is closest to (　　).

A) 5.66%

B) 12.59%

C) 10.48%

D) 17.56%

57. Which of the following statements about probability distributions is not true? (　　)

A) A probability distribution is, by definition, normally distributed.

B) One of the key properties of a probability function is $0 \leqslant p \leqslant 1$.

C) In a binomial distribution, each observation has only two possible outcomes that are mutually exclusive.

D) A probability distribution includes a listing of all the possible outcomes of an experiment.

58. A series of investors want to be sure to always earn at least a 6% rate of return on their investments. They are looking at an investment that has a normally distributed probability distribution with an expected rate of return of 12% and a standard deviation of 6%. The probability of meeting or exceeding the investors desired return in any given year is closest to (　　).

A) 50%

B) 98%

C) 84%

D) 68%

59. Given the probabilities $N(-0.75)=0.2266$, $N(1)=0.8413$, and $N(1.75)=0.9599$ from a table, the probability of 0.1587 corresponds to (　　).

A) N (0.25)

B) N (−1)

C) N (−1.75)

D) N (0.75)

60. To apply the central limit theorem to the sampling distribution of the sample mean, the sample is usually considered to be large if nis greater than (　　).

A) 18

B) 30

C) 35

D) 25

61. A normal distribution can be completely described by its (　　).

A) mean and mode

B) skewness and kurtosis

C) mean and variance

D) standard deviation

62. An investor has a portfolio that mean return is 15% and a standard deviation of returns equal to 10%. Which of the following statements is most likely? The probability of obtaining a return (　　).

A) greater than 5% is 0.7882

B) greater than 25% is 0. 8413

C) between 15% and 35% is 0. 9772

D) less than 25% is 0. 8413

63. An economist has determined that the probability that the Shanghai composite index will increase on any given day is 0. 55 and the probability that it will decrease is 0. 45. The expected value and variance of the number of up days in an 8-day period are closest to (　　).

A) 3. 5 and 1. 19

B) 3. 0 and 1. 26

C) 2. 5 and 0. 55

D) 4. 4 and 1. 98

64. A famous fashion company is considering the introduction of A brand new brand. In the past year, the success rate for new brand has been 40 percent. Extensive market research has produced positive marketing for the brand under consideration. Historically, 80 percent of reports before introduction have been favorable given successful brand. Only 25 percent have received favorable reports given unsuccessful brand. What is the probability that the new brand will be successful given a favorable report? (　　)

A) 73%

B) 25%

C) 18%

D) 68%

65. Bonds rated A has a 15% chance of default in five years. Bonds rated BBB have a 25% chance of default in five years. A portfolio consists of 40% A and 60% BBB-rated bonds. If a randomly selected bond NOT defaults in five years, what is the probability that it was an A-rated bond? (　　)

A) 0. 29

B) 0. 25

C) 0. 43

D) 0. 64

66. James Simons was graduated last month. He has applied to both Apple and Google; Simons has determined that probability of getting into Apple is 30% and the probability of getting into Google (his brotherworkingoogle) is 52%. Simons has also determined that the probability of being accepted both companies is 5. 6%. What is the probability of Simons being accepted at either Appleor Google? (　　)

A) 64.2%
B) 7.7%
C) 76.4%
D) 10.5%

67. The probability of a new Seven eleven convenience store being built in front of the company is 70%. If Seven eleven convenience store comes to town, the probability of the new KFC restaurant being built is 90%. What is the probability of a new Seven eleven convenience store and a new KFC restaurant being built? (　　)
A) 0.63
B) 0.24
C) 0.36
D) 0.57

68. An investor is choosing one of twenty securities. Half of the securities are stocks and bonds. Three of the ten stocks were issued by Private enterprises; the other seven were issued by State-owned enterprises. Four of the ten bonds were issued by Private enterprises; the other six were issued by State-owned enterprises. What the probability that security is a bond or security issued by a State-owned enterprise If the investor chooses security at random? (　　)
A) 0.75
B) 0.60
C) 0.85
D) 0.80

69. The following chart describes the availability of smartphone with Professional camera and Environmentally battery dealership.

	Environmentally battery	No Environmentally battery	Total
Professional camera	70	35	105
No Professional camera	65	55	120
Total	135	90	225

What is the probability of selecting a smartphone at random that has either Professional camera or Environmentally battery? (　　)
A) 106.6%
B) 50%
C) 75.6%
D) 34%

第 6 单元

假设检验与线性回归

70. What does a hypothesis test at the 5% significance level mean? (　　)
A) P(not reject H_0 | H_0 is true) $=0.05$
B) P(not reject H_0 | H_0 is false) $=0.05$
C) P(reject H_0 | H_0 is true) $=0.05$
D) P(reject H_0 | H_0 is false) $=0.05$

71. When testing a hypothesis, which of the following statements is correct when the level of significance of the test is decreased? (　　)
A) The likelihood of rejecting the null hypothesis when it is true decreases.
B) The likelihood of making a type 1 error increases.
C) The null hypothesis is rejected more frequently, even when it is false.
D) The likelihood of making a type 2 error decreases.

72. A population has a known mean of 1,000. Suppose 1,600 samples are randomly drawn (with replacement) from this population. The mean of the observed samples is 998.7, and the standard deviation of the observed samples is 100. What is the standard error of the sample mean? (　　)
A) 0.025
B) 0.25
C) 2.5
D) 25

73. Consider the following linear regression model: $Y = a + bX + e$. Suppose $a = 0.05$, $b = 1.2$, $SD(Y) = 0.26$, and $SD(e) = 0.1$. What is the correlation between X and Y? (　　)
A) 0.923
B) 0.852
C) 0.701
D) 0.462

A statistician wants to investigate two samples were drawn from a normally distributed population. The first sample, the mean was \$55, and the standard deviation was \$6. The second sample, the mean was \$58, and the standard deviation was \$8. The first sample consists of 16 observations, and the second sample consists of 25 observations. (Note: In the following Questions, the subscripts "A" and "B" indicate the first and second sample, respectively.) Answer the following three question.

74. Consider the hypotheses structured as $H_0: \mu_a = \$50$ versus $H_a: \mu_a \neq \$50$. At a 1 percent level of significance, the null hypothesis (　　).
A) should neither be rejected nor fail to be rejected
B) should be rejected
C) cannot be rejected
D) cannot be tested using this sample information provided

75. Adjust the significant level from 1 percentto 5 percent and a hypothesis test structure of $H_0: \sigma_a^2 \leqslant 24$ versus $H_A: \sigma_a^2 > 24$, the null hypothesis (　　). (Population standard deviation = 5)
A) should be rejected
B) cannot be rejected
C) cannot be tested using this sample information provided
D) should neither be rejected nor fail to be rejected

76. Consider the hypotheses structured as $H_0: \mu_b \leqslant \$56$ versus $H_a: \mu_b > \$56$. At a 10 percent level of significance, the null hypothesis (　　).
A) cannot be tested using the sample information provided
B) should neither be rejected nor fail to be rejected
C) cannot be rejected
D) should be rejected

77. If the variance of the sampling distribution of an estimator is smaller than all other estimators of the parameter of interest, which of the following statement about the estimator is most accurate? (　　)
A) consistent
B) efficient
C) reliable
D) unbiased

78. Which value is the most accurate of the test statistic that follows an F-distribution when two variances are equal, and the level of significance is 0.1? (　　)

A) 0.10
B) 0.90
C) 1.00
D) 0.05

79. A series of firms in the technology industry have a different annual return in the following chart. Given the information about the sample of returns, what are the sample variance and standard deviation? (　　)

Firm 1	Firm 2	Firm 3	Firm 4	Firm 5
14%	6%	5%	7%	(−2%)

Variance	Standard Deviation
A) 64.5	8.0
B) 25.0	5.0
C) 49.6	7.1
D) 32.5	5.7

80. The mean and variance of a sample average help identify the distributional characteristics of sample distribution and when the sample size is large allow assumptions to be made about this distribution. Which of the following choices represent the standard deviation of a sample average? (　　)

A) $\sigma(X)/\sqrt{n}$
B) $1/n$
C) $\sigma(X)2/n$
D) $\sigma(X)2$

81. Williams a head of Investment department for a large regional invest bank. Last year, he hired John Brinkley as atrader. Part of the compensation package was the chance to earn one of the following two bonuses: if Brinkley can increase Operating income tomore than 40%, he will receive a 35% bonus. If he can increase Operating income to more than 25%, he will receive a 20% bonus (using a significance level of 10%). Assume Operating income is normally distributed. The population standard deviation of Operating income is 16%. A recent sample of 100 branch offices resulted in an average Operating income of 24.2%. Which of the following statements is most accurate? (　　)

A) Brinkley should not receive either bonus.
B) For the 20% bonus level, the test statistic is −0.5 and should give Brinkley a 20% bonus.

C) For the 25% bonus level, the test statistic is −1.65.

D) For the 35% bonus level, the critical value is −1.65 and Huffman should give Brinkley a 50% bonus.

82. A Type Ⅱ error occurs when the null hypothesis ( ).

A) is rejected when it is false

B) fails to be rejected when it is false

C) fails to be rejected when it is true

D) is rejected when it is true

83. A Type I error ( ).

A) fails to reject a false null hypothesis

B) rejects a false null hypothesis

C) fails to reject a true null hypothesis

D) rejects a true null hypothesis

84. A random sample of 64 technology stocks earned an average of 15%. Assuming the distribution of equity returns is normal and the population standard deviation is 4%, the 95% confidence interval for the population mean is ( ).

A) 14.02% to 15.98%

B) 9.62% to 12.98%

C) 9.50% to 10.50%

D) 4.00% to 14.00%

85. A survey is taken to determine whether the startling average salaries of FRM candidates is equal to or greater than $60,000 per year. What is the test statistic given a sample of 145 newly acquired FRM candidates with a mean startling salary of $66,000 and a standard deviation of $5,500? ( )

A) 0.91

B) −0.91

C) 13.14

D) −13.14

86. The first step in the process of hypothesis testing is ( ).

A) selecting the test statistic

B) the collection of the sample

C) to state the hypotheses

D) the calculation of sample statistics

87. The average CAD/Euro exchange rate from a sample of 49 monthly observations is \$0. 9/ Euro. The population variance is 0. 36. Which of the following is most accurate about the 95% of the confidence interval for the mean CAD/Euro exchange rate? (　　)

A) \$0. 807 to \$1. 192

B) \$0. 792 to \$1. 068

C) \$0. 845 to \$1. 143

D) \$0. 771 to \$1. 287

88. Given the following hypothesis:

The null hypothesis is H_0: $\mu = 6$

The alternative is H_1: $\mu \neq 6$

The mean of a sample of 25 is 7. 5

The population standard deviation is 4. 0

Calculate the calculated z-statistic. (　　)

A) 6. 25

B) 4. 12

C) 1. 88

D) 1. 65

89. James is comparing the return on equity for two food company. Heis convinced that the return on equity for the Nutritious food (NF) is greater than that of the Junk food (JF). Which describe is most likely about the hypotheses for a test of his comparison of return on different food? (　　)

A) H_0: $\mu NF \leqslant \mu JF$ versus H_a: $\mu NF > \mu JF$.

B) H_0: $\mu NF \neq \mu JF$ versus H_a: $\mu NF = \mu JF$.

C) H_0: $\mu NF = \mu JF$ versus H_a: $\mu NF \neq \mu JF$.

D) H_0: $\mu NF = \mu JF$ versus H_a: $\mu NF < \mu JF$.

90. A sample of size 36 is selected from a normal population. This sample has a mean of 9 and the population standard deviation is 6. Using this information, calculate a 95% confidence interval for the population mean. (　　)

A) $9 \pm 1.96(0.5)$

B) $9 \pm 1.96(0.8)$

C) $9 \pm 1.96(1)$

D) $9 \pm 1.96(4)$

91. A stock analysis wants to test weather Stock A is more volatile than Stock B; prices of both stocks are observed to construct the sample variance of the two stocks. The most appropriate test statistics to carry out the test is the (　　).

A) Chi-square test

B) T-test

C) Z test

D) F test

92. The approximate 95% confidence interval for the population mean based on the 36-day returnand sample returns with a mean of 9% and a sample standard deviation of 24% is closest to (   ).

A) 1. 44% to 18. 58%

B) 1. 16% to 16. 84%

C) −1. 22% to 15. 5%

D) 0. 54% to 13. 4%

93. The mean equity risk premium over 38 years is equal to 12. 0 percent. The standard deviation of the sample is 16 percent. Calculate the standard error of the sample mean (   ).

A) 1. 86%

B) 8. 40%

C) 0. 30%

D) 2. 60%

94. Vic observe the following pairs of month returns on a sample of two stocks in Dow Jones index: [(0. 06, 0. 02), (0. 05, 0. 09), (0. 02, 0. 02), (0. 13, 0. 04)] and the correlation coefficient is 0. 56. calculatethe covariance of the returns on the two stocks (   ).

A) 0. 00165

B) 0. 00133

C) 0. 00086

D) 0. 00064

95. A return series with 360 observations has a sample mean of 16 percent and a standard deviation of 18 percent. The standard error of the sample means is closest to (   ).

A) 3. 87%

B) 0. 95%

C) 33. 3%

D) 0. 68%

96. For the 99 percent confidence interval of the sample mean of the Hedge fund return for a hedge fund is 20 to 37. There are over 1,000 fund and the sample size of this

test is 81. Given that the expected value of the Hedge fund return is 28.5, the standard error of the ratio is closest to (　　).

A) 5.38

B) 1.96

C) 3.32

D) 12.50

97. The mean annual return for an equity portfolio over 16 years is 2.5%. The standard deviation is 3.0%. The value of the test statistic to test the hypothesis that means annual return is equal to zero is closest to (　　).

A) 6.87

B) 33.00

C) 0.50

D) 3.33

98. In a two-tailed test of a hypothesis concerning whether a population mean is one, Willian computes a t-statistic of 2.8 based on a sample of 20 observations where the distribution is normal. If a 1% significance level is chosen, Willan should (　　).

A) reject the null hypothesis and conclude that the population means is significantly different from one

B) reject the null hypothesis and conclude that the population means is not significantly different from one

C) failto reject the null hypothesis that the population means is not significantly different from one

D) not make a conclusion pending additional observations

99. A bottler of milk tea wishes to ensure that an average of 11milliliter of milk tea is in each bottle. Wantto analyze the accuracy of the bottling process, a random sample of 180 bottles is taken. Using a t-distributed test statistic of −1.39 and a 5% level of significance, the bottler should (　　).

A) reject the null hypothesis and conclude that bottles do not contain an average of 11 ounces of tea

B) reject the null hypothesis and conclude that bottles contain an average 11 ounces of tea

C) not reject the null hypothesis and conclude that bottles do not contain an average of 11 ounces of tea

D) not reject the null hypothesis and conclude that bottles contain an average 11 ounces of tea

100. Brown believes that the average return on equity in the manufacturing industry, μ, is less than 8%. Which following is true about the appropriate null (H_0) and alternative (H_a) hypothesis to test? (　　)

A) H_0: $\mu < 0.08$ versus H_a: $\mu > 0.08$.

B) H_0: $\mu < 0.08$ versus H_a: $\mu \geqslant 0.08$.

C) H_0: $\mu \geqslant 0.08$ versus H_a: $\mu < 0.08$.

D) H_0: $\mu > 0.08$ versus H_a: $\mu < 0.08$.

101. The test statistic for an F-test of the equality of two sample variances is the (　　).

A) plus of the two sample variances.

B) ratio of the two sample variances.

C) ratio of the two samples standard error.

D) product of the two sample standard deviations.

102. The assumptions underlying linear regression include all of the following EXCEPT (　　).

A) Dependent variable and independent variable are linearly related.

B) Disturbance term is homoskedastic and is independently distributed.

C) Disturbance term is normally distributed with an expected value of 0.

D) Independent variable is linearly related to the residuals (or disturbance term).

103. Which of the following statements is least likely? (　　)

A) Failing to reject the null when it is false is an example of a Type Ⅱ error.

B) The probability of committing a Type I error is the significance level of the test.

C) If a person is presumed innocent unless proven otherwise, finding a guilty person innocent is an example of a Type I error.

D) A Type I error is rejecting the null when it is true.

104. An analyst conducts a two-tailed z-test to determine if big cap returns are significantly different from 12%. The sample size was 100. The computed z-statistic is 1.4. Using a 5% level of significance, which statement is not least likely? (　　)

A) A sample size of 100 indicates that we should fail to reject the null.

B) You cannot determine what to do with the information given.

C) Reject the null hypothesis and conclude that small-cap returns are significantly different from 12%.

D) Fail to reject the null hypothesis and conclude that small-cap returns are close enough to 12% that we cannot say they are significantly different from 12

A stock analyst is conducting a hypothesis test to determine whether the mean time spent on investment research is different from 5 hours per day. The test is performed at the 1 percent level of significance and uses a random sample of 36 portfolio managers, where the mean time spent on research is round to be 4.5 hours. The population standard deviation is 2.5 hours. Answer the following five question.

105. The appropriate null hypothesis for the described test is (　　).

A) H_0: $\mu \neq 5$ hours

B) H_0: $\mu = 5$ hours

C) H_0: $\mu \leqslant 5$ hours

D) H_0: $\mu \geqslant 5$ hours

106. Which type of test is this? (　　)

A) One-tailed test.

B) Two-tailed test.

C) Equity of variance test.

D) Chi-square test.

107. The calculated z-statistic is (　　).

A) ± 1.20

B) -1.20

C) -2.13

D) $+0.33$

108. The critical z-value(s) of the test statistic is (are) (　　).

A) ± 2.56

B) -2.56

C) ± 1.58

D) $+1.96$

109. Which of the following decisions is the accurate decision for this case? (　　)

A) No decision is possible because the sample standard deviation was not given.

B) Fail to reject the null hypothesis.

C) Reject the null hypothesis.

D) The sample size is too small, so increase the sample size.

The ANOVA table above; I regressed Male Math scores (explained) on Male Verbal scores (explanatory). The OLS regression equation produced is: MATHM = 269.76 + 0.52 × VERBM. Here is the ANOVA table produced by Excel, Answer the following two question.

ANOVA					
	df	ss	ms	F	Singnificance
Regression	1	947. 906	947. 906	168. 5	0. 00
Residual	22	124. 094	5. 641		
Total	23	1,072			

	Coefficients	Standard error	T-stat	P-value	Low 95%	Upper 95%
Intercept	262. 8	18. 30	14. 36	0. 00	224. 84	300. 76
X Variable 1	0. 5386	0. 04155	12. 96	0. 00	0. 45	0. 62

110. Show how the 95% confidence interval for each coefficient (slope and intercept) is calculated. (　　)

A) [231. 606; 307. 73], [0. 335567; 0. 565404]
B) [231. 696; 307. 82], [0. 433576; 0. 606424]
C) [201. 696; 307. 73], [0. 335567; 0. 565404]
D) [231. 606; 327. 73], [0. 433576; 0. 606424]

111. Confirm this by using the ANOVA table to calculate the R^2. (　　)

A) 0. 86
B) 0. 91
C) 0. 88
D) 0. 80

112. Consider the regression results from the regression of Y against X for 30 observations: $Y = 0.89 + 1.5X$.

The standard error of the estimate is 0. 45 and the standard error of the coefficient is 0. 55. Which of the following reports the correct value of the t-statistic for the slope and correctly evaluates its statistical significance with 99 percent confidence? (　　)

A) $t = 1.200$; the slope not significantly difference from zero.
B) $t = 2.727$; the slopeis not significantly difference from zero.
C) $t = 3.000$; the slopeis significantly difference from zero.
D) $t = 2.667$; the slopeis significantly difference from zero.

113. Which of the following are included in a sample regression function? (　　)

Ⅰ. The intercept.
Ⅱ. The error term.
Ⅲ. The slope coefficient.

Ⅳ. The independent variable.

A) Ⅰ and Ⅲ only

B) Ⅲ and Ⅳ only

C) Ⅰ, Ⅲ, and Ⅳ only

D) Ⅰ, Ⅱ, Ⅲ, and Ⅳ

114. Consider the following estimated regression equation:

Income(t) = 1.89 + 1.22 Salary(t)

The standard error of the coefficient is 0.45 and the number of observations is 24. The 95 percent confidence interval for the slope coefficient, b_1, is (　　).

A) $\{0.454 < b_1 < 2.696\}$

B) $\{-0.766 < b_1 < 3.406\}$

C) $\{0.286 < b_1 < 2.153\}$

D) $\{0.910 < b_1 < 1.840\}$

115. Simple linear regression is run to quantify the relationship between the return on the individual stocks of small-sized companies (small Caps) and the return on the Shanghai composite index, using the monthly return on small Cap stocks as the dependent variable and the monthly return on the Shanghai composite index as the independent variable. The results of the regression are shown below:

	Coefficient	Standard Error of Coefficient	t-Value
Intercept	1.68	2.85	0.48
Shanghai composite index	1.42	0.16	12.69
$R^2 = 0.599$			

Use the regression statistics presented above and assume this historical relationship still holds in the future period. If the expected return on the Shanghai composite index over the next period were 12%, the expected return on small Cap stocks over the next period would be (　　).

A) 33.85%

B) 18.72%

C) 22.36%

D) 25.61%

116. Consider the regression results from the regression of A against B for 49 observations: $A = 6.0 - 1.3B$. The standard error of the estimate is 0.90 and the standard error of the coefficient is 0.55. What is the predicted value of A if B is 10 is? (　　)

A) −12

B) 20

C) −7

D) 3.5

117. Which term is not accurate to apply to a regression model? (　　)

A) Goodness of fit.

B) Coefficient of determination.

C) Coefficient of variation.

D) R^2.

118. Which following about the R^2 of a simple regression of two variables measure is most accurate and what calculation is used to equate the correlation coefficient to the coefficient of determination?

R^2 measures (　　).	Correlation coefficient
A) percent of the variability of the dependent variable that is explained by the variability of the independent variable	$R^2 = r^2$
B) percent of the variability of the independent variable that is explained by the variability of the dependent variable	$R^2 = r^2$
C) percent of the variability of the dependent variable that is explained by the variability of the independent variable	$R^2 = r \times 2$
D) percent of the variability of the independent variable that is explained by the variability of the dependent variable	$R^2 = r \times 2$

119. In the estimated regression equation $Y = 0.88 - 1.3X$, which of the following is true when interpreting the slope coefficient? (　　)

A) If the value of X is 0, the value of Y will be −1.3.

B) 0.88 is the elasticity of X with respect to Y.

C) The independent variable declines by −1.5 units if X increases by 1 unit.

D) The dependent variable increases by 1.3 units if X decreases by 1 unit.

120. If the correlation between two variables is 1.0, the scatter plot would appear along a (　　).

A) a curved line running northwest to southeast

B) a curved line centered in the scatter plot

C) a straight line running from southwest to northeast

D) straight line running from southwest to northeast

121. When interpreting the results of a multiple analysis, which of the following terms

represents the value of the dependent variable when the independent variables are all equal to zero? ( )

A) slope coefficient

B) P-Value

C) T-value

D) intercept term

122. Paul Benson is an analyst for the auto industry. He is examining the role if television advertisement for car on the sales of car shop. He gathered data and estimated the following regression of sales (millions of dollars) on the number of hours advertisement on TV (TV, in hours per week): Salest = 2.85 + 1.5TVt

The predicted sales if advertisement on TV is 5 hours per week is ( ).

A) \$9.15 million

B) \$10.35 million

C) \$12.65 million

D) \$8.75 million

123. Bob, FRM and Joy, FRM are planning to do a regression analysis. They discuss specifying the stock return equation they wish to estimate. Bob proposes the specification $E(Y_i \mid X_i) = B_0 + (B_1) \times (X^2)$. Joy process the specification $(Y_i \mid X_i) = B_0 + (B_1 \times X_i)^2$. Which, or either, is appropriate when applying linear regression? ( )

A) Neither the specification of Bob nor that of Joy.

B) The specification of Bob but not that of Jay.

C) Both the specification of Bob and Jay.

D) The specification of Jay but not that of Bob.

124. The independent variable in a regression equation is called all the following EXCEPT ( ).

A) Predicted variable

B) Explanatory variable

C) Endogenous variable

D) Predicting variable

125. The Y variable is regressed against the X variable resulting in a regression line that is flat with the plot of the paired observations widely dispersed about the regression line. Based on this information, which statement is most accurate? ( )

A) The R^2 of this regression is close to 100%.

B) X is perfectly positively correlatedto Y.

C) The correlation between X and Y is close to zero.

D) X is perfectly negatively correlated to Y.

126. Consider two stocks, A and B. Assume their annual returns are jointly normally distributed, the marginal distribution of each stockhas mean 2% and standard deviation 10%, and the correlation is 0.9. What is the expected annual return of stockA if the annual return of stock B is 3%? ( )

A) 2%

B) 2.9%

C) 4.7%

D) 1.1%

127. Whichof following about sample covariance of two random variables is true? ( )

A) Estimate the "pure" measure of the tendency of two variables to move together over a period of time.

B) Identify and measure strong nonlinear relationships between the two variables.

C) Demonstrate either the presence or absence of spurious correlation of the variables.

D) Calculatethe correlation coefficient, which is a measure of the strength of their linear relationship.

128. To evaluate the potential of a linear relationship between portfolio returns and a benchmark index, your colleague Richard conducted a univariate regression analysis. He regressed the benchmark index returns, $B(i)$, as the dependent (aka, response) variable against portfolio returns, $R(i)$, as the independent (aka, explanatory) variable. Here is his summary output:

Predictor	Coefficient	Standard Error	t-stat
Intercept	21.88	18.88	14.56
Portfolio Return	0.86	0.45	9.56
Source of Variation	Degrees of Freedom(df)	Sum of squares(ss)	Mean of squares (Mss)
Regression	1	1.728	1.728
Residual	18	2.714	0.151
Total	19	4.442	0.234

Which is nearest to the correlation coefficient between portfolio returns, $R(i)$, and the benchmark returns, $R(b)$? ( )

A) 0.4937

B) 0.5150

C) 0.6237

D) We cannot know without the adjusted R^2

129. For the last three years, we regressed monthly dollar change in gasoline prices (regressand; dependent) against the monthly change in oil prices (regressor; independent). The number of observations (n) is 36. If the coefficient of determination (R^2) is 0.18 and the total sum of squares (TSS) is 3.23 dollars^2, what is the standard error of the regression (SER)? (　　)

A) \$0.28

B) \$0.42

C) \$2.65

D) \$3.23

130. We regressed daily returns of a stock (the regressand or dependent variable) against a market index (e.g., S&P 1,500; regressor or independent variable). The regression produced a beta for the stock, with respect to the market index, of 1.050. The stock's volatility was 30.0% and the market's volatility was 20.0%. If the regression's total sum of squares (TSS) is 0.300, what is the regression's explained sum of squares (ESS)? (　　)

A) 0.0960

B) 0.1470

C) 0.4900

D) 1.2500

131. A five-year regression of monthly cotton price changes, such that the number of observations (n) equals 60, against average temperature changes produced a standard error of the regression (SER) of \$1.20. If the total sum of squares (TSS) was \$90.625 dollars^2, what is the implied correlation coefficient? (　　)

A) 0.08

B) 0.16

C) 0.28

D) 0.77

132. A portfolio manager is interested in the systematic risk of a stock portfolio, so he estimates the linear regression: $R_{Pt} - R_F = \alpha_P + \beta_P[R_{Mt} - R_F] + \epsilon_{Pt}$. where R_{Pt} is the return of the portfolio at time t, R_{Mt} is the return of the market portfolio at time t, and R_F is the risk-free rate, which is constant over time. Suppose that $\alpha = 0.008$, $\beta = 0.977$, $\sigma(R_P) = 0.167$, and $\sigma(R_M) = 0.156$. What is the approximate coefficient of determination in this regression? (　　)

A) 0.913
B) 0.834
C) 0.977
D) 0.955

133. Which of the following statements about the linear regression of the return of a portfolio over the return of its benchmark presented below are correct? (　　)

Portfolio Parameter	Value
Beta	1.25
Alpha	0.26
Coefficient of determination	0.66
Standard deviation of error	2.42

Ⅰ. The correlation is 0.71.
Ⅱ. About 34% of the variation in the portfolio return is explained by variation in the benchmark return.
Ⅲ. The portfolio is the dependent variable.
Ⅳ. For an estimated portfolio return of 12%, the confidence interval at 95% is (7.16%; 16.84%).
A) Ⅱ and Ⅳ
B) Ⅲ and Ⅳ
C) Ⅰ, Ⅱ, and Ⅲ
D) Ⅱ, Ⅲ, and Ⅳ

134. You built a linear regression model to analyze annual salaries for a developedcountry. You incorporated two independent variables, age, and experience, into your model. Upon reading the regression results, you notice that the coefficient of experience is negative, which appears to be counterintuitive. In addition, you discover that the coefficients have low t-statistics but the regression model has a high R^2. What is the most likely cause of these results? (　　)
A) incorrect standard errors
B) heteroskedasticity
C) serial correlation
D) multicollinearity

135. Which of the following statements regarding linear regression is false? (　　)
A) Heteroskedasticity occurs when the variance of residuals is not the same across all observations in the sample.

B) Unconditional heteroskedasticity leads to inefficient estimates, whereas conditional heteroskedasticity can lead to problems with both inference andestimation.

C) Serial correlation occurs when the residual terms are correlated with each other.

D) Multicollinearity occurs when a high correlation exists between or among two or more of the independent variables in a multiple regression.

136. Under what circumstances could the explanatory power of regression analysis be overstated? ( )

A) The explanatory variables are not correlated with one another.

B) The variance of the error term decreases as the value of the dependent variable increases.

C) The error term is normally distributed.

D) An important explanatory variable is omitted that influences the explanatory variables included and the dependent variable.

137. Regarding the relationship between the number of scenarios run in a simulation and the accuracy of a simulation model, which of the following statements is correct when increasing the number of scenarios from 1,000 to 4,000? ( )

A) The confidence interval will be reduced by 80%.

B) The confidence interval will increase by 50%.

C) The confidence interval will be reduced by 50%.

D) The confidence interval will double.

138. Which of the following is not accurate an assumption of linear regression? ( )

A) The residuals are normally distributed.

B) The variance of the residuals is constant.

C) There is a linear relationship between the dependent and independent variables.

D) The independent variable is correlated with the residuals.

139. A simple linear regression equation had a coefficient of determination (R^2) of 0.75. When the variance of the independent variable is 5 and the variance of the dependent variable is 8. What is the correlation coefficient between the dependent and independent variables and what is the covariance between the two variables? ( )

Correlation	Coefficient Covariance
A) 0.81	4.8
B) 0.87	5.3
C) 0.87	5.5
D) 0.91	5.5

140. In a regression analysis, the effects from independent variables that are not included in the model are embodied in the (   ).

A) scattergram

B) error term

C) slope coefficient

D) intercept

141. Linear regression is based on a series of assumptions. Which of the following is not accurate an assumption of linear regression? (   )

A) There is at least some correlation between the error terms from one observation to the next.

B) Values of the independent variable are not correlated with the error term.

C) The variance of the error terms each period remains the same.

D) A linear relationship exists between the dependent and independent variables.

142. Which of the following statements not describes the procedure for testing a hypothesis? (   )

A) Compute the sample value of the test statistic, set up a rejection (critical) region, and make a decision.

B) Develop a hypothesis, compute the test statistic, and make a decision.

C) Select the level of significance, formulate the decision rule, and make a decision.

D) Select the level of significance, compute the test statistic, and make a decision, Analyze the results

143. Each of the following is true about the adjusted R^2 EXCEPT which? (   )

A) Adjusted $R^2 = 1 - (SSR/TSS) * [(n-1)/(n-k-1)]$.

B) Adding a regressor (independent variable) always causes the adjusted R^2 to decrease.

C) Adjusted R^2 is always less than R^2.

D) The adjusted R^2 can be negative.

144. A multiple regression model, on a small sample of monthly returns for one year, has two regressors and is given by: $Y(i) = 10.0 + 1.46 * X(1, i) - 0.82 * X(2, i) + u(i)$. The number of observations (n) is 12. The sum of squared residuals (SSR) is 106.0. The total sum of squares (TSS) is 166.0. What are, respectively, the standard error of the regression (SER) and the adjusted R^2? (   )

A) $SER = 0.89$ and Adjusted $R^2 = -0.11$

B) $SER = 2.25$ and Adjusted $R^2 = 0.64$

C) $SER = 3.43$ and Adjusted $R^2 = 0.22$

D) $SER = 11.87$ and Adjusted $R^2 = 0.64$

145. EACH of the following is TRUE EXCEPT for? (　　)

A) As the degrees of freedom (df) increase, the standard error of regression (SER) increases

B) As RSS decreases, coefficient of determination (R^2) increases

C) SER must be less than *RSS*

D) Both standard error of regression (SER) and coefficient of determination (R^2) are valid measures of "goodness of fit" of the estimated regression line

146. In a two-variable regression with sample size of ten ($n = 10$) given by $Y(i) = b_1 + b_2 * X(i)$, the sample variance of $Y(i)$ is 66.67. The explained sum of squares is 238. What is the correlation coefficient? (　　)

A) 0.40

B) 0.52

C) 0.58

D) 0.63

第 7 单元

时间序列分析

147. An analyst has determined that monthly refrigerator sales in the Chongqing has been increasing over the last 2 years, but the growth rate has been relatively constant in the future. Which choice is most appropriate to predict future the refrigerator sales? (　　)

A) $Re(salest) = \beta_0 + \beta_1(t)$

B) $\ln Re(salest) = \beta_0 + \beta_1(t)$

C) $Re(salest) = \beta_0 + \beta_1(t) + \beta_2(t)2$

D) $\ln Re(salest) = \ln(\beta_0) + \beta_1(t)$

148. Regarding the conditions for model selection criteria to demonstrate consistency, which of the following statements is most accurate? (　　)

Ⅰ. The most consistent selection criteria with the greatest penalty factor for degrees of freedom is unbiased mean squared error.

Ⅱ. If we consider the fact that the true model may be much more complicated than the models under consideration, then the Akaike information criterion (AIC) measure should be examined.

A) Ⅰ only

B) Ⅱ only

C) Both Ⅰ and Ⅱ

D) Neither Ⅰ nor Ⅱ

149. John, FRM CFA, wants to use a regression model to forecast in-sample data. Heis concerned about data mining and over-fitting the data. Which of the following criteria provides the highest penalty factor based on degrees of freedom? (　　)

A) Unbiased mean squared error (s^2).

B) Akaike information criterion (AIC).

C) Schwarz information criterion (SIC).

D) Mean squared error (MSE).

150. Assume that a sample of 450 observations has degrees of freedom of 36. What is the

penalty factor associated with the Schwarz information criterion (SIC)? (　　)

A) 1.153

B) 1.630

C) 1.145

D) 1.564

151. Which of the following statements does lease likely describe the mean squared error (*MSE*) statistical measure? (　　)

A) Scaling the sum of squared residuals by $1/T$ changes the ranking of the models based on squared residuals.

B) The residuals in the numerator of the *MSE* calculation are defined as the difference between the actual value observed and the predicted value based on the regression model.

C) The best regression model based on minimizing the *MSE* will also be the one that maximizes R^2.

D) The regression model with the smallest *MSE* is also the model with the smallest sum of squared residuals.

152. Suppose a trend model over one hundred observations has eight parameters and its sum of squared residuals is equal to 1,435; i. e., $T=100$, $k=8$, *SSR* (aka, residual sum of squares) = 1,435. Let's define "corrected *MSE*" as the mean squared error (*MSE*) thatis penalized for degrees of freedom used. Which are nearest, respectively, to (i) the mean squared error (*MSE*), (ii) the corrected *MSE*, and (iii) the standard error of the regression, *SER*? (　　)

A) *MSE* = 13.29; corrected *MSE* = 14.35; *SER* = 3.85

B) *MSE* = 14.35; corrected *MSE* = 15.60; *SER* = 3.97

C) *MSE* = 14.35; corrected *MSE* = 26.43; *SER* = *NA* (not available with information given)

D) *MSE* = 179.38; corrected *MSE* = 14.35; *SER* = *NA*

153. Consider the fitting of a polynomial trend model with (p) powers of time, $T(t) = B(0) + B(1) * TIME(t) + B(2) * TIME(t)^2 + B(p) * TIME(t)^p$. Each of the following is true EXCEPT which? (　　)

A) As we include higher powers of time, the sum of squared residuals can't rise, because the estimated parameters are explicitly chosen to minimize the sum of squared residuals; therefore, the more variables we include in a forecasting model, the lower the sum of squared residuals will be, and therefore the lower MSE will be, and the higher R^2 will be.

B) The mean squared error (*MSE*) is a biased estimator of out-of-sample 1 − step-ahead prediction error variance: the reduction in mean squared error (*MSE*) as higher powers of time are included in the model occurs even if they are, in fact, of no use in forecasting the variable of interest.

C) While *MSE* and *SIC* are inconsistent, *AIC* is consistent.

D) In-sample overfitting (aka, data mining) refers to the idea that including more variables in a forecasting model won't necessarily improve its out-of-sample forecasting performance, although it will improve the model's fit on historical data.

154. You would like to describe an account that begins at TIME(0) = \$100.00 and compounds continuously at 9.0% per annum. What is a function that characterizes the value of this account, $A(t)$, over time according to such a continuous and constant growth trend? (　　)

A) $A(t) = \$100 * \exp[0.090 * \text{TIME}(t)]$

B) $\ln[A(t)] = \ln(100) + 0.09 * \text{TIME}(t)$

C) Neither (A) nor (B)

D) Both (A) and (B)

155. Consider the following quadratic trend model.

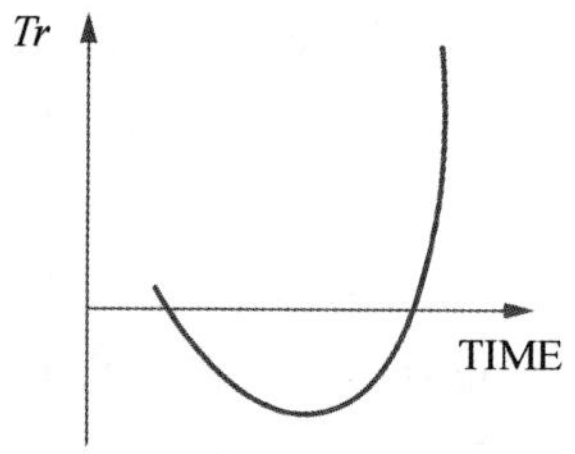

Which of the following functions correctly characterizes this trend? (　　)

A) $Tr = 10 + 0.3 * \text{TIME} + 0.3 * \text{TIME}^2$

B) $Tr = 10 + 30 * \text{TIME} - 0.3 * \text{TIME}^2$

C) $Tr = 10 - 0.4 * \text{TIME} - 0.4 * \text{TIME}^2$

D) $Tr = 10 - 30 * \text{TIME} + 0.5 * \text{TIME}^2$

156. For a time series with T observations, the bands displayed on a graph of its correlogram are most likely to be located at plus-or-minus (　　).

A) $1/T$

B) $2/T$

C) $1/\sqrt{T}$

D) $2/\sqrt{T}$

157. A forecaster is not accurate to remove seasonality (and focus on forecasting nonseasonal fluctuations) in the case of a time series related to (　　).

A) corporate earnings

B) unemployment rates

C) the consumer price index (CPI)

D) gross domestic product (GDP)

158. Joy is an analyst in the Cosmetics industry. She is modeling a company's sales over time and has noticed a quarterly seasonal pattern. If Joy includes an intercept term in her model, how many dummy variables should she use to model the seasonality component? (　　)

A) 1

B) 2

C) 3

D) 4

159. Consider the following regression equation utilizing dummy variables for explaining quarterly INCOMES in terms of the quarter of their occurrence: INCOMESt = β_0 + $\beta_1 D_1$, t + $\beta_2 D_2$, t + $\beta_3 D_3$, t + £ $_t$ where INCOMESt = a quarterly observation of EPS.

$D_1 t$ = 1 if period t is the first quarter, D_1 t = 0 otherwise.

$D_2 t$ = 1 if period t is the second quarter, D_2 t = 0 otherwise.

$D_3 t$ = 1 if period t is the third quarter, D_3 t = 0 otherwise.

The intercept term β_0 represents the average value of sales for the (　　).

A) first quarter

B) second quarter

C) third quarter

D) fourth quarter

160. Which of the following time series is MOST LIKELY to contain a seasonal pattern? (　　)

A) price of solar panels

B) employment participation rate

C) climate data data recorded from a weather station once per year

D) return on average assets (ROA) for the large commercial bank sector

161. In order to forecast housing starts, your colleague Brett is going to use the following seasonal model that employs a regression on seasonal dummies:

$$y_t = \sum_{i=1}^{s} \gamma_i D_{it} + \varepsilon_t$$

About this model, each of the following is true EXCEPT? ( )

A) This model does not contain a trend.

B) If the model includes twelve monthly seasons (January, February, ..., December) such that $s = 12$, then seasonal factor $\gamma(5)$ is probably greater than either $\gamma(1)$ or γ (12).

C) If the model includes four seasons (spring, summer, fall and winter) such that $s = 4$, then he should include four (4) seasonal dummy variables plus an intercept.

D) If this is a quarterly model such that $y(t) = D_1 + D_2 + D_3 + 9.0 * D_4$, and the standard error of day (4) = 9.0 coefficient is 15.0, then we can infer that average housing starts in the 4th quarter are not statistically different than average housing starts in the first quarter.

162. Jack works for the International Monetary Fund in Washington DC, monitoring Singapore's real consumption expenditures. Using a sample of real consumption data (measured in billions of 2005 Singapore dollars), $y(t)$, t = 1990: $Q1$, 1990: $Q2$, ..., 2006: $Q3$, 2006: $Q4$, you estimate the linear consumption trend model, $y(t) = \beta(0) + \beta(1) * \text{TIME}(t) + e(i)$, where $e(i) \sim N(0, \sigma^2)$, obtaining the estimates $\beta(0) = 0.510$, $\beta(1) = 2.30$, and $\sigma^2 = 16$. Based on your estimated trend model, which is nearest to the 95.0% interval forecast 2010: Q1? ( )

A) 39 to 54

B) 153 to 216

C) 177 to 192

D) 181 to 189

163. The conditions for a time series to exhibit covariance stationarity least likely include ( ).

A) a stable mean

B) a finite variance

C) auto covariances that do not depend on time

D) a finite number of observations

164. Which of the following statements about white noise is TURE? ( )

A) All serially uncorrelated processes are white noise.

B) All Gaussian white noise processes are independent white noise.

C) All independent white noise processes are Gaussian white noise.

D) All serially correlated Gaussian processes are independent white noise.

165. Consider the following conditions for a model selection criteria to demonstrate consistency.

Ⅰ. When the true model (that is, the data-generating process, or DGP) is among the models considered, the probability of selecting the true DGP approaches one as the sample size gets large, and

Ⅱ. When the true model is not among those considered, so that it's impossible to select the true data-generating process (DGP), the probability of selecting the best approximation to the true DGP approaches one as the sample size gets large

Which of these conditions is (are) TRUE? (　　)

A) Neither

B) Ⅰ only

C) Ⅱ Only

D) Both

166. In regard to modeling and forecasting seasonality, each of the following is true EXCEPT which is not accurate? (　　)

A) A seasonal time series is, by definition, covariance stationary.

B) Trading-day variation is a type of seasonality that refers to the fact that different months contain different numbers of trading days.

C) A key technique for modeling seasonality is regression on seasonal dummy variables; dummy variables assume a value of zero or one.

D) Log transformation is useful in both trend models and seasonal models, but for different reasons; in a seasonal model, log transformation can stabilize seasonal patterns whose variance is growing over time.

167. Based on a regression analysis, the following model was produced to predict housing starts (given in thousands) within a certain geographical region; e.g., one of the larger U.S. states. The time series model contains both a trend and a seasonal component and is given by the following:

$y_t = 0.3 * \text{Time}_t + 20.10 + 4.70 * D_{2t} + 5.80 * D_{3t} + 0.9 * D_{4t}$

The trend component is reflected in the variable, TIME(t), where (t) is the month. Seasonality is reflected by the intercept (20.10) plus the three seasonal dummy variables (D_2, D_3 and D_4) in order to capture quarterly seasonality. Winter includes December, January and February. Spring includes March, April and May and is indicatedby dummy $D(2t)$. Summer includes June, Julyand August and is indicated by dummy $D(3t)$. Finally, fall includes September, October and November and is indicated by $D(4t)$. The model starts in November 2016; for example, $y(T+1)$ refers to December 2016 and $y(T+2)$ refers to January 2017. What does the model predict for October 2018? (　　)

A) 24,700
B) 26,100
C) 27,900
D) 30,500

168. In regard to covariance stationary stochastic processes each of the following statements is true EXCEPT? (　　)

A) In time series analysis, "cycles" refer to a general, all-encompassing notion of cyclicality: any sort of dynamics with some persistence that is not captured by trends or seasonality.

B) An upward trend corresponds to a steadily increasing mean, and seasonality corresponds to means that vary with the season; both of which are violations of covariance stationarity.

C) Due to the stringent requirements for covariance stationarity, and a practical inability to transform non-stationary series, forecasting models avoid applying covariance stationarity in practice.

D) In a stationary process, distributions depend on displacement (i. e., the difference between time subscripts) but do not depend on the time subscripts. A "strictly stationary" stochastic process requires that the multivariate distribution function, including skew and kurtosis, be stable and finite; but "weak stationarity" (aka, covariance stationarity) only requires means and covariances to be stable and finite.

169. Each of the following is a requirement for a series to be covariance stationary (aka, weak stationarity, second-order stationarity) EXCEPT? (　　)

A) The mean of the series is stable over time; $E[y(t)] = \mu(t)$.

B) The covariance structure of the series is stable over time; $\text{cov}[y(t), y(t-\pi)] = \gamma(t, \pi)$.

C) The variance of the series (i. e., the autocovariance at displacement 0) is finite.

D) The autocovariance depends on time (t), but does not depend on the displacement (π).

170. Regarding white noise, each of the following statements is true EXCEPT? (　　)

A) If a process is zero-mean white noise, then it must be Gaussian white noise.

B) If a process is Gaussian (aka, normal) white noise, then it must be (zero-mean) white noise.

C) If a process is Gaussian (aka, normal) white noise, then it must be independent white noise.

D) If a process is stationary, has zero mean, has constant variance and it serially uncorrelated, then the process is white noise.

171. If a time series is reasonably approximated as white noise, then each of the following is true EXCEPT? (　　)

A) Serial correlations (aka, autocorrelations) are zero.

B) Observations in the time series are normally distributed.

C) In a large sample, the distribution of the sample autocorrelations is approximately normal with meanof zero.

D) In a large sample, the distribution of the sample autocorrelations is approximately normal with variance of 1/T.

172. If a forecaster is using a time series model and notices periodic spikes in autocorrelations as they gradually decay, this is most likely a sign of (　　).

A) a structural shift in the time series

B) seasonality in the data

C) autoregressive conditional heteroskedasticity (ARCH)

D) first differencing lag operators

173. Which of the following statements is a key differentiator between a moving average (*MA*) representation and an autoregressive (*AR*) process? (　　)

A) An autoregressive process shows evidence of autocorrelation cutoff.

B) An unadjusted moving average process shows evidence of gradual autocorrelation decay.

C) An autoregressive process is never covariance stationary.

D) A moving average representation shows evidence of autocorrelation cutoff.

174. Which following is most accurate about the qth -order moving average process? (　　)

A) Add exactly two additional lagged variables to the original specification.

B) Add a second error term to an *MA*(1) process.

C) Invert the moving average process to make the formula more useful.

D) Add as many additional lagged variables as needed to more robustly estimate the data series.

175. What is the difference between autocorrelation and partial autocorrelation? (　　)

A) In the time series context, autocorrelation and partial autocorrelation are synonyms; i. e. , there is no real difference, they are identical concepts.

B) The partial autocorrelation is the correlation between $y(t)$ and $y(t-\pi)$ multiplied by the variance of $y(0)$, an operation which standardizes the association across cycles.

C) In the time series context, partial autocorrelation is the second moment of autocorrelation; if autocorrelation is positive (negative), then partial autocorrelation must be positive (negative).

D) Autocorrelation is the typical correlation between $y(t)$ and $y(t-\pi)$ while partial autocorrelation measures the association between $y(t)$ and $y(t-\pi)$ after controlling for the effects of $y(t-1)$, ..., $y(t-\pi+1)$.

176. Wold's representation theorem points to an appropriate model for a covariance stationary residual such that (　　).

A) any autoregressive process of (p) order can be expressedas a rational polynomial of lagged errors

B) any purely nondeterministic covariance-stationary process is a linear regression of $y(t)$ on a lagged conditional mean

C) any purely nondeterministic covariance-stationary process is some linear combination of lagged values of a white noise process

D) any autoregressive moving average model, $ARMA(p, q)$, can be shown as the sum of autoregressive (AR) and moving average (MA) processes

177. In regard to rational distributed lag models, each of the following is true EXCEPT? (　　)

A) It is possible to approximate the Woldrepresentation using a rational distributed lag.

B) ARMA and ARIMA forecasting models are simply rational approximations to the Wold representation.

C) Rational distributed lags produce models that are parsimonious yet provide accurate approximations to the Wold representation.

D) ARMA(1, 1) is not practical for two reasons: it cannot be covariance stationary; and its unconditional mean is time-varying while its conditional mean is fixed.

178. For a certain time series, you have produced a correlogram with an autocorrelation function that includes twenty four monthly observations; m = degrees of freedom = 24. Your calculated Box-Pierce Q-statistic is 19.50 and your calculated Ljung-Box Q-statistic is 27.90. You want to determine if the series is white noise. Which is your best conclusion (please note this requires a lookup)? (　　)

A) With 95.0% confidence, you accept the series as white noise (more accurately, you fail to reject the null).

B) With 95.0% confidence, you accept the series as partial white noise (due to Box-Pierce) but reject the null (due to Ljung-Box).

C) With 95.0% confidence, you reject both null hypotheses and conclude the series is not white noise.

D) With 95.0% confidence, you reject both null hypotheses but conclude the series is white noise because the sum of the statistics is greater than the critical value.

179. In regard to the Box-Pierce and Ljung-Box Q-statistics, each of the following is TRUE except which is false? (　　)

A) The Box-Pierce Q-statistic is used to test whether the residuals in a time series are white noise.

B) The Ljung-Box Q-statistic is used to test whether a time series exhibits a linear trend under the null hypothesis of a unit root.

C) The Box-Pierce Q-statistic is approximately distributed as a chi-squared random variable under the null hypothesis that autocorrelations are jointly zero in a time series.

D) Selection of the number of lags being tested (aka, maximum displacement, m) in the Ljung-Box test is a balance between conducting a joint test (i.e., can't be too small) and quality of the distribution approximations (i.e., can't be too large).

第 8 单元

波动率、相关性和模拟

180. An economic analyst investigates three different stocks, his researchers found that the stock's GARCH equations:

Stock1: $\sigma_n^2 = 0.83 + 0.04\mu_{n-1}^2 + 0.94\sigma_{n-1}^2$

Stock 2: $\sigma_n^2 = 0.06 + 0.05\mu_{n-1}^2 + 0.94\sigma_{n-1}^2$

Stock 3: $\sigma_n^2 = 0.60 + 0.10\mu_{n-1}^2 + 0.94\sigma_{n-1}^2$

Following statements regarding these equations. Which is (are) most accurate? (　　)

Ⅰ. Stock 1 is a stationary model.

Ⅱ. Stock 2 shows no mean reversion.

Ⅲ. Volatility will revert to a long run mean level slower with Stock 1 than it will for Stock 2.

Ⅳ. Volatility will revert to a long run level faster with Stock 3 than it will for Stock 2.

A) Ⅰ only

B) Ⅲ only

C) Ⅱ and Ⅳ only

D) Ⅱ and Ⅲ only

181. Consider a stock with daily returns that follow a random walk. The annualized volatility is 34%. Estimate the weekly volatility of this stock assuming that the year has 52 weeks. (　　)

A) 6.80%

B) 5.83%

C) 4.85%

D) 4.71%

182. Assume we calculate a one-week VAR for a natural gas position by rescaling the daily VAR using the square root of time rule. Let us now assume that we determine the true gas price process to be mean reverting and recalculate the VAR. Which of the following statements is true? (　　)

A) The recalculated VAR will be less than the original VAR.

B) The recalculated VAR will be equal to the original VAR.

C) The recalculated VAR will be greater than the original VAR.

D) There is no necessary relationship between the recalculated VAR and the original VAR.

183. Consider a portfolio with 40% invested in asset X and 60% invested in asset Y. The mean and variance of return on X are 0 and 25 respectively. The mean and variance of return on Y are 1 and 121 respectively. The correlation coefficient between X and Y is 0.3. What is the nearest value for portfolio volatility? (　　)

A) 9.51

B) 8 60

C) 13.38

D) 7.45

184. Suppose σ_t^2 is the estimated variance at time t and μ_t is the realized return at t. Which of the following GARCH (1, 1) models will take the longest time to revert to its mean? (　　)

A) $\sigma_t^2 = 0.04 + 0.02\mu_{t-1}^2 + 0.92\sigma_{t-1}^2$

B) $\sigma_t^2 = 0.02 + 0.04\mu_{t-1}^2 + 0.94\sigma_{t-1}^2$

C) $\sigma_t^2 = 0.03 + 0.02\mu_{t-1}^2 + 0.95\sigma_{t-1}^2$

D) $\sigma_t^2 = 0.03 + 0.03\mu_{t-1}^2 + 0.93\sigma_{t-1}^2$

185. Assume you are using a GARCH model to forecast volatility that you use to calculate the one-day VAR. If volatility is mean reverting, what can you say about the T-day VAR? (　　)

A) It is less than the $\sqrt{T}\times$one-day VAR.

B) It is equal to $\sqrt{T}\times$one-day VAR.

C) It is greater than the $\sqrt{T}\times$one-day VAR.

D) It could be greater or less than the $\sqrt{T}\times$one-day VAR.

186. A risk manager estimates daily variance b_t using a GARCH model on daily returns r_t: $b_t = \alpha_0 + \alpha_1 r_{t-1}^2 + \beta b_{t-1}$, with $\alpha_0 = 5\times10^{-7}$, $\alpha_1 = 0.04$, $\beta = 0.94$. The long-run annualized volatility is approximately (　　), assuming there are 252 trading days a year.

A) 13.54%

B) 7.94%

C) 72.72%

D) 25.00%

187. Which of the following statements is incorrect regarding the volatility term structure predicted by a GARCH(1, 1) model: $\sigma_t^2 = \omega + \alpha\mu_{t-1}^2 + \beta\sigma_{t-1}^2$, where $\alpha + \beta < 1$? (　)

A) When the current volatility estimate is below the long-run average volatility, this GARCH model estimates an upward-sloping volatility term structure.

B) When the current volatility estimate is above the long-run average volatility, this GARCH model estimates a downward-sloping volatility term structure.

C) Assuming the long-run estimated variance remains unchanged as the GARCH parameters and α increase, the volatility term structure predicted by this GARCH model reverts to the long-run estimated variance more slowly.

D) Assuming the long-run estimated variance remains unchanged as the GARCH parameters and β increase, the volatility term structure predicted by this GARCH model reverts to the long-run estimated variance faster.

188. A bank uses the exponentially weighted moving average (EWMA) technique with λ of 0.9 to model the daily volatility of a security. The current estimate of the daily volatility is 1.5%. The closing price of the security is USD 20 yesterday and USD 18 today. Using continuously compounded returns, what is the updated estimate of the volatility? (　)

A) 3.62%

B) 1.31%

C) 2.96%

D) 5.44%

189. Using a daily RiskMetrics EWMA model with a decay factor X 0.95 to develop a forecast of the conditional variance, which weight will be applied to the return that is four days old? (　)

A) 0.000

B) 0.043

C) 0.048

D) 0.950

190. TheVasicek model defines a risk-neutral process for r that is $dr = a(b - r)dt + \sigma dz$, where a, b, and σ are constant, and r represents the rate of interest. From this equation we can conclude that the model is a (　).

A) Monte Carlo type model

B) single-factor term-structure model

C) two-factor term-structure model

D) decision tree model

191. An analyst wants to estimate the following GARCH model:

$$\sigma_n^2 = 0.05 + 0.4\mu_{t-1}^2 + 0.32\sigma_{n-1}^2$$

If the most recent volatility estimate and error term are 0.15 and 0.02, respectively, the long-run average variance is closest to (　　).

A) 0.43

B) 0.22

C) 0.06

D) 0.18

192. The current estimate of daily volatility is 2.5%. The closing price of an asset yesterday was \$28.00. The closing price of the asset today is \$29.50. Using the EWMA (Exponentially Weighted Moving Average) model (with $\lambda = 0.92$), the updated estimate of volatility is (　　).

A) 2.96%

B) 2.82%

C) 1.59%

D) 2.58%

193. The λ of an exponentially weighted moving average (EWMA) model is estimated to be 0.85. Daily standard deviation is estimated to be 2.5%, and today's stock market return is 0.7%. What is the new estimate of the standard deviation? (　　)

A) 2.88%

B) 1.65%

C) 1.44%

D) 2.32%

194. Given λ of 0.93, under an infinite series, what is the weight assigned to the seventh prior daily squared return? (　　)

A) 4.53%

B) 4.41%

C) 4.34%

D) 3.69%

195. A fundamental assumption of the random walk hypothesis of market returns is that returns from one time period to the next are statistically independent. This assumption implies (　　).

A) returns from one time period to the next can never be equal

B) returns from one time period to the next are uncorrelated

C) knowledge of the returns from one time period does not help in predicting returns from the next time period

D) both b. and c. are true

196. Until February, 2004 the historical volatility for The Japanese yen versus the US dollar had been very small for several years. On February 15th, Japan abandoned the defense of the currency peg. Using the data from the close of business on February 15th, which of the following methods for calculating volatility would have shown the greatest jump in measured historical volatility? (　　)

A) 252 days equal weight

B) 60 days equal weight

C) All of the above

D) Exponentially weighted with a daily decay factor of 0.94

197. Consider the following probability matrix that displays four joint probabilities, Prob(X, Y):

Y\X	1	2	
3	40%	20%	60%
4	10%	30%	40%
	50%	50%	

Which is nearest to the correlation between (X) and (Y)? (　　)

A) 0.35

B) Zero

C) 0.29

D) 0.41

198. You have assumed a single-index model and regressed the returns for two stocks, stock (A) and stock (B), against the index in separate univariate regressions. This produced the following two linear functions, such that $\beta(A)$ is 0.80 and $\beta(B)$ is 1.40:

$$R_A = 0.02 + 0.8 * R_m + e_A$$
$$R_B = 0.05 + 1.4 * R_m + e_B$$

Additionally, the volatility of the index, $\sigma(M)$, is 20.0%, the volatility of stock A, $\sigma(A)$, is 32.0% and the volatility of stock B, $\sigma(B)$, is 40.0%. Which of the following is the implied correlation between the two stocks? (　　)

A) 0.2240

B) 0.3500

C) 0.4900

D) 1.1200

199. The general single-factor model below, given by $U(i)$, characterizes both $U(1)$ and $U(2)$ which are both dependent on a common factor, (F):

$$U_i = \alpha_i F + \sqrt{1-\alpha_i^2} Z_i$$

$$U_1 = 0.12F + \sqrt{1-0.12^2} Z_1$$

$$U_2 = 0.7F + \sqrt{1-0.7^2} Z_2$$

What is the coefficient of correlation between $U(1)$ and $U(2)$? (   )

A) −0.4900

B) 0.0840

C) 0.5044

D) 0.8200

200. Yesterday's volatility, $\sigma(n-1)$, and the return data for two assets is shown below.

	Asset A	Asset B
$\sigma(n-1)$	2%	3%
Yesterday's price, $p(n-1)$	30	50
Today's price, $p(n)$	29.40	47.50
Return, $[p(n)/p(n-1)]-1$	−2%	−5%
Correlation, $\rho(A, B)$ on $(n-1)$	0.5	
EWMA lambda, λ	0.85	

Yesterday's correlation, $\rho(A, B)$, between the asset was 0.50. If we assume a lambda, λ, parameter of 0.850, which is nearest to the updated correlation between the two assets if we use an exponentially weighted moving average (EWMA) model to update the correlation? (   )

A) 0.500

B) 0.533

C) 0.600

D) 0.731

201. Suppose that the yesterday daily volatilities of asset A and asset B are 3.0% and 5.0%, respectively. The prices of the assets at close of trading yesterday were

\$10.00 and \$20.00 and the estimate of the coefficient of correlation between the returns on the two assets made at that time was 0.30. The lambda (λ) parameter used in the EWMA model is 0.80. The prices of the assets at close of trading today are \$11.00 and \$21.00. Which is nearest to the updated correlation estimate? (   )

A) 0.018

B) 0.0032

C) 0.044

D) 0.5148

202. Suppose that the yesterday daily volatilities of asset X and asset Y are 3.0% and 6.0%, respectively. The prices of the assets at close of trading yesterday were \$50.00 and \$70.00 and the estimate of the coefficient of correlation between the returns on the two assets made at this time was 0.50. Correlations and volatilities are updated using a GARCH(1, 1) model. The estimates of the model's parameters are: alpha (α) = 0.040 and beta (β) = 0.940. For the correlation, omega (ω) = 0.000001 and for the volatilities omega (ω) = 0.000003. If the prices of the two assets at close of trading today are \$55.00 and \$84.00, which is nearest to the updated correlation estimate? (   )

A) 0.0331

B) 0.0482

C) 0.6454

D) 0.0733

203. In a one-factor model, each $U(i)$ has a component dependent on a common factor, F, and a component that is uncorrelated with the other variables. Formally, $U(i) = a(i) * F + \text{sqrt}[1 - a(i)^2] * Z(i)$, where ($F$) and $Z(i)$ have standard normal distributions and $a(i)$ is a constant between −1.0 and +1.0. The $Z(i)$ are uncorrelated with each other and uncorrelated with (F). Consider two variables, $U(1)$ and $U(2)$ as follows:

$$U(1) = a(1) * F + \text{sqrt}[1 - a(1)^2] * Z(1)$$
$$= 0.650 * F + \text{sqrt}[1 - 0.650^2] * Z(1)$$
$$U(2) = a(2) * F + \text{sqrt}[1 - a(2)^2] * Z(2)$$
$$= 0.480 * F + \text{sqrt}[1 - 0.480^2] * Z(2)$$

Which is nearest to the coefficient of correlation between $U(1)$ and $U(2)$? (   )

A) 0.0973

B) 0.1498

C) 0.2028

D) 0.3120

204. In regard to copulas, each of the following is true EXCEPT which is false? (　　)

A) A copula is a way of defining the correlation between variables with known distributions.

B) Copulas cannot be used to define a correlation structure between more than two variables.

C) The one-factor Gaussian copula model leads to very little tail dependence, which is a limitation of the model.

D) The Gaussian copula is just one copula that can be used to define a correlation structure between marginal distributions; there are many other copulas leading to many other correlation structures.

205. Consider the following three statements about tail dependence.

Ⅰ. Tail dependence is the tendency for extreme values for two or more variables to occur together.

Ⅱ. The choice of the copula affects tail dependence.

Ⅲ. The tail dependence is higher in a bivariate Student t-distribution than in a bivariate normal distribution.

Which of the above is (are) TRUE? (　　)

A) None are true

B) Only Ⅰ is true

C) Only Ⅲ is true

D) All are true

206. Suppose you simulate the price path of stock HHF using a geometric Brownian motion model with drift $\mu = 0$, volatility $\sigma = 0.14$, and time step $\Delta t = 0.01$. Let S_t be the price of the stock at time t. If $S_0 = 100$, and the first two simulated (randomly selected) standard normal variables are $\epsilon_1 = 0.263$ and $\epsilon_2 = -0\ 475$, what is the simulated stock price after the second step? (　　)

A) 96.79

B) 99.79

C) 99.97

D) 99.70

207. In the geometric Brown motion process for a variable S, which is true? (　　)

Ⅰ. S is normally distributed.

Ⅱ. $d\ln(S)$ is normally distributed.

Ⅲ. dS/S is normally distributed.

Ⅳ. S is lognormally distributed.

A) Ⅰ only

B) Ⅱ, Ⅲ, and Ⅳ

C) Ⅳ only

D) Ⅲ and Ⅳ

208. Consider that a stock price S that follows a geometric Brownian motion $dS = aSdt + bSdz$, with b strictly positive. Which of the following statements is false? (　　)

A) If the drift a is positive, the price one year from now will be above today's price.

B) The instantaneous rate of return on the stock follows a normal distribution.

C) The stock price S follows a lognormal distribution.

D) This model does not impose mean reversion.

209. Which group of term-structure models do the Ho-Lee, Hull-White, and Heath-Jarrow-Morton models belong to? (　　)

A) no-arbitrage models

B) two-factor models

C) lognormal models

D) deterministic models

210. A plausible stochastic process for the short-term rate is often considered to be one where the rate is pulled back to some long-run average level. Which one of the following term-structure models does not include this characteristic? (　　)

A) The Vasicek model

B) The Ho-Lee model

C) The Hull-White model

D) The Cox-Ingersoll-Ross model

211. Which one of the following statements about Monte Carlo simulation is false? (　　)

A) Monte Carlo simulation can be used with a lognormal distribution.

B) Monte Carlo simulation can generate distributions for portfolios that contain only linear positions.

C) One drawback of Monte Carlo simulation is that it is computationally very intensive.

D) Assuming the underlying process is normal, the standard error resulting from Monte Carlo simulation is inversely related to the square root of the number of trials.

212. A risk manager has been requested to provide some indication of the accuracy of a Monte Carlo simulation. Using 1,000 replications of a normally distributed variable S, the relative error in the one-day 99% VAR is 5%. Under these conditions which is true? (   )

A) Using 1,000 replications of a long option position on S should create a larger relative error.

B) Using 10,000 replications should create a larger relative error.

C) Using another set of 1,000 replications will create an exact measure of 5.0% forrelative error.

D) Using 1,000 replications of a short option position on S should create a larger relative error.

213. The measurement error in VAR, due to sampling variation, should be greater with (   ).

A) more observations and a high confidence level (e. g. , 99%)

B) fewer observations and a high confidence level

C) more observations and a low confidence level (e. g. , 95%)

D) fewer observations and a low confidence level

214. Consider a stock that pays no dividends, has a volatility of 25% pa, and has an expected return of 13% pa. The current stock price is $S_0 = \$30$. This implies the model $S_{t+1} = S_t(1 + 0.13\Delta t + 0.25\sqrt{\Delta t}\epsilon)$, where e is a standard normal random variable. To implement this simulation, you generate a path of the stock price by starting at $t = 0$, generating a sample for ϵ, updating the stock price according to the model, incrementing t by 1, and repeating this process until the end of the horizon is reached. Which of the following strategies for generating a sample for ϵ will implement this simulation properly? (   )

A) Generate a sample for ϵ by using the inverse of the standard normal cumulative distribution of a sample value drawn from a uniform distribution between 0 and 1.

B) Generate a sample for ϵ by sampling from a normal distribution with mean 0.13 and standard deviation 0.25.

C) Generate a sample for ϵ by using the inverse of the standard normal cumulative distribution of a sample value drawn from a uniform distribution between 0 and 1. Use Cholesky decomposition to correlate this sample with the sample from the previous time interval.

D) Generate a sample for ϵ by sampling from a normal distribution with mean 0.13 and standard deviation 0.25. Use Cholesky decomposition to correlate this sample with the sample from the previous time interval.

第三部分

金融市场和产品

第 9 单元

金 融 机 构

1. The minimum amount of capital a bank needs to maintain, according to its own estimates, models, and risk assessments can be best described as its ( ).
   A) equity capital
   B) financial capital
   C) economic capital
   D) regulatory capital

2. The intention of a "Chinese wall" in banking is to ( ).
   A) preventa bank failure from endangering other banks
   B) prevent a bank's departments from sharing information
   C) restrict companies from offering both banking and securities services
   D) restrict companies from engaging in both commercial and investment banking

3. Which of the following actions in the banking system is most likely intended to Deal with the problem of moral hazard? ( )
   A) Deposit insurers charge risk-based premiums.
   B) Banks increase loans to higher-risk borrowers.
   C) Governments implement deposit insurance programs.
   D) Banks increase the interest rates they offer to depositors.

4. An investment bank is most likely to earn a trading profit from buying and selling securities if it involved a ( ).
   A) dutch auction
   B) private placement
   C) best efforts offering
   D) firm commitment offering

5. Which of the following arrangements would allow the bank to sell only part of the issue without being obligated to buy the unsold portion for a new securities

underwriting? (　　)

A) firm commitment

B) private placement

C) dutch auction process

D) best efforts basis

6. Regarding the originate-to-distribute model of a bank, which of the following statements is not associated with a benefit of this mode? (　　)

A) It increases liquidity in the sectors of the lending market where it is used.

B) It can free up capital with which banks can meet regulatory requirements or make new loans.

C) It can be applied to the residential mortgage market, student loans, credit card balances, and commercial loans and mortgages.

D) It can let banks to loosen lending standards.

7. Which of the following statements About the difference between economic capital and regulatory capital is correct? (　　)

A) Even if economic capital is less than regulatory capital, a bank must maintain its capital at the regulatory minimum or greater.

B) In terms of bank regulation, subordinated long-term debt is referred to as Tier 1 capital.

C) Regulatory capital refers to the amount of capital that a bank believes is adequate based on its own.

D) Economic capital is greater than regulatory capital.

8. Which of the following statements About the differences between the bank's trading book and banking bank is correct? The trading book (　　).

A) refers to loans made, which are the primary assets of a commercial bank

B) refers to assets and liabilities related to a bank's trading activities

C) does not include accrued interest for nonperforming loans

D) uses marked to market model to evaluate all asset prices

9. Which of the following forms of insurance is most likely exposed to long-tail risk? (　　)

A) health insurance

B) life insurance

C) liability insurance

D) property insurance

10. The following information about a property and casualty (P&C) insurance company:

Investment income	5%
Dividends	2%
Loss ratio	74%
Expense ratio	23%

Based on the information provided, calculate the company's operating ratio (　　).

A) 90%

B) 94%

C) 97%

D) 99%

11. Which of the following problems would most likely be a concern for life insurance companies that are worried about identifying between good risks and bad risks? (　　)

A) adverse selection

B) catastrophic risk

C) longevity risk

D) moral hazard

12. A system of deposit insurance May potentially creates a moral hazard problem. Which of the following statements is Most likely wrong regarding moral hazard? (　　)

A) In the banking context, with deposit insurance in place, the moral hazard arises when depositors pay more attention to banks' financial health than they otherwise would

B) One way of mitigating moral hazard is by making insurance premiums risk-based

C) Deposit insurance allows banks to offer higher interest rates on deposits and make higher-risk loans with the funds they attract

D) Moral hazard suggests that insured parties take greater risks than they would normally take if they were not insured

13. Assume that the relevant interest rate for insurance contracts is 4% per annum (semiannual compounding applies), and all premiums are paid annually at the beginning of the year. A $250,000 term insurance contract is being proposed for a 50-year-old man in average health. Assuming that payouts occur halfway throughout the year, calculate the insurance company's breakeven premium for a one-year term. Note that the probability of death within one year for a 50-year-old man is 0.005038. (　　)

A) $1,211.44

B) $1,259.50

C) \$1,234.80

D) \$1,615.38

14. An employer is researching the differences between a defined benefit plan and a defined contribution plan. Which of the following statements within the company's policies Most likely shows that the pension plan is a defined benefit plan? A defined benefit plan (　　).

A) does not explicitly state the amount of the pension that the employee will receive upon retirement

B) involves one individual account associated with one employee

C) risks underperformance of the plan's investments, and this risk is borne solely by the employee

D) involves one pooled account for all employees as all contributions go into and all payments come out of the one account

15. Which of the following statements about the differences between mortality risk and longevity risk Regarding an insurance company is correct? (　　)

A) Mortality risk refers to the risk of policyholders living longer than expected due to better healthcare and healthier lifestyle choices.

B) Regarding mortality risk, the risk of losses increases due to the longer-than-expected annuity payout period.

C) Longevity risk refers to the risk of policyholders dying earlier than expected due to illness or disease.

D) Longevity risk is bad for the annuity business but is good for the life insurance business due to the delayed payout.

16. For a property-casualty insurance company, how to calculate a company's operating ratio? (　　)

A) Payouts minus premiums generated.

B) Combined ratio plus dividends minus investment income.

C) Loss ratio plus expense ratio.

D) Combined ratio minus dividends.

17. Which of the following Description about a major risk facing insurance company is not accurate? (　　)

A) By transacting with banks and reinsurance companies, insurance companies face credit risk if the counterparty defaults on its obligations.

B) Insurance companies often invest in short-term debt securities, so if defaults decrease, insurance companies will incur losses.

C) Insurance companies face losses due to failure of its systems and procedures or from external events outside the company's control.

D) It is always possible that insurance companies will have a sudden surge of payouts in a short period of time.

18. Which of the following statements is Least likely correct regarding investment funds available to all investors? (　　)

A) Open-end mutual funds always transact at the next available net asset value.

B) Stop orders can be used on closed-end funds.

C) Open-end mutual funds can be purchased with a limit order.

D) Short selling is available for some exchange-traded funds.

19. Which of the following characteristics is an important difference between mutual funds and hedge funds? (　　)

A) professional asset management

B) immediate access to withdrawals from the fund

C) charging a fee for providing investment services

D) easy diversification for an investor

20. Calculating the expected return to a hedge fund if the fund uses a standard 2 and 20 incentive fee structure with an investment that has a 35% probability of making 55% and a 65% probability of losing 45%? (　　)

A) 5. 71%

B) 6. 12%

C) 3. 78%

D) 5. 28%

21. Which of the following hedge fund strategies would most likely include market neutral fund and factor neutral funds? (　　)

A) Merger arbitrage

B) Long/short equity

C) Distressed securities

D) Managed futures

22. Assume ABZ mutual fund is an open-end fund that owns $450 million in equities, $100 million in bonds, and $25 million in cash. Itowes $10. 5 million in management fees payable at this point in the quarter and has 24 million shares outstanding. What is this fund's net asset value(NAV)? (　　)

A) $53. 23

B) $29.55

C) $30.43

D) $22.48

23. A hedge fund manager uses a strategy that attempts to infer patterns from past price movements and use those patterns as a basis for predictions. The Fund manager often uses historical data to back test his trading rules. Which of the following strategies is this hedge fund manager most likely utilizing? ( )

A) managed futures

B) fixed income arbitrage

C) convertible arbitrage

D) dedicated short

24. An analyst is Concluding the essential differences and similarities between hedge funds and mutual funds. Which of the following statements should be considered correct? ( )

A) Hedge funds are marketed to any and all investors, while mutual funds are restricted to only wealthy and sophisticated investors.

B) Both mutual funds and hedge funds are permitted to use leverage.

C) Mutual funds offer professional management, instant diversification, and the ability to commingle funds with other investors, while hedge funds do not offer all of these features.

D) Unlike mutual funds, hedge funds do not need to provide the redemption of shares at any time the investor chooses or a daily calculated net asset value.

25. If Hedge fund ssetting a complex compensation structure centered on incentive fees. Which of the following items would not act as a safeguard for investors to soften this incentive fee structure? ( )

A) 2 plus 20% structure.

B) Clawback clause.

C) Hurdle rates.

D) High-water mark.

第 10 单元

衍生品分析——远期、期货和互换

26. Which one is the payoff at expiration to a put option buyer? (　　)
    A) max (0, $S_T - X$)
    B) max (0, $X - S_T$)
    C) $-$max (0, $X - S_T$)
    D) $-$max (0, $S_T - X$)

27. A call option gives a holder (　　).
    A) the right to sell at a specific price
    B) the right to buy at a specific price
    C) an obligation to buy at a certain price
    D) an obligation to sell at a certain price

28. Comparing the over-the-counter (OTC) market with the traditional exchange market, which One is bigger, and what would be a key advantage of OTC trading compared with traditional exchange trading? (　　)
    A) OTC market is smaller, and a key OTC advantage is that terms are not set by any exchange.
    B) OTC market is smaller, and a key OTC advantage is calls are recorded, to prevent miscommunications.
    C) OTC market is larger, and a key OTC advantage is that credit risk is eliminated or largely mitigated.
    D) OTC market is larger, and a key OTC advantage is participants flexibility to negotiate.

29. Which following about Arbitrageurs is ture? (　　)
    A) Earn significant profits by making market bets regarding securities price.
    B) Earn a riskless profit through the exploitation of security mispricings.
    C) Neutralize financial exposure as part of a risk management strategy.
    D) Earn a long-term profit by making consistent long term investments.

30. Calculate the payoff and profit, respectively, to the call buyer on a stock, given the following specifics: Call strike price: \$62; Put strike price: \$63; Stock price: \$70; Call premium: \$3.25; Put premium: \$2.75. ( )

A) Payoff: \$8.00; Profit: \$4.75

B) Payoff: \$8.00; Profit: \$12.75

C) Payoff: \$0; Profit: \$0

D) Payoff: \$7.00; Profit: \$2.75

31. To prevent arbitrage profits, the theoretical future price of a stock index should befully determined by which of the following? ( )

Ⅰ. Cash market price.

Ⅱ. Financing cost.

Ⅲ. Inflation.

Ⅳ. Dividend Yield

A) Ⅰ and Ⅱ only

B) Ⅱ and Ⅲ only

C) Ⅰ, Ⅱ and Ⅳ only

D) All of the above

32. The highest price a dealer is willing to pay to purchase a security is called ( ).

A) exercise price

B) bid price

C) offer price

D) strike price

33. An investor has been bullish on AAPL for quite some time and has accumulated a large position totaling 1.2 million shares. The current stock price is \$575 per share. If the investor is concerned about a decline in the price of the stock and wants to hedge the position by purchasing a 3-month put option, calculate what the profit is on a per share basis if the stock price is \$541 in 3 months, the strike price on the put is \$575, and the put premium is \$3.70? ( )

A) \$30.30

B) - \$3.70

C) - \$34.00

D) \$3.70

34. Which of the following is most likely wrong? ( )

A) The initial investment in futures consists of the premium.

B) Futures contracts have a symmetrical payoff.

C) Speculators use derivatives due to the low initial investment required.

D) Option contracts have an asymmetrical payoff.

35. Which of the following statements about arbitrage opportunities is correct? (　　)

A) There can never be an opportunity to make profits from arbitrage.

B) Engaging in arbitrage requires a large amount of capital for the investment.

C) Pricing errors in securities are instantaneously corrected by the first arbitrageur to recognize them.

D) When an opportunity exists to profit from arbitrage, it usually lasts for several trading days.

36. From the point of view of a company that uses derivatives to hedge foreign exchange risk, the main advantage of futures contracts over forward contracts is that (　　).

A) futures are typically available for longer maturities

B) futures are less standardized

C) futures have less credit risk due to "marking-to-market"

D) futures usually have smaller notional amounts

37. Novation is the process of (　　).

A) creating a new trade between two counterparties

B) terminating an existing trade between two counterparties

C) discharging a contract between the original counterparties and creating two new contracts, each with a central counterparty

D) assigning a trade to another party

38. What is the purpose of margin payments associated with futures contracts? (　　)

A) to reduce the maintenance cost for participants

B) to reduce the credit risk for participants

C) to reduce the market risk for participants

D) none of the above

39. A trader buys one wheat contract (underlying = 5,000 bushels) at a price of \$3.05 per bushel. The initial margin on the contract is \$4,500 and the maintenance margin is \$3,750. At what price will the trader receive a maintenance margin call? (　　)

A) \$2.30

B) \$2.90

C) \$3.20

D) \$3.80

40. To utilize the cash position of assets under management, a portfolio manager enters into a long futures position on the S&P 500 index with a multiplier of 250.
The cash position is $15 million which at the current futures value of 1,000, requires the manager to be long 60 contracts. If the current initial margin is $12,500 per contract, and the current maintenance margin is $10,000 per contract, what variation margin does the portfolio manager have to advance if the futures contract value falls to 995 at the end of the first day of the position being placed? (　　)

A) $30,000

B) $0

C) $300,000

D) $75,000

41. The practice of adjusting the margin balance in a futures account for the daily change in the futures price is best described as (　　).

A) the daily call

B) a margincall

C) marking to market

D) setting up

42. To equalize the cash portion of assets under management, a portfolio managerenters into a long futures position on the S&P 500 Index with a multiplier of 250. The cash position is $5,000,000, which at the current futures value of 1,000 requires the manager to be long 20 contracts. If the current initial margin is $12,500 per contract, and the current maintenance margin is $10,000 per contract, the variation margin the portfolio manager needs to advance if the futures contract value falls to 985 at the end of the first day of the position is closest to (　　).

A) $25,000

B) $30,000

C) $50,000

D) $75,000

43. Simon bought a futures contract on a commodity on the New York Commodity Exchange on June 1. The futures price was USD 500 per unit and the contract size was 100 units per contract. Alan set up a margin account with initial marginof USD 2,000 per contract and maintenance margin of USD 1,000 per contract. The futures price of the commodity varied as shown below. Which following about the balance in Simon's margin account at end of June 2? (　　)

Day	Futures Price (USD)
June1	504. 30
June2	503. 10

A) USD 1,880
B) USD 0
C) USD 780
D) USD 2,310

44. Which statement about the futures contracts is correct? (　　)
A) Futures contracts are used to hedge commodity and financial product risk, are organized between two parties privately, and can be established in any quantity or product.
B) Futures contracts require a margin deposit, the position is marked to market daily, and are standardized according to exchange guidelines.
C) Futures contracts do not trade on organized exchange, do not require margin deposits, and are not regulated by any agencies.
D) One counterparty agrees to buy another counterparty agrees to sell, a given asset, at an agreed price, and there always exists risk that one party may default.

45. In the commodity spot and futures markets, what effect on price fluctuations and market liquidity Can speculators provide? (　　)
A) Expand market breadth, reduce volatility, increase price volatility.
B) Smooth price fluctuation, provide market liquidity.
C) Increase volume, volatility and liquidity risk, while providing market depth.
D) Lower margin rates, increase price volatility.

46. Joe Mannes, FRM believes he has found an arbitrage opportunity between the NASDAQ and the London Stock Exchange (LSE). The stock he is looking at, Pharma PLC, is trading on NASDAQ for $76 and trading on the LSE for 52. 03 GBP. The current exchange rate is 1. 557 $ / GBP. Is there a Potential arbitrage profit exist, and if so, compute it. (　　)
A) Yes; $4. 75.
B) Yes; $2. 50.
C) Yes; $5. 00.
D) No.

47. Which of the following is an instance of an arbitrage opportunity? (　　)
A) A portfolio of two securities that will produce a certain return that is greater than

the risk-free rate of interest.

B) A stock with the same price as another has a higher expected rate of return.

C) A stock with the same price as another has a higher rate of return.

D) A put option on a share of stock has the same price as a call option on an identical share.

48. Which of the following trade(s) contain basis risk? (　　)

Ⅰ. Long 1,000 lots Nov 07 ICE Brent Oil contracts and short 1,000 lots Nov 07 NYMEX WTI Crude Oil contracts

Ⅱ. Long 1,000 lots Nov 07 ICE Brent Oil contracts and long 2,000 lots Nov 07 ICE Brent Oil at-the-money put

Ⅲ. Long 1,000 lots Nov 07 ICE Brent Oil contracts and short 1,000 lots Dec 07 ICE Brent Oil contracts

Ⅳ. Long 1,000 lots Nov 07 ICE Brent Oil contracts and short 1,000 lots Dec 07 NYMEX WTI Crude Oil contracts

A) Ⅱ and Ⅳ only

B) Ⅰ and Ⅲ only

C) Ⅰ, Ⅲ and Ⅳ only

D) Ⅲ and Ⅳ only

49. The process that ensures two securities positions with identical future payoffs, regardless of future events, will have the same price is called (　　).

A) the law of one price

B) payoff parity

C) arbitrage

D) exchange parity

50. An investor enters into a short position in a gold futures contract at USD 294.20. Each futures contract controls 100 troy ounces. The initial margin is USD 3,200, and the maintenance margin is USD 2,900. At the end of the first day, the futures price drops to USD 286.6. Which of the following is the amount of the variation margin at the end of the first day? (　　)

A) 0

B) USD 34

C) USD 334

D) USD 760

51. Which one of the following statements is incorrect regarding the margin of exchange-traded futures contracts? (　　)

A) Day trades and spread transactions require lower margin levels.

B) If an investor fails to deposit variation margin in a timely manner, the positions may be liquidated by the carrying broker.

C) Initial margin is the amount of money that must be deposited when a futures contract is opened.

D) A margin call will be issue donly if the investor's margin account balance becomes negative.

52. The standard deviation of monthly changes in the spot price and futures price of silver is, respectively, \$3. 20 and \$5. 10. The correlation between them is 0. 80. An industrial firm will need to purchase one million silver in six months, but wants to hedge their price risk with silver futures, the silver futures are trading at 10 and multiplier is 250, how many long contracts are optimal? (　　)

A) 10 contracts

B) 63 contracts

C) 100 contracts

D) 200 contracts

53. A wheat farmer hedged her future sale of 100,000 bushels of wheat by selling forward 10 contracts, each contract for 5,000 bushels; hedge ratio is 0. 86. The standard deviation of monthly changes in the spot and futures price of wheat is, respectively, \$0. 60 and \$0. 30. What was her correlation assumption? (　　)

A) 0. 67

B) 0. 43

C) 0. 80

D) 0. 90

54. An investment manager holds a large cap equity portfolio with a current market value of \$55 million. The portfolio has a return volatility of 40% compared to S&P 500 index volatility of 20%. The correlation between the portfolio returns and index returns is 0. 75. Finally, the near-term maturity of the S&P 500 futures price is 1,320. (multiplier is 250) The manager wants to hedge against overall market exposure (i. e. , the S&P 500 is the imperfect proxy of the overall market). What is the hedge trade? (　　)

A) long 125 S&P futures contracts

B) short 125 S&P futures contracts

C) long 250 S&P futures contracts

D) short 250 S&P futures contracts

55. An investment manager owns a large-cap equity portfolio with a market value of \$10 million. The portfolio has a beta, with respect to the S&P 500 (as a proxy for the market), of 0.30. The S&P 500 index futures price is 1,380 (multiplier is 250). The manager wants to increase the portfolio's beta to 1.0. What is the trade? (   )

A) long 9 S&P 500 futures contracts

B) short 9 S&P 500 futures contracts

C) long 20 S&P 500 futures contracts

D) short 20 S&P 500 futures contracts

56. An investor holds 10,000 shares of Apple (AAPL), each with a price of \$350.00. The beta of Apple's stock is 1.14. the market will be very volatile over the next month but that Apple has a good chance of outperforming the market. The investor decides to use short-term futures contracts on the S&P 500 to hedge the position during the one-month period. The current one-month futures price, F(1/12), is 1,343. What is the hedge trade? (multiplier is 250) (   )

A) long 10 contracts

B) short 10 contracts

C) long 12 contracts

D) short 12 contracts

57. An oil producer wants to employ a stack-and-roll hedge, by rolling over one-month contracts, in order to minimize (hedge) the price risk of 1.2 million barrels of oil that will be sold (by the oil producer) in 12 months. The spot price of oil is \$106, the one-month futures price is \$102 (each contract has 1,000 barrels) and the 12-month futures price is \$98. The correlation between changes in the spot and futures price is 0.9 and both the spot and futures price have the same 20% volatility. If the oil producer wants to tail the hedge, what is the initial trade? (   )

A) short 90 contracts

B) short 94 contracts

C) short 1,080 contracts

D) short 1,122 contracts

58. An investor buys a Treasury bill maturing in one month for \$987. On the maturity date the investor collects \$1,000. Calculate effective annual rate (EAR). (   )

A) 17.0%

B) 15.8%

C) 13.0%

D) 11.6%

59. Lisa Smith, the treasurer of Bank AAA, has $100 million to invest for one year. She has identified three alternative one-year certificates of deposit (CDs), with different compounding periods and annual rates. CD1: monthly, 7.82%; CD2: quarterly, 8.00%; CD3: semiannually, 8.05%; and CD4: continuous, 7.95%. Which CD has the highest effective annual rate (EAR)? (　　)

A) CD1

B) CD2

C) CD3

D) CD4

60. Consider a savings account that pays an annual interest rate of 8% Calculate the amount of time it would take to double your money. Round to the nearest year. (　　)

A) 7 years

B) 8 years

C) 9 years

D) 10 years

61. A five-year corporate bond paying an annual coupon of 8% is sold at a price reflecting a yield to maturity of 6%. One year passes and the interest rates remain unchanged. Assuming a flat term structure and holding all other factors constant, the bond's price during this period will have (　　).

A) increased

B) decreased

C) remained constant

D) cannot be determined with the data given

62. A zero-coupon bond with a maturity of 10 years has an annual effective yield of 10%. What is the closest value for its modified duration? (　　)

A) 9 years

B) 10 years

C) 99 years

D) 100 years

63. Interest rates (bond yields) are currently below 6.0%. Which of the following bonds will the short position in U.S. Treasury bond futures contract be most likely to deliver; i.e., which will be CTD? (　　)

A) short-maturity with low coupon

B) short-maturity with high coupon

C) long-maturity with low coupon

D) long-maturity with high coupon

64. Which of the following statements is correct regarding the effects of interest rateshift on fixed-income portfolios with similar durations? (　　)

A) A barbell portfolio has greater convexity than a bullet portfolio because convexity increases linearly with maturity.

B) A barbell portfolio has greater convexity than a bullet portfolio because convexity increases with the square of maturity.

C) A barbell portfolio has lower convexity than a bullet portfolio because convexity increases linearly with maturity.

D) A barbell portfolio has lower convexity than a bullet portfolio because convexity increases with the square of maturity.

65. The yield curve is upward sloping and a portfolio manager has a long position in 10-year Treasury notes funded through overnight repurchase agreements. The risk manager is concerned with the risk that market rates may increase further and reduce the market value of the position. What hedge could be put on to reduce the position's exposure to rising rates? (　　)

A) Enter into a 10-year pay-fixed and receive-floating interest rate swap.

B) Enter into a 10-year receive-fixed and pay-floating interest rate swap.

C) Establish a long position in 10-year Treasury note futures.

D) Buy a call option on 10-year Treasury note futures.

66. A portfolio manager has a bond position worth USD 100 million. The position has a modified duration of eight years and a convexity of 150 years. Assume that the term structure is flat. By how much does the value of the position change if interest rates increase by 25 basis points? (　　)

A) USD −2,046,875

B) USD −2,187,500

C) USD −1,953,125

D) USD −1,906,250

67. A portfolio manager uses her valuation model to estimate the value of a bond portfolio at USD 125.482 million. The term structure is flat. Using the same model, she estimates that the value of the portfolio would increase to USD 127.723 million if all interest rates fell by 30bp and would decrease to USD 122.164 million if allinterest rates rose by 30bp. Using these estimates, the effective duration of the bond portfolio is closest to (　　).

A) 8.38

B) 16.76

C) 7.38

D) 14.77

68. Suppose the face value of a three-year option-free bond is USD 1,000 and the annual coupon is 10%. The current yield to maturity is 5%. What is the modified duration of this bond? (　　)

A) 2.62

B) 2.85

C) 3.00

D) 2.75

69. A Treasury bond has a coupon rate of 6% per annum (the coupons are paid semiannually) and a semiannually compounded yield of 4% per annum. The bond matures in 18 months and the next coupon will be paid 6 months from now. Which number of years is closest to the bond's Macaulay duration? (　　)

A) 1.023 years

B) 1.457 years

C) 1.500 years

D) 2.915 years

70. A and B are two perpetual bonds; that is, their maturities are infinite. A has a coupon of 4% and B has a coupon of 8%, Assuming that both are trading at the same yield, what can be said about the duration of these bonds? (　　)

A) The duration of A is greater than the duration of B.

B) The duration of A is less than the duration of B,

C) A and B both have the same duration,

D) None of the above.

71. A manager wants to swap a bond for a bond with the same price but higher duration. Which of the following bond characteristics would be associated with a higher duration? (　　)

Ⅰ. A higher coupon rate

Ⅱ. More frequent coupon payments

Ⅲ. A longer term to maturity

Ⅳ. A lower yield

A) Ⅰ, Ⅱ, and Ⅲ

B) Ⅱ, Ⅲ, and Ⅳ

C) Ⅲ and Ⅳ

D) Iand Ⅱ

72. When the maturity of a plain coupon bond increases, its duration increases (　　).

A) indefinitely and regularly

B) up to a certain level
C) indefinitely and progressively
D) in a way dependent on the bond being priced above or below par

73. Consider the following bonds:

Bond Number	Maturity (Years)	Coupon Rate	Frequency	Yield (Annual)
1	10	6%	1	6%
2	10	6%	2	6%
3	10	0%	1	6%
4	10	6%	1	5%
5	9	6%	1	6%

How would you rank the bonds from the shortest to longest duration? (　　)
A) 5-2-1-4-3
B) 1-2-3-4-5
C) 5-4-3-1-2
D) 2-4-5-1-3

74. The price of a zero-coupon six-month Treasury bill is \$98.00. The price of a one-year Treasury bill that pays a 2.0% semi-annual coupon is \$97.00. Using the bootstrap method, what is the one-year Treasury zero (spot) rate expressed in continuous compounding? (　　)
A) 4.0405%
B) 4.9405%
C) 5.0564%
D) 5.6564%

75. Assume the following continuously compounded zero rates: 1.0% at 0.5 years; 1.6% at 1.0 year; 1.9% at 1.5 years; and 2.5% at 2.0 years. What is the theoretical price of a bond with a \$100 principal that pays coupons at the rate of 2.0% semiannually? (　　)
A) \$98.03
B) \$99.03
C) \$100.03
D) \$101.03

76. Assume the following theoretical continuously compounded spot rates: 2.0% at

0.5 years; 3.0% at 1.0 year; 4.0% at 1.5 years; and 5.0% at 2.0 years. What is the two-year PAR YIELD with continuous compounding? (　　)

A) 4.88%

B) 4.94%

C) 5.00%

D) 5.04%

77. Let $r(0, 1)$ and $r(0, 2)$ be the one- and two-year spot rates; a.k.a., zero rates. Let $r(2.0, 3.0)$ be the implied forward rate from year two to year three; i.e., the one-year interest rate two years forward. Assume the following zero rate curve: $r(0, 0.5) = 2.0\%$, $r(0, 1.0) = 2.4\%$, $r(0, 1.5) = 2.8\%$ and $r(0, 2.0) = 3.0\%$. If all rates are per annum expressed with continuous compounding, what is the implied forward rate, $r(1.0, 2.0)$? (　　)

A) 2.8%

B) 3.2%

C) 3.4%

D) 3.6%

78. The price of a \$100 par zero-coupon bond with four (4) years to maturity is \$88.00. The price of a \$100 par zero-coupon bond with five (5) years to maturity is \$82.00. Under continuous compounding, what is the implied forward rate, $r(4.0, 5.0)$? (　　)

A) 4.06%

B) 5.06%

C) 6.06%

D) 7.06%

79. The price of a \$100 par zero-coupon bond with six months (0.5) to maturity is \$97.00. The price of a \$100 par zero-coupon bond with one year (1.0) to maturity is \$94.00. Finally, the price of a \$100 par bond that pays a 4.0% semi-annual coupon and matures in eighteen months (1.5 years) is \$95.00. What is the continuously compounded implied forward rate, $r(1.0, 1.5)$; the six-month rate one year forward? (　　)

A) 8.05%

B) 9.05%

C) 10.05%

D) 11.05%

80. Suppose that U.S. interest rates rise from 3% to 4% this year. The spot exchange rate quotes at 112.5 JPY/USD and the forward rate for a one-year contract is at

110.5. What is the Japanese interest rate? (   )

A) 1.81%

B) 2.15%

C) 3.84%

D) 5.88%

81. A trader runs a cash and future arbitrage book on the S&P 500 index. Which of the following are the major risk factors? (   )

Ⅰ. Interest rate

Ⅱ. Foreign exchange

Ⅲ. Equity price

Ⅳ. Dividend assumption risk

A) Ⅰ and Ⅱ only

B) Ⅰ and Ⅲ only

C) Ⅰ, Ⅲ, and Ⅳ only

D) Ⅰ, Ⅱ, Ⅲ, and Ⅳ

82. Consider a forward contract on a stock market index. Identify the false statement. everything else being constant. (   )

A) The forward price depends directly on the level of the stock market index.

B) The forward price will fall if underlying stocks increase the level of dividend payments over the life of the contract.

C) The forward price will rise if time to maturity is increased.

D) The forward price will fall if the interest rate is raised.

83. A three-month futures contract on an equity index is currently priced at USD 1,000. The underlying index stocks are valued at USD 990 and pay dividends at acontinuously compounded rate of 2%. The current continuously compounded risk-free rate is 4%. The potential arbitrage profit per contract, given this set of data, is closest to (   ).

A) USD 10.00

B) USD 7.50

C) USD 5.04

D) USD 1.50

84. Suppose the price for a six-month S&P index futures contract is 552.3. If the risk-free interest rate is 7.5% per year and the dividend yield on the stock index is 4.2% per year, and the market is complete and there is no arbitrage, what is the price of the index today? (   )

A) 543.26

B) 552.11

C) 555.78

D) 560.02

85. A stock index is valued at USD 750 and pays a continuous dividend at the rate of 2% per annum. The six-month futures contract on that index is trading at USD 757. The risk-free rate is 3.50% continuously compounded. There are no transaction costs or taxes. Is the futures contract priced so that there is an arbitrage opportunity? If yes, which of the following numbers comes closest to the arbitrage profit you could realize by taking a position in one futures contract? (　　)

A) $4.18

B) $1.35

C) $12.60

D) There is no arbitrage opportunity.

86. Which of the following statements is/are true? (　　)

Ⅰ. The convexity of a 10-year zero-coupon bond is higher than the convexity of a 10-year 6% bond.

Ⅱ. The convexity of a 10-year zero-coupon bond is higher than the convexity of a 6% bond with a duration of 10 years.

Ⅲ. Convexity grows proportionately with the maturity of the bond.

Ⅳ. Convexity is always positive for all types of bonds.

Ⅴ. Convexity is always positive for straight bonds.

A) Ionly

B) Ⅰ and Ⅱ only

C) Ⅰ and Ⅴ only

D) Ⅱ, Ⅲ, and Vonly

87. A bond portfolio has the following composition:

1. Portfolio A: price $90,000, modified duration 2.5, long position in 8 bonds

2. Portfolio B: price $110,000, modified duration 3, short position in 6 bonds

3. Portfolio C: price $120,000, modified duration 3.3, long position in 12 bonds

All interest rates are 10%. If the rates rise by 25 basis points, then the bond portfolio value will decrease by (　　).

A) $11,430

B) $21,330

C) $12,573

D) $23,463

88. Consider the following portfolio of bonds (par amounts are in millions of USD).

Bond	Price	Par Amount Held	Modified Duration
A	101.43	3	2.36
B	84.89	5	4.13
C	121.87	8	6.27

What is the value of the portfolio's DV01 (dollar value of 1 basis point)? (　　)

A) $8,019

B) $8,294

C) $8,584

D) $8,813

89. Long-dated forward contracts on short-term deposits (　　).

A) imply lower rates than Eurodollar futures contracts for the same maturity

B) imply higher rates than Eurodollar futures contracts for the same maturity

C) imply the rates as Eurodollar futures contracts for the same maturity

D) may imply higher or lower rates than Eurodollar futures contracts for the same maturity

90. Consider a 6-month futures contract on the S&P 500, and suppose the current value of the index is 1,330. Suppose the dividend yield is 1.5% annually for the stocks underlying the index, and that the continuously compounded risk-free interest rate is 5.5% annually. What is the cost of carry for this futures contract? (　　)

A) 4.0%

B) −4.0%

C) 2.0%

D) −2.0%

91. The S&P 500 index is trading at 1,025. The S&P 500 pays an expected dividend yield of 1.2% and the current risk-free rate is 2.75%. The value of a 3-month futures contract on the S&P 500 index is closest to (　　).

A) $1,028.98

B) $1,108.59

C) $984.86

D) $1,025.00

92. Which of the following statements describing the role of a convenience yield inpricing commodity futures is true? The convenience yield (　　).

Ⅰ. Will cause contango in the futures pricing relationship.

Ⅱ. Effectively reduces the cost of carry in the futures pricing relationship.

Ⅲ. Eliminates the potential for arbitrage between the futures and spot price.

Ⅳ. Accounts for additional costs for storing an asset in the futures pricing relationship.

A) Ⅰ only

B) Ⅱ only

C) Ⅱ, Ⅲ, and Ⅳ only

D) Ⅰ and Ⅱ only

93. A stock index is valued at USD 800 and pays a continuous dividend at the rate of 3% per year. The 6-month futures contract on that index is trading at USD 758. The continuously compounded risk free rate is 2.5% per year. There are no transaction costs or taxes. Is the futures contract priced so that there is an arbitrage opportunity? If yes, which of the following numbers comes closest tothe arbitrage profit you could realize by taking a position in one futures contract? (　　)

A) 38

B) 40

C) 42

D) There is no arbitrage opportunity

94. A forward contract on a stock index was created three months ago. The current price of the index is \$1,100. Expressed on a continuously compounded annual basis, the risk-free rate of interest is 4% and the index pays a dividend of 2%. The contract requires delivery three months from today at a price of \$1,080. The value of the contract is closest to (　　).

A) \$8.97

B) \$14.44

C) \$25.26

D) \$30.44

95. The one-year U.S. dollar interest rate is 2.75% and one-year Canadian dollar interest rate is 4.25%. The current USD/CAD spot exchange rate is 1.0221—1.0225. Calculate the one-year USD/CAD forward rate (　　). Assume annual compounding.

A) 1.0076

B) 1.0074

C) 1.0075

D) 1.03722

96. In March 2011, an investor shorts 10,000 shares of Cisco (CSCO) when the price is \$16.00 per share. In April, CSCO pays a dividend of \$0.06 per share. In June (three months after initiating the short), the investors close out the short when the price drops to \$12.00 per share. During the three months (one quarter), the short also earns a short rebate (interest) of 0.375% on the initial short proceeds; i.e., 1.5% per annum divided by four. Ignoring time value of money, what are the net profits to the short investor? ( )

A) \$38,800

B) \$39,400

C) \$40,000

D) \$40,600

97. With respect to short sales, which of the following is true EXCEPT ( ).

A) A short squeeze is most likely when the short interest (or short interest ratio) is low and the security price is dropping.

B) A loss in a short position leads to larger exposure such that, unlike a long position, a short position implies an inverse relationship between performance and exposure.

C) While a long position has a limited downside, a short position has an unlimited downside.

D) The SEC abolished the uptick rule in 2007, but recently adopted the "alternative uptick rule" which is triggered if a security declines by 10% during the day.

98. Under what condition should the price of a FORWARD contract equal the price of a FUTURE contract, if the commodity and specifics of the contracts (e.g., maturity) are otherwise identical? (Best answer) ( )

A) If the financing cost (r), storage cost (u), income (q) and convenience yield (y) are identical.

B) If the counterparty (credit) risk on the forward contract is virtually zero.

C) If the riskfree interest rate is constant and the rate curve is flat.

D) If the riskfree interest rate is constant and the rate curve is flat; and if the counterparty (credit) risk on the forward contract is virtually zero.

99. The spot price of corn is \$7.00 per bushel. Corn has a market beta of 0.40 and a storage cost of 2.0% per annum (continuous). The market return is 9.0% and the riskfree rate is 4.0% per annum. A corn farmer plans to sell corn in six months and therefore hedges with a short position in corn futures. What is the expected future gain per bushel on the corn futures contract? ( )

A) Loss of \$0.07 per bushel.

B) Loss of $0.02.

C) No expected gain/loss.

D) Gain of $0.05.

100. Assume that corn has the following properties: positive storage cost, no convenience yield, and positive systemic risk (i. e., beta > 0). According to Hull, which is most likely with respect to, respectively, the observed forward curve (contango = normal; backwardation = inverted) and the relationship between the futures price, $F(0, X)$, and the expected future spot price, $E[S(X)]$? (　　)

A) Contango and normal contango

B) Contango and normal backwardation

C) Backwardation and normal contango

D) Backwardation and normal backwardation

101. Consider an FRA (forward rate agreement) with the same maturity and compounding frequency as a Eurodollar futures contract. The FRA has a LIBOR underlying. Which of the following statements are true about the relationship between the forward rate and the futures rate? (　　)

A) The forward rate is normally higher than the futures rate.

B) They have no fixed relationship.

C) The forward rate is normally lower than the futures rate.

D) They should be exactly the same.

102. What can be said about the settlement risk of a Eurodollar futures contract and aFRA with the same term? (　　)

A) The Eurodollar futures contract and a FRA have the same settlement risk.

B) The Eurodollar futures contract has less settlement risk than a FRA

C) The Eurodollar futures contract has more settlement risk than a FRA

D) The Eurodollar futures contract may have more or less settlement risk.

103. An interest rate cap runs for 12 months based on three-month LIBOR with a strike price of 4%. Which of the following is generally true? (　　)

A) The cap consists of three caplet options with maturities of three months, the first one starting today based on three-month LIBOR set in advance and paid in arrears.

B) The cap consists of four caplets starting today, based on LIBOR set in advance and paid in arrears.

C) The implied volatility of each caplet will be identical no matter how the yield curve moves.

D) Rate caps have only a single option based on the maturity of the structure.

104. What are the differences between Forward Rate Agreements (FRAs) and Eurodollar Futures? (　　)

Ⅰ. FRAs are traded on an exchange while Eurodollar Futures are not.

Ⅱ. FRAs have better liquidity than Eurodollar Futures.

Ⅲ. FRAs have standard contract sizes while Eurodollar Futures do not.

A) Ⅰ only

B) Ⅰ and Ⅱ only

C) Ⅱ and Ⅲ only

D) None of the above

105. The party with the short position in a U. S. Treasury bond futures contract wants to identify the cheapest-to-delivery (CTD) bond. The settlement date is March 4th, 2011 and the settlement price is 106-04 (i. e. , 106. 125). The two bonds eligible for delivery are:

✓ Bond A: Matures in 20 years (7/1/2031), pays a 5. 0% semiannual coupon, has a conversion factor (CF) of 0. 87, and has a Quoted Price of $88. 00;

✓ Bond B: Matures in 29 years (7/1/2040), pays a 7. 0% semiannual coupon, has a conversion factor (CF) of 1. 13, and has a Quoted Price of $113. 00

All bonds pay coupons on January 1st and July 1st (Numbers are approximately accurate but rounded for convenience). Which bond is the cheapest-to-deliver (CTD)? (　　)

A) Bond A is the CTD because it costs the short only $900 per contract to deliver

B) Bond A is the CTD because it profits the short $2,125 per contract to deliver

C) Bond B is the CTD because it costs the short only $4,329 per contract to deliver

D) Bond B is the CTD because it profits the short $6,921 per contract to deliver

106. The settlement price of a U. S. Treasury bond futures contract is $98. 50 (98-16). The two bonds eligible for delivery are: (　　)

✓ Bond A: Quoted Price of $97. 00 and conversion factor (CF) of 0. 96;

✓ Bond B: Quoted Price of $102. 00 and conversion factor (CF) of 1. 03.

Which bond is cheapest-to-deliver (CTD)?

A) Bond A is the CTD because it cost the short $2,440 per contract to deliver

B) Bond A is the CTD because it profits the short $5,500 per contract to deliver

C) Bond B is the CTD because it costs the short $545 per contract to deliver

D) Bond B is the CTD because it profits the short $1,316 per contract to deliver

107. The following four bonds can be delivered by the party with the short position in a

U. S. Treasury bond futures contract：

√ Bond A：15 year maturity and 5. 0% semi-annual coupon

√ Bond B：20 year maturity and 6. 5% semi-annual coupon

√ Bond C：25 year maturity and 6. 0% semi-annual coupon

√ Bond D：30 year maturity and 5. 5% semi-annual coupon

Which of these bonds has the HIGHEST conversion factor? (　　)

A) Bond A

B) Bond B

C) Bond C

D) Bond D

108. The current quoted price (Q) of a September 2016 Eurodollar futures contract is 95. 940. What is the associated contract price? (　　)

A) $938,600

B) $959,400

C) $989,850

D) $999,887

109. The table below shows quoted fixed borrowing rates (adjusted for taxes) in two different currencies for two different firms：

	Yen	Pounds
Company A	2%	4%
Company B	3%	6%

Which of the following is true? (　　)

A) Company A has a comparative advantage borrowing in both yen and pounds.

B) Company A has a comparative advantage borrowing in pounds.

C) Company A has a comparative advantage borrowing in yen.

D) Company A can arbitrage by borrowing in yen and lending in pounds.

110. Which of the following achievable swap positions could be used to transform a floating-rate asset into a fixed-rate asset? (　　)

A) Receive the floating-rate leg and receive the fixed-rate leg of a plain vanilla interest-rate swap.

B) Pay the fixed-rate leg and receive the floating-rate leg of a plain vanilla interest-rate swap.

C) Pay the floating-rate leg and pay the fixed-rate leg of a plain vanilla interest-rate swap.

D) Pay the floating-rate leg and receive the fixed-rate leg of a plain vanilla interest-rate swap.

111. A multinational corporation is considering issuing a fixed-rate bond. However, byusing interest swaps and floating rate notes, the issuer can achieve the same objective. To do so, the issuer should consider ( ).

A) issuing a floating rate note of the same maturity and enter into an interest rate swap paying fixed and receiving float

B) issuing a floating rate note of the same maturity and enter into an interest rate swap paying float and receiving fixed

C) buying a floating rate note of the same maturity and enter into an interest rate swap paying fixed and receiving float

D) buying a floating rate note of the same maturity of and enter into an interest rate swap paying float and receiving fixed

112. Two banks enter into a 1-year plain vanilla interest-rate swap with the following terms:

Notional principal is \$500,000,000.

The fixed component of the swap is 7%, which is the current market rate.

The floating component of the swap is LIBOR + 200bps.

If the current risk-free rate is 4%, the value for this swap at inception is closest to ( ).

A) \$500,000,000

B) \$8,750,000

C) \$35,000,000

D) \$0

113. Assume an investor has a position in a currency swap. He receives euro in exchange for paying yen. What are the conditions for the swap to bein-the-money? ( )

Ⅰ. The value of yen falls

Ⅱ. The value of yen rises

Ⅲ. The euro interest rate falls

Ⅳ. The euro interest rate rises

A) Ⅰ and Ⅲ

B) Ⅰ and Ⅳ

C) Ⅱ and Ⅲ

D) Ⅱ and Ⅳ

114. Consider the following plain vanilla swap. Party A pays a fixed rate 8.29% per

annum on a semiannual basis (180/360), and receives from Party B30 basis point. The current six-month LIBOR rate is 7.35% per annum. The notional principal is $25M. What is the net swap payment of Party A? (　　)

A) $20,000

B) $40,000

C) $80,000

D) $110,000

115. You are given the following information about an interest rate swap:

✓ 2-year term

✓ Semi-annual payment

✓ Fixed rate = 6%

✓ Floating rate = LIBOR + 50 basis points

✓ Notional principal USD 10 million

Calculate the net coupon exchange for the first period if LIBOR is 5% at the beginning of the period and 5.6% at the end of the period. (　　)

A) Fixed-rate payer pays USD0.

B) Fixed-rate payer pays USD25,000.

C) Fixed-rate payer pays USD50,000.

D) Fixed-rate payer receives USD25,000.

116. Cooper Industries (Cooper) is the pay-fixed counterparty in an interest rate swap. The swap is based on a notional value of $2,000,000, and Cooper receives a floating rate based on the 6-month Hong Kong Interbank Offered Rate (HIBOR). Cooper pays a fixed rate of 7% semiannually. A swap payment has just been made. The swap has a remaining life of 18 months, with pay dates at 6, 12, and18 months. Continuously compounded spot HIBOR rates are shown in the table below.

6-month HIBOR	6.5%
12-month HIBOR	6.8%
18-month HIBOR	7.5%
24-month HIBOR	7.7%

The value of the swap to Cooper is closest to (　　).

A) $0

B) $6,346

C) $17,093

D) $72,486

117. Consider the following 3-year currency swap, which involves exchanging annual interest of 2.75% on 10 million US dollars for 3.75% on 15 million Canadian dollars. The CAD/USD spot rate is 1.52. The term structure is flat in both countries. Calculate the value of the swap in USD if interest rates in Canada are 5% and in the United States are 4%. Assume continuous compounding. Round to the nearest dollar. (　　)

A) \$152,000

B) \$145,693

C) \$131,967

D) \$127,818

118. A financial institution has entered into a plain vanilla currency swap with one ofits customers. The period left on the swap is two years with the institution paying 4.5% on USD120 million and receiving 2% on JPY3,500 million annually. The current exchange rate is 120 JPY/USD, and the flat term structure in both countries generates a 3% rate in the U.S. and a 0.5% rate in Japan. The current value of this swap to the institution is closest to (　　).

A) \$93,300,000

B) − \$118,090,000

C) − \$93,300,000

D) \$118,090,000

119. You have entered into a currency swap in which you receive 4% per annum in yen and pay 6% per annum in dollars once a year. The principals in the two currencies are 1,000 million yen and 10 million dollar. The swap will last for another two years, and the current exchange rate is 115 yen for 1 dollar. Suppose that the annualized spot rates (with continuous compounding) are given as in the table below, what is the value of the swap to you in million dollars? (　　)

	1 Year	2 Year
Japan	2%	2.5%
United States	4.5%	4.75%

A) 1.277

B) −0.447

C) 0.447

D) −1.270

120. A company plans to borrow \$3.0 million for three months starting in one year. The

Eurodollar futures contract that matures in one year has a quoted price of 98. 00 and the company wants to (net) effectively lock-in this 2. 0% LIBOR interest rate. At the end of one year, LIBOR increases to 3. 0%. The company's borrowing (at the higher 3. 0% LIBOR) will increase but will be hedged by the gain on the Eurodollar futures contract. What is the futures trade and what is the gain on the futures contract only? (　　)

A) Long one contract for a gain of $2,500

B) Long three contracts for a gain of $7,500

C) Short one contract for a gain of $2,500

D) Short three contracts for a gain of $7,500

121. A Eurodollar futures price changes from 98. 00 to 97. 20. What is the gain/loss to an investor who LONGS one contract? (　　)

A) LIBOR decreased by 80 basis point for a loss (to the long position) of $2,000

B) LIBOR increased by 80 basis point for a loss (to the long position) of $2,000

C) LIBOR decreased by 80 basis point for a gain (to the long position) of $2,000

D) LIBOR increased by 80 basis point for a gain (to the long position) of $2,000

122. The payoff to a swap where the investor receives fixed and pays floating can be replicated by all of the following except (　　).

A) a short position in a portfolio of FRAs

B) a long position in a fixed-rate bond and a short position in a floating-rate bond

C) a short position in an interest rate cap and a long position in a floor

D) a long position in a floating-rate cap and a short position in a floor

123. As your company's risk manager, you are looking for protection against adverse interest rate changes in five years. Using Black's model for options on futures to price a European swap option (swaption) that gives the option holder the right to cancel a seven-year swap after five years, which of the following would you use in the model? (　　)

A) The two-year forward par swap rate starting in five years' time

B) The five-year forward par swap rate starting in two years' time

C) The two-year par swap rate

D) The five-year par swap rate

124. To hedge against future, unanticipated, and significant increases in borrowing rates, which of the following alternatives offers the greatest flexibility for the borrower? (　　)

A) interest rate collar

B) fixed for floating swap

C) call swaption

D) interest rate floor

125. A bank entered into a three-year interest rate swap for a notional amount of USD 250 million, paying a fixed rate of 7.5% and receiving LIBOR annually. Just after the payment was made at the end of the first year, the continuously compounded spot one-year and two-year LIBOR rates are 8% and 8.5%, respectively, The value of the swap at that time is closest to (　　).

A) USD 14 million

B) USD −6 million

C) USD −14 million

D) USD 6 million

126. Each of the following is true about corporate bond interest payments EXCEPT which? (　　).

A) The three main interest payment classifications of domestically issued corporate bonds are straight-coupon bonds, zero-coupon bonds, and floating-rate (aka, variable-rate) bonds.

B) Two variations on the zero-coupon bond are deferred-interest bonds (DIB) and pay-in-kind (PIK) bonds.

C) The day count convention day count basis for corporate bonds issued in the United States is 30/360.

D) A floating-rate bond tends to have a higher duration than a straight-coupon bond with an equivalent current yield.

127. Each of the following is TRUE about the Eurodollar futures contract EXCEPT which? (　　).

A) A Eurodollar is a dollar denominated deposit in a bank that is not located in the United States.

B) The long position in a Eurodollar future contract promises to borrow $1,000,000 at maturity and repay this principal three months later.

C) The notional value of a single Eurodollar futures contract is $1,000,000 with delivery months of March, June, September and December.

D) The short position in a Eurodollar futures contract gains when the LIBOR interest rate increases.

128. If the volatility of the short interest rate (LIBOR) is 4.0%, what is the convexity adjustment for a five (5)-year Eurodollar futures contract? (　　)

A) 0.75%
B) 1.1%
C) 2.1%
D) 4.2%

129. The four (4)-year Eurodollar futures quote is 97.00. The volatility of the short-term interest rate (LIBOR) is 1.0%, expressed with continuous compounding. What is the equivalent forward rate, adjusted for convexity, given in ACT/360-day count with continuous compounding (i.e., the Eurodollar futures contract gives LIBOR in quarterly compounding ACT/360, so convert to continuous but a day count conversion is not needed)? (　　)
A) 2.90%
B) 2.95%
C) 2.99%
D) 3.00%

130. With respect to the convexity adjustment applied to a Eurodollar futures contract that has a final settlement at time (T), which of the following is TRUE? (　　)
A) The forward rate (per FRA) is greater than the Eurodollar futures rate because (i) the futures contract settles daily and (ii) the FRA probably settles at $T+0.25$ years.
B) The forward rate (per FRA) is greater than the Eurodollar futures rate because (i) the Eurodollar has additional currency risk and (ii) the FRA probably settles at $T-0.25$ years.
C) The Eurodollar futures rate is greater than the forward rate (per FRA) because (i) the Eurodollar has additional currency risk and (ii) the FRA probably settles at $T-0.25$ years.
D) The Eurodollar futures rate is greater than the forward rate (per FRA) because (i) the futures contract settles daily and (ii) the FRA probably settles at $T+0.25$ years.

第 11 单元

衍生品分析——期权

131. Robert purchases an equity option on a major trading exchange when the underlying share price is $96. 00. Each of the following specifications is a plausible entry in the option contract EXCEPT which is not a contract specification or element? (　　)
   A) Strike prices of $90. 00, $95. 00 or $100. 00
   B) Underlying: 100 shares of the equity security
   C) Implied volatility: limited to 25. 00% or the average of last twenty trading days
   D) Exercise Style: American; may be exercised on any business day up to and including on the expiration date

132. In regard to option mechanics, each of the following is true EXCEPT? (　　)
   A) A margin account is required when clients write (ie, sell) options but not when the buy options.
   B) An American option is always worth at least as much as a European option on the same asset with the same strike price and exercise date.
   C) To hedge foreign exchange risk, a long binary option on the currency provides insurance that is identical to a short foreign exchange futures contract.
   D) While the exercise of an exchange-traded option typically does not cause dilution of the underlying company's equity, exercise of an employee stock option (ESO) typically does cause dilution.

133. A trader has a put option contract to sell 100 shares of a stock for a strike price of $50. 00. Each of the following is true EXCEPT? (　　)
   A) If there is a 4-for-1 stock split, the option contract becomes one to sell 400 shares with an exercise price of $12. 50.
   B) If there is an 10. 0% stock dividend, the option contract becomes one to sell 90. 0 shares with an exercise price of $55. 56.
   C) If there is $2. 00 cash dividend declared, there is no effect on the contract.
   D) If there is a reverse 1-for-5 stock split, the option contract becomes one to sell 20 shares with an exercise price of $250. 00.

134. In regard tooptions markets, with which of the following statements would most disagree? (　　)

A) If an investor sells a stock at a loss then buys a call option within 30 days, the "wash sale rule" disallows the loss as a tax deduction.

B) Convertible bonds (aka, convertibles) are bonds issued by a company that can be converted into equity at certain times using a predetermined exchange ratio.; therefore, they are therefore bonds with an embedded call option on the company's stock.

C) Because vanilla executive stock options (i. e. , ESOs with a fixed strike price) profit when the company's stock increases, ESOs are an optimal tool for aligning a public company's executive compensation with its shareholders, and for rewarding performance relative to industry peers.

D) Warrants are options issued by a financial institution or nonfinancial corporation. A common use of warrants by a nonfinancial corporation is at the time of a bond issue; the corporation issues call warrants on its own stock and then attaches them to the bond issue to make it more attractive to investors.

135. A trader has a call option contract to sell 100 shares of a stock for a strike price of $60, each option's value is $6. Which of the following causes the option premium to rise? (　　)

A) a $2 dividend being declared

B) a $2 dividend being paid

C) a 5-for-2 stock split

D) volatility increase

136. Suppose you believe that Company A's stock price is going to decline from its current level of $82. 50 sometime during the next 5 months. For $510. 25 you could buy a 5-month put option giving you the right to sell 100 shares at a priceof $83. 00 per share. If you bought the put option contract for $510. 25 and Company A's stock price actually dropped to $63. 00, your profit net of the premium paid would be (　　).

A) $1,950. 00

B) $1,439. 75

C) $1,489. 75

D) $2,000. 00

137. You have been asked to verify the pricing of a two-year European call option with a strike price of USD 45. You know that the initial stock price is USD 50, and the continuous risk-free rate is 3%. To verify the possible price range of this call, you

consider using price bounds. What is the difference between the upper and lower bounds for that European call? (　　)

A) 0.00

B) 7.62

C) 42.38

D) 45.00

138. You are looking at two options on a non-dividend paying stock that are identical in all respects except one is a European put and the other is a European call option. If the assumed volatility of the stock price increases, (　　).

A) the call will increase more than the put in value

B) the put will increase more than the call in value

C) the call will increase, but the put will decrease in value

D) the call and the put will increase equally

139. SCU stock is currently priced at \$106 per share, and the risk-free interest rate is 3.25%. Assuming that SCU does not pay any dividends, what is the lower bound of an American put option on SCU that expires in three months and has an exercise price of \$110? (　　)

A) \$0

B) \$0.48

C) \$3.11

D) \$4.00

140. For American options prior to maturity, the difference between the price of a call option and the price of a put option with the same underlying stock, strike price, and maturity must be less than or equal to the (　　).

A) stock price minus the present value of the exercise price

B) stock price minus the exercise price

C) present value of exercise price minus stock price

D) exercise price minus stock price

141. If the current USD/AUD rate is 0.6650 (1 AUD = 0.6650USD) and the risk-freerates for the USD and AUD are 1.0% and 4.5% respectively, what is the lower bound of a 5-month European put option on the AUD with a strike price of 0.6880? (　　)

A) 0.0135

B) 0.0245

C) 0.0325

D) 0.0455

142. Which of the following statements about options on futures is true? ( )
A) An American call is equal in value to a European call.
B) An American put is equal in value to a European put.
C) Put-call parity holds for both American and European options.
D) None of the above.

143. The price of an American call stock option is equal to an otherwise equivalent European call stock option at time t when ( ).
Ⅰ. The stock pays continuous dividends from t to option expiration T.
Ⅱ. The interest rates follow a mean-reverting process between t and T.
Ⅲ. The stock pays no dividends from t to option expiration T.
Ⅳ. Interest rates are non-stochastic between t and T.
A) Ⅱ and Ⅳ
B) Ⅲ only
C) Ⅰ and Ⅲ
D) None of the above, an American option is always worth more than a European option.

144. Which of the following is most true about American options? ( )
A) Early exercise is never optimal.
B) Early exercise of an American call on a non-dividend paying stock is never optimal.
C) Early exercise of an American put on a non-dividend paying stock is never optimal.
D) Before exercise, the value of the American call is always equal to the European call.

145. Given strictly positive interest rates, the best way to close out a long American call option position early (option written on a stock that pays no dividends) would be to ( ).
A) exercise the call
B) sell the call
C) deliver the call
D) none of the above

146. Which two of the following four statements are correct about the early exercise of American options on non-dividend-paying stocks? ( )
Ⅰ. It is never optimal to exercise an American call option early.
Ⅱ. It can be optimal to exercise an American put option early.

Ⅲ. It can be optimal to exercise an American call option early.

Ⅳ. It is never optimal to exercise an American put option early.

A) Ⅰ and Ⅱ

B) Ⅰ and Ⅳ

C) Ⅱ and Ⅲ

D) Ⅲ and Ⅳ

147. Each of the following is NECESSARILY TRUE about relationship between "time to expiration" (T) and option price EXCEPT ( ).

A) An increase in time to expiration (T) implies an increase in the option price for an American call on a non-dividend-paying stock.

B) An increase in time to expiration (T) implies an increase in the option price for a European call on a non-dividend-paying stock.

C) An increase in time to expiration (T) implies an increase in the option price for an American put on a dividend-paying stock.

D) An increase in time to expiration (T) implies an increase in the option price for a European put on a dividend-paying stock.

148. Each of the following is true about the RISK-FREE RATE, ceteris paribus, with respect to option value EXCEPT which? ( ).

A) An increase in the risk-free rate must increase the lower bound (minimum value) of a European PUT option on a non-dividend-paying stock.

B) An increase in the risk-free rate must increase the lower bound (minimum value) of a European CALL option on a non-dividend-paying stock.

C) An increase in the risk-free rate will increase the value of an American and European CALL on either dividend- or non-dividend-paying stock.

D) An increase in the risk-free rate will decrease the value of an American and European PUT on either dividend or non-dividend-paying stock.

149. According to put-call parity, buying a put option on a stock is equivalent to ( ).

A) buying a call option and buying the stock with funds borrowed at the risk-free rate

B) selling a call option and buying the stock with funds borrowed at the risk-free rate

C) buying a call option, selling the stock, and investing the proceeds at the risk-free rate

D) selling a call option, selling the stock, and investing the proceeds at the risk-free rate

150. Each of the following is true about option volatility EXCEPT ( ).

A) The lower bound for a European call option is equal to the Black-Scholes-Merton option value where the volatility input is zero.

B) The historical volatility, as in input into Black-Scholes-Merton, tends to converge on implied volatility as the option is nearer to being "at the money" (ATM).

C) Option value is an increasing function with volatility for an American or European CALL on a both a dividend- or non-dividend-paying stock.

D) Option value is an increasing function with volatility for an American or European PUT on a both a dividend- or non-dividend-paying stock.

151. A one-year European put option on a non-dividend-paying stock with strike at EUR 25 currently trades at EUR 3.19. The current stock price is EUR 23 and its annualvolatility is 30%. The annual risk-free interest rate is 5%. What is the price of a European call option on the same stock with the same parameters as those of this put option? Assume continuous compounding. ( )

A) EUR 1.19

B) EUR 3.97

C) EUR 2.41

D) cannot be determined with the data provided

152. The current price of stock ABC is \$42 and the call option with a strike at \$44 is trading at \$3. Expiration is in one year. The corresponding put is priced at \$2. Which of the following trading strategies will result in arbitrage profits? Assume that the risk-free rate is 10% and that the risk-free bond can be shorted costlessly. There are no transaction costs. ( )

A) Long position in both the call option and the stock, and short position in the put option and risk-free bond.

B) Long position in both the call option and the put option, and short position in the stock and risk-free bond.

C) Long position in both the call option and the risk-free bond, and short position in the stock and the put option.

D) Long position in both the put option and the risk-free bond, and short position in the stock and the call option.

153. Jeff is an arbitrage trader, who wants to calculate the implied dividend yield on astock while looking at the over-the-counter price of a five-year European put and call on that stock. He has the following data: $S = \$85$, $K = \$90$, $r = 5\%$, $c = \$10$, $p = \$15$. What is the continuous implied dividend yield of that stock? ( )

A) 2.48%
B) 4.69%
C) 5.34%
D) 7.71%

154. An American investor holds a portfolio of French stocks. The market value of the portfolio is € 10 million, with a beta of 1.35 relative to the CAC index. In November, the spot value of the CAC index is 4,750. The exchange rate is USD 1.25/€. The dividend yield, euro interest rates, and dollar interest rates are all equal to 4%. Which of the following option strategies would be most appropriate to protect the portfolio against a decline of the euro that week? March Euro options (all prices in US dollars per €) (　　)

Strike	Call euro	Put euro
1.25	0.018	0.022

A) Buy calls with a premium of USD 180,000.
B) Buy puts with a premium of USD 220,000.
C) Sell calls with a premium of USD 180,000.
D) Sell puts with a premium of USD 220,000.

155. Consider the following call option with 6-months till expiry. The strike price is \$50, the current stock price is \$55 and the value of the option is \$5. What does this imply about the level of 6-month interest rates? (　　)
A) Interest rates are positively sloped around the 6-month period.
B) Interest rates are negatively sloped around the 6-month period.
C) Interest rates are at zero for the 6-month period.
D) Cannot be determined from the information given.

156. Put option values increase as a result of increases in which of the following factors? (　　)
Ⅰ. Volatility
Ⅱ. Dividends
Ⅲ. Stock Price
Ⅳ. Time to expiration
A) Ⅰ, Ⅱ, and Ⅳ only
B) Ⅰ, Ⅲ, and Ⅳ only
C) Ⅱ and Ⅳ only
D) Ⅰ and Ⅲ only

157. Which of the following factors will not necessarily increase the price of a European call option on a dividend paying stock as this factor increases in value? (　　)

A) the risk free rate

B) the stock price

C) the time to expiration

D) the volatility of the stock price

158. According to Put-Call parity, buying a call option on a stock is equivalent to (　　).

A) writing a put, buying the stock, and selling short bonds (borrowing)

B) writing a put, selling the stock, and buying bonds (lending)

C) buying a put, selling the stock, and buying bonds (lending)

D) buying a put, buying the stock, and selling short bonds (borrowing)

159. According to put-call parity, buying a put option on a stock is equivalent to (　　).

A) buying a call option and buying the stock with funds borrowed at the risk-free rate

B) selling a call option and buying the stock with funds borrowed at the risk-free rate

C) buying a call option, selling the stock, and investing the proceeds at the risk-free rate

D) selling a call option, selling the stock, and investing the proceeds at the risk-free rate

160. According to put-call parity, writing a put is like (　　).

A) buying a call, buying stock, and lending

B) writing a call, buying stock, and borrowing

C) writing a call, buying stock, and lending

D) writing a call, selling stock, and borrowing

161. A six-month call option sells for \$30, with a strike price of \$120. If the stock price is \$100 per share and the risk-free interest rate is 5%, what is the price of a 6-month put option with a strike price of \$120? (　　)

A) \$39.20

B) \$44.53

C) \$46.28

D) \$47.04

162. A 3 month European call option on DEF stock with a strike price of \$50 is trading

for \$2. 25. The risk free rate is 10%. The current stock price of DEF stock is \$48. Calculate the value of a corresponding put with the same strike and maturity. (   )

A) \$2. 00

B) \$2. 25

C) \$3. 02

D) \$3. 57

163. A 2-year European call option has a market price of \$50 with a strike price of \$140. The underlying stock price is \$100 with a two-year annualized interest rate of 5% and a dividend yield of 2% (annualized). What is the number closest to the market price of a two-year European put struck at \$140? (   )

A) \$77

B) \$10

C) \$90

D) \$81

164. Consider a 1-year European call option with a strike price of \$27. 50 that is currently valued at \$4. 10 on a \$25 stock. The 1-year risk-free rate is 6% compounded annually. Which of the following is closest to the value of the corresponding put option (assume continuous compounding)? (   )

A) \$0. 00

B) \$4. 95

C) \$5. 00

D) \$5. 04

165. Jeff is an arbitrage trader, and he wants to calculate the implied dividend yield on a stock while looking at the over-the-counter price of a 5-year put and call (both European-style) on that same stock. He has the following data:

- Initial stock price = USD 85
- Strike price = USD 90
- Continuous risk-free rate = 5%
- Underlying stock volatility = unknown
- Call price = USD 10
- Put price = USD 15

What is the continuous implied dividend yield of that stock? (   )

A) 2. 48%

B) 4. 69%

C) 5. 34%

D) 7. 71%

166. The current price of stock ABC is USD 42 and the call option with a strike at USD 44 is trading at USD 3. Expiration is in one year. The put option with the same exercise price and same expiration date is priced at USD 2. Assume that the annual risk-free rate is 10% and that there is a risk-free bond paying the risk-free rate that can be shorted costlessly. There are no transaction costs. Which of the following trading strategies will result in arbitrage profits? (　　)

A) Long position in both the call option and the stock, and short position in the put option and risk-free bond.

B) Long position in both the call option and the put option, and short position in the stock and risk-free bond.

C) Long position in both the call option and risk-free bond, and short position in the stock and the put option.

D) Long position in both the put option and the risk-free bond, and short position in the stock and the call option.

167. On the OTC market there are two options available on Microsoft stock: a European put with premium of USD 2.25 and an American call option with premium of USD 0.46. Both options have a strike price of USD 24 and an expiration date 3 months from now. Microsoft's stock price is currently at USD 22 and no dividend is due during the next 6 months. Assuming that there is no arbitrage opportunity, which of the following choices is closest to the level of the risk-free rate? (　　)

A) 0.25%

B) 1.76%

C) 3.52%

D) insufficient information to determine

168. What are the minimum values of an American-style and a European-style 3-month call option with a strike price of $80 on a non-dividend-paying stock trading at $86 if the risk-free rate is 3%? (　　)

	American	European
A)	$6.00	$6.00
B)	$6.00	$5.96
C)	$6.59	$6.00
D)	$6.59	$6.59

169. What is the lower pricing bound for a European call option with a strike price of 80 and one year until expiration? The price of the underlying asset is 90, and the 1-year interest rate is 5% per annum. Assume continuous compounding of interest. (　　)

A) 14. 61
B) 13. 90
C) 10. 00
D) 5. 90

170. Consider a European call option on a non-dividend paying stock. The current market price is \$100, the strike price is \$102, the time to maturity is 9 months and the risk free rate is 7. 25%. Calculate the lower bound of the option price. (　　)
A) \$3. 40
B) \$3. 22
C) \$2. 75
D) \$2. 00

171. A long position in a put option can be synthetically produced by (　　).
A) long position in the underlying and a short position in a call.
B) short position in the underlying and a long position in a call.
C) long position in the underlying and a long position in a put.
D) short position in the underlying and a short position in a put.

172. Identify the false statement. (　　)
A) The difference in American call prices of same maturity cannot exceed the difference in their exercise prices.
B) The price difference between two European puts of same maturity can exceed the difference in their exercise prices.
C) Before expiration, an American put must be worth at least the exercise price less the stock price.
D) The longer until expiration, the more valuable an American put.

173. A covered call position is equivalent to (　　).
A) a long position in the stock and a long position in the call option
B) a short put position
C) a short position in the stock and a long position in the call option
D) a short call position

174. Which of the following will create a bull spread? (　　)
A) Buy a put with a strike price of $X = 50$, and sell a put with a strike price of 55
B) Buy a put with a strike price of $X = 55$, and sell a put with a strike price of 50.
C) Buy a call with a premium of 5, and sell a call with a premium of 7
D) Buy a call with a strike price of $X = 50$, and sell a put with a strike price of 55

175. Consider a bullish spread option strategy of buying one call option with a \$30 exercise price at a premium of \$3 and writing a call option with a \$40 exercise price at a premium of \$1.50. If the price of the stock increases to \$42 at expiration and the optionis exercised on the expiration date, the net profit per share at expiration (ignoring transaction costs) will be (   ).

A) \$8.50

B) \$9.00

C) \$9.50

D) \$12.50

176. Long a call on stock and short a call on the same stock with a higher strike price and same maturity is called (   ).

A) a bull spread

B) a bear spread

C) a calendar spread

D) a butterfly spread

177. Your bank is an active player in the commodity market. The view of the economist of the bank is that inflation is expected to rise moderately in the near term and market volatility is expected to remain low. The traders are advised to undertake deals on the metals exchange to align your book to conform with the expectations of the economist of the bank. As a risk manager, you are asked to monitor the positions of the traders to make sure that they have the exposures to inflation and market volatility sought by the bank. Which trader has taken an appropriate position among the traders you are monitoring? (   )

A) Trader A bought a call and a put, both with 90 days to expiration and with strike price equal to the existing spot level.

B) Trader B bought a put option with a down-and-in knock in feature.

C) Trader C bought a call option at the existing spot levels and sold a call at a higher strike price, both with 90 days to expiration.

D) Trader D sold a call option and bought a put at the existing levels, both with 90 days to expiration.

178. An investor sells a June 2008 call of ABC Limited with a strike price of USD 45 for USD 3 and buys a June 2008 call of ABC Limited with a strike price of USD 40 for USD 5. What is the name of this strategy and the maximum profit and loss the investor could incur? (   )

A) Bear Spread, Maximum Loss USD 2, Maximum Profit USD 3

B) Bull Spread, Maximum Loss Unlimited, Maximum Profit USD 3

C) Bear Spread, Maximum Loss USD 2, Maximum Profit Unlimited

D) Bull Spread, Maximum Loss USD 2, Maximum Profit USD 3

179. A bear spread is an option strategy in which the option trader (　　).

A) purchases a high strike call option and sells a lower strike call option

B) sells a low strike call option and sells a higher strike put option

C) purchases a low strike put option and sells a higher strike call option

D) sells a low strike put option and buys a higher strike call option

180. Research and model projections indicate that a specific event is likely to move the CHF against the USD. While the direction of the move is highly uncertain, it is highly likely that magnitude of the move will be significant. Based on this information, which of the following strategies would provide the largest economic benefit? (　　)

A) Long a call option on USD/CHF and long a put option on USD/CHF with the same strike price and expiration date.

B) Long a call option on USD/CHF and short a put option on USD/CHF with the same strike price and expiration date.

C) Short a call option on USD/CHF and short a put option on USD/CHF with the same strike price and expiration date.

D) Short a call option on USD/CHF and long a put option on USD/CHF with the same strike price and expiration date.

181. Which one of the following four trading strategies limits the investor's upside potential and downside risk? (　　)

A) A long position in a put combined with a long position in a stock.

B) A short position in a put combined with a short position in a stock.

C) Buying a call option on a stock with a certain strike price and selling a call option on the same stock with a higher strike price and the same expiration date.

D) Buying a call and a put with the same strike price and expiration date.

182. An option trader constructs the following position: buys 1 call with a strike price at X_1, buys 1 call with a strike price at X_2 and sells 2 calls with a strike X_3. Where $X_1 < X_3 < X_2$. This strategy is referred to as a (　　).

A) Butterfly Spread

B) Bull Spread

C) Strap Spread

D) Strip Spread

183. A butterfly spread involves positions in options with three difference strike prices. It can be created by buying a call option with a low strike of X; buying a call option with a high strike Y; and selling two call options with a strike X halfway between X and Y. What can be said about the upside and downside of the strategy? (　　)

A) Both the upside and downside is unlimited.

B) Both the upside and downside is limited.

C) The upside is unlimited but the downside is limited.

D) The upside is limited but the downside is unlimited.

184. Consider the following option strategy of buying one at-the-money put with a strike price of \$43 for \$6, selling two puts with a strike price of \$37 for \$4 each and buying one put with a strike price of \$32 for \$1. If the stock price plummets to \$19 at expiration, calculate the net profit/loss per share of the strategy. (　　)

A) −2.00 per share

B) Zero-no profit or loss

C) 1.00 per share

D) 2.00 per share

185. The payoff on a calendar spread is most similar to which of the following option strategies? (　　)

A) Bull spread.

B) Bear spread.

C) Long straddle.

D) Butterfly spread.

186. A portfolio manager wants to hedge his bond portfolio against changes in interest rates. He intends to buy a put option with a strike price below the portfolio'scurrent price in order to protect against rising interest rates. He also wants to sella call option with a strike price above the portfolio's current pricein order to reduce the cost of buying the put option. What strategy is the manager using? (　　)

A) Bear spread

B) Strangle

C) Collar

D) Straddle

187. Which of the following regarding option strategies is/are not correct? (　　)

Ⅰ. A long strangle involves buying a call and a put with equal strike prices

Ⅱ. A short bull spread involves selling a call at lower strike price and buying another call at higher strike price

Ⅲ. Vertical spreads are formed by options with different maturities

Ⅳ. A long butterfly spread is formed by buying two options at two different strike prices and selling another two options at the same strike price

A) Ⅰ only

B) Ⅰ and Ⅲ only

C) Ⅰ and Ⅱ only

D) Ⅲ and Ⅳ only

188. An investor owns a stock and is bullish over the short term. 'Which of the following strategies will be the most appropriate one for this investor if the primary concern is to make a bet on the volatility of the stock? (　　)

A) A covered call

B) A protective put

C) An at-the-money strip

D) An at-the-money strap

189. Which of the following statements about a floor is true? (　　)

A) Floor is a put option and protects against a fall in interest rates.

B) Floor is a call option and protects against a fall in interest rates.

C) Floor is a put option and protects against a rise in interest rates.

D) Floor is a call option and protects against a rise in interest rates.

190. An interest rate collar can be structured by (　　).

A) buying an interest rate cap and selling an interest rate floor

B) buying an interest rate cap and buying an interest rate floor

C) selling an interest rate cap and selling an interest rate floor

D) selling an interest rate cap and buying an interest rate floor

191. Which of the following is the riskiest form of speculation using option contracts? (　　)

A) setting up a spread using call options

B) buying put options

C) writing naked call options

D) writing naked put options

192. Tom and Jerry both are working for a portfolio managers at a regional investment firm based on California.

Jim Bob is examining employing a covered call strategy on a particular oil stock, and tells his colleague that he likes this approach, since it will increase expected returns on the portfolio while at the same time reducing downside risk.

Joe Bob is considering another approach. He is looking at an oil services firm and would like to employ a protective put strategy. He tells his colleague that this approach will permit his investors to have an unlimited profit potential while limiting potential losses to an amount equal to the initial stock priceless the put premium. Are Jim Bob and/or Joe Bob correct in their statements? (　　)

A) Tom is incorrect; Jerry is also incorrect.

B) Tom is correct; Jerry is incorrect.

C) Tom is incorrect; Jerry is correct.

D) Tom is correct; Jerry is also correct.

193. An investor sells a June 2008 call of ABC Limited with a strike price of USD 45 for USD 3 and buys a June 2008 call of ABC Limited with a strike price of USD 40 for USD 5. What is the name of this strategy and the maximum profit and loss the investor could incur? (　　)

A) Bear spread, maximum loss USD 2, maximum profit USD 3

B) Bull spread, maximum loss unlimited, maximum profit USD 3

C) Bear spread, maximum loss USD 2, maximum profit unlimited

D) Bull spread, maximum loss USD 2, maximum profit USD 3

194. Consider a bearish option strategy of buying one \$50 strike put for \$7, selling two \$42 strike puts for \$4 each, and buying one \$37 put for \$2. All options have the same maturity. Calculate the final profit per share of the strategy if the underlying is trading at \$33 at expiration. (　　)

A) \$1 per share

B) \$2 per share

C) \$3 per share

D) \$4 per share

195. According to an in-house research report, it is expected that USDJPY (quoted as JPY/USD) will trade near 97 at the end of March. Frankie Shiller, the investment director of a house fund, decides to use an option strategy to capture this opportunity. The current level of the USDJPY exchange rate is 97 on February 28. Accordingly, which of the following strategies would be the most appropriate for the largest profit while the potential loss is limited? (　　)

A) Long a call option on USDJPY and long a put option on USDJPY with the same strike price of USDJPY 97 and expiration date.

B) Long a call option on USDJPY with strike price of USDJPY 97 and short a call option on USDJPY with strike price of USDJPY 99 and the same expiration date.

C) Short a call option on USDJPY and long a put option on USDJPY with the same strike price of USDJPY 97 and expiration date.

D) Long a call option with strike price of USDJPY 96, long a call option with strike price of USDJPY 98, and sell two call options with strike price of USDJPY 97, all of them with the same expiration date.

196. Which of the following options is strongly path-dependent? (　　)

A) an Asian option

B) a binary option

C) an American option

D) a European call option

197. All else being equal, which of the following options would cost more than plain-vanilla options that are currently at-the-money? (　　)

Ⅰ. Lookback options

Ⅱ. Barrier options

Ⅲ. Asian options

Ⅳ. Chooser option

A) Ionly

B) Ⅰ and Ⅳ

C) Ⅱ and Ⅲ

D) Ⅰ, Ⅲ, and Ⅳ

198. Of the following options, which one does not benefit from an increase in the stock price when the current stock price is \$100 and the barrier has not yet been crossed? (　　)

A) a down-and-out call with barrier at \$90 and strike at \$110

B) a down-and-in call with barrier at \$90 and strike at \$110

C) an up-and-in put with barrier at \$110 and strike at \$100

D) an up-and-in call with barrier at \$110 and strike at \$100

199. In the Black-Scholes expression for a European call option, the term used to compute option probability of exercise is (　　).

A) d_1

B) d_2

C) $N(d_1)$

D) $N(d_2)$

200. Using the Black-Scholes model, calculate the value of a European call option given the following information: spot rate = 100; strike price = 110; risk-free rate = 10%; time to expiry = 0.5 years; $N(d_1) = 0.457185$; $N(d_2) = 0.374163$. (　　)

A) \$10.90

B) \$9.51

C) \$6.57

D) \$4.92

201. Each of the following is a possible motive to trade a barrier option EXCEPT which? (　　)

A) Reduce the option's cost.

B) Implement static hedge.

C) Add leverage to a directional view.

D) Reduce the cost of tail insurance.

202. If the cash-or-nothing call option pays (Q), what is the value of the binary option? bonus: explain the formula intuitively. (　　)

A) $Q * N(d_1)$

B) $Q * \text{EXP}(-rT) * N(d_1)$

C) $Q * N(d_2)$

D) $Q * \text{EXP}(-rT) * N(d_2)$

203. A cash-or-nothing call with strike = \$30 and payoff (Q) = \$30 is equivalent to a short European call option (same strike) PLUS (　　).

A) long asset-or-nothing call

B) short asset-or-nothing call

C) long cash-or-nothing call

D) short cash-or-nothing call

204. Which of the following statements about lookback options is FALSE? (　　)

A) The MAX (.) function is employed by a floating lookback put and fixed lookback call, while the MIN(.) function is employed by a floating lookback call and fixed lookback put

B) The basic exotic lookback (in Hull) is European-style

C) Due to the max/min function, a lookback can always be exercised for at least some gain

D) The key drawback to the buyer of a lookback (the long) is the premium cost

205. In regard to a shout option, which of the following statements is TRUE? (　　)

A) It is always better to shout arbitrarily, when in the money, than to never shout.
B) A shout option must be a call
C) Neither the floating (strike) lookback option nor the shout option can expire underwater
D) The Black-Scholes formula is best suited to pricing a shout

206. What is the most likely relationship among the prices of a call option, ceteris paribus. ( )
A) Shout<Vanilla call<Lookback; i. e. , shout less expensive than regular call is less expensive than lookback)
B) Lookback<Shout<Vanilla call
C) Vanilla call<Shout<Lookback
D) Vanilla call<Lookback<Shout

207. Each of the following is true about Asian options EXCEPT which? ( )
A) Average price options are less expensive than their vanilla option analogs.
B) It is easier to price an Asian option if the geometric average is used.
C) Most market traded options use a geometric average.
D) Like the lookback option, the Asian is path dependent.

第 12 单元

中央对手方交易机制

208. Which of the following is not an advantage of establishing CCPs? (　　)
 A) CCPs allow netting of contracts.
 B) CCPs can be applied to some types of OTC trades.
 C) CCPs can create more transparency in trading.
 D) CCPs eliminate all counterparty risk in the financial system.

209. Describe the characteristic of a clearing ring. Which of the following statement is TURE? (　　)
 A) improve liquidity
 B) are designed to mitigate counterparty risk
 C) benefit all exchange members
 D) facilitate the close-out process

210. Identify the difference between exchanged-traded and over-the-counter (OTC) derivatives, which of the following statement is likely? (　　)
 A) Novation of contracts may be problematic given the lack of fungibility in the OTC markets.
 B) OTC derivatives are standardized contracts with a liquid, active, and regulated market.
 C) Exchange-traded derivatives are privately negotiated bilateral contracts transacted in a market with little or no regulation.
 D) OTC derivatives are typically shorter term and are settled within a few days.

211. Taking about the functions of exchanges, which of the following statements is incorrect? (　　)
 A) Entities trading on an exchange may opt out of the exchange's rules and conditions.
 B) Exchanges report transaction prices to various entities, including trading participants, vendors, and subscribers.

C) Exchange may be physical locations or electronic platforms that provide a central location for trading, which then facilities price discovery.
D) Exchanges set the terms of traded, standardized products.

212. Counterparties must post both initial margin and variation margin with a central counterparty (CCP). Describe the margin. Variation margin means to (　　).
A) adjusts contract prices to changes in the market value of the underlying asset, or to changes in the reference rate or currency
B) cannot be rehypothecated or reused as margin for other transactions
C) is the first line of defense against potential losses in a member default scenario
D) acts as the first buffer against member defaults and reduces counterparty risk

213. When consider the counterparty risk, which choice about mechanisms is like that of a monoline? (　　)
A) structured investment vehicles(SⅣs)
B) derivatives product companies (DPCs)
C) special purpose vehicles(SPVs)
D) credit derivative product companies(CDPCs)

214. In a comparison between exchange-traded derivatives and over-the-counter (OTC) derivatives, which of the following statements is TRUE? (　　)
A) Customized OTC derivatives are exotic and exotic products are not socially useful.
B) Compared to an exchange-traded derivative, a customized OTC derivative offers better liquidity but greater basis risk.
C) Due to the leverage inherent in customized OTC derivatives, the total market value of OTC derivatives is nearly 100% of their gross notional outstanding.
D) Compared to an exchange-traded derivative, a disadvantage of OTC derivatives is their relative lack of fungibility; i. e., difficulty in unwinding position or assigning to another counterparty.

215. If a company wants to be separated from its parent company, it will not be affected when the parent company goes bankrupt. Which choice is ture? (　　)
A) MICs
B) DPCs
C) SPVs
D) CDPCs

216. What risks are the SPVS most likely to suffer? (　　)

A) Model Risk
B) Legal Risk
C) Operational Risk
D) Market Risk

217. Derivatives Product Companies are generally rated? (　　)
A) AAA
B) BBB
C) CCC
D) Aa

218. Which of the following risks can be avoided by Derivatives Product Companies? (　　)
A) Legal Risk
B) Model Risk
C) Bankruptcy risk
D) Operational Risk

219. Which of the following statement will lend moral hazard and/or adverse selection in the central clearing process? (　　)
A) By transacting through a CCP, duplicate bilateral contracts can be offset, which improves flexibility for new transactions and reduces costs.
B) Member defaults are centrally managed through the auction process which minimizes price disruptions.
C) A member's losses are distributed among all surviving members, which spread the impact of losses, reduce costs, and minimize market impact and systemic risk.
D) The daily margining of products in a centrally-cleared market ensures greater transparency in product valuation, which increases product liquidity.

220. Regarding margining in centrally cleared and bilateral markets, Which following is error? (　　)
A) Variation margin is typically cash posted by a member to cover the daily net change of the member's position.
B) Margining by CCPs is stricter than in the OTC derivative markets.
C) CCPs normally set margin requirements based only on the risks of the members' transactions.
D) Members with different credit risk will always post different amounts of initial margin.

221. Corn producer X owes wheat producer Y 140, wheat Y owes soybean producer Z 185, and soybean producer Z owes corn producer X 245. If a central counterparty (CCP) is used to net these obligations, which choice is most accurate? (　　)

A) Counterparty Y pays the CCP 25.

B) Counterparty Z pays the CCP 50.

C) The CCP pays counterparty X 105.

D) The CCP pays counterparty Z 25.

222. A central counterparty (CCP) interjects itself between over-the-counter (OTC) trades. Describe the CCP's functions, Which choice is incorrect? (　　)

A) Acts as the seller to each buyer and the buyer to each seller.

B) Increases the interconnectedness of trades and of participants.

C) Reduces the risk of default or non-payment by a counterparty.

D) Increases trade liquidity and transparency.

223. Which is TRUE of clearing? (　　)

A) By definition, clearing is central.

B) Clearing occurs between execution and settlement.

C) Clearing refers to the exchange of securities and/or cash and fulfillment of legal obligations.

D) On most exchanges, clearing is an intraday dynamic with an occasional maximum time horizon of several days.

224. Novation, which is critical to central clearing, is the legal process whereby the central counterparty (CCP) positions itself between the buyer and seller by replacing a contract with one or more other contracts. After novation, which risk (s) does the CCP bear? (　　)

A) Market risk

B) Conditional market risk

C) Novation implies that the CCP inherits only market risk

D) Novation ensures that the CCP is immunized from credit and market risk

225. According to Gregory, which of the following is a potential DISADVANTAGE of a central counterparty (CCP)? (　　)

A) Bifurcations

B) Market liquidity

C) Loss mutualization

D) Default management

226. A central counterparty (CCP) is evaluating a new derivative instrument as a possible candidate for trading on its central clearing platform. The following four features are associated with the candidate derivative instrument. Which of the following is MOST LIKELY to render the instrument incompatible with central clearing? (　　)

A) The candidate derivative instrument requires heterogeneous (ie, non-standard) legal terms such that each contract is unique.

B) The candidate derivative instrument is simple (ie, not complex) however valuation models are quite sensitive to input assumptions.

C) Several of the counterparties, who are interested to trade the candidate derivative instrument, are not currently members of the CCP.

D) The candidate derivative instrument has an historical price volatility that is significantly above average, although volume has been deep.

227. Describe the non-member of a central counterparty (CCP) properties. The following statements Which is incorrectly about non-member of a central counterparty? (　　)

A) It is possible that clearing members are able to pass on losses to non-members, which would reduce the gains of non-members.

B) Non-members are required to contribute to default funds.

C) If a CCP fails, a non-member may be able to avoid losses so long as its counterparty is solvent.

D) Non-members face the risk of not being able to port their trades should the counterparty member default.

228. Regarding FICO score is needed to qualify a borrower as prime rather than subprime. Which following is most likely? (　　)

A) Above 660.

B) Above 620.

C) Above 600.

D) Above 640.

229. Central clearing through central counterparties (CCPs) have many advantages for counterparty. Which of the following statements does not describe a potential benefit of central clearing? Which of the describe is not merit of central clearing? (　　)

A) CCPs and clearinghouses manage margin requirements and quire both initial margin and variation margin payments.

B) Multilateral netting of trades allows entities to reduce their counterparty risk.

C) CCPs represent a single point in the market system through which counterparty risk is concentrated.

D) Losses arising from a counterparty's default are spread across all central clearing members.

230. A risk officer is evaluating lessons learned from previous central counterparty (CCP) failures. The the risk officer should reject which statement about mitigate the risk from CCP failures? (　　)

A) Eliminating cross-margining linkage arrangements between CCPs will minimize liquidity problems.

B) CCPs must actively monitor positions, penalize overly concentrated positions, and promptly liquidate or hedge extremely large positions.

C) Variation margins should be recalculated often and collected quickly.

D) Initial margins and default funds should be sufficiently large in order to withstand significant negative asset value declines.

231. Regarding the following central counterparty functions. Which of the following will increase potentially systematic risk? (　　)

A) Improve liquidity for the market.

B) Provide transparency for the market.

C) Address counterparty risk by providing offsetting positions through netting.

D) Require members to post higher initial margin during times of increased market volatility.

232. Regarding risks faced by central counterparties (CCPs), describes characteristics of the concentration risk, which of following is TRUE? (　　)

A) The risk that a foreign government could default on its debt obligations, thereby causing members to fail.

B) The risk that exposure to a counterparty is negatively correlated with the credit quality of the counterparty.

C) The risk of clearing members, margins, or both that are located in a single geographic area.

D) The risk of losses of margin funds resulting from investment actions performed within or outside of the stated investment policy.

233. Each of the following arguments about the future of central counterparties (CCPs) is true, according to Gregory, except which is FALSE? (　　)

A) CCP disadvantages include vulnerability to moral hazard and adverse selection, and the possibility of pro-cyclical effects.

B) It seems likely that there will be a relatively large number of CCPs due to bifurcation on two levels: regional and product.

C) CCPs are unlikely to fail, due to margins, but if a CCP fails, a redeeming quality is that its bailout should be relatively simple.

D) In accordance with a sort of "conservation of risk" principal, CCP will not so much reduce counterparty risk as transform it into different forms.

234. Which OTC derivatives class has the LARGEST amount of gross notional outstanding? (　　)

A) Equity derivatives

B) Credit default swaps

C) Interest rate derivatives

D) Foreign exchange derivatives

235. Among the following, what is the MOST COMMON method for quantifying counterparty risk into the price of a transaction? (　　)

A) Novation

B) Vertical setup

C) Trade compression

D) Credit value adjustment (CVA)

236. To which risk are central counterparties (CCPs) MOST exposed when they require margin—especially initial margin because initial margin generally imposes linearity—such that problems can arise "with respect to volatility, tail risk, complex dependencies and wrong-way risk"? (　　)

A) Legal risk

B) Model risk

C) Default risk

D) Liquidity risk

237. Each of the following is a risk faced by central counterparties (CCPs) EXCEPT which is not? (　　)

A) Reputational risk associated with remedying a clearing member default

B) Hindsight bias risk implied by increased transparency of network interconnectedness

C) Liquidity risk due to variation margin, investment of financial resources, and liquidity support

D) Knock-on effects ensuing from the default of a clearing member including failed auctions and resignations

238. Each of the following is a lesson learned from prior central counterparty (CCP) failures EXCEPT which is not? ( )

A) Operational risk must be controlled as much as possible.

B) Variation margins should be recalculated frequently and collected promptly.

C) Excessive reliance on external liquidity tends to promote adverse selection by bad agents.

D) Initial margin and default funds should be resilient to large negative asset shocks or gaps.

第 13 单元

常见金融资产——大宗商品、外汇、债券和房贷

239. Which commodities have seasonal production and constant demand properties? (　　)
 A) Gold
 B) Oil
 C) Natural gas
 D) Corn

240. Electricity is unique among commodities for each of the following three reasons EXCEPT which? (　　)
 A) More difficult to store than most consumption commodities (mostly non-storable).
 B) At any point in time, maximum supply of electricity is fixed (can produce less but not more).
 C) Demand for electricity is highly elastic.
 D) Demand for electricity is highly seasonal.

241. Financial assets are stored (please note this is different than having a storage cost) but electricity is effectively non-storable. Consider three possible implications of electricity's non-storability:
 Ⅰ. The electricity forward curve performs a price discovery function (it contains unique information not already contained in the spot price of electricity)
 Ⅱ. Unlike the forward curve of a financial asset, we expect the electricity forward curve to contain swings
 Ⅲ. Unlike a financial commodity where the forward price can be expressed as a function of the expected future spot price, $F(0) = E[S(t)] * \exp[(r - a)T]$ where (r) is the riskfree rate and (a) is the discount rate, the electricity forward price cannot be similarly expressed. Which of the statements is TRUE about the electricity forward curve? (　　)
 A) Ⅰ. Only

B) Ⅰ. and Ⅱ. Only

C) Ⅰ. and Ⅲ. Only

D) All three are true

242. The spot price and one-year futures price of silver, respectively, is \$40 and \$47 per ounce; i. e. , $S(0) = \$40.00$, $F(0,1) = \$47.00$. The riskless rate is 3.0%. A speculator (investor) assumes a discount rate of 8.0%. From the perspective of this speculator, if she considers the futures price to be fair, what is the expected future spot price of silver in one year, $E[S(1)]$? ( )

A) \$41.22

B) \$43.33

C) \$47.00

D) \$44.7

243. Each of the following statements is true about the commodity lease rate EXCEPT which? ( )

A) In a carry market, the lease rate should equal the negative of the storage cost

B) In a lease market, the lease rate (delta) informs the forward price in a way similar to a dividend does a financial commodity: $F(0, T) = S(0) * [\exp(\text{riskfree} - \text{delta})T]$

C) We should be able to infer the lease rate of gold from the gold forward curve

D) The lease rate is given by: commodity growth rate (g)-discount rate (alpha)

244. Analysis finds that current cornprice for a commodity is \$22. The annual lease rate is 5 percent for the commodity. The appropriate continuously compounding annual risk-free rate for the commodity is equivalent to 8 percent. What is the two year commodity forward price? ( )

A) \$23.82

B) \$23.36

C) \$25.22

D) \$24.12

245. An investor attempt to effectively counterbalance risk and to manage volatility and takes a position in two different markets with essentially equal amount positions in each market, what is this strategy? ( )

A) Cross spread

B) Swap spread

C) Interest hedge

D) Cross hedge

246. The market is a normal backwardation. Futures prices tend to (　　).

A) fall over the life of the contract because speculators are net short and have to receive compensation for bearing risk

B) rise over the life of the contract because speculators are net long and have to receive compensation for bearing risk

C) fall over the life of the contract because hedgers are net short and have to receive compensation for bearing risk

D) rise over the life of the contract because hedgers are net long and have to receive compensation for bearing risk

247. The spot price of gold is \$1,822 and the six-month forward price is \$1,830; $S(0) = 1{,}822$, $F(0, 0.5) = 1{,}830$. The riskless rate is 2.0%. What is the implied per annum lease rate under, respectively, an assumption of Ⅰ. continuous compounding and Ⅱ. annual (discrete) compounding? (　　)

A) 1.124% (continuous) and 1.110% (annual)

B) 1.248% (continuous) and 1.220% (annual)

C) 1.362% (continuous) and 1.346% (annual)

D) 1.444% (continuous) and 1.428% (annual)

248. Identify the difference between a strip and a stack hedge and Which following statement about stack hedge is TURE? (　　)

A) out-of-the-money put options

B) a combination of long and short positions in different futures expiration

C) futures contracts that are concentrated in a single futures expiration

D) futures contracts on assets that are related to, but different, from the hedged asset

249. Which of the following commodities is most likely to imply a forward curve in backwardation? (　　)

A) low risk-free rate, low lease rate, low storage cost, low convenience yield

B) high risk-free rate, low lease rate, high storage cost, low convenience yield

C) low risk-free rate, high lease rate, low storage cost, high convenience yield

D) high risk-free rate, high lease rate, high storage cost, high convenience yield

250. Consider the following statements about the commodity lease rate:

Ⅰ. A positive lease rate, convenience yield and dividend yield are similar in that they all, ceteris paribus, tend to push the commodity forward curve down (toward backwardation)

Ⅱ. A lease rate (on a consumption commodity) is like a dividend yield (on a financial commodity like a stock index) in that both are observable, require a storable commodity, and are earned by the owner regardless of whether the commodity is loaned, which of the statements is (are) true? (   )

A) Ⅰ. only
B) Ⅱ. Only
C) Both Ⅰ. and Ⅱ.
D) Neither Ⅰ. nor Ⅱ.

251. The spot price and one-year futures price of wheat, respectively, is \$7 and \$8 per bushel; $S(0) = \$7.00$, $F(0, 1) = \$8.00$. The riskless rate is 4.0% per annum with continuous compounding. Which trade create a synthetic position in wheat that would be equivalent to buying wheat in the spot market with the intent to hold the wheat for one year? (   )

A) Short a riskless zero-coupon bond with current price of \$7.69 (* number of bushels) plus short the one-year wheat futures contract
B) Long a riskless zero-coupon bond with current price of \$8.00 (* number of bushels) plus short the one-year wheat futures contract
C) Long a riskless zero-coupon bond with current price of \$7.69 (* number of bushels) plus long the one-year wheat futures contract
D) Long a riskless zero-coupon bond with current price of \$8.00 (* number of bushels) plus long the one-year wheat futures contract

252. Each of the following is an example of a commodity product (non calendar) spread trade EXCEPT (   ).

A) long crude oil futures plus short gasoline and heating oil futures
B) long cocoa and milk futures plus short hardwood pulp futures
C) long soybeans futures plus short soybean meal (soymeal) and soybean oil (soyoil)
D) long feeder cattle and corn futures plus short live cattle futures

253. The December oil futures price is \$100 per barrel. The December unleaded gasoline futures price is \$270 per gallon, and the December heating oil futures price is \$280 per gallon. What is the gross margin that can be locked-in with a "3-2-1" crack spread trade per barrel? (   )

A) Zero
B) \$156
C) \$173
D) \$240

254. An oil producer has an obligation to deliver 100,000 barrels per month at a fixed price for the next three years. Which of the following circumstances, ceteris paribus, favors a stack hedge over a strip hedge? (　　)

A) Bid-ask spreads (on the oil futures contracts) are atypically constant over time (spreads do not widen with maturity).

B) The oil futures curve exhibits contango.

C) There is uncertainty with respect to the future shape of the oil futures curve.

D) There is justifiable conviction that current oil futures curve is too steep and will flatten.

255. Each of the following is a major risk in commodity SPOT markets EXCEPT (　　).

A) Price risk

B) Basis risk

C) Delivery risk

D) Credit risk

256. Which risk is most difficult to hedge or insure? (　　)

A) Ordinary transportation risk

B) Extraordinary transportation risk

C) Cost of transportation risk

D) Delivery risk

257. Geman defines "basis risk" as the variance of the basis where, if (S) is the spot price and(F)is the futures price, the variance of the basis is equal to the variance (S − F). If the spot price has a volatility of 20%, the futures price has a volatility of 30%, and if their correlation is 0.70, what is the basis risk? (　　)

A) 0.0460

B) 0.0820

C) 0.2140

D) 0.2145

258. The very difficult to store and transport commodities is? (　　)

A) Natural gas

B) Corn

C) Oil

D) Gold

259. A commodities analyst is studying storage costs, lease rates and convenience yield. In determining a forward price in a non-arbitrage forward pricing formula, what is

the convenience yield, and how would it be related to inventory levels? (　　)

A) Convenience yield is the cost-of-carry adjustment, and is directly related to levels of inventory.

B) Convenience yield is equal to storage costs minus the lease rate, and is inversely related to levels of inventory.

C) convenience yield is the benefit of holding the physical asset, and is inversely related to levels of inventory.

D) Convenience yield is the reverse cost-of-carry adjustment which quantifies the benefit of going forward the asset, and is directly related to levels of inventory.

260. What effect does the fact that electricity is a non-storable commodity have on overall electricity pricing? (　　)

A) Price is set by supply and demand at a given point in time, and futures prices fluctuate more during the day compared to financial futures.

B) Arbitrage opportunities are only available long-term, and price fluctuations are much higher compared to all other commodities.

C) Short-term arbitrages are possible, but daily price fluctuations are higher compared to financial futures.

D) price is set according to supply and electricity production source, and daily price fluctuations are lower compared to financial futures.

261. A US bank has the following pound sterling exposures: GBP 10.0 billion in assets, GBP 7.0 billion in liabilities, GBP 5.0 billion bought, GBP 6.0 billion sold. The bank is concerned that the pound sterling will fall in value relative to the US dollar. Which of the following will reduce the bank's exposure to pound sterling depreciation? (　　)

A) Nothing, its net exposure implies a benefit if GBP depreciates.

B) Add +2 billion in assets to the balance sheet that are denominated in pound sterlings.

C) Add +2 billion in liabilities to the balance sheet that are denominated in pound sterlings.

D) Add +2 billion in long forward exposure to the pound sterling; i.e., promises to buy GBP in the future.

262. A US bank raises USD $10 million (liabilities) and invests this amount into a Russian project denominated in Russian rubles (asset) with an expected foreign rate of return of 12%. The bank remains unhedged with respect to this currency risk. If there is an sudden increase in the Russian inflation rate, without any corresponding impact on the project's nominal, foreign 12% return on the project, according to purchasing power parity (PPP), what is the impact on the bank? (　　)

A) No impact

B) Ruble should appreciate, translating into a gain for the bank

C) Ruble should depreciate, translating into a gain for the bank

D) Ruble should depreciate, translating into a loss for the bank

263. The current EURUSD spot exchange rate is \$1.1111 and the one-year forward exchange rate is \$1.2240; i.e., EUR is the base rate and USD is the quote rate. If you convert \$500,000 U.S. dollars to euros in the spot foreign exchange market and purchase a one-year forward contract to convert euros into dollars, which is nearest to the effective annual return? (　　)

A) −1.50%

B) 2.08%

C) 5.79%

D) 10.16%

264. A bank has the following currency positions in the Brazilian real, expressed in Brazilian real (\$R):

Assets = R\$125,000

Liabilities = R\$78,000

FX Bought = R\$27,000

FX Sold = R\$5,000

The spot exchange rate USDBRL is \$R 3.497 (i.e., USD is the base currency). If the Brazilian real depreciates by 3.0%, approximately what is the gain (loss) on the currency position expressed in US dollars? (　　)

A) Loss of \$3,365

B) Loss of \$592

C) Gain of \$1,270

D) Gain of \$4,822

265. City Bank issued \$200.0 million of one-year CDs in the United States at a rate of 3.50%. It invested part of this money, \$100.0 million, in the purchase of a one-year bond issued by a U.S. firm at an annual rate of 4.0%. The remaining \$100.0 million was invested in a one-year Brazilian government bond paying an annual interest rate of 5.0%. The exchange rate at the time of the transaction was USDBRL R\$3.5000. If the Brazilian real appreciates (against the dollar) from R\$3.5000 to R\$3.0000, what is the net return on this \$200.0 million investment? (　　)

A) 3.470%

B) 5.833%

C) 9.750%

D) 12.930%

266. A bank purchases a six-month, \$1.0 million Eurodollar deposit at an interest rate of 2.5% per annum with semiannual compounding. It invests the funds in a six-month Swedish krone AA-rated bond paying 3.5% per annum. The current SEKUSD spot rate is \$0.1140 per 1.0 krona. The six-month forward rate on the Swedish krone is being quoted at SEKUSD \$0.1210. If the bank covers its foreign exchange exposure using the FX forward market, which is nearest to the net spread earned on this investment per annum with semiannual compounding? (　　)

A) 2.38%

B) 4.75%

C) 7.93%

D) 13.50%

267. Assume that interest rates are 1.0% per annum with annual compounding in the United States and 9.0% in Brazil. A bank can borrow (by issuing CDs) or lend (by purchasing CDs) at these rates. The USDBRL spot exchange rate is R \$3.500 per 1.0 US dollar. Which is nearest to the forward exchange rate implied by the interest rate parity theorem (quoted USDBRL with Brazilian real as the quote currency)? (　　)

A) R \$2.85

B) R \$3.54

C) R \$3.78

D) R \$4.07

268. Suppose the current EUR/USD spot exchange rate is \$1.1300. Eurozone inflation is 5.0% while U.S. inflation is only 2.0%. According to purchasing power parity (PPP), which is nearest to the new EUR/USD spot exchange rate that should result from the difference in inflation rates? (　　)

A) \$1.0961

B) \$1.1128

C) \$1.1300

D) \$1.1403

269. Each of the following is true about the corporate trustee in a corporate bond issuance EXCEPT? (　　)

A) The trustee is paid by bondholders.

B) The trustee acts in a fiduciary capacity for investors who own the bond issue.

C) The trustee must, at the time of issue, authenticate the bonds issued (i. e., keep track of all the bonds sold) and make sure that they do not exceed the principal amount authorized by the indenture.

D) If a corporate issuer fails to pay interest or principal, the trustee may declare a default and take such action as may be necessary to protect the rights of bondholders.

270. Six months ago Brian Smith purchased a zero-coupon bond with a face value of $100.00 and a remaining term to maturity of seven (7.0) years. When he purchased the bond, the yield curve was flat at 3.0% per annum with semi-annual compounding. While today the yield curve remains flat, it has shifted up by 40 basis points. If Brian sells the bond today, what is his per annum return with semi-annual compounding and approximately how much of the return is due to reinvestment risk? (　　)

A) −6.70% with about 30% due reinvestment risk

B) −4.54% with about 50% due reinvestment risk

C) −2.13% with no reinvestment risk

D) +0.40% with no reinvestment risk

271. What is an advantage of a fixed-spread tender offer over a fixed-price tender offer? (　　)

A) No significant advantage.

B) It is easier for bondholders to assess the value of a fixed-spread tender offer.

C) Significantly less counterparty credit risk to bondholders in a fixed-spread tender offer.

D) Fixed-spread tender offers eliminate the exposure to interest-rate risk for both bondholders and the issuer during the tender offer window.

272. Consider which of the following statements are true about bond reinvestment risk and bond duration (interest rate risk) (　　).

Ⅰ. Less bond reinvestment risk implies greater interest rate risk (duration), ceteris paribus

Ⅱ. Due to reinvestment risk, the yield-to-maturity on a bond is unlikely to equal the bond's realized return

Ⅲ. Reinvestment risk is eliminated in a zero-coupon bond

A) Ⅰ Only

B) Ⅱ and Ⅰ

C) Ⅱ and Ⅲ

D) All three

273. Which of the following is most likely to cause an increase (i. e. , widening) in a corporate bond credit spread? (　　)

A) Economic expansion in the business cycle.

B) Increase in the bond's liquidity.

C) Flight to quality.

D) Addition of embedded put option feature to the bond.

274. Each of the following is true about corporate bond recovery rates EXCEPT? (　　)

A) Measuring recovery rates is not a simple task.

B) In one possible method, recovery rate measure = credit spread divided by hazard rate.

C) In one possible method, recovery rate measure = trading price at time of default divided by the par value.

D) The higher the level of seniority, in general the greater is the recovery rate.

275. Each of the following is an example of a high-yield bond issuer EXCEPT (　　).

A) issuer with a credit rating of "BBB－"

B) original issuer

C) fallen angel

D) leveraged buyout

276. Each of the following is true about a bond indenture EXCEPT? (　　)

A) A bond indenture is a legal contract that details the obligations (promises) of the bond issuer and the rights of investors.

B) A bond indenture is a corporate bond that is unsecured by collateral.

C) Bond indenture terms are a compromise between issuer (wants to pay lowest rate; prefers fewer covenants) and bond holders (want to earn highest possible rate; prefer more covenants).

D) The Trust Indenture Act requires a corporate trustee for all corporate bond offerings in the amount of more than $5 million sold in interstate commerce.

277. Regarding have greater price volatility than the pass-through from which they are derived? (　　)

A) Interest only strops.

B) Neither interest only strips nor principal only strips.

C) Interest only and principal only strips.

D) Principal only strips.

278. A US corporate bond that matures on October 1st, 2017 with a par value of $100.00 pays a semi-annual coupon with a coupon rate of 9.0% per annum. It pays coupons on April and October 1st and it offers a yield to maturity (yield) of 4.0% per annum. If it settles on September 1st 2015, which is nearest to the bond's clean price? (　　)

A) $109.89

B) $111.78

C) $113.64

D) $115.53

279. Which of the following debt instruments has the lowest interest rate when all other things are the same? (　　)

A) Mortgage Bond

B) Collateral Trust Bond

C) Equipment Trust Certificates

D) Noneofall

280. Each of the following is true about a corporate mortgage bond EXCEPT? (　　)

A) A mortgage bond grants the bondholders a first-mortgage lien on substantially all its properties.

B) A lien is a legal right to sell mortgaged property to satisfy unpaid obligations to bondholders.

C) As a result of a first-mortgage lien, which provides additional security for the bondholder, the issuer is able to borrow at a lower rate of interest than if the debt were unsecured.

D) In a corporate mortgage bond, the lien tends to create negative convexity at lower yields.

281. Each of the following is generally true about a collateral trust bond EXCEPT? (　　)

A) Collateral trust bonds are secured by assets, referred to as collateral, which are pledged to bondholders as security.

B) The collateral in a collateral trust bond might include stocks, securities in the issuer's subsidiary(ies), notes, bonds, or whatever other kinds of obligations owned by the issuer.

C) The issuer delivers to a corporate trustee under a bond indenture the securities pledged, and the trustee holds them for the benefit of the bondholders.

D) When voting common stocks are included in the collateral, the indenture permits the bondholders to vote the stocks.

282. Which of the following is TRUE of a corporate debenture bond? (　　)

A) Debentures are unsecured bonds; i. e. , they are not secured by a specific pledge of designated property.

B) Debenture bondholders have no claim(s) on the property of the the issuer (or its earnings).

C) Very few ("almost none") corporate bonds are debentures.

D) Debentures are bonds that lack provisions designed to afford protection to bondholders.

283. Which of the following is TRUE about a Guaranteed Corporate Bond? (　　)

A) Guaranteed bonds are free of default risk.

B) The safety of a guaranteed bond depends on the financial capability of the guarantor AND the financial capability of the issuer.

C) A guaranteed bond may not have more than one corporate guarantor.

D) A guarantee may call for the guarantor to guarantee the repayment of principal, but is NOT permitted to call for the guarantor to guarantee the payment of interest.

284. As a zero-coupon bond approaches its maturity date (i. e. , as the term to maturity decreases) EACH of the following is necessarily true EXCEPT? (　　)

A) the price increases

B) the price volatility decreases

C) the Macaulay duration decreases

D) the dollar value of an '01 (DV01) decreases

285. A analysis knows the single monthly mortality rate (SMM) of 0. 55 percent, a mortgage pool with a $250, 000 principal balance outstanding at the beginning of the 30th month, and a scheduled monthly principal payment of $80. 00 for the 30th month, which following is Ture about the estimated prepayment (　　).

A) $1,374. 56

B) $887. 89

C) $1,250. 70

D) $1,326. 38

286. Which of the following statement about a fixed-rate level payment and fully amortized mortgage loan is most accurate? (　　)

A) Principal repayment falls as interest payments rise over the life of the loan.

B) Interest payments fall as principal payments rise over the life of the loan.

C) Payments are equal over the life of the loan.

D) Each payment consists of an interest component and a principal component.

287. Which of the following description about the creation of agency or private-label mortgage-backed security pools are least likely? (　　)

A) The loans that do not meet government agency requirements are securitized in private label transactions.

B) Although there is no agency guarantee on private label securities, there is insurance through the creation of subordinate classes.

C) After a pool of mortgage is securitized, it is sold to investors as a pass-through investment.

D) The loans that meet government agency requirements are charged an insurance premium by the agency and then sold as private label transactions.

288. If you want to use the Monte Carlo simulation model for valuing mortgage-backed securities. Which of the following description is ture? (　　)

A) The Monte-Carlo simulation model is not designed to be arbitrage-free.

B) Monte Carlo models must be calibrated so that the current price generated by the paths in the model is equal to the market price of the on-the-run benchmark issues.

C) The critical refinancing rate spread (spread relationship between the refinancing rate and the 1-month interest rates along each of the simulated paths) is allowed to vary.

D) The key difference between the various suppliers of the Monte-Carlo-based simulation programs is the assumed level of refinancing rates.

289. What does a stripped MBS's mean? (　　)

A) It provides no interest payments.

B) Its distribution of principal and interest has been altered from a pro rata distribution to an unequal distribution.

C) It provides no principal payments.

D) Its distribution of principal and interest has been altered from an unequal distribution to a pro rata distribution.

290. Which of the following description about the prepayments or curtailments is correct? (　　)

A) have no influence on the amount of interest the lender receive over the life of the loan

B) cause the duration of the original mortgage to lengthen or increase

C) will increase the amount of interest the lender receives over the life of the loan

D) will decrease the amount of interest the lender receives over the life of the loan

291. What is the influence about the price of a principal-only mortgage strip? If mortgage rate is declining in the market? ( )

A) may increase or decrease

B) decreases

C) unaffected

D) increases

292. Consider the mortgage passthrough security, which is most likely? ( )

A) A futures contract on a pool of mortgages of a certain type.

B) A participation certificate in a pool of mortgages.

C) An option on a pool of mortgages.

D) A security that pays off the full amount of the mortgage if the borrower defaults.

293. Consider using Monte Carlo simulation for valuing a mortgage-backed security. Which choice is TRUE? ( )

A) Creating a trinomial interest rate tree that is used for the valuation.

B) Generating a series of interest rates paths used to discount the known cash flows.

C) Creating a binomial interest rate tree that is used for the valuation.

D) Generating a series of cash flows based on simulated mortgage refinancing rates.

294. Regarding to MBS, refinancing burnout means ( ).

A) A number of falls in interest rates.

B) Lenders tightening their underwriting after a boom period.

C) A fall in the supply of mortgage funding.

D) Interest rates rising after having fallen.

295. Which of the following about the Interest only (IO) strip cash flow is most accurate? ( )

A) starts out big and gets smaller over time

B) starts out small and gets bigger over time

C) have longer effective lives than principal only (PO) strips

D) are the same throughout the life of the security

296. Which of the following most correctly describes a mortgage loan? ( )

A) An unsecured loan to enable the borrower to finance a real estate property.

B) An unsecured commercial loan to enable the borrower to finance a real estate property.

C) A loan secured by the collateral of some specified real estate property.

D) A commercial loan secured by the collateral of some specified real estate property.

297. The following statements describe the principal-only (PO) and interest-only (IO) strips. Which is Ture? (　　)

Ⅰ. The IO price is positively related to mortgage rates at low current rates.

Ⅱ. The IO exhibit some negative convexity at low rates.

Ⅲ. PO strips are sold at moderate discount to par.

Ⅳ. PO prices increase when interest rates fall.

A) Ⅱ and Ⅲ.

B) Ⅰ and Ⅳ.

C) Ⅰ and Ⅱ.

D) Ⅲ and Ⅳ.

298. If a pool of mortgages starts the year with a principal balance of $10.0 million and the single monthly mortality rate, SMM(n), is constant at 1.0%, which is nearest to the principal that prepays over the next twelve months (not including scheduled principal)? (　　)

A) $1,136,151

B) $1,200,000

C) $8,800,000

D) $8,863,849

299. If the monthly payment on a 15-year fully-amortizing mortgage loan, with $100,000 principal, is $740, what is the loan's yield (YTM)? (　　)

A) 4.0%

B) 4.2%

C) 4.4%

D) 4.8%

300. Vic gives the monthly payment of a fully-amortizing mortgage as: original balance * $[i*(1+i)^{T}]/[(1+i)^{T-1}]$, where ($i$) is the interest rate and (T) is the loan term. If the interest rate on a $200,000 fully amortizing mortgage loan is 6.0% on a 30-year fully-amortizing mortgage loan, what is the monthly payment? (　　)

A) $599.55

B) $1,099.55

C) $1,199.10

D) $1,99.55

301. What principal-only (PO) mortgage strip properties about the investment characteristics is true? (　　)

A) The higher the coupon the higher the investor's return.

B) The lower the coupon the higher the investor's return.

C) The slower the prepayments the higher the investor's return.

D) The faster the prepayments the higher the investor's return.

302. A collateralized mortgage obligation (CMO) bond structure includes three tranches, with the following characteristics:

Trache	OAS (in BP)	Option Cost (in BP)
Trache1	54	73
Trache2	55	94
Trache3	68	71

which tranches appears to be cheap? (　　)

A) Trache1

B) Trache2

C) Trache3

D) Not above

303. Which of the following about Principal-only strips is most accurate? (　　)

A) sold at par

B) sold at a considerable discount to par

C) sold at a considerable premium to par

D) could be sold at a discount or a premium, depending on economic conditions

304. Which of the following necessarily participates in the PRIMARY mortgage market? (　　)

A) Collateralized mortgage obligation (CMO)

B) Mortgage-backed security (MBS)

C) Fannie Mae

D) Originator

305. What is the essential (defining) feature of a mortgage? (　　)

A) Duration

B) Collateral type

C) Prepayment option

D) Amortization style

306. What is the essential (defining) feature of a pass-through? ( )

A) Cash flows distributed pro rata

B) Cash flows are structured

C) Loans are fixed-rate

D) Loans are conforming

307. Under a constant maturity mortality approach, the monthly rate of prepayment (p) on a mortgage (aka, single month mortality rate, SMM) is found to be 0.40%. What is the annualized conditional prepayment rate (CPR)? ( )

A) 4.70%

B) 4.80%

C) 6.00%

D) 95.30%

308. A pass-through mortgage-based security (MBS) assumes a 200% PSA prepayment speed. The pool has an original weighted average maturity (WAM) of 360 months but now has an age of 60 months (five years). What is the model's assumption, at this month 60, for the single month mortality (SMM) rate? ( )

A) 0.92%

B) 1.00%

C) 1.06%

D) 1.14%

第四部分

估值和风险模型

第 14 单元

市场风险计量

1. If the daily, 90% confidence level, value-at-risk (VaR) of a portfolio is correctly estimated to be USD 5,000, one would expect that in one out of (　　).
   A) 10 days, the portfolio value will decline by USD 5,000 or less
   B) 90 days, the portfolio value will decline by USD 5,000 or less
   C) 10 days, the portfolio value will decline by USD 5,000 or more
   D) 90 days, the portfolio value will decline by USD 5,000 or more

2. Consider a portfolio with a one-day VaR of $1 million. Assume that the market is trending with an autocorrelation of 0.1. Under this scenario, what would you expect the two-day VaR to be? (　　)
   A) $2 million
   B) $1.414 million
   C) $1.483 million
   D) $1.449 million

3. Which of following descriptions about value at risk is incorrect? (　　)
   A) VaR represents the necessary economic capital to guarantee commercial bank solvency.
   B) VaR(5%) means the number of days that a loss in portfolio value will exceed 5%.
   C) For the diversified holding of a financial institution and capital requirements reduction, VaR can be used.
   D) The VaR (5%) of 100K means there's a 5% chance on any given day, there's a loss of 100K or more.

4. Which of the following statements about trader limits are correct? (　　)
   Ⅰ. Stop loss limits are useful if markets are trending.
   Ⅱ. Exposure limits do not allow for diversification.
   Ⅲ. VaR limits are not susceptible to arbitrage.
   Ⅳ. Stop loss limits are effective in preventing losses.

A) Ⅰ and Ⅱ

B) Ⅲ and Ⅳ

C) Ⅰ and Ⅲ

D) Ⅱ and Ⅳ

5. If one portfolio has an expected return of \$10,000 and a standard deviation of \$22,500. what is the portfolio's VaR given a 95 percent confidence level? ( )

A) \$27,125.

B) \$21,750.

C) \$37,125.

D) \$47,125.

6. The 10-Q report of ABC Bank states that the monthly VaR of ABC Bank is USD 10 million at the 95% confidence level. What is the proper interpretation of this statement? ( )

A) If we collect 100 monthly gain/loss data of ABC Bank, we will always see five months with losses larger than \$10 million.

B) There is a 95% probability that the bank will lose less than \$10 million over a month.

C) There is a 5% probability that the bank will gain less than \$10 million each month.

D) There is a 5% probability that the bank will lose less than \$10 million over a month.

7. If a portfolio of \$200 M has 12% expected return over one year with a standard deviation of 8 percent. Calculate the VaR for this portfolio at the 99 percent confidence level. ( )

A) \$4.0 M

B) \$25.2 M

C) \$3.6 M

D) \$13.216 M

8. An equity portfolio value is \$1 million and has a daily standard deviation of returns equal to 0.8%. Calculate the portfolio's weekly dollar VaR at the 95% confidence level assuming five trading days in a week. ( )

A) \$28,200

B) \$29,516

C) \$106,240

D) \$22,430

9. Consider a stock with daily returns that follow a random walk. The annualized volatility is 34%. Estimate the weekly volatility of this stock assuming that the year has 52 weeks. (　　)

A) 6.80%

B) 5.83%

C) 4.85%

D) 4.71%

The next two questions are based on the following information:

A Bank has a position in a 5-year, zero-coupon bond with the following characteristics:

The par value of the bond: 10 million.

- The market value of the bond: \$8,219,271.
- The yield to maturity of the bond: 4%.
- The historical mean change in daily yield is 0.0%.
- The standard deviation of the position is 0.8%.

10. Calculate the one-day VaR for this bond at the 95% confidence level (　　).

A) \$106,132

B) \$108,494

C) \$420,377

D) \$290,456

11. The VaR measure calculated from percentiles from a set of hypothetical returns is called (　　).

A) Conditional VaR

B) Prospective VaR

C) Historical VaR

D) Monte Carlo VaR

12. Which of the following statements is false about VaR? (　　)

A) VaR increases with longer holding periods.

B) VaR is dependent on the probability level.

C) VaR is dependent on the holding period.

D) VaR decreases with lower significance levels.

13. An investor has a portfolio with \$200,000 invests in fund 1 and \$300,000 invests in fund 2. The correlation of returns of the two funds is − 0.30. Calculate the portfolio's VaR at the 95% confidence level based on the information in the table. (　　)

Fund	E(R)	σ
Fund1	8%	16.0%
Fund2	12%	24.0%

A) \$23,748
B) \$62,592.5
C) \$81,364
D) \$39,814

14. A portfolio consists of \$200,000 bonds and \$800,000 stocks, the correlation between the stock and the bond component is 0.3. The expected return and the standard deviation of the bond component is 6% and 10%. In contrast, the expected return and the standard deviation of the stock component is 10% and 15%. Calculate the portfolio's annual VaR at the 99% confidence level. (　　)
A) \$123,432
B) \$235,512
C) \$204,842
D) \$152,230

15. A portfolio consists of U.S. bond and Japanese bond. The correlation of returns for the two kinds of bonds is 0.2. Based on the information in the table, calculate the portfolio's annual value at risk (VaR) at the 95% confidence level. (　　)

Bond	Value	E(R)	σ
U.S. bond	\$600,000	10.0%	10.0%
Japanese bond	\$400,000	15.0%	20.0%

A) \$120,321
B) \$130,141
C) \$60,180
D) \$123,721

16. A portfolio has an expected return of 15% per month and a 10 percent probability 1-month VaR of \$1,000. Which of the following statements is true? (　　)
A) The portfolio's maximum monthly loss is \$1,000.
B) The portfolio's minimum monthly loss is \$1,000
C) The maximum loss for the worst 10% of the month is \$1,000.
D) The portfolio will lose more than \$1,000 only 10% of the time.

17. A bond portfolio's PVBP is 50,000. Calculate the bond portfolio's VaR at the 99% confidence level based on the information in the table? (　　)

Expected Change in Interest rates	Probability
＞+1.20%	1%
+1%—1.2%	28%
0.01%—1%	21%
-0.1%—0.01%	42%
＜-0.1%	8%

A) $7,000,500
B) $6,000,000
C) $2,000,000
D) $4,000,000

18. Which of the following statements is (are) TRUE about fat-tail distributions? (　　)
Ⅰ. Fat-tailed distributions have a smaller probability in the tails than the normal distribution.
Ⅱ. The most likely explanation for "fat tails" is that the mean return is time-varying
Ⅲ. The most likely explanation for "fat tails" is that the second moment or volatility is time-varying
A) Ⅰ and Ⅱ
B) Ⅰ and Ⅲ
C) Ⅲ only
D) Ⅰ only

19. Which of the following statements is true about Value at risk (VaR)? (　　)
A) The actual losscannot exceed VaR.
B) The actual loss has an inverse relationship with VaR.
C) The actual loss is the average of the expected return of the portfolio and VaR.
D) The actual loss may be larger than VaR

20. Calculate the 9-day VaR on this bond at the 95% confidence level, if one-day VaR (95%) for a bond is 10 849.4. (　　)
A) $325,483
B) $435,434
C) $879,133
D) $327,676

21. Assume that the P&L distribution of a liquid asset is i.i.d. normally distributed. The position has a one-day VaR at the 95% confidence level of $100,000. Estimate the 10-day VaR of the same position at the 99% confidence level. (　　)

A) $1,000,000

B) $450,000

C) $320,000

D) $220,000

22. Which of the following deviations from normality will result in underestimating the distribution variance? (　　)

A) The mean of the distribution is conditional on the economic conditions.

B) The variance of the distribution is conditional on the economic conditions.

C) Higher probability of extreme return.

D) Higher probability of mean returns.

23. Calculate portfolio's standard deviation. (　　)

- Total assets of $7 million
- Expected return of 6. 25 percent.
- Historical VaR at 5 percent probability level is $1,200,000

A) 8. 99%

B) 14. 18%

C) 6. 25%

D) 7. 87%

24. The 95%, one-day RiskMetrics VaR for a bank trading portfolio is $1,000,000. What is the approximate general market risk charge, as defined in 1996? (　　)

A) $3,000,000

B) $9,500,000

C) $4,200,000

D) $13,400,000

25. Consider a portfolio with 40% invested in asset X and 60% invested in asset Y. The mean and variance of return on X are O and 25 respectively. The mean and variance of return on Y are 1 and 121 respectively. The correlation coefficient between X and Y is 0. 3. What is the nearest value for portfolio volatility? (　　)

A) 9. 51

B) 8 60

C) 13. 38

D) 7. 45

26. A fundamental assumption of the random walk hypothesis of market returns is that returns from one time period to the next are statistically independent. This assumption implies that ( ).

A) returns from one time period to the next can never be equal

B) returns from one time period to the next are uncorrelated

C) knowledge of the returns from one time period does not help in predicting returns from the next time period

D) both B and C are true

27. Multidimensional scenario analysis can take two general forms: historical or prospective. The historical approach is backward looking, while the prospective approach is forward looking. Which of the following statements is correct regarding prospective and historical scenario approaches? ( )

A) The historical approach uses an exponential smoothing model to weight market data over the relevant time period.

B) The prospective approach ignores correlations between risk factors.

C) The factor push method of historical scenario analysis uses a constant multiple of historic correlations to forecast correlations during an economic crisis.

D) None of the above statements are correct.

28. Fat-tailed asset return distributions are most likely the result of time-varying ( ).

A) volatility for the unconditional distribution

B) means for the unconditional distribution

C) volatility for the conditional distribution

D) means for the conditional distribution

29. Which of the following VaR methodologies most closely resembles the approach followed by RiskMetrics? ( )

A) Structured Monte Carlo

B) Stress testing

C) Delta-normal method

D) Historical simulation

30. You are asked by your Chief Risk Officer to evaluate arguments he has heard to switch from VaR to conditional VaR as your firm' main risk measurement tool. Which of the following arguments is not correct? ( )

A) Conditional VaR is a coherent risk measure in contrast to VaR.

B) Conditional VaR estimated for a confidence level corresponding to one minus the probability of default for the firm's target rating provides an unbiased measure of the amount of the economic capital required above the firm's bankruptcy threshold point to achieve the probability of default associated with the firm's target rating.

C) A low VaR does not mean that the firm will make small losses when VaR is exceeded, but a low conditional VaR means that the firm will make small losses when VaR is exceeded.

D) For the same confidence level, conditional VaR is greater than VaR.

31. Assume that portfolio daily returns are independently and identically normally distributed, Avatar Mathews, a new quantitative analyst, has been asked by the portfolio manager to calculate the portfolio Value-at-Risk (VaR) measure for 10, 15, 20 and 25 day periods. The portfolio manager notices something mistake with Sam's calculations displayed below. Which one of following VaRs on this portfolio is inconsistent with the others? (　　)

A) VaR(10-day) = USD 316M

B) VaR(15-day) = USD 465M

C) VaR(20-day) = USD 537M

D) VaR(25-day) = USD 600M

32. Consider the following levels of sophistication in Risk Management Models and Procedures:

Ⅰ. Mark to Market Analysis.

Ⅱ. Stress/Scenario Analysis.

Ⅲ. Simulation Value at Risk.

Ⅳ. Parametric Value at Risk.

Which of the following lists these models in order of increasing sophistication? (　　)

A) Ⅱ, Ⅰ, Ⅳ, Ⅲ

B) Ⅰ, Ⅳ, Ⅲ, Ⅱ

C) Ⅰ, Ⅱ, Ⅲ, Ⅳ

D) Ⅰ, Ⅲ, Ⅳ, Ⅱ

33. It is often possible to estimate the Value at Risk of a vanilla European options portfolio by using a delta-gamma methodology rather than exact valuation formulas because (　　).

A) delta and gamma are the first two terms in the Taylor series expansion of the change in an option price as a function of the change in the underlying and the remaining terms are often insignificant

B) it is only delta and gamma risk that can be hedged

C) unlike the price, delta and gamma for a European option can be computed in closed form

D) both A and C, but not B

34. The hybrid approach for estimating VaR is the combination of a parametric and a nonparametric approach. It specifically combines the historical simulation approach with (　　).

A) the delta normal approach

B) the exponentially weighted moving average approach

C) the multivariate density estimation approach

D) the generalized autoregressive conditional heteroskedasticity approach

35. In the presence of fat tails in the distribution of returns, VaR based on the delta-normal method would (for a linear portfolio) (　　).

A) underestimate the true VaR

B) be the same as the true VaR

C) overestimate the true VaR

D) cannot be determined from the information provided

36. An institution has a fixed-income desk and an exotic-options desk. Four risk reports were produced, each with a different methodology. With all four methodologies readily available, which of the following would you use to allocate economic capital? (　　)

A) Simulation applied to both desks.

B) Delta-normal applied to both desks.

C) Delta-gamma for the exotic-options desk and the delta-normal for the fixed-income desk.

D) Delta-gamma applied to both desks.

37. The historical simulation approach is more likely to provide an accurate estimate of the VaR than the RiskMetrics approach for a portfolio that consists of (　　).

A) a small number of emerging market securities

B) a small number of broad market indexes

C) a large number of emerging market securities

D) a large number of board market indexes

38. There exist two portfolios A and B. Each has their individual VaR. When putting them together in a new portfolio C, which of the following will be always true? (　　)

A) $VaR(C) < VaR(A) + VaR(B)$

B) $VaR(C) > VaR(A) + VaR(B)$

C) $VaR(C) = VaR(A) + VaR(B)$

D) None of the above

39. The measurement error in VaR due to sampling variation should be greater with ( ).

A) more observations and a high confidence level (e.g. 99%)

B) fewer observations and a high confidence level

C) more observations and a low confidence level (e.g. 95%)

D) fewer observations and a low confidence level

40. An analyst at Bergman International Bank has been asked to explain the calculation of VaR for linear derivatives to the newly hired junior analysts. Which of the following statements best describes the calculation of VaR for a linear derivative on the S&P 500 Index? ( )

A) For a futures contract, multiply the VaR of the S&P 500 Index by a sensitivity factor reflecting the percent change in the value of the futures contract for a 1% change in the index value.

B) For an options contract, multiply the VaR of the S&P 500 Index by a sensitivity factor reflecting the percent change in the value of the futures contract for a 1% change in the index value.

C) For a futures contract, divide the VaR of the S&P 500 Index by a sensitivity factor reflecting the absolute change in the value of the futures contract per absolute change in the index value.

D) For an options contract, divide the VaR of the S&P 500 Index by a sensitivity factor reflecting the percent change in the value of the futures contract for a 1% change in the index value.

41. A portfolio of investment securities for a regional bank has a current market value equal to USD 6,247,000 with a daily variance of 0.0002. Assuming there are 250 trading days in a year and that the portfolio returns follow a normal distribution, the estimate of the annual VaR at the 95% confidence level is closest to which of the following? ( )

A) USD 32,595

B) USD 145,770

C) USD 2,297,507

D) USD 2,737,868

42. Assume that we calculate a one-week VAR for a natural gas position by rescaling the daily VAR using the square root of time rule. Let us now assume that we determine the true gas price process to be mean reverting and recalculate the VAR. Which of the following statements is true? (　　)

A) The recalculated VAR will be less than the original VAR.

B) The recalculated VAR will be equal to the original VAR.

C) The recalculated VAR will be greater than the original VAR.

D) There is no necessary relationship between the recalculated VAR and the original VAR.

43. Assume you are using a GARCH model to forecast volatility that you use to calculate the one-day VAR. If volatility is mean reverting, what can you say about the T-day VAR? (　　)

A) It is less than the $\sqrt{T}$ × one-day VAR.

B) It is equal to $\sqrt{T}$ × one-day VAR.

C) It is greater than the $\sqrt{T}$ × one-day VAR.

D) It could be greater or less than the $\sqrt{T}$ × one-day VAR.

44. Suppose σ_t^2 is the estimated variance at time t and μ_t is the realized return at t. Which of the following GARCH(1, 1) models will take the longest time to revert to its mean? (　　)

A) $\sigma_t^2 = 0.04 + 0.02\mu_{t-1}^2 + 0.92\sigma_{t-1}^2$

B) $\sigma_t^2 = 0.02 + 0.04\mu_{t-1}^2 + 0.94\sigma_{t-1}^2$

C) $\sigma_t^2 = 0.03 + 0.02\mu_{t-1}^2 + 0.95\sigma_{t-1}^2$

D) $\sigma_t^2 = 0.03 + 0.03\mu_{t-1}^2 + 0.93\sigma_{t-1}^2$

45. A risk manager estimates daily variance b_t using a GARCH model on daily returns r_t: $b_t = \alpha_0 + \alpha_1 r_{t-1}^2 + \beta b_{t-1}$, with $\alpha_0 = 0.005$, $\alpha_1 = 0.04$, $\beta = 0.94$. The long-run annualized volatility is approximately (　　).

A) 13.54%

B) 7.94%

C) 72.72%

D) 25.00%

46. Which of the following statements is incorrect regarding the volatility term structure predicted by a GARCH(1,1) model: $\sigma_t^2 = \omega + \alpha\mu_{t-1}^2 + \beta\sigma_{t-1}^2$, where $\alpha + \beta < 1$? (　　)

A) When the current volatility estimate is below the long-run average volatility, this

GARCH model estimates an upward-sloping volatility term structure.

B) When the current volatility estimate is above the long-run average volatility, this GARCH model estimates a downward-sloping volatility term structure.

C) Assuming the long-run estimated variance remains unchanged as the GARCH parameters and p increase, the volatility term structure predicted by this GARCH model reverts to the long-run estimated variance more slowly.

D) Assuming the long-run estimated variance remains unchanged as the GARCH parameters and B increase, the volatility term structure predicted by this GARCH model reverts to the long-run estimated variance faster.

47. A bank uses the exponentially weighted moving average (EWMA) technique with λ of 0.9 to model the daily volatility of a security. The current estimate of the daily volatility is 1.5%. The closing price of the security is USD 20 yesterday and USD 18 today. Using continuously compounded returns, what is the updated estimate of the volatility? (　　)

A) 3.62%

B) 1.31%

C) 2.96%

D) 5.44%

48. Using a daily RiskMetrics EWMA model with a decay factor 0.95 to develop a forecast of the conditional variance, which weight will be applied to the return that is four days old? (　　)

A) 0.000

B) 0.043

C) 0.048

D) 0.950

49. Until January 1999 the historical volatility for the Brazilian real versus the U.S. dollar had been very small for several years. On January 13, Brazil abandoned the defense of the currency peg. Using the data from the close of business on January 13, which of the following methods for calculating volatility would have shown the greatest jump in measured historical volatility? (　　)

A) 250-day equal weight

B) Exponentially weighted with a daily decay factor of 0.94

C) 60-day equal weight

D) All of the above

50. Which of the following four statements on models for estimating volatility is incorrect? (　　)

A) In the EWMA model, some positive weight is assigned to the long-run average variance rate.

B) In the EWMA model, the weights assigned to observations decrease exponentially as the observations become older.

C) In the GARCH(1,1) model, a positive weight is estimated for the long-run average variance rate.

D) In the GARCH(1,1) model, the weights estimated for observations decrease exponentially as the observations become older.

51. A portfolio manager of an endowment wants to calculate a daily VAR for the portfolio. The € 10,000,000 portfolio is restricted from using derivative securities. The annual return is expected to be 10%, with a standard deviation of 15%. If the manager assumes there are 250 trading days in a year and uses a 1% level of significance, which of the following amounts is closest to the daily VAR using the delta-normal method? (　　)

A) € 217,043

B) € 221,350

C) € 241,100

D) € 245,100

52. A portfolio's expected return and standard deviation is 8% and 15%. The market value of the portfolio is 2,000,000. Calculate the portfolio's VAR at the 95% confidence level. (　　)

A) $153,000

B) $335,000

C) $110,000

D) $143,500

53. A portfolio manager invests 35% of his salary in bond and 65% in stock. The daily standard deviations of the bond and stock is 2% and 5% respectively. The portfolio manager estimates the correlation between bond and stock is about 0. 2. Calculate the portfolio's daily VAR at the 97. 5 confidence level. (　　)

A) 3. 15%

B) 6. 78%

C) 1. 47%

D) 2. 37%

54. What is the characteristic of a fat-tailed distribution comparing to a normal

distribution? ( )

A) a different standard deviation and mean

B) At more than three standard deviations, the probability mass is lower

C) an equal probability mass close to the mean

D) At around one standard deviation, the probability mass is lower

55. Please select the most restrictive approach for asset return distribution assumptions. ( )

A) multivariate density estimation

B) nonparametric approach

C) parametric approach

D) hybrid approach

56. The standard VAR calculation for extension to multiple periods also assumes that positions are fixed. If risk management enforces loss limits, the true VAR will be ( ).

A) the same

B) greater than calculated

C) less than calculated

D) unable to be determined

57. The ten lowest return of a fund for the last 100 trading days are listed below:

−20%, −18%, −16%, −11%, −8%, −5%, −4%, −2%, 0%, 1%

Calculate the fund's percent VaR at the 95% confidence level based on historical simulation approach. ( )

A) −8%

B) −2%

C) −20%

D) −18%

58. To calculate value at risk, the assumption of normality is required by which method? ( )

A) Historical method

B) Monte Carlo simulation

C) Rounding estimation

D) Variance/covariance method

59. Which of the following statements is true about nonparametric methods and parametric methods for quantifying volatility? ( )

A) Nonparametric models assume that portfolio returns are normally distributed.
B) Data is used less efficiently with parametric methods than nonparametric methods.
C) In the estimation process for parametric methods, fat tails and skewness from some assumed distribution are not a concern.
D) Multivariate density estimation (MDE) allows for weights to vary based on how relevant the data is to the current market environment, regardless of the timing of the most relevant data.

60. Which of the following EWMA models will have the greatest day-to-day volatility and the slowest to respond to new data respectively? ( )

Model 1: $\sigma_n^2 = 0.03\mu_n - 1^2 + 0.97\sigma_n - 1^2$

Model 2: $\sigma_n^2 = 0.01\mu_n - 1^2 + 0.99\sigma_n - 1^2$

Model 3: $\sigma_n^2 = 0.22\mu_n - 1^2 + 0.78\sigma_n - 1^2$

Model 4: $\sigma_n^2 = 0.12\mu_n - 1^2 + 0.88\sigma_n - 1^2$

A) Model 1 and model 2 respectively
B) Model 1 and model 4 respectively
C) Model 3 and model 4 respectively
D) Model 3 and model 2 respectively

61. Select one CORRECT statement about value at risk (VAR). ( )
A) VAR is irrelevant to holding period.
B) If confidence level is lower, VAR decreases.
C) VAR depends on probability level.
D) If holding period is longer, VAR will decrease.

62. Over the next year, an operational process model predicts an 95% probability of no loss occurrence and a 5% probability of a single loss occurrence. If the single loss occurs, the severity is characterized by three possible outcomes: \$10.0 million loss with 20% probability, \$18.0 million loss with 50% probability, and \$25.0 million loss with 30% probability. What is the model's one-year 90% expected shortfall (ES)? ( )
A) \$9.25 million
B) \$10.00 million
C) \$13.88 million
D) \$18.50 million

63. Given the following 30 ordered percentage returns of an asset, calculate the VAR and expected shortfall at a 90% confidence level: −16, −14, −10, −7, −7,

−5, −4, −4, −4, −3, −1, −1, 0, 0, 0, 1, 2, 2, 4, 6, 7, 8, 9, 11, 12, 12, 14, 18, 21, 23. ( )

A) VAR (90%) = 10, expected shortfall = 14
B) VAR (90%) = 10, expected shortfall = 15
C) VAR (90%) = 14, expected shortfall = 15
D) VAR (90%) = 18, expected shortfall = 22

64. Which of the following statements comparing VAR with expected shortfall is true? ( )

A) Expected shortfall is sub-additive while VAR is not.
B) Both VAR and expected shortfall measure the amount of capital an investor can expect to lose over a given time period and are, therefore, interchangeable as risk measures.
C) Both VAR and expected shortfall depend on the assumption of a normal distribution of returns.
D) VAR can vary according to the confidence level selected, but expected shortfall will not.

65. Worse-than-VAR scenarios are defined as scenarios that lead to losses in the extreme left tail of the return distribution equal to or exceeding VAR at a given level of confidence. Which of the following statements is an accurate description of VAR? ( )

A) VAR is the average of the worse-than-VAR scenario returns.
B) VAR is the standard deviation of the worse-than-VAR scenario returns.
C) VAR is the most pessimistic scenario return (maximum loss) from the worse-than-VAR scenarios.
D) VAR is the most optimistic scenario return (minimum loss) from the worse-than-VAR scenarios.

66. Which of the following statements is false about Monte Carlo VaR and historical VaR? ( )

A) Monte Carlo VaR uses more inputs into the model than historical VaR.
B) Monte Carlo VaR and historical VaR.
C) Monte Carlo VaR computes VaR from percentiles from a set of hypothetical returns.
D) Historical VaR computes VaR from percentiles from a set of realized returns.

67. If λ is 0.96, calculate the K-value that equates the most recent weight between RiskMetrics and historical standard deviation models. ( )

A) $K = 25$

B) $K = 0.96$

C) $K = 26$

D) $K = 24$

68. Monte Carlo simulation is different from historical simulation, because (　　).

A) Monte Carlo uses random variables generated by computer

B) Monte Carlo requires priori principles.

C) Monte Carlo selects variables randomly from future distributions.

D) Roulette odds based variables are used by Monte Carlo

69. Which of the following examples cannot explain why returns distributions can deviate from the normal distribution? (　　)

A) positive skew

B) unstable parameters

C) symmetrical distribution

D) fat tails

70. Which of the following statements is false about VAR methodologies? (　　)

A) GARCH approachuses time varying weights on historic returns to calculate distribution parameters.

B) Nonparametric models do not require assumptions regarding the entire distribution of returns.

C) The implied-volatility based approach uses historical market prices to estimate volatility.

D) The parametric approach is typically defined by the calculation of the distribution parameters: mean and variance.

第 15 单元

期权定价模型

71. Amtek Company issued a bond which is priced at $95 now. If interest rates decline, the bond price will rise to $97, and if interest rates increase, its price will decline to $93. The 6-month period spot rate is 2%. What is the risk-neutral probabilities of the rates going down by using binomial interest-rate tree? ( )

A) 73.75%

B) 75.76%

C) 26.25%

D) 13.95%

72. Assume that a binomial interest-rate tree indicates a 6-month period spot rate of 2.5% and the price of the bond if rates decline is $98.45, and if rates increase is $96. The risk-neutral probabilities respectively associated with a decline and increase in rates if the market price of the bond is $97 correspond to ( ).

A) 0.1/0.9

B) 0.9/0.1

C) 0.2/0.8

D) 0.8/0.2

73. Amy, a manager of Bank Montgomery is considering buying a non-dividend paying stock ABC. The current stock price is USD 50. The stock price can go up or down by 10% each period. Each period is 6 months. The annual risk-free rate is 10% with continuous compounding. What is the risk-neutral probability of the stock price going up in a single period? ( )

A) 39.5%

B) 47.1%

C) 55.9%

D) 75.6%

74. There is a 1-year European put option of which the underlying asset is Hurst stock.

The current price of the stock is S0, and it pays a continuous dividend yield of 4%. The continuously compounded risk-free rate is 6%. Assume the stock value in "up" state is 1.05 S0. The risk-neutral probability of an up-move for the put option is (　　).

A) 0.69

B) 0.98

C) 0.53

D) 0.37

75. There is a 6-month European call option on Stock Cora and the stock currently trades at \$10. At the end of 6 months, the stock will either be \$12 or \$8. The continuously compounded risk-free rate of interest is 4% per year. The value of the call option is closest to (the strike price is 10) (　　).

A) \$1.7936

B) \$1.5849

C) \$0.9465

D) \$1.0792

76. A non-dividend paying stock is priced at \$10 now. A 3-year European call option on this stock has a strike price of \$11. The annual volatility of the stock is 9.531%, and the current continuously compounded risk-free interest rate is 4%. Assuming that the price of the stock will rise or fall by a fixed proportional amount each year, and that the probability of the stock rising in any one year is 40%, what is the value of the European call option? (　　)

A) \$1.5625

B) \$0.1311

C) \$3.9248

D) \$2.6543

77. Wilburn King, a chief manager for bank Noah, is considering writing a 6 month European call option on a non-dividend paying stock Wolfe. The current stock price is USD 36.2 and the strike price of the option is USD 39.3. Wilburn King try to find the no-arbitrage price of the option by using a two-step binomial tree model. The stock price can go up or down by 15% each period. From Wilburn King's point of view, the stock price has an 31.4% probability of going up each period and a 68.6% probability of going down. The risk-free rate is 8% per annum with continuous compounding.

What is the risk-neutral probability of the stock pricing going up in a single step? (　　)

A) 34.17%

B) 89.05%

C) 56.73%

D) 23.61%

78. Viola Buck, a deputy manager for Bank Gomez, is considering writing a 6 month European call option on a non-dividend paying stock Myra. The current stock price is USD 100 and the strike price of the option is USD 110. In order to find the no-arbitrage price of the option, Viola Buck uses a two-step binomial tree model. The stock price can go up or down by 10% each period. The annual risk-free rate is 12% with continuous compounding. The no-arbitrage price of the option is closest to ( ).

A) USD 2.6975

B) USD 2.8447

C) USD 4.4075

D) USD 5.8695

79. Consider a non-dividend paying stock currently priced at \$48. Assuming that the price of the stock will rise or fall by 6% every three months. The continuously compounded risk-free rate is 8%. Calculate the value of a 6-month European call option with a strike price at \$50 by using a two-step binomial tree model. ( )

A) \$1.0457

B) \$1.2342

C) \$1.6878

D) \$2.9836

80. A risk manager for Bank XYZ, Mark is considering writing a 6 month American put option on a non-dividend paying stock ABC. The current stock price is USD 50 and the strike price of the option is USD 52. In order to find the no-arbitrage price of the option Mark uses a two-step binomial tree model. The stock price can go up or down by 20% each period. Mark's view is that the stock price has an 80% probability of going up each period and a 20% probability of going down. The annual risk-free rate is 12% with continuous compounding. The no-arbitrage price of the option is closest to ( ).

A) USD 2.00

B) USD 2.93

C) USD 5.22

D) USD 5.86

81. An American call option has strike price of \$110. Its underlying asset is a stock with a spot price of \$100. Using an one-step binomial tree to evaluate the option. Suppose the stock price will go up or down by \$20 in 6 month, the risk-free rate is 6% with continuously compounding, what is the value of this American call? (　　)

A) USD 8. 96

B) USD 7. 37

C) USD 5. 59

D) USD 13. 75

82. Which of the following statements about American options is incorrect? (　　)

A) American options cannot be valued with Monte Carlo simulation.

B) American options can be exercised at any time until maturity.

C) American options are always worth at least as much as European options .

D) American options can be valued with binomial trees.

83. Which of the following statements about the early exercise of American options is correct? (　　)

A) It is always optimal to exercise an American call option on a non-dividend-paying stock before the expiration date.

B) It can be optimal to exercise an American call option on a non-dividend-paying stock before the expiration date.

C) It can be optimal to exercise an American put option on a non-dividend-paying stock before the expiration date.

D) It is never optimal to exercise an American put option on a non-dividend-paying stock before the expiration date.

84. Suppose you simulate the price path of stock HHF using a geometric Brownian motion model with drift $\mu=0$, volatility $\sigma=0.14$, and time step $\Delta t=0.01$. Let S_t be the price of the stock at time t. If $S_0=100$, and the first two simulated (randomly selected) standard normal variables are $\epsilon_1=0.263$ and $\epsilon_2=-0\ 475$, what is the simulated stock price after the second step? (　　)

A) 96. 79

B) 99. 79

C) 99. 97

D) 99. 70

85. In the geometric Brown motion process for a variable S, which of the following is correct?

Ⅰ. S is normally distributed.

Ⅱ. dln(S) is normally distributed.

Ⅲ. dS/S is normally distributed.

Ⅳ. S is lognormally distributed.

A) Ⅰ only

B) Ⅱ, Ⅲ, and Ⅳ

C) Ⅳ only

D) Ⅲ and Ⅳ

86. Consider that a stock price S that follows a geometric Brownian motion $dS = aSdt + bSdz$, with b strictly positive. Which of the following statements is false? ( )

A) If the drift a is positive, the price one year from now will be above today's price.

B) The instantaneous rate of return on the stock follows a normal distribution.

C) The stock price S follows a lognormal distribution.

D) This model does not impose mean reversion.

87. Which of the following is not an assumption of the Black-Scholes options pricing model? ( )

A) The price of the underlying moves in a continuous fashion.

B) The interest rate changes randomly over time.

C) The instantaneous variance of the return of the underlying is constant.

D) Markets are perfect, i.e. short sales are allowed, there are no transaction costs or taxes, and markets operate continuously.

88. Which of the following statement is not an assumption of the BSM model? ( )

A) The expected real-world rate of return on the stock is known and the value of the option is an increasing function of this rate of return.

B) Asset price follows a geometric Brownian motion (GBM) which is a continuous process without jumps.

C) The continuously compounded rate of return on the stock is normally distributed, but the distribution of the future stock prices is lognormal.

D) The expected rate of return on the stock and volatility are constant.

89. Which of the following statement is not an assumption of the BSM model? ( )

A) The price of the underlying asset moves without jump.

B) Markets are perfect. Short sales are allowed and there are no transaction costs or taxes, and markets operate continuously.

C) The interest rate changes randomly over time

D) The variance of the return of the underlying asset is constant.

90. Using the Black-Scholes-Merton (BSM) model, a 1-year, European-style call option on a non-dividend-paying stock is valued at USD 1. 65. The stock is currently trading at USD 40. In the BSM model, $N(d_1) = 0.23378$, $N(d_2) = 0.23556$. The risk free rate is 5% continuously compounding. The next day, the company announces that it will pay a dividend of USD 0. 5 per share to holders of the stock 1 month from now. This new information does not affect the current stock price, but the parameter of BSM model changes, so that: $N(d_1) = 0.29876$, $N(d_2) = 0.23556$. The new BSM call price is closest to (　　).

A) USD 0. 89

B) USD 1. 67

C) USD 2. 88

D) USD 3. 95

91. Sonja Norris, anoption trader in Burke bank, is analyzing the impact of dividends on the options held by the options desk. She wants to figure out which options are the most sensitive to dividend payments. By using the Black-Scholes model adjusted for dividends, which of the following statement is correct? (　　)

A) Keeping the type of option constant, at-the-money options experience the largest absolute change in value and out of-the-money options the smallest absolute change in value as a result of dividend payment.

B) Keeping the type of option constant, in-the-money options experience the greatest absolute change in value and out-of-the-money options the smallest absolute change in value as expected dividends increase.

C) Holding everything else equal, out-of-the-money call options experience a larger decrease in value than in-the-money call options as expected dividends increase.

D) Holding everything else equal, the increase in the value of in-the-money put options caused by an increase in expected dividends is always larger than the decrease in value of in-the-money call options.

92. A put option on a stock with a $30 strike price that expires in six months is available. The current price of a stock is $35. The current risk-free rate is 4% continuously compounding. $N(d_1) = 0.8976$ and $N(d_2) = 0.8517$. The underlying stock has an annual standard deviation of 20%. According to Black-Scholes-Merton model, the value of the put is closest to (　　).

A) $3. 4355

B) $1. 9856

C) $0. 6541

D) $0. 7769

93. According to BSM model, what is the price of a three month European put option on a non-dividend-paying stock with a strike price of $60 assuming the annual volatility is 20%, the risk-free annual interest rate is 4%, and its underlying stock price is $60 currently? ( )

A) 1.57

B) 2.87

C) 2.09

D) 3.66

94. Using the Black-Scholes model, calculate the value of a European call option given the following information: spot rate = 100; strike price = 110; risk-free rate = 10%; time to expiry = 0.5 years; $N(d_1) = 0.457185$; $N(d_2) = 0.374163$. ( )

A) $10.90

B) $9.51

C) $6.57

D) $4.92

95. A three months call option is available with a $26 strike price. The current price of its underlying stock is $30. The current risk-free rate is 5%, $N(d_1) = 0.9546$, and $N(d_2) = 0.9279$, the Black-Scholes-Merton value of the call is closest to ( ).

A) $3.56

B) $4.81

C) $5.37

D) $6.84

96. Assume that 1-year options on a non-dividend paying stock has a strike price of USD 60. The underlying stock price is USD 50. The risk-free rate is 8%. $N(d_1) = 0.5417$ and $N(d_2) = 0.4862$, According to the Black-Scholes Model, which of the following statement may be correct? ( )

A) Value of American put option is USD 12 and of American call option is USD 0.35.

B) Value of American put option is USD 12 and of American call option is USD 0.12.

C) Value of American put option is USD 9 and of American call option is USD 0.35.

D) Value of American put option is USD 9 and of American call option is USD 0.12.

97. In the Black-Scholes expression for a European call option, the term used to compute option probability of exercise is ( ).

A) d_1

B) d_2

C) $N(d_1)$

D) $N(d_2)$

98. A non-dividend-paying stock is currently trading at USD 40 and has an expected return of 12% per year. Using the Black-Scholes-Merton (BSM) model, a 1-year, European-style call option on the stock is valued at USD 1. 78. The parameters used in the model are: $N(d_1) = 0.29123$ $N(d_2) = 0.20333$. The next day, the company announces that it will pay a dividend of USD 0. 5 per share to holders of the stock on an ex-dividend date 1 month from now and has no further dividend payout plans for at least 1 year. This new information does not affect the current stock price, but the BSM model inputs change, so that: $N(d_1) = 0.29928$ $N(d_2) = 0.20333$. If the risk-free rate is 3% per year, what is the new BSM call price? ( )

A) USD 1. 61

B) USD 1. 78

C) USD 1. 95

D) USD 2. 11

99. The dividend yield of an asset is 10% per annum. What is the delta of a long forward contract on the asset with six months to maturity? ( )

A) 0. 95

B) 1. 00

C) 1. 05

D) Cannot determine without additional information

100. Which two of the following four statements are correct about the early exercise of American options on non-dividend-paying stocks? ( )

Ⅰ. It is never optimal to exercise an American call option early.

Ⅱ. It can be optimal to exercise an American put option early.

Ⅲ. It can be optimal to exercise an American call option early.

Ⅳ. It is never optimal to exercise an American put option early.

A) Ⅰ and Ⅱ

B) Ⅰ and Ⅳ

C) Ⅱ and Ⅲ

D) Ⅲ and Ⅳ

101. Ms. Zheng is responsible for the options desk in a London bank. She is concerned about the impact of dividends on the options held by the options desk. She asks you to assess which options are the most sensitive to dividend payments. What would be

your answer if the value of the options is found by using the Black-Scholes model adjusted for dividends? (   )

A) Everything else equal, out-of-the-money call options experience a larger decrease in value than in-the-money call options as expected dividends increase.

B) The increase in the value of in-the-money put options caused by an increase in expected dividends is always larger than the decrease in value of in-the-money call options.

C) Keeping the type of option constant, in-the-money options experience the largest absolute change in value and out-of-the-money options the smallest absolute change in value as expected dividends increase.

D) Keeping the type of option constant, at-the-money options experience the largest absolute change in value and out-of-the-money options the smallest absolute change in value as a result of dividend payment.

102. Use the Black-Scholes model to analyze which kind of options are the most sensitive to dividend payments. Which of the following statement is correct? (   )

A) Keeping the type of option constant, at-the-money options experience the largest absolute change in value and out-of-the-money options the smallest absolute change in value as a result of dividend payment.

B) Out-of-the-money call options experience a larger decrease in value than in-the-money call options as expected dividends increase, holding everything else equal.

C) Holding everything else equal, the increase in the value of in-the-money put options caused by an increase in expected dividends is larger than the decrease in value of in-the-money call options.

D) Keeping the type of option constant, in-the-money options experience the largest absolute change in value and out-of-the-money options the smallest absolute change in value as expected dividends increase.

103. A company with 1 million shares worth \$40 each is considering issuing 200,000 warrants each giving the holder the right to buy one share with a strike price of \$60 in 5 years. It wants to know the cost of this. The value of a 5-year European call option on the stock is \$7.04. In this case, $N = 1{,}000{,}000$ and $M = 200{,}000$, so that the value of each warrant is (   ).

A) 5.77

B) 5.87

C) 5.97

D) 6.07

104. You are given the following information about a European call option: Time to maturity = two years; continuous risk-free rate = 4%; continuous dividend yield = 1%; $N(d_1) = 0.64$. Calculate the delta of this option. (　　)

A) 0.64

B) 0.36

C) 0.63

D) 0.64

105. An analyst is doing a study on the effect on option prices of changes in the price of the underlying asset. The analyst wants to find out when the deltas of calls and puts are most sensitive to changes in the price of the underlying. Assume that the options are European and that the Black-Scholes formula holds. An increase in the price of the underlying has the largest absolute value impact on delta for (　　).

A) deep in-the-money calls and deep out-of-the-money puts

B) deep in-the-money puts and calls

C) deep out-of-the-money puts and calls

D) at-the-money puts and calls

106. A 90-day European put option on Microsoft has an exercise price of \$30, The current market price for Microsoft is \$30. The delta for this option is close to (　　).

A) −1

B) −0.5

C) 0.5

D) 1

107. Which of the following Greeks contributes most to the risk of an option that is close to expiration and deep in the money? (　　)

A) Vega

B) Rho

C) Gamma

D) Delta

108. An at-the-money European call option on the DJ EURO STOXX 50 index with a strike of 2,200 and maturing in 1 year is trading at EUR 350, where contract value is determined by EUR 10 per index point. The risk-free rate is 3% per year, and the daily volatility of the index is 2.05%. If we assume that the expected return on the DJ EURO STOXX 50 is 0%, the 99% 1-day VaR of a short position on a single call option calculated using the delta-normal approach is closest to (　　).

A) EUR 8
B) EUR 53
C) EUR 84
D) EUR 525

109. An option on the Bovespa stock index is struck on 3,000 Brazilian reals (BRL). The delta of the option is 0.6, and the annual volatility of the index is 24%. Using delta-normal assumptions, what is the 10-day VAR at the 95% confidence level? Assume 260 days per year. (　　)
A) 44 BRL
B) 139 BRL
C) 2,240 BRL
D) 278 BRL

110. An investor is long a short-term at-the-money put option on an underlying portfolio of equities with a notional value of USD 100,000. If the 95% VAR of the underlying portfolio is 10.4%, which of the following statements about the VAR of the option position is correct when second-order terms are considered? (　　)
A) The VAR of the option position is slightly more than USD 5,200.
B) The VAR of the option position is slightly more than USD 10,400.
C) The VAR of the option position is slightly less than USD 5,200.
D) The VAR of the option position is slightly less than USD 10,400.

111. The current stock price of a company is USD 80. A risk manager is monitoring call and put options on the stock with exercise prices of USD 50 and 5 days to maturity. Which of these scenarios is most likely to occur if the stock price falls by USD 1? (　　)

Scenario	Call Value	Put Value
A	Decrease by USD 0.94	Increase by USD 0.08
B	Decrease by USD 0.94	Increase by USD 0.89
C	Decrease by USD 0.07	Increase by USD 0.89
D	Decrease by USD 0.07	Increase by USD 0.08

A) Scenario A
B) Scenario B
C) Scenario C
D) Scenario D

112. To hedge a short call option position that exhibits a delta of 0.5, which of the following choice is most effective? (　　)

A) Buy two shares of the underlying for each option sold.
B) Sell two shares of the underlying for each option sold.
C) Buy one share of the underlying for every 2 options sold.
D) Sell one share of the underlying for every 2 options sold.

113. If the current market price of a stock is USD 50, which of the following options on the stock has the highest gamma? (　　)
A) Call option expiring in 30 days with strike price of USD 50
B) Call option expiring in 5 days with strike price of USD 30
C) Call option expiring in 5 days with strike price of USD 50
D) Put option expiring in 30 days with strike price of USD 30

114. Deborah Copeland, a risk manager of Oswaldo Bank, is analyzing call and put options on a stock with exercise prices of USD 20 and 3 days to maturity. The current stock price is USD 60. If the stock price falls by USD 1 now, which of these scenarios is most likely to occur? (　　)

Scenario	Call value	Put value
A	Decrease by USD 0.96	Increase by USD 0.92
B	Decrease by USD 0.96	Increase by USD 0.06
C	Decrease by USD 0.05	Increase by USD 0.92
D	Decrease by USD 0.05	Increase by USD 0.06

A) Scenario A
B) Scenario B
C) Scenario C
D) Scenario D

115. Rhonda Owen, a trader of Buckley Bank, buys an at-the-money call option in order to delta hedge it to maturity. Which of the following situation the trader is expecting to see most? (　　)
A) The underlying price drifting back and forth on a small scale around the strike price over the life of the option.
B) A decrease in implied volatility.
C) A large rise of the underlying price over the life of the option.
D) A large decrease of the underlying price over the life of the option.

116. Calculate the delta of this option given the following information below about a call option. (　　)

Time to maturity = 4 years
Continuous risk-free rate = 8%
Continuous dividend yield = 1%
$N(d_1) = 0.6$

A) −0.6
B) 0.5765
C) 0.4832
D) 0.6

117. Herminia Reeves, a risk manager of Harding Bank, is analyzing the stock of Colon company and the forward contracts on it. Assume the dividend yield of the stock is 5% per annum. What is the delta of a 6-month long forward contract on the stock? (　　)

A) 0.8749
B) 1.00
C) 0.9753
D) Cannot be determined without further information.

118. According to the Black-Scholes formula, an increase in the price of the underlying has the largest absolute value impact on delta of a European option for (　　).

A) deep in-the-money calls and deep out-of-the-money puts
B) at-the-money puts and calls
C) deep in-the-money puts and calls
D) deep out-of-the-money calls and deep out-of-the-money calls

119. Suppose an existing short option position is delta-neutral, but has a gamma of −600. Also assume that there exists a traded option with a delta of 0.75 and a gamma of 1.50. In order to maintain the position gamma-neutral and delta-neutral, which of the following is the appropriate strategy to implement? (　　)

A) Buy 400 options and sell 300 shares of the underlying asset.
B) Buy 300 options and sell 400 shares of the underlying asset.
C) Sell 400 options and buy 300 shares of the underlying asset.
D) Sell 300 options and buy 400 shares of the underlying asset.

120. The 90-day call option on Branden Company now trades at USD 2.67. A trader sells 200 call option contracts, each option has a delta of 0.6873. To delta-hedge the position, the dealer purchases 13,746 shares of the stock in the current market. 2 days later, the prices of the stock changes and as a result, the delta increases to 0.9831. What should the trader do to maintain the delta hedge? (　　)

A) sell 5,916 shares
B) sell 19,962 shares
C) purchase 5,916 shares
D) purchase 19,962 shares

121. A bank's position in options on the dollar/euro exchange rate has a delta of 30,000 and a gamma of −80, 000. The exchange rate (dollars per euro) is 0.90. After a short period of time, the exchange rate moves to 0.93. What is the new delta, and what trade is necessary to keep the position delta neutral? Assuming the bank did set up a delta-neutral position originally, has it gained or lost money from the exchange-rate movement? (　　)

A) 27,600, short 27,600 dollars, it gained money from the exchange-rate movement.
B) 33,000, long 33,000 euros, it lost money from the exchange-rate movement.
C) 27,600, short 27,600 euros, it lost money from the exchange-rate movement.
D) 33,000, long 33,000 dollars, it gained money from the exchange-rate movement.

122. Which of the following statement about delta hedge is correct? (　　)

A) The interest cost of carrying the delta hedge will be highest when the options are deep in-the-money.
B) The interest cost of carrying the delta hedge will be highest when the options are deep out-of-the-money.
C) The interest cost of carrying the delta hedge will be lowest when the options are at-the-money.
D) The interest cost of carrying the delta hedge will be highest when the options are at-the-money.

123. Deon Faulkner, a dealer of an investment bank, is analyzing options with delta-gamma method. Which of the following position is the least risky? (　　)

A) Gamma-negative, delta-positive
B) Gamma-positive, delta-neutral
C) Gamma-negative, delta-neutral
D) Gamma-positive, delta-positive

124. Clara Harmon, an expert on option trading, has a position that is delta-neutral, but has a gamma of negative 150. Assume that there exists a traded option with a delta of 0.4 and a gamma of 1.50. In order to create a position of both gamma-neutral and delta-neutral, which of the following strategy is correct? (　　)

A) Buy 150 options and sell 60 shares of the underlying asset.

B) Buy 100 options and sell 40 shares of the underlying asset.

C) Sell 100 options and buy 40 shares of the underlying asset.

D) Sell 150 options and buy 60 shares of the underlying asset.

125. A bank has sold USD 300,000 of call options on 100,000 equities. The equities trade at 50, the option strike price is 49, the maturity is in three months, volatility is 20%, and the interest rate is 5%. How should the bank delta-hedge? (　　)

A) Buy 65,000 shares

B) Buy 100,000 shares

C) Buy 21,000 shares

D) Sell 100,000 shares

126. A trader wants to create a portfolio with options. He views that the volatility of the underlying stock will increase but he does not want to create a portfolio with an exposed long or short position because of market risk. Which following strategy would the trader most likely prefer? (　　)

A) Buy short dated options and sell long dated options

B) Sell short dated options and buy long dated options

C) Sell short dated options and sell long dated options

D) Buy short dated options and buy long dated options

127. There is a portfolio consisting of a stock and options on it. It is currently delta neutral, but has a positive gamma. To make the portfolio both delta and gamma neutral, which of the following strategy is appropriate? (　　)

A) Buy call options on stock A and sell stock A

B) Sell put options on stock A and sell stock A

C) Sell call options on stock A and sell stock A

D) Buy put options on stock A and buy stock A

128. Rita Leonard has been informed by his client to hedge on the short position of a put option on the Dow Jones index. Which of the following statements about the hedging strategy are not correct? (　　)

A) A long position in a traded option on the index will help hedge the volatility risk of the option he has written.

B) He can make his portfolio delta neutral by shorting index futures contracts.

C) There is a short position in an index futures contract that will make his portfolio insensitive to both small and large moves in the index.

D) To make his hedged portfolio gamma neutral, he needs to take positions in options as well as futures.

129. Eunice Forbes, a hedge fund manager, holds a portfolio of stock Morse and options on it. The portfolio is currently delta neutral, but has a positive gamma. How to make the portfolio both delta neutral and gamma neutral? (　　)

A) Buy call options and sell stock.

B) Sell call options and sell stock.

C) Sell put options and sell stock.

D) Buy put options and buy stock.

130. Fannie Freeman, an individual investor, holds a portfolio which is delta neutral but has a negative gamma. To create a gamma neutral, he buys 2,000 deep-in-the-money call options. Then he wants to keep delta neutral, too. Which of the following strategy should he choose? (　　)

A) Sell 1,000 shares of the underlying asset.

B) Sell 2,000 shares of the underlying asset.

C) Buy 1,000 shares of the underlying asset.

D) Buy 2,000 shares of die underlying asset.

131. Which of the following statements is true regarding options Greeks? (　　)

A) Theta tends to be large and positive when buying at-the-money options.

B) Gamma is greatest for in-the-money options with long maturities.

C) Vega is greatest for at-the-money options with long maturities.

D) Delta of deep in-the-money put options tends toward +1.

132. Which of the following statements regarding option "Greeks" is incorrect? (　　)

A) Vega is highest when options are at-the-money.

B) Forward instruments cannot be used to create gamma-neutral positions.

C) Rho is higher for at-the-money versus in-the-money options.

D) Gamma represents the expected change in delta for a change in the value of the underlying instrument.

133. Which of the following statements is incorrect? (　　)

A) The vega of a European-style call option is highest when the option is at-the-money.

B) The delta of a European-style put option moves toward zero as the price of the underlying stock rises.

C) The gamma of an at-the-money European-style option tends to increase as the remaining maturity of the option decreases.

D) Compared to an at-the-money European-style call option, an out-of-the-money European-style option with the same strike price and remaining maturity has a greater negative value for theta.

134. There is a long call option of a stock with strike at $100. the current price of the stock is $99.50. The maturity of the option is within 20 minutes. Which of the following Greeks poses the highest risk to the call option? ( )

A) Gamma

B) Rho

C) Delta

D) Theta

135. If the current market price of a stock is USD 50, which of the following options on the stock has the highest gamma? ( )

A) call option expiring in 30 days with strike price of USD 50

B) put option expiring in 30 days with strike price of USD 30

C) call option expiring in 5 days with strike price of USD 30

D) call option expiring in 5 days with strike price of USD 50

136. Which of the following options has the highest gamma if the current price of its underlying stock is USD 148? ( )

A) call option expiring in 20 days with strike USD 100

B) call option expiring in 20 days with strike USD 150

C) put option expiring in 20 days with strike USD 100

D) put option expiring in 50 days with strike USD 150

137. There is a portfolio that is delta-neutral, but has a negative 3,000 gamma. An option has a delta of 0.8 and a gamma of 3. Which following strategy can create a both delta-neutral and gamma-neutral position? ( )

A) Go long 1,000 options and sell 800 shares of the underlying stock.

B) Go long 1,000 options and buy 800 shares of the underlying stock.

C) Go long 1,500 options and sell 400 shares of the underlying stock.

D) Go long 1,500 options and buy 400 shares of the underlying stock.

138. Which of the following statement about Greeks is false? ( )

A) Short a plain vanilla put option is equivalent to short vega.

B) Short a coupon bond is equivalent to long effective duration and short effective convexity.

C) Long a deep in the money up and out call option is equivalent to long delta and short vega.

D) Long a plain vanilla call option is equivalent to long delta and long gamma.

139. A financial institution has the following portfolio of over-the-counter options on

sterling.

Type	Position	Delta	Gamma	Vega
Call	−1,000	0.5	2.2	1.8
Call	−500	0.8	0.6	0.2
Put	−2,000	−0.4	1.3	0.7
Call	−500	0.7	1.8	1.4

A traded option is available with a delta of 0.6, a gamma of 1.5, a vega of 0.8. What position in the traded option and in sterling would make the portfolio both gamma neutral and delta neutral? (　　)

A) Short position in 4,000 traded options, long position in 1950 sterling.

B) Long position in 4,000 traded options, short position in 1950 sterling.

C) Long position in 4,000 traded options, long position in 1950 sterling.

D) Short position in 4,000 traded options, short position in 1950 sterling.

140. Pasquale Stark, a risk manager of Davila Securities, is analyzing the risk of a portfolio composed of different options. He is informed by his assistant that the position is positive gamma and negative vega. Which of the following portfolios conform to this position? (　　)

A) Long long-expiry call and short short-expiry put.

B) Long long-expiry put and short long-expiry call.

C) Long short-expiry call and short long-expiry call.

D) Long long-expiry call and short short-expiry call.

141. If a deep in-the-money option is closed to its expiration date, which of the following Greeks contributes most to the risk of an option? (　　)

A) Gamma

B) Delta

C) Rho

D) Vega

142. Which of the following type of option experiences accelerating time decay as expiration date come near? (　　)

A) At-the-money

B) In-the-money

C) Out-of-the-money

D) None of the above

143. Tonia Schultz, an option dealer, wants to produce a short vega, long gamma position. Which of the following strategy is appropriate for him? (　　)

A) Buy and sell options of short maturity.

B) Buy and sell options of long maturity.

C) Buy short-maturity options, sell long-maturity options.

D) Buy long-maturity options, sell short-maturity options.

144. In which of the following situation, value of the options are most sensitive to changes in the volatility? (　　)

A) Both calls and puts are at-the-money.

B) Both calls and puts are deep in-the-money.

C) Both puts and calls are deep out-of-the-money.

D) Calls are deep out-of-the-money and puts are deep in-the-money.

145. Greeks reflect properties of options in different ways. Which of the following statements is true about Greeks of option? (　　)

A) Delta of deep in-the-money put options tends toward +1.

B) Gamma is greatest for in-the-money options with long maturities.

C) Theta tends to be large and positive when buying at-the-money options.

D) Vega is greatest for at-the-money options with long maturities.

146. According to the definition of vega, what is the purpose to neutralize vega of the option? (　　)

A) To minimize the potential loss as a result of a change in the volatility of the underlying source of risk.

B) To minimize the adverse effect due to the government regulation.

C) To minimize the potential loss as a result of a large movement in the underlying source of risk.

D) To minimize the possibility of counterparty default risk.

147. Which of the following statements about greeks is correct? (　　)

Ⅰ. Theta is always negative for long calls and long puts while it is always positive for short calls and short puts.

Ⅱ. The rho of a call option changes with the passage of time and will approach zero as expiration approaches, but this is not true for the rho of put options.

A) Ⅰ only

B) Ⅱ only

C) Neither

D) Both

148. Sonya Tanner, a risk manager of Willy Bank, has a option portfolio with the following position greeks: gamma = −470, vega = +286,000 and theta = +31,500. Which of the following additional trades will neutralize all these three greeks (Assuming all the options below are at the money)? (　　)

A) Buy short-term options + sell long-term options.

B) Sell short-term options + buy long-term options.

C) Sell short-term options + sell long-term options.

D) Buy short-term options + buy long-term options.

149. Shelton Meza, an option dealer, write an at-the-money call option. Which of the following statements is correct? (　　)

Ⅰ. The option dealer has a negative gamma and negative vega exposure.

Ⅱ. If the option moves away from the money, gamma and vega will have less impact on the value of the option.

A) Ⅰ only

B) Ⅱ only

C) Neither Ⅰ nor Ⅱ

D) Both Ⅰ and Ⅱ

150. For a European option on a non-dividend paying stock, which option Greek would be identical for both a call and a put option, holding strike price, time to maturity, implied volatility and risk free interest rate constant? (　　)

A) vega only

B) Theta and rho

C) Gamma and vega

D) Gamma Vega Theta Rho

151. A European put option on a non-dividend paying stock has a remaining life of 6 months with a strike of USD 50 and the risk-free rate of 1%, after 3 months which of the following stock prices has the highest time-value of the option (in% of stock price)? (　　)

A) USD 10

B) USD 40

C) USD 50

D) USD 60

152. There is a 6-month European call option on a non-dividend paying stock with a strike price of USD 150. The risk-free rate of 3%. Which of the following current stock prices makes the highest time-value of the option? (　　)

A) USD 120
B) USD 130
C) USD 140
D) USD 150

153. Which greeks contribute to the risk (defined as unexpected loss) of a short call option position? (　　)
A) Delta, Vega, Gamma, Theta, Rho
B) Vega, Rho
C) Delta, Vega, Rho
D) Delta, Vega, Gamma, Rho

154. Option value is composed of time value and option value. Which of the following statements about option time value is correct? (　　)
A) At-the-money options have higher time value than either out-of-the-money or in-the-money options with the same time to expiration.
B) Deeply out-of-the-money options have more time value than at-the-money options with the same time to expiration.
C) Deeply in-the-money options have more time value than at-the-money options with the same time to expiration.
D) At-the-money options have no time value.

155. Humberto Medina, a Portfolio manager, has a position in option portfolio with the following Greeks: theta = + 30,000; vega = + 400,000 and gamma = − 350. Now Humberto Medina wants to neutralize the portfolio's theta, vega and gamma. Which of the following strategy is appropriate, assuming all the option below is roughly at the money? (　　)
A) Buy short-term options and sell long-term options.
B) Buy short-term options and buy long-term options.
C) Sell short-term options and sell long-term options.
D) Sell short-term options and buy long-term options.

156. The following statements are about option greeks, which of them is false? (　　)
A) The gamma of an at-the-money European-styled option tends to increase as the remaining maturity of the option decreases.
B) Compared to an at-the-money European-styled call option, an out-of-the-money European option with the same strike price and remaining maturity would have a greater negative value for theta.
C) European-style call and put options are most affected by changes in vega when

they are at-the-money.

D) The delta of a European-styled put option on an underlying stock would move towards zero as the price of the underlying stock rises.

157. Kris Fry, an expert on option trading, is explaining option greeks to his client. Which of the following statements about option "Greeks" is/are correct? (   )

Ⅰ. Vega is highest when options are at-the-money.

Ⅱ. Forward instruments cannot be used to create gamma-neutral positions.

Ⅲ. Rho is higher for at-the-money versus in-the-money put options.

Ⅳ. Theta represents the expected change in delta for a change in the value of the underlying instrument.

A) Ⅰ, Ⅱ and Ⅲ only

B) Ⅰ and Ⅱ only

C) Ⅳ only

D) Ⅰ, Ⅱ, and Ⅳ only

158. Kendra James, an investor who is interested in derivatives, is looking to create an option portfolio on Barrett stock. He hopes that the portfolio will have virtually zero vega the portfolio will profit from increases in interest rates. If the current stock price is $100, which of the following portfolio would satisfy his will? (   )

A) Sell a call with a strike price of $100.

B) Sell a put with a strike price of $100.

C) Buy a call with a strike price of $40.

D) Buy a put with a strike price of $40.

159. Fay Zamora, FRM in Wilton Bank, is considering using options to hedge financial risk on the position of a stock portfolio. Which of the following statement about the "Greeks" of the option is true? (   )

A) Theta is the most negative for out-of-the-money options.

B) A vega of 10 suggests that for a 0.01 increase in volatility, the option price will increase by 0.10.

C) Call option deltas range from −1 to 1.

D) Rho for fixed income options is small.

160. Steve, a market risk manager at Marcat Securities, is analyzing the risk of its S&P 500 index options trading desk. His risk report shows the desk is net long gamma and short Vega. Which of the following portfolios of options shows exposures consistent with this report? (   )

A) The desk has substantial long-expiry long call positions and substantial short-expiry short put positions.
B) The desk has substantial long-expiry long put positions and substantial long-expiry short call positions.
C) The desk has substantial long-expiry long call positions and substantial short-expiry short call positions.
D) The desk has substantial short-expiry long call positions and substantial long-expiry short call positions.

161. How can a trader produce a short vega, long gamma position? (　　)
A) Buy short-maturity options, sell long-maturity options.
B) Buy long-maturity options, sell short-maturity options.
C) Buy and sell options of long maturity.
D) Buy and sell options of short maturity.

162. An option portfolio exhibits high unfavorable sensitivity to increases in implied volatility and while experiencing significant daily losses with the passage of time. Which strategy would the trader most likely employ to hedge the portfolio? (　　)
A) Sell short-dated options and buy long-dated options.
B) Buy short-dated options and sell long-dated options.
C) Sell short-dated options and sell long-dated options.
D) Buy short-dated options and buy long-dated options.

第 16 单元

债券定价和模型

163. A bond has a 10% coupon rate that pays interest semiannually and matures in three years. Calculate the bond price per 100 of par value assuming the required rate of return is 12%. (　　)

A) 95. 08

B) 96. 10.

C) 104. 50

D) 95. 00

164. A bond will mature in seven years, it pays interest semiannually and the annual coupon rate is 6%. Calculate the bond price per 100 of par value assuming the market discount rate is 4%. (　　)

A) 112. 10.

B) 89. 59

C) 114. 90

D) 100

165. A 30 years mature zero-coupon bond has a market discount rate of 4. 5% per year and compound annually, calculate the bond price per 100 of par value. (　　)

A) 26. 70

B) 26. 31

C) 100

D) 51. 00

166. Two bonds pay interest annually.

- Bond A: Coupon Rate = 10%, Time-to-maturity = 2 years.
- Bond B: Coupon Rate = 6%, Time-to-maturity = 2 years.

Calculate the price difference between Bond A and Bond B per 100 of par value, assuming market discount rate is 4%. (　　)

A) 7. 55

B) 4.00
C) 0.75
D) 2.00

The following information relates to the next two questions.

Bond	Price	Coupon Rate	Time-to-Maturity
A	105	5%	2 years
B	100	6%	2 years
C	95	5%	4 years

167. The yield-to-maturity is lowest for (　　).
A) Bond A
B) Bond B
C) Bond C
D) Can't judge

168. If the market discount rate raises by 100 basis points, which bond will show the smallest percent change in price? (　　)
A) Bond A
B) Bond B
C) Bond C
D) Can't judge

169. An investor buys a Treasury bill maturing in one month for \$987. On the maturity date the investor collects \$1,000. Calculate effective annual rate (EAR). (　　)
A) 17.0%
B) 15.8%
C) 13.0%
D) 11.6%

170. Lisa Smith, the treasurer of Bank AAA, has \$100 million to invest for one year. She has identified three alternative one-year certificates of deposit (CDs), with different compounding periods and annual rates. CD1: monthly, 7.82%; CD2: quarterly, 8.00%; CD3: semiannually, 8.05%; and CD4: continuous, 7.95%. Which CD has the highest effective annual rate (EAR)? (　　)
A) CD1
B) CD2
C) CD3
D) CD4

171. Consider a savings account that pays an annual interest rate of 8% Calculate the amount of time it would take to double your money. Round to the nearest year. (　　)

A) 7 years
B) 8 years
C) 9 years
D) 10 years

172. Two bonds are currently trading at par value.
Bond A: coupon rate = 4%, maturity = 5 years
Bond B: coupon rate = 8%, maturity = 5 years
Comparing to Bond B, for a 100 basis points decrease in the required rate of return, the percentage price change of Bond A will be (　　).

A) equal to Bond B
B) greater than Bond B
C) smaller than Bond B
D) uncertain

173. If the market discount rates for all three bonds increase by 100 basis points, which bond will have the greatest percentage change in price? (　　)

Bond	Coupon Rate	Maturity (years)
X	4%	15
Y	4%	5
Z	8%	5

A) Bond X
B) Bond Y
C) Bond Z
D) uncertain

174. Given the following information, which of the following is closest to d(1.0), the discount factor for the 1st year? (　　)

	Bond A	Bond B	Bond C
Bond maturity in years	0.5	1	2
Coupon	6%	12%	9%
Price	101.182	102.341	99.573

A) 0.9099
B) 0.9138
C) 0.9655
D) 0.9823

175. A 2-year bond has a 6% coupon rate and pays interest annually. What is the bond price with below sequence of spot rate? (　　)

Time-to-Maturity	Spot Rates
1 year	2%
2 years	4%

A) 103.89
B) 101.39
C) 102.58
D) 104.81

176. Consider a bond with par value of EUR 1,000 and maturity in three years, and that pays a coupon of 5% annually. The spot rate curve is as follows: 1-year, 6%; 2-year, 7%; and 3-year, 8%. The value of the bond is closest to (　　).
A) 904
B) 924
C) 930
D) 950

177. A 3-year bond has a 10% coupon rate and pays interest annually. What is the bond price? (　　)

Time-to-Maturity	Spot Rates
1 year	8.0%
2 years	9.0%
3 years	10.0%

A) 100.32
B) 99.98.
C) 102.46.
D) 102.25.

The following information relates to the next three questions.
All three bonds pay interest annually.

Bond	Coupon Rate	Time-to-Maturity
X	8%	3 years
Y	7%	3 years
Z	6%	3 years

Time-to-maturity	Spot Rates
1 year	8%
2 years	9%
3 years	10%

178. Based upon the given sequence of spot rates, the price of Bond X is closest to (　　).
A) 95. 02
B) 95. 28
C) 96. 29
D) 97. 63

179. Based upon the given sequence of spot rates, the price of Bond Y is closest to (　　).
A) 87. 50
B) 92. 54
C) 92. 76
D) 94. 82

180. Based upon the given sequence of spot rates, the yield-to-maturity of Bond Z is closest to (　　).
A) 9. 00%
B) 9. 92%
C) 10. 67%
D) 11. 93%

181. All other things being equal, which of the following would you expect to increase the yield-to-maturity (YTM) of a corporate bond? (　　)
Ⅰ. An increase in the risk-free interest rate
Ⅱ. An increase in the company's business risk
Ⅲ. An increase in the company's leverage ratio
A) Ⅲ only
B) Ⅰ and Ⅱ only
C) Ⅰ and Ⅲ only
D) Ⅰ, Ⅱ and Ⅲ

182. One bond has 9% coupon rate and pays interest annually, calculate bond price base on the sequence of spot rates. (　　)

Time-to-maturity	Spot Rates
1 year	8%
2 years	9%
3 years	10%

A) 97.80

B) 92.02

C) 96.28

D) 98.63

183. In building a portfolio of fixed income securities for one of your clients, you determine that the use of STRIPS (separate trading of registered interest and principal securities) issued by the Treasury would assist in reducing reinvestment risk. Which of the following statements regarding STRIPS is correct? (　　)

A) STRIPS tend to trade at a premium.

B) Shorter-term C-STRIPS (coupon) tend to trade at a discount.

C) Longer-term C-STRIPS (coupon) tend to trade at a premium.

D) STRIPS tend to have significant risk of illiquidity.

184. One bond has 7% coupon rate and pays interest annually, calculate bond price base on the sequence of spot rates. (　　)

Time-to-maturity	Spot Rates
I year	8%
2 years	9%
3 years	10%

A) 97.80

B) 92.02.

C) 96.28.

D) 92.76

185. If a 91-day U. S. Treasury bill (T-bill) is priced at a discount of 6.8%, what will an investor actually pay for a \$10,000 bill at issuance? (　　)

A) \$9,320

B) \$9,828

C) \$9,830

D) \$9,832

186. Calculate the yield-to-maturity of one bond which has coupon rate of 6%, pays interest annually and has below spot rate. (　　)

Time-to-maturity	Spot Rates
1 year	8%
2 years	9%
3 years	10%

A) 8.00%
B) 10.00%
C) 11.39%
D) 9.92%

187. Which is the most popular quote by bond dealers? (　　)
A) full price
B) full price plus accrued interest
C) flat price
D) full price minus accrued interest

188. A 5-year corporate bond paying an annual coupon of 8% is sold at a price reflecting a yield-to-maturity of 6% per year. One year passes and the interest rates remain unchanged. Assuming a flat term structure and holding all other factors constant, the bond's price during this period will (　　).
A) increase
B) decrease
C) remaine constant
D) cannot be determined with the data given

189. Calculate bond full price assume the settlement date is 14 June 2018. (　　)

Annual Coupon	5%
Coupon Payment Frequency	Semiannual
Interest Payment Dates	10 April and 10 October
Maturity Date	10 October 2020
Day Count Convention	30/360
Annual Yield-to-Maturity	4%

A) 103.08
B) 106.32

C) 104.65

D) 100

190. Assume that the settlement date is 14 June 2018, calculate the accrued interest. (　　)

Annual Coupon	5%
Coupon Payment Frequency	Semiannual
Interest Payment Dates	10 April and 10 October
Maturity Date	10 October 2020
Day Count Convention	30/360
Annual Yield-to-Maturity	4%

A) 0.89

B) 0.64

C) 0.93

D) 0.82

191. Assume that the settlement date is 14 June 2018, calculate bond flat price. (　　)

Annual Coupon	5%
Coupon Payment Frequency	Semiannual
Interest Payment Dates	10 April and 10 October
Maturity Date	10 October 2020
Day Count Convention	30/360
Annual Yield-to-Maturity	4%

A) 102.19

B) 103.18

C) 104.01

D) 101.25

192. Which bond is suitable for matrix pricing? (　　)

A) Not actively traded

B) coupon rates not same

C) credit quality not same

D) actively traded

193. For new bonds, matrix pricing can be used to estimate (　　).

A) market discount rate

B) yield-to-maturity of similar bond

C) required yield spread over the benchmark rate.

D) benchmark rate

194. A bond has a 6% coupon rate and pays interest semiannually. If there are 20 years remaining until maturity and current trading price is 111. 00, calculate annual yield-to-maturity (　　).

A) 2. 56%

B) 5. 12%

C) 4. 50%

D) 2. 25%

195. Calculate the annual yield-to-maturity of a 4-year, zero-coupon bond priced at 80 per 100 of par value, which pays interest monthly. (　　)

A) 5. 59%

B) 6. 52%

C) 7. 12%

D) 7. 64%

196. A 5-year, 5% semiannual coupon payment corporate bond is priced at 104. 967 per 100 of par value. The bond's yield-to-maturity, quoted on a semiannual bond basis, is 3. 897%. An analyst has been asked to convert to a monthly periodicity. Under this conversion, the yield-to-maturity is closest to (　　).

A) 3. 87%

B) 4. 95%

C) 7. 67%

D) 8. 42%

197. Calculate the bond's annual yield-to-maturity. (　　)

- There are 5 years remaining until maturity.
- Bond price is 101 per 100 of par value.
- The coupon rate is 8% and paid semiannually.
- The bond is first callable in 3 years, then callable according to schedule.

End of Year	Call Price
3	102
4	101
5	100

A) 2.88%
B) 5.77%
C) 3.88%
D) 7.75%

198. Calculate the bond's annual yield-to-first-call. ( )

- There are 5 years remaining until maturity.
- Bond price is 101 per 100 of par value.
- The coupon rate is 8% and paid semiannually.
- The bond is first callable in 3 years, then callable according to schedule.

End of Year	Call Price
3	102
4	101
5	100

A) 3.12%
B) 6.11%
C) 4.30%
D) 8.20%

199. Calculate the bond's annual yield-to-second-call. ( )

- There are 5 years remaining until maturity.
- Bond price is 101 per 100 of par value.
- The coupon rate is 8% and paid semiannually.
- The bond is first callable in 3 years, then callable according to schedule.

End of Year	Call Price
3	102
4	101
5	100

A) 3.12%
B) 6.11%
C) 7.92%
D) 3.96%

200. Calculate the bond's yield-to-worst. ( )

- There are 5 years remaining until maturity.
- Bond price is 101 per 100 of par value.

- The coupon rate is 8% and paid semiannually.
- The bond is first callable in 3 years, then callable according to schedule.

End of Year	Call Price
3	102
4	101
5	100

A) 8.60%
B) 7.92%
C) 7.75%
D) 8.00%

201. Which FRN (floating rate notes) will be priced at a premium on the next reset date, if issued at par value with 3-month Libor as a reference rate? (　　)

Floating Rate Note	Quoted Margin	Discount Margin
A	0.41%	0.32%
B	0.35%	0.35%
C	0.65%	0.72%

A) FRN A
B) FRN B
C) FRN C
D) Either one

202. Calculate bond equivalent yield. (　　)

- A 365-day year bank certificate of deposit.
- Initial principal amount of USD 95 million.
- Redemption amount due at maturity of USD 100 million.
- The number of days between settlement and maturity is 320.

A) 5.48%
B) 5.65%
C) 5.78%
D) 6.00%

203. Calculate bond equivalent yield. (　　)

- 180-day banker's acceptance.
- Quoted at a discount rate of 5.20%.
- 360-day year.

A) 5.31%

B) 5.34%

C) 5.50%

D) 5.40%

204. Select one correct statement about a par curve. (　　)

A) It is obtained from a spot curve.

B) A par curve is a sequence of yields-to-maturity which prices each bond at premium value.

C) A par curve is a sequence of yields-to-maturity which prices each bond at discount value.

D) All bonds on a par curve are assumed to have different credit risk.

205. Suppose that the 6-month, 12-month, 18-month, and 24-month zero rates are 5%, 6%, 6.5%, and 7%, respectively. What is the 2-year par yield? (　　)

A) 6.872%

B) 6.972%

C) 7.072%

D) 7.172%

206. Spot curve is a yield curve constructed from a sequence of yields-to-maturity on (　　).

A) zero-coupon bond

B) floating rate notes

C) government bond

D) corporate bond

207. Which rate is the incremental return by extending the investment time-to-maturity for an additional time period? (　　)

A) Forward rate.

B) Add-on rate.

C) Spot rate.

D) Yield-to-maturity.

208. The price of a three-year zero-coupon government bond is \$85.16. The price of a similar four-year bond is \$79.81. What is the one-year implied forward rate from year 3 to year 4? (　　)

A) 5.4%

B) 5.5%

C) 5.8%

D) 6.7%

209. Suppose that the yield curve is upward sloping. Which of the following statements is true? (　　)

A) The forward rate yield curve is above the zero-coupon yield curve, which is above the coupon-bearing bond yield curve.

B) The forward rate yield curve is above the coupon-bearing bond yield curve, which is above the zero-coupon yield curve.

C) The coupon-bearing bond yield curve is above the zero-coupon yield curve, which is above the forward rate yield curve.

D) The coupon-bearing bond yield curve is above the forward rate yield curve, which is above the zero-coupon yield curve.

210. Calculate the 3-year implied spot rate. (　　)

Time Period	Forward Rate (effective annual rates)
0	0.90%
1	1.13%
2	3.95%
3	3.29%
4	3.15%

A) 1.28%

B) 2.34%

C) 3.28%

D) 1.98%

211. Calculate the price of a two-year, 3.6% coupon bond, with interest payments paid annually. (　　)

Time Period	Forward Rate (effective annual rates)
0	0.81%
1	1.13%
2	3.95%
3	3.29%
4	3.15%

A) 101.68

B) 105.91

C) 105.72

D) 105.19

212. The specific bond's yield-to-maturity will not be impacted by changes of ( ).

A) inflation

B) tax

C) quality rating

D) call provision

213. Which spread is the yield spread of a specific bond over the standard swap rate? ( )

A) I-spread

B) Z-spread

C) G-spread

D) N-spread

214. The term structure of swap rates is: 1-year, 2.50%; 2-year, 3.00%; 3-year, 3.50%; 4-year, 4.00%; 5-year, 4.50%. The two-year forward swap rate starting in three years is closest to ( ).

A) 3.50%

B) 4.50%

C) 5.51%

D) 6.02%

215. In managing a portfolio of domestic corporate bonds, which of the following risks is least important? ( )

A) Interest rate risks

B) Concentration risks

C) Spread risks

D) Foreign exchange risks

216. Calculate G-spread (bps) of the US corporate bond which pays interest annually. ( )

Bond	Coupon Rate	Time-to-Maturity	Price
US Government Benchmark	4%	3 years	100.25
Bond	5%	3 years	100.65

A) 270 bps

B) 264 bps

C) 83 bps

D) 300 bps

217. A corporate bond has 3 years remaining to maturity with a 5% coupon rate paid annually. If Z-spread is 100 bps, calculate bond price base on benchmark spot curve. (　　)

Time-to-maturity	Spot Rate
I year	4.86%
2 years	4.95%
3 years	5.65%

A) 95.38
B) 97.35
C) 104.56
D) 95.74

218. What is OAS (option-adjusted spread) on a callable bond? (　　)
A) Z-spread minus the standard swap rate of the same tenor.
B) Z-spread over the benchmark spot curve.
C) Z-spread minus the embedded call option.
D) Z-spread plus the embedded call option.

219. For "buy-and-hold" investment strategy till maturity, which source of return is not available forfixed rate bond? (　　)
A) Principal payment
B) Reinvestment of coupon payments
C) Capital gain
D) Principal + coupon reinvestment

220. Your boss wants to devise a fixed-income strategy such that there is no reinvestment risk over five years. Reinvestment risk will not occur if (　　).
Ⅰ. Interest rates remain constant over the time period the bonds are held.
Ⅱ. The bonds purchased are callable.
Ⅲ. The bonds purchased are issued at par.
Ⅳ. Only zero-coupon bonds with a five-year maturity are purchased.
A) Ionly
B) Ⅰ and Ⅱ only
C) Ⅲ only
D) Ⅰ and Ⅳ

221. If a fixed-rate bond is held until maturity, which sources of return is exposed to

interest rate risk? (　　)

A) Capital gain

B) Capital loss

C) Redemption of principal

D) Reinvestment of coupon payments

222. A bond is purchased at a price above par value and sold four years later. How to measure capital gain or loss? (　　)

A) Compare to carrying value.

B) Compare to purchase price.

C) Compare to purchase price plus the amortized amount of the premium.

D) Compare to purchase price plus premium.

223. A five-year corporate bond paying an annual coupon of 8% is sold at a price reflecting a yield to maturity of 6%. One year passes and the interest rates remain unchanged. Assuming a flat term structure and holding all other factors constant, the bond's price during this period will (　　).

A) increase

B) decrease

C) remain constant

D) cannot be determined with the data given

224. A 9-year, 7% annual coupon payment bond is purchased at a price equal to par value. If interest rates increase to 9% before the first coupon payment and the bond is sold after five years. Calculate the future value of the reinvested coupon payments at the end of the holding period (reinvestment rate based on 9%). (　　)

A) 35.00

B) 44.26

C) 41.89

D) 6.89

225. A 9-year, 7% annual coupon payment bond is purchased at a price equal to par value. If interest rates increase to 9% before the first coupon payment and the bond is sold after five years. Calculate the capital gain/loss (reinvestment rate based on 9%). (　　)

A) loss of 9.45

B) loss of 2.31

C) gain of 3.75

D) loss of 6.48

226. Consider a $1,000-face value, 12-year, 8%, semiannual coupon bond with a YTM of 10.45%. The change in value for a decrease in yield of 38 basis points is closest to (　　).

A) increase of $22.76

B) decrease of $22.76

C) increase of $23.06

D) decrease of $23.06

227. An investor buys a three-year bond with a 5% coupon rate paid annually. The bond, with a yield-to-maturity of 3%, is purchased at a price of 105.657223 per 100 of par value. Assuming a 5-basis point change in yield-to-maturity, the bond's approximate modified duration is closest to (　　).

A) 2.78

B) 2.86

C) 3.56

D) 4.18

228. A zero-coupon bond with a maturity of 10 years has an annual effective yield of 10%. What is the closest value for its modified duration? (　　)

A) 9 years

B) 10 years

C) 99 years

D) 100 years

229. Suppose the face value of a three-year option-free bond is USD 1,000 and the annual coupon is 10%. The current yield to maturity is 5%. What is the modified duration of this bond? (　　)

A) 2.62

B) 2.85

C) 3.00

D) 2.75

230. A Treasury bond has a coupon rate of 6% per annum (the coupons are paid semiannually) and a semiannually compounded yield of 4% per annum. The bond matures in 18 months and the next coupon will be paid 6 months from now. Which number of years is closest to the bond's Macaulay duration? (　　)

A) 1.023 years

B) 1.457 years

C) 1.500 years

D) 2.915 years

231. Select one correct description of bond's duration. ( )

A) yield duration is measured by effective duration

B) curve duration is measured by modified duration

C) Macaulay duration cannot be less than modified duration

D) None of the above

232. A portfolio manager uses her valuation model to estimate the value of a bond portfolio at USD 125.482 million. The term structure is flat. Using the same model, she estimates that the value of the portfolio would increase to USD 127.723 million if all interest rates fell by 30bp and would decrease to USD 122.164 million if allinterest rates rose by 30bp. Using these estimates, the effective duration of the bond portfolio is closest to ( ).

A) 8.38

B) 16.76

C) 7.38

D) 14.77

233. An investor buys a 6% annual payment bond with three years to maturity. The bond has a yield-to-maturity of 8% and is currently priced at 94.845806 per 100 of par. The bond's Macaulay duration is closest to ( ).

A) 2.62

B) 2.78

C) 2.83

D) 2.95

234. A bank has \$500 million in assets with a modified duration of 7 and \$400 million in liabilities with a modified duration of 5. Accounting only for duration effects, the impact of a 50-basis-point parallel upward shift in the yield curve on the bank's equity value is closest to a ( ).

A) \$7.5 million decrease

B) \$7.5 million increase

C) \$15 million decrease

D) \$15 million increase

235. A bond portfolio has the following composition:

1. Portfolio A: price \$90,000, modified duration 2.5, long position in 8 bonds
2. Portfolio B: price \$110,000, modified duration 3, short position in 6 bonds
3. Portfolio C: price \$120,000, modified duration 3.3, long position in 12 bonds

All interest rates are 10%. If the rates rise by 25 basis points, then the bond portfolio value will decrease by (　　).

A) \$11,430

B) \$21,330

C) \$12,573

D) \$23,463

236. Which of the following can measure the interest rate risk of a fixed-rate bond with an embedded call option? (　　)

A) Macaulay duration.

B) effective duration.

C) modified duration.

D) None of the above

237. A trading portfolio consists of two bonds, A and B. Both have modified duration of 3 years and face value of USD 1,000, but A is a zero-coupon bond and its current price is USD 900, and bond B pays annual coupons and is priced at par. What do you expect will happen to the market prices of A and B if the risk-free yield curve moves up by 1 basis point? (　　)

A) Both bond prices will move up by roughly the same amount.

B) Both bond prices will move up, but bond B will gain more than bond A.

C) Both bond prices will move down by roughly equal amounts.

D) Both bond prices will move down, but bond B will lose more than bond A.

238. A money markets desk holds a floating-rate note with an eight-year maturity. The interest rate is floating at the three-month LIBOR rate, reset quarterly. The next reset is in one week. What is the approximate duration of the floating-rate note? (　　)

A) 8 years

B) 4 years

C) 3 months

D) 1 week

239. Which of the following can measure a bond's sensitivity to shaping risk? (　　)

A) effective duration

B) key rate duration

C) modified duration

D) Macaulay duration

240. A and B are two perpetual bonds; that is, their maturities are infinite. A has a

coupon of 4% and B has a coupon of 8%. Assuming that both are trading at the same yield, what can be said about the duration of these bonds? (　　)

A) The duration of A is greater than the duration of B.

B) The duration of A is less than the duration of B.

C) A and B both have the same duration.

D) None of the above.

241. A manager wants to swap a bond for a bond with the same price but higher duration. Which of the following bond characteristics would be associated with a higher duration? (　　)

Ⅰ. A higher coupon rate

Ⅱ. More frequent coupon payments

Ⅲ. A longer term to maturity

Ⅳ. A lower yield

A) Ⅰ, Ⅱ, and Ⅲ

B) Ⅱ, Ⅲ, and Ⅳ

C) Ⅲ and Ⅳ

D) Ⅰ and Ⅱ

242. When the maturity of a plain coupon bond increases, its duration increases (　　).

A) Indefinitely and regularly

B) Up to a certain level

C) Indefinitely and progressively

D) In a way dependent on the bond being priced above or below par

243. Consider the following bonds:

Bond Number	Maturity (Years)	Coupon Rate	Frequency	Yield (Annual)
1	10	6%	1	6%
2	10	6%	2	6%
3	10	0%	1	6%
4	10	6%	1	5%
5	9	6%	1	6%

How would you rank the bonds from the shortest to longest duration? (　　)

A) 5－2－1－4－3

B) 5－2－3－4－5

C) 5－4－3－1－2

D) 2－4－5－1－3

244. You are using key rate shifts to analyze the effect of yield changes on bond prices. Suppose that the 10-year yield has increased by 10 basis points and that this shock decreases linearly to zero for the 20-year yield. What is the effect of this shock on the 14-year yield? (　　)

A) Increase of 0 basis points

B) increase of 4 basis points

C) increase of 6 basis points

D) increase of 10 basis points

245. Calculate effective duration with a base rate of 7%. (　　)

Interest Rate Assumption	Present Value of Liabilities
6%	USD 520 million
7%	USD 450 million
8%	USD 370 million

A) 14. 49.

B) 16. 67.

C) 18. 97.

D) 33. 34

246. A 10-year zero-coupon bond is callable annually at par (its face value) starting at the beginning of year 6. Assume a flat yield curve of 10%. What is the bond duration? (　　)

A) 5 years

B) 7. 5 years

C) 10 years

D) Cannot be determined based on the data given

247. Select correct description about Macaulay duration (　　).

A) there's positive relation between coupon rate and Macaulay duration

B) there's no relation between yield-to-maturity and Macaulay duration

C) there's inverse relation between Macaulay duration and yield-to-maturity.

D) The Macaulay duration of a zero-coupon bond is not equal to its time-to-maturity.

248. What is the impact of embedded put option if there's no change in the credit risk of a bond, if interest rate increase? (　　)

A) Effective duration of the bond will be reduced.

B) Effective duration of the bond will be increased.
C) No change to effective during of the bond.
D) Uncertain.

249. Calculate the bond portfolio's modified duration. (　　)

Bond	Maturity	Market Value	Price	Coupon	Yield-to-Maturity	Modified Duration
X	5 years	100,000	85.0000	2.00%	4%	6.42
Y	10 years	200,000	80.0000	2.40%	5%	9.44
Z	15 years	300,000	100.0000	5.00%	6%	11.38

A) 8.62.
B) 7.08.
C) 9.20.
D) 9.91

250. What is the assumption when calculating a bond portfolio's duration as the weighted average of the yield durations of the individual bonds? (　　)
A) Parallel shift to the yield curve.
B) Yield curve is steeply sloped.
C) Yield curve is flat.
D) Bonds with embedded options.

251. According to the pure expectation hypothesis, which of the following statements is correct concerning the expectations of market participants in an upward-sloping yield curve environment? (　　)
A) Interest rates will increase and the yield curve will flatten.
B) Interest rates will increase and the yield curve will steepen.
C) Interest rates will decrease and the yield curve will flatten.
D) Interest rates will decrease and the yield curve will steepen.

252. Calculate money duration per 100 of par value assuming annual coupon payments and no accrued interest.
- Time-to-Maturity 6 years.
- Price Per 100 of Par Value 95.00.
- Coupon Rate 2.00%.
- Yield-to-Modified 6.95%.
- Maturity Duration 5.22.

A) 460.70
B) 575.20
C) 660.88
D) 495.90

253. A bond with exactly nine years remaining until maturity offers a 3% coupon rate with annual coupons. The bond, with a yield-to-maturity of 5%, is priced at 85.784357 per 100 of par value. The estimated price value of a basis point for the bond is closest to (　　).
A) 0.0086
B) 0.0648
C) 0.1295
D) 0.1873

254. If market discount rate decreases by 100 basis points, a bond's price is expected to increase by 6%. If the bond's market discount rate increases by 100 basis points, what will be the change of bond price? (　　)
A) 6%
B) less than 6%
C) more than 6%
D) uncertain

255. Which of the following explain the "second-order" effect on a bond's percentage price change if there's a change in yield-to-maturity (　　).
A) effective duration
B) modified duration.
C) convexity.
D) yield volatility.

256. Calculate bond convexity. (　　).
- Currently trading for 98 per 100 of par value.
- If YTM goes up by 100 basis points, price will fall to 97
- If YTM goes down by 100 basis points, price will raise to 100

A) 1.02
B) 102
C) 102,040
D) 10.2

257. A bond has an annual modified duration of 7.020 and annual convexity of 65.180.

If the bond's yield-to-maturity decreases by 25 basis points, the expected percentage price change is closest to (　　).

A) 1.73%

B) 1.76%

C) 1.78%

D) 1.81

258. A bond has an annual modified duration of 7.140 and annual convexity of 66.200. The bond's yield-to-maturity is expected to increase by 50 basis points. The expected percentage price change is closest to (　　).

A) −3.40%

B) −3.49%

C) −3.57%

D) −3.68%

259. If the term structure of yield volatility is downward sloping, what will happen to yield volatility? (　　)

A) short-term bonds price will fluctuate more than long-term bonds.

B) long-term rates are lower than short-term rates.

C) rates are not relevant to terms.

D) short-term yields are less stable than long-term yields.

260. If a bond's coupon reinvestment risk could offset the market price risk, which of the following can explain the holding period? (　　)

A) Effective duration

B) duration gap.

C) modified duration.

D) Macaulay duration.

261. What will happen if investment horizon is shorter than the Macaulay duration of the bond? (　　)

A) Interest rate risk can be hedged

B) Reinvestment risk is higher due to the risk of lower rates.

C) Market price risk is higher due to the risk of higher rates.

D) Uncertain

262. Calculate duration gap. (　　)

- An annual coupon bond with a 8% coupon rate and exactly 20 years remaining until maturity at a price equal to par value.

- The investment horizon is eight years.
- The modified duration of the bond is 12. 5 years.

A) 5. 5

B) −7. 8

C) 3. 5

D) 4. 2

263. Select CORRECT description about duration of a bond. (　　)

A) How sensitive the value of the bond is relative to an interest rate change

B) Maturity of a bond portfolio calculated by weighted average

C) How sensitive the value of the bond is relative to maturity change

D) How sensitive the value of the bond is relative to a change in the value of market portfolio

264. A 12-year, 5 percent semiannual coupon bond with \$100 par value currently yields 8. 00 percent. What is the duration of the bond given a 100 basis increase and decrease in yield? (　　)

A) 12. 56

B) 8. 38

C) 16. 78

D) 7. 80

265. Immunization is the process of offsetting the effects of interest-rate changes on the value of assets and liabilities. Coverage of liabilities with significant convexity may be more effectively matched with a (　　).

A) mortgage portfolio, especially in a highly volatile rate environment

B) barbell portfolio with positive convexity

C) bullet portfolio withe little convexity

D) callable bond portfolio, especially in a declining-rate environment

266. With any other factors remaining unchanged, which of the following statements regarding bonds is not valid? (　　)

A) The price of a callable bond increases when interest rates increase.

B) Issuance of a callable bond is equivalent to a short position in a straight bond plus a long call option on the bond price.

C) The put feature in a puttable bond lowers its yield compared with the yield of an equivalent straight bond.

D) The price of an inverse floater decreases as interest rates increase.

267. Which of the following statements is correct regarding the effects of interest rate shift on fixed-income portfolios with similar durations? (　　)

A) A barbell portfolio has greater convexity than a bullet portfolio because convexity increases linearly with maturity.

B) A barbell portfolio has greater convexity than a bullet portfolio because convexity increases with the square of maturity.

C) A barbell portfolio has lower convexity than a bullet portfolio because convexity increases linearly with maturity.

D) A barbell portfolio has lower convexity than a bullet portfolio because convexity increases with the square of maturity.

268. Calculate bond price change percentage for 50 bp rate change. (　　)

- A bond with 15-year maturity is currently priced at \$905 to yield 9.5%.
- Coupon rate is 8% and paid semi-annually.
- If the yield declines to 9%, the bond's price will increase to \$935.
- If the yield increases to 10%, the bond's price will decrease to \$875.

A) 1.13%

B) 6.35%

C) 7.41%

D) 6.63%

269. Select one CORRECT description about negative convexity (　　).

A) As interest rates fall, there's larger increase of the bond's price.

B) As interest rates rise, the bond's price becomes lowest.

C) As interest rates fall, the bond's price increases slower.

D) As interest rates rise, the bond's price decreases lower.

270. From the time of issuance until the bond matures, which of the following bonds is most likely to exhibit negative convexity? (　　)

A) a puttable bond

B) a callable bond

C) an option-free bond selling at a discount

D) a zero-coupon bond

271. Which of following bonds might demonstrate negative convexity? (　　)

A) zero coupon bonds

B) treasury bonds

C) municipal bonds

D) callable bonds

272. Effective duration is more suitable than modified duration except for (　　).

A) option-free bond

B) puttable bond

C) callable bond

D) convertible bond

273. Which of following bonds has the greatest convexity assuming the same yield? (　　)

A) 5% coupon bond of 10-year duration

B) 10-year zero-coupon bond

C) callable 6% coupon bond of 10-year duration

D) uncertain

274. Which of the following statements about a puttable bond and a callable bond is correct? (　　)

A) The put option of a puttable bond is more expensive than the call option of the callable bond.

B) A puttable bond will have a lower yield than a comparable callable bond.

C) The value of a callable bond increases when interest rate volatility increases.

D) Long position in a puttable bond has more interest rate risk than a long position in a callable bond.

275. Select one FALSE description about portfolio duration. (　　)

A) Portfolio duration is the weighted average of the asset duration in the portfolio.

B) Market prices of the bonds can be used to measure portfolio duration.

C) Portfolio duration is calculated as a simple average of the asset duration.

D) Portfolio duration can be used to measure interest rate risk.

276. Consider the following portfolio of bonds (par amounts are in millions of USD).

Bond	Price	Par Amount Held	Modified Duration
A	101.43	3	2.36
B	84.89	5	4.13
C	121.87	8	6.27

What is the value of the portfolio's DV01 (dollar value of 1 basis point)? (　　)

A) \$8,019

B) \$8,294

C) \$8,584

D) \$8,813

277. An investor has a short position in a 20-year 5% coupon, U.S Treasury bond (T-bond) with a yield to maturity YTM) of 6% and par value of \$100. Assume discounting occurs on a semiannual basis. Which of the following amounts is closest to the dollar value of a basis point (DV01)? ( )

A) 0.1053

B) 0.1061

C) 0.1351

D) 0.1360

278. A portfolio consists of two zero coupon bonds, each with a current value of \$10. The first bond has a modified duration of one year and the second has a modified duration of nine years. The yield curve is flat, and all yields are 5%. Assume all moves of the yield curve are parallel shifts. Given that the daily volatility of the yield is 1%, which of the following is the best estimate of the portfolio daily VAR at the 95% confidence level? ( )

A) USD 1.65

B) USD 2.33

C) USD 1.16

D) USD 0.82

279. If yield to maturity decrease, what will happen? ( )

- Bond X sells at par, annual coupon payment is \$100, will mature in 5 years
- Bond Y sells at par, annual coupon payment is \$100, will mature in 6 years

A) Bond A will decrease more than bond B.

B) Bond B will decrease more than bond A.

C) Bond B will increase more than bond A.

D) Bond A will increase more than bond B.

280. Which investment market has more concerns about interest rate risk? ( )

A) Fixed income

B) Futures

C) Commodity

D) Equity

281. Which of the following statements is/are true? ( )

Ⅰ. The convexity of a 10-year zero-coupon bond is higher than the convexity of a 10-year 6% bond.

Ⅱ. The convexity of a 10-year zero-coupon bond is higher than the convexity of a 6% bond with a duration of 10 years.

Ⅲ. Convexity grows proportionately with the maturity of the bond.

Ⅳ. Convexity is always positive for all types of bonds.

Ⅴ. Convexity is always positive for straight bonds.

A) Ⅰ only

B) Ⅰ and Ⅱ only

C) Ⅰ and Ⅴ only

D) Ⅱ, Ⅲ, and Ⅴ only

282. If all spot interest rates are increased by one basis point, a value of a portfolio of swaps will increase by $1,100. How many Eurodollar futures contracts are needed to hedge the portfolio? (　　)

A) 44

B) 22

C) 11

D) 1,100

283. On June 2, a fund manager with USD 10 million invested in government bonds is concerned that interest rates will be highly volatile over the next three months. The manager decides to use the September Treasury bond futures contract to hedge the portfolio. The current futures price is USD 95.0625. Each contract is for the delivery of USD 100,000 face value of bonds. The duration of the manager's bond portfolio in three months will be 7.8 years. The cheapest-to-deliver (CTD) bond in the Treasury bond futures contract is expected to have a duration of 8.4 years at maturity of the contract. At the maturity of the Treasury bond futures contract, the duration of the underlying benchmark Treasury bond is nine years. What position should the fund manager undertake to mitigate his interest rate risk exposure? (　　)

A) Short 94 contracts

B) Short 98 contracts

C) Short 105 contracts

D) Short 113 contracts

284. Albert Henri is the fixed income manager of a large Canadian pension fund. The present value of the pension fund's portfolio of assets is CAD 4 billion while the expected present value of the fund's liabilities is CAD 5 billion. The respective modified durations are 8.254 and 6.825 years. The fund currently has an actuarial deficit (assets＜liabilities) and Albert must avoid widening this gap. There are currently two scenarios for the yield curve: The first scenario is an upward shift of 25bp, with the second scenario a downward shift of 25bp. The most liquid interest rate futures contract has a present value of CAD 68,336 and a duration of 2.1468 years. Analyzing both scenarios separately, what should Albert Henri do to avoid widening the pension fund gap? Choose the best option. (　　)

	First Scenario	Second Scenario
A)	Do nothing.	Buy 7,559 contracts.
B)	Do nothing.	Sell 7,559 contracts.
C)	Buy 7,559 contracts.	Do nothing.
D)	Do nothing.	Do nothing.

285. Which statement is correct about convexity? (　　)

A) Convexity is critical when rates are unstable.

B) Convexity is critical when rates are low.

C) Convexity is critical depending on selling at a premium or a discount.

D) Convexity is critical when rates are high.

286. Why does non-callable bond prices go up faster than they go down? (　　)

A) positive convexity

B) negative convexity

C) embedded benefits

D) inverse features

287. A 12-year, 8 percent annual coupon bond with $100 par value currently sells at par. The bond is callable at 102. What is the effective duration of the bond assuming interest rates change by 100 basis points? (　　)

A) 5.85

B) 10.50

C) 4.58

D) 7.55

288. For an option-free bond, what will happen if there's large change of interest-rate? (　　)

A) The duration measure will overestimate bond's price increase from a given increases in interest rates.

B) The duration measure will overestimate the change in the bond's rating.

C) The duration measure will overestimate bond's price decrease from a given increase in interest rates.

D) No impact to duration measure.

289. Which of the following bonds may have negative convexity? (　　)

A) High yield bonds.
B) Callable bonds.
C) Mortgage backed securities.
D) All of these choices are correct.

290. When (in what situation) is convexity adjustment required? (　　)
A) The non-linearity of the slope of the price yield curve.
B) To measure non-callable bonds volatility.
C) To calculate optimal hedge ratio.
D) The backward bending of the slope of the callable bond price/yield curve.

291. A portfolio manager has a bond position worth USD 100 million. The position has a modified duration of eight years and a convexity of 150 years. Assume that the term structure is flat. By how much does the value of the position change if interest rates increase by 25 basis points? (　　)
A) USD −2,046,875
B) USD −2,187,500
C) USD −1,953,125
D) USD −1,906,250

292. What is the price-yield relationship for callable bond and option-free bond? (　　)
A) concave for low yields for the callable bond
B) always concave for the callable bond
C) concave for an option-free bond
D) always same

293. The price value of a basis point (PVBP) for a 18 year, 8 percent annual pay bond with a par value of $1,000 and yield of 9 percent is closest to (　　).
A) $0.82
B) $0.63
C) $0.80
D) $0.4

294. Select one CORRECT description about bond convexity. (　　)
A) Convexity positively relate to yield change.
B) Increase with the square of maturity.
C) Convexity is not relevant to coupon rate.
D) Convexity is the first derivative of price with respect to yield.

295. Which of the following can measure interest-rate risk? (　　)

A) duration

B) yield

C) maturity

D) coupon

296. Select one CORRECT description about positive convexity. (　　)

A) When yields drop, the price increase will be larger than price drop when yields rise by the same amount.

B) No matter yield increases or decreases, price changes are the same.

C) Yield change and price change are positively related.

D) Price change are quicker than yield change.

297. Which description is correct for the convexity of a U.S Treasury bond? (　　)

A) negative

B) positive

C) additional information is required

D) zero

298. For a given change in yields, the difference between the actual change in a bond's price and that predicted using the duration measure will be greater for (　　).

A) a bond with less convexity

B) a bond with greater convexity

C) inverse convexity

D) a short-term bond

299. If the yield of one bond goes up by 1 bps and the bond's price value of a basis point (PVBP) is \$0.60, the price of the bond will (　　).

A) go down by \$0.60

B) go up by \$0.60

C) no change

D) uncertain

300. A bond is selling at \$100 par value, which pays 8% coupon annually and matures in 10 years, calculate bond convexity. (　　)

A) 60.0

B) 92.0

C) 100.0

D) 102.0

301. Investors may benefit from convexity because ( ).

A) high convexity bond is more sensitive to interest rate changes than low convexity bond.

B) high convexity bond has better price changes no matter which direction the yield changes.

C) low convexity bond is usually overpriced.

D) the estimation for high convexity bond is more accurate.

302. Select one FALSE description about positive convexity. ( )

A) Changes in yield have a larger effect on bond prices when yields increase.

B) Changes in yield have a smaller effect on bond prices when yields increase.

C) Changes in yield have a larger effect on bond prices when yields decrease.

D) The level of market yields is inversely related to non-callable bonds price volatility.

303. For one basis point change in yield, the dollar value of bond will be ( ).

A) greater for a yield decrease

B) greater for a yield increase

C) equal for a yield change

D) not relevant

The following information is used by the next three questions.

A 10-year maturity Treasury bond has a par value of $10,000 and a 5 percent coupon. The yield on the bond is 4.5 percent. Assume that the yield can fall to 4.45 percent of rise to 4.55 percent.

304. The effective duration for the bond is closest to ( ).

A) 7.24

B) 7.86

C) 8.07

D) 7.61

305. The effective convexity of the bond is closest to ( ).

A) 57.69

B) 38.46

C) 76.93

D) 19.23

306. Given your answers to the two prior questions, the percentage price change

associated with a 20-baisi-point increase in yield is closest to a (   ).

A) decrease of 1.58%

B) decrease of 1.54%

C) decrease of 1.56%

D) decrease of 1.60%

307. Which of the following would not cause an upward-sloping yield curve? (   )

A) an investor preference for short-term instruments

B) an expected decline in interest rates

C) an improving credit risk outlook

D) an expected increase in the inflation rate

308. What assumptions does a duration-based hedging scheme make about the way in which interest rates move? (   )

A) All interest rates change by the same amount.

B) A small parallel shift occurs in the yield curve.

C) Any parallel shift occurs in the term structure.

D) Interest rates' movements are highly correlated.

309. Select one CORRECT description about positive convexity. (   )

A) For a given change in market yields, bond price sensitivity is lowest when market yields are high and highest when market yields are low.

B) For a given change in market yields, bond price sensitivity is highest when market yields are high and lowest when market yields are low.

C) Changes in interest rates is inversely related to the price of a fixed-coupon bond.

D) None of the above.

310. A fixed-coupon bond portfolio has a face value of $120 million and a current market value of $116 million. Suppose the interest rates are going to change by 100 basis points, the portfolio's value will increase to $118 million if interest rates fall and will decrease to $114 million if interest rates rise. Calculate the portfolio's effective duration. (   )

A) 4.4

B) 3.4

C) 0.5

D) 1.7

311. How to determine key rate duration? (   )

A) Parallel shift the yield curve.

B) Linearly shift the yield curve.
C) Change the yield of a specific maturity.
D) Change the curvature of the yield curve.

312. To model the term structure of interest rates with key rate shifts, the 1-year, 7-year, and 20-year yields have been selected. If the 7-year yield increases by 20 bps, which is the impact to 10-year yield? (　　)
A) 4. 6 basis points increase
B) 10 basis point increase
C) 15. 4 basis point increase
D) 5 basis points increase

313. For a security with a 2-year key rate exposure of $2. 78, how to hedge this position with a security that has a 2 year key rate exposure of 1. 67 per $100 of face value? (　　)
A) Face value should be $166.
B) Face value should be $60.
C) Face value should be $278.
D) Face value should be $339.

314. Select one INCORRECT description about the key rate shift approach in analyzing nonparallel shifts of yield curve. (　　)
A) In reality, shifts are not always perfectly linear.
B) Key rate shift makes very strong assumptions about how the term structure behaves.
C) The important information to be collected from these calculations is the bond's pricesensitivity to shifts in each key rate.
D) Key rates are mostly affected by the few rates closest to it.

315. Select one correct description about key rate shifts and bucket shifts. (　　)
A) Many potential effects within a region of the yield curve will be required by the key rate shift approach.
B) Parallel changes in the forward rates of yield curve is required by the bucket shift approach.
C) Swaps portfolio prefers the key rate shift approach.
D) The key rate shift approach assumes no changes in rates.

316. What is the definition of forward bucket 01s? (　　)
A) To shift the forward rate of the term structure over each region.

B) To expand key rates along the yield curve.
C) To calculate the lump sum of asset value changes.
D) To fit the swap rates to the yield curve.

317. Which can manage the interest rate risk of a swaps portfolio? (　　)
A) bucket shift
B) key rate shift
C) effective duration
D) key rate duration

318. Assume only one interest rate on the yield curve changes for a portfolio of bonds, how to calculate the change of bond portfolio value? (　　)
A) Multiply the rate change by the specific key rate duration for rate that changed.
B) Multiply the rate change by simple average of the key rate durations.
C) Multiply the rate change by median of the key rate durations.
D) Multiply the rate change by weighted average of the key rate durations.

319. Select one correct description about key rate and bucket analysis. (　　)
A) More interest rate factors are required by key rate.
B) Parallel change of forward rates is required by bucket analysis.
C) The key rate shift approach assumes no changes in rates.
D) Bucket technique required fewer inputs and correlations.

320. Select one correct description about key rate shifts and bucket shift approaches. (　　)
A) Parallel changes in forward rates of the yield curve is required by bucket shift approach.
B) Key rate shifts assume no change in key rates.
C) Key rate shifts require a large of number of key rates for analysis.
D) Non-Parallel changes in forward rates of the yield curve is required by bucket shift approach.

321. To model the term structure of interest rates, key rates of the 1-year, 5-year, and 10-year yields have been selected by investor. For one 3-year bond, there will be impacts by key rate changes of (　　).
A) 1-year and 5-year
B) 5-year and 10-year
C) 5-year
D) 10-year

第 17 单元

信用风险和操作风险

322. Which of the following statement is correct about sovereign default in foreign currency debt? (　　)
    A) Countries are less likely to default on funds borrowed from banks than on sovereign bond issues.
    B) Over the past hundreds of years, there have been few instances of default.
    C) A large proportion of sovereign defaults are foreign currency defaults.
    D) Eastern Europe has the most sovereign defaults in the last 50 years.

323. During 2002, an Argentinean pension fund with 80% of its assets in dollar-denominated debt lost more than 40% of its value. Which of the following reasons could explain all of the 40% loss? (　　)
    A) The assets were invested in a diversified portfolio of AAA firms in the United States.
    B) The assets invested in local currency in Argentina lost all of their value, while the value of the dollar-denominated assets stayed constant.
    C) The dollar-denominated assets were invested in U. S. Treasury debt, but the fund had bought credit protection on sovereign debt from Argentina.)
    D) The fund had invested 80% of its funds in dollar-denominated sovereign debt from Argentina.

324. An investment analyst is required to research and report on the factors that influence the level of sovereign default risk. Which of the following statements is true? (　　)
    A) Countries with more pension commitments and health care commitments are less likely to default.
    B) The amount the country owes its own citizens is very important for evaluating default risk.
    C) A country is less capable to make debt payments if greater tax are collected.
    D) Countries with less diversified economies are more capable of stable tax receipts.

325. Which of the following statements is true a country's risk exposure? (　　)

A) Continuous versus discontinuous risks is one component of political risk.

B) Too much reliance on a single commodity or service in an economy will decrease a country's risk exposure, when considering economic structure.

C) The protection of property rights do not affect default risk, when regarding legal risks.

D) Mature companies are riskier than firms in the early stages of growth, based on economic growth life cycle.

326. Which is not true about the consequences of sovereign default? (　　)

A) After a sovereign default, gross domestic product (GDP) growth will falls between 0.5% and 2.0% and it will be recovered in a short time.

B) Trade war will happen after a sovereign default.

C) Ratings of countries that have defaulted are usually one grades lower than the ratings of similar countries that have not defaulted.

D) After a sovereign default, Currency devaluation often happen.

327. Traders may use sovereign default risk spread as a predictor of defaults. What is true about the advantages of this strategy? (　　)

A) Default risk spreads are more reliable since they are not volatile.

B) Calculating A default risk spread does no require a risk-free rate.

C) Default risk spreads change can provide information about the market's view to the risk of bonds.

D) Traders can compare local currency bonds with each other more timely.

328. What is true about an at-the-point approach? It tends to be (　　).

A) more counter-cyclical

B) more pro-cyclical

C) both counter-nor pro-cyclical

D) neither counter-nor pro-cyclical

329. What is true about the relationship between a firm's bond rating and stock price? (　　)

A) A bond downgrade will raise stock price, while an upgrade will lower stock price.

B) A bond downgrade will lower stock price; while an upgrade has little or no impact on stock price.

C) A bond downgrade will have little impact on the stock price; while an upgrade produces will raise stock price.

D) Bond downgrades and upgrades are both having little impact on stock price.

330. A company has a credit rating of B1. Which rating agency gives this kind of rating? (　　)

A) World Bank.

B) Standard & Poors.

C) Fitch.

D) Moody's.

331. Banks may use internal ratings for credit risk management. Internal ratings by banks tend to (　　).

A) lead the economic cycle

B) coincide with the economic cycle

C) lag behind the economic cycle

D) be unrelated to the economic cycle

332. Six months ago, an investor purchased a bond that was rated BB. Today the bond is upgraded to a BBB rating. The *most likely* effect of this upgrade is (　　).

A) increased call risk

B) an increase in yield to maturity

C) a higher spot price

D) increased liquidity risk

333. What rating downgrade means falling from an investment grade to a non-investment grade, in the Moody's bond rating system? (　　)

A) A3 to Baa1.

B) Baa1 to Baa3.

C) Baa3 to Ba1.

D) Caa to D.

334. Regarding bond ratings, which of the following statements is **TRUE**? (　　)

A) Bond ratings are given by biggest market participants.

B) If an issuer fails to make interest or principal payments as scheduled in the indenture, it's called "technical default".

C) If a bond issuer defaults, the bondholders will lose all of his/her investment.

D) When downgraded by a rating agency, a bond's price usually falls.

335. What is correct about the impact of ratings change? (　　)

A) More significant for stock prices than it is for bond prices.

B) More significant for bond prices than it is for stock prices.

C) Neither significant for bond nor for stock prices.

D) Equally significant for both bond and stock prices.

336. What is the highest speculative grade rating in the following ratings? (　　)

A) A

B) Baa

C) Ba

D) B

337. What is the lowest investment grade in Moody's credit rating scheme? (　　)

A) Aa

B) A

C) Baa

D) Ba

338. In the S&P credit rating scheme, the least risky speculative investment rating is (　　).

A) AAA

B) Aaa

C) Baa

D) BB

339. Which of the following ratings is investment grade in S&P's credit rating scheme? (　　)

A) BBB

B) BB

C) B

D) CCC

340. What is the relationship between external ratings and default probability? (　　)

A) Higher-rated firms do have higher default rates.

B) Lower-rated firms do have higher default rates.

C) Firms with lower ratings do have lower probability of downgrade in the future.

D) No significant relationship exists.

341. Which internal rating credit systems is more likely to be procyclical? (　　)

A) At-the-point approach.

B) Through-the-cycle approach.

C) Both of the approaches.

D) Neither of the approaches.

342. Which of the following internal rating credit systems is suitable for long time

horizons (more than one year)? ( )

A) At-the-point approach.

B) Through-the-cycle approach.

C) Both of the approaches.

D) Neither of the approaches.

343. Which of the following is true about the horizons of through-the-cycle and at-the-point approaches of rating bonds? ( )

A) Typically, through-the-cycle approaches have longer horizons.

B) Typically, at-the-point approaches have longer horizons.

C) There is little relationship between the horizons of through-the cycle and at-the-point approaches.

D) The horizons of through-the cycle and at-the-point approaches are equal.

344. Which of the following statements is most likely to be true about loan losses and economic capital? ( )

A) Unexpected loss > economic capital.

B) Expected loss > economic capital.

C) Economic capital > unexpected loss.

D) Economic capital = expected loss.

345. You are considering an investment in one of three different bonds. Your investment guidelines require that any bond you invest in carry an investment grade rating from at least two recognized bond rating agencies. Which, if any, of the bonds listed below would meet your investment guidelines? ( )

A) Bond A carries an S&P rating of BB and a Moody's rating of Baa.

B) Bond B carries an S&P rating of BBB and a Moody's rating of Ba.

C) Bond C carries an S&P rating of BBB and a Moody's rating of Baa.

D) None of the above.

346. If there's rating upgrade for one company, what factor will lead to price increase of its fixed-rate bond? ( )

A) liquidity spread increase

B) credit spread decrease

C) credit spread increase

D) benchmark rate increase

347. Given the following ratings transition matrix, calculate the two-period cumulative probability of default for a 'B' credit. ( )

Beginning Rating	End Rating			
	A	B	C	D
A	0.95	0.05	0.00	0.00
B	0.03	0.90	0.05	0.02
C	0.01	0.10	0.75	0.14
Default	0.00	0.00	0.00	1.00

A) 2.0%
B) 2.5%
C) 4.0%
D) 4.5%

348. Bank AAA has an adjusted exposure of \$15 million, a probability of default of 2%, and a recovery rate of 20%. What is the expected loss for Bank AAA? (　　)

A) \$240,000
B) \$60,000
C) \$300,000
D) \$3,000,000

349. What is the definition of unexpected loss? It is (　　).

A) actual losses less than expected losses
B) expected losses exceeding actual losses
C) expected losses less than actual losses
D) actual losses exceeding expected losses

350. How to calculate Expected Loss? (　　)

A) Exposure × Recovery rate × Probability of default.
B) Exposure × (1 − Recovery rate) × Probability of default
C) Exposure × (1 − Loss give default) × (1 − Probability of default).
D) Exposure × Loss given default × (1 − Probability of default).

351. Which of the following pairs represent the correct effects on expected loss from increasing both loss given default (LGD) and draw down? (　　)

	LGD	Draw down
A)	Increase	Increase
B)	No effect	Increase
C)	Increase	No effect
D)	No effect	No effect

352. What is the impact of decreasing the recovery rate to the unexpected loss? (　　)

A) Increase the unexpected loss.

B) Decrease the unexpected loss.

C) No influence to the unexpected loss.

D) Either increase or decrease the unexpected loss, based on the type of assets.

353. Please compute the loss given default and recovery rate, based on the following information: (1) Expected loss = \$200,000. (2) Exposure = \$5,000,000. (3) Probability of loss = 5%. (　　)

	Loss given default	Recovery rate
A)	0.02	0.08
B)	0.08	0.02
C)	0.80	0.20
D)	0.20	0.80

354. If the adjusted exposure for Bank X is \$15 million, the probability of default is 2%, the recovery rate is 20%, and the standard deviation of EDF and LGD is 5% and 3%, respectively. What is the unexpected loss for Bank X? (　　)

A) \$240,000

B) \$603,366

C) \$24,270

D) \$302,242

355. A loan portfolio is made up of ten noncorrelated loans, each with a value of \$1 million and an estimated probability of default of 3% in any given year. Recovery in the case of default is expected to be zero. Which of the following amounts is closest to the cumulative expected loss on the loan portfolio over two years? (　　)

A) \$0.03 million

B) \$0.059 million

C) \$0.30 million

D) \$0.591 million

356. As the number of assets in an equally-weighted portfolio increases, the contribution of each individual asset's variance to the volatility of the portfolio (　　).

A) increases

B) decreases

C) remains the same

D) cannot judge

357. With respect to an equally-weighted portfolio made up of a large number of assets, which of the following contributes the most to the volatility of the portfolio? ( )

A) Average variance of the individual assets.

B) Standard deviation of the individual assets.

C) Average covariance between all pairs of assets.

D) Correlation between individual assets and the whole portfolio.

358. What is unexpected loss? It is ( ).

A) variance of expected loss

B) variance of unanticipated loss

C) standard deviation of expected loss

D) standard deviation of unanticipated loss

359. What capital is used to buffer unexpected losses for a bank? ( )

A) regulatory capital

B) unexpected capital

C) economical capital

D) risk-adjusted capital

360. For given loan portfolio, which of the following will unambiguously increase expected loss? ( )

A) Increase recovery rate and increase probability of default.

B) Increase recovery rate and decrease probability of default.

C) Decrease recovery rate and increase probability of default.

D) Decrease recovery rate and decrease probability of default.

361. Which of the following may NOT increase expected loss? ( )

A) Decrease recovery rate and decrease probability of default.

B) Decrease recovery rate and increase probability of default.

C) Increase recovery rate and decrease probability of default.

D) Increase recovery rate and increase probability of default.

362. Identify the effect of increasing LGD on expected loss. ( )

A) Increase.

B) LGD is not a component of expected loss.

C) No effect.

D) Decrease.

363. In comparison to the bottom-up approach to measuring operational risk exposure, the top-down approach would be most appropriate for which of the following? (　　)

A) determining firm-wide economic capital levels.

B) designing risk reduction techniques at the business-unit level.

C) diagnosing specific weak points in a process.

D) incorporating changes in the risk environment.

364. It is very important to accumulate loss data for a financial institution. Which of the following is least likely a reason for accumulating? (　　)

A) It can help to the understanding of future expected loses.

B) It can provide necessary data for empirical analysis.

C) Past losses are almost always repeated in the future.

D) It can help management to pay attention to the magnitude and effect or risk.

365. Which of the following is/are characteristic of self-insurance as a means to hedge against catastrophic and operational losses? (　　)

Ⅰ. Using captive insurers has tax benefits associated with self-insurance.

Ⅱ. Exercising risk prevention and control is a form of self-insurance.

Ⅲ. Establishing a contingent line of credit that becomes available in the event of a large operational loss is one method of self-insurance.

A) Ⅰ only

B) Ⅱ only

C) Ⅱ and Ⅲ only

D) Ⅰ, Ⅱ, and Ⅲ

366. One of the basic requirements of a risk control process that a risk and control self-assessment program (RCSA) fails in is the (　　).

A) expert opinion of managers

B) independent verification of risk identification and measurement

C) identification of expected losses

D) ongoing assessment of the effectiveness of risk management activities

367. Jennifer is evaluating operational risk and plans to model risk frequency. She can (　　).

A) use a Poisson distribution

B) assume risk frequency and severity are the same distribution

C) assume that risks are highly correlated

D) use most recent loss data to simulate

368. John Diamond is evaluating the existing risk management system of Rome Asset Management and identified the following two risks:

Ⅰ. Rome Asset Management's derivative pricing model consistently undervalues call options.

Ⅱ. Swaps with counterparties exceed counterparty credit limit.

These two risks are most likely to be classified as (   ).

A) market

B) credit

C) liquidity

D) operational

369. Canadian Bank Inc. (CBI) has the following annual gross income amounts in its business lines over its most recent three years.

	Retail banking	Commercial banking	Investment banking:
2009	\$380 million	\$712 million	\$846 million
2008	\$344 million	\$645 million	\$777 million
2007	\$326 million	\$599 million	\$687 million

Using the standardized approach, which of the following amounts represents CBI's operational risk capital requirement for 2010? (   )

A) \$253.2 million.

B) \$265.8 million.

C) \$274.9 million.

D) \$278.4 million.

370. Your supervisor is an expert in market and credit risk. He recruits you to manage the operational risk department. He would like to use VaR to measure the firm's operational risk and proposes that you use the same VaR framework previously developed for market and credit risk. Which of the following arguments is a valid argument for why it is difficult to estimate an operational VaR using the same framework as market and credit VaR? (   )

A) Market risk events are easier to map to risk factors than operational risk events.

B) Quantitative methods for estimating operational risk VaR do not exist.

C) Market and credit VaRs are estimated using only frequency distribution, but operational VaR is estimated using both a frequency distribution and a severity distribution.

D) Monte Carlo techniques cannot be used for an operational risk VaR because the underlying risk factors are not normally distributed.

371. Which of the following is least likely to be true about scorecard data? (   )

A) It is forward looking rather than backward looking.

B) It is more subjective because it relies upon the judgment of business line managers.

C) It usually results in higher capital charges than the use of historical data.

D) It more accurately captures the future benefits of risk management activities.

372. Which of the followings is the source of scorecards? (　　)

A) Internal loss databases.

B) External loss databases.

C) Industry standards and guidelines.

D) Surveys of the managers of the various business lines.

第 18 单元

压力测试

373. Which of the following statements is most likely correct about the key aspects of stress testing governance? (　　)

A) Stress testing coverage can be applied to entire institution, or sublevels within an institution, or individual exposures.

B) Stress testing coverage must be applied on a long-term basis.

C) Stress testing should detect risk concentrations and find causes of risk that could positively impact the institution.

D) Stress testing results must include important factors, including portfolios, liabilities, and exposures.

374. Which of the following statements is true about senior management, when discussing the responsibilities of the board of directors and senior management in stress testing activities? The management (　　).

A) members should be actively challenging assumptions of stress tests

B) should establish robust policies and procedures to ensure compliance with stress testing these activities, reviewing and coordinating stress test activities, and remedying, and issues

C) should have enough stress testing knowledge to ask informed questions

D) oversight an organization's key strategies and decisions for the entire organization

375. Regarding the key elements of effective governance and controls over stress testing, which of the following statements is most likely incorrect? (　　)

A) Key elements of effective governance and controls over stress testing include the governance structure, policies and procedures, documentation, validation and independent review, and internal audit.

B) Effective governance and controls are critical to ensuring that stress tests are conducted appropriately under adequate oversight.

C) Oversight should be tailored according to the complexity and characteristics of the specific institution.

D) Proper governance and controls are especially important for stress tests that are qualitative or require only a small number of assumptions.

376. Prudent governance should also incorporate ongoing validation and independent review of stress testing activities. Which is incorrect about the ways to tackle challenges with model validation? (　　)

A) expert-based judgment

B) sensitivity analysis and simulation techniques

C) putting greater emphasis on ensuring that stress tests remain sound

D) benchmarking to the S&P 500 Index

377. Regarding the internal audit's role, which of the following statements is most likely incorrect? The internal audit (　　).

A) has the right to assess the integrity and reliability of an institution's policies and procedures, including those related to stress tests

B) is not required to have sufficient knowledge and technical expertise to review, because they can depend on other business departments

C) should review the procedures related to the documentation, review, and approval of stress tests

D) should verify that stress tests are conducted thoroughly and as planned, and that the staff in charge has necessary expertise and follows the appropriate policies and procedures

378. Which of the following statements about stress testing are true? (　　)

Ⅰ. Stress testing can complement VAR estimation in helping risk managers identify crucial vulnerabilities in a portfolio.

Ⅱ. Stress testing allows users to include scenarios that did not occur in the lookback horizon of the VAR data but are nonetheless possible.

Ⅲ. A drawback of stress testing is that it is highly subjective.

Ⅳ. The inclusion of a large number of scenarios helps management better understand the risk exposure of a portfolio.

A) Ⅰ and Ⅱ only

B) Ⅲ and Ⅳ only

C) Ⅰ, Ⅱ, and Ⅲ only

D) Ⅰ, Ⅱ, Ⅲ, and Ⅳ

379. Which of the following would least likely be used in a stress test? (　　)

A) Monte Carlo simulations to generate extreme values.

B) Tail values(1%) of factors.

C) Market values and relationships observed during the 07-09 Financial Crisis.

D) 99% VaR where kurtosis is three and skewness is zero.

380. Sandy is a risk manager of Venus Fund. He estimated that the weekly value at risk (VAR) for an \$80 million equity portfolio of Venus Fund is \$1.02 million (at the 95% confidence level). How to understand this VAR measurement? (　　)

A) Increasing the time period used in the calculation will not increase the VAR.

B) During extreme market time, losses could be much greater than \$1.02 million.

C) The interpretation of the VAR measure is different for different asset categories.

D) The measure is backward looking.

381. Stress testing is usually viewed as an intuitive risk management tool. What can be a possible reason for this viewpoint? (　　)

A) Business line managers have expectation of major structural shifts, which is very helpful for estimating scenarios in stress time.

B) Scenario selection is mainly focus on recent historical data.

C) Correlation between underlying exposures is not very important in a scenario.

D) Scenarios are usually selected according to factors that would likely impact portfolio value.

382. Which of the following is not suitable for stress testing? (　　)

A) Yield curve twist of 50 basis points.

B) Treasury yield curve shift of 100 basis points.

C) Exchange rate depreciation of 10% between USD relative to GBP.

D) S&P 500 index drop of 2%.

383. Which of the following is **NOT** suitable for stress testing? (　　)

A) Stress testing can be used to complement value at risk (VAR).

B) Stress testing can help the risk manager to eliminate all risk from an investment.

C) Stress testing can reflect weaknesses in contingency planning and assumptions.

D) Stress testing can help allocating capital among business units.

384. Which of the following is true about stress testing? (　　)

Ⅰ. It is used to evaluate the potential impact on portfolio values of unlikely, although plausible, events or movements in a set of financial variables.

Ⅱ. It is a risk management tool that directly compares predicted results to observed actual results. Predicted values are also compared with historical data.

A) Statement Ⅰ is true

B) Statement Ⅱ is true

C) Both Ⅰ and Ⅱ are true.

D) Neither Ⅰ nor Ⅱ are true.

385. Although stress testing is an indispensable complementary method to VaR, it has several disadvantages. Which of the following does **NOT** correctly mention a disadvantage? Stress testing may ( ).

A) exclude the simultaneous adverse movements of risk factors

B) fail to recognize how does a change in one factor affect anothers

C) reflect normal circumstances more than abnormal ones

D) reflect unintentional or even intentional misspecification of the model

386. Which of the following methodologies would be most appropriate for stress-testing your portfolio? ( )

A) delta-gamma valuation

B) full revaluation

C) marking to market

D) delta-normal VAR

387. Manuela Burnett is studying how to use of stress testing properly. He writes several statements in his notebooks. Which of the statements *best* describes the uses of stress analysis? ( )

A) Stress analysis can be used to model hypothetical events that can happen once but not likely to recur.

B) Scenario analysis is a special case of stress analysis.

C) Comparing with VaR, stress analysis has the ability to forecast probability of rare but damaging events because it can highlighton unpractical assumptions.

D) Stress analysis can be used to enhance VAR analysis by focusing on the extent of loss in an extreme event.

388. John Flag, the manager of a $150 million distressed bond portfolio, conducts stress tests on the portfolio. The portfolio's annualized return is 12%, with an annualized return volatility of 25%. In the past two years, the portfolio encountered several days when the daily value change of the portfolio was more than 3 standard deviations. If the portfolio would suffer a 4-sigma daily event, estimate the change in the value of this portfolio. ( )

A) $9. 48 million

B) $23. 70 million

C) $37. 50 million

D) $150 million

389. Alexandra Lindsey is an expert of implementing stress testing. He is now reviewing a document written by a staff from Bank Wolfe. Alexandra picks up several statements from the document and plans to correct them. Which one(s) of these statements does(do) not to be corrected? (　　)

Ⅰ. Before 07-09 Crisis, stress testing methodology assumpts that risk is generated by unknown and non-stochastic processes.

Ⅱ. In a reverse testing, analysts shoulduse an outcome to identify likely events that may produce the outcome and evaluation of effectiveness of risk mitigating strategies to deal with the risk outcome.

Ⅲ. Basis risk is the difference between the cash market price and the futures marketprice(or interest rate).

Ⅳ. Contingent risk arises due to contractual agreements only.

A) Ⅰ, Ⅱ and Ⅲ

B) Ⅲ only

C) Ⅰ only

D) Ⅱ only

390. Bank AYA is planning to implement a stress test. Which of the following is *least likely* included in a stress test? (　　)

A) Choosing the market factors.

B) Choosing the time period over which the stress will take place.

C) Adjusting the correlations of risk factors.

D) Computing market value at risk.

391. Stress testing plans should take into consideration inter-correlations between (　　).

Ⅰ. reputational and liquidity risks.

Ⅱ. funding and market risk.

Ⅲ. market and securitization risks.

Ⅳ. basis and liquidity risks.

A) Ⅰ, Ⅱ and Ⅲ

B) Ⅰ and Ⅱ

C) Ⅰ only

D) Ⅰ, Ⅱ, Ⅲ and Ⅳ

392. An implementation principle recommended by the Basel Committee to banks for the governance of sound stress testing practices is that stress testing reports should (　　).

A) not be passed up to senior management without first being approved by middle management

B) have limited input from their respective business areas to prevent biasing of the results

C) challenge prior assumptions to help foster debate among decision makers

D) be separated by business lines to help identify risk concentrations

393. Regarding stress testing principles for supervisors, which of the following statements is most likely to be wrong? ( )

A) To be prudent, supervisors should conduct additional stress tests using common scenarios within a bank's jurisdiction.

B) Supervisors don't need tocheck stress tests with unrealistic results or inconsistent with a bank's risk appetite because these stress tests are not useful.

C) Supervisors should make frequent and comprehensive assessments of a bank's stress testing procedures.

D) Supervisors should consult with other experts to identify potential stress vulnerabilitiesto expand knowledge of stress testing.

394. Under which scenario is basis risk likely to exist? ( )

A) A hedge (which was initially matched to the maturity of the underlying) is lifted before expiration.

B) The correlation of the underlying and the hedge vehicle is less than one and their volatilities are unequal.

C) The underlying instrument and the hedge vehicle are dissimilar.

D) All of the above are correct.

395. Typically, reverse stress testing methodology has three phases. Which of the following is not included in the three phases? ( )

A) outcome

B) impact

C) events

D) hedging

396. Stress test sometimes are used to describe the wrong-way risk. Considering the stress testing principles for banks, which of the following statements is an example of wrong-way risk? ( )

A) The probability of default of counterparties increases as a result of exposure increase

B) A company buys options on its own stock to support stock price.

C) There are changes in basis between the opening and closing of a futures position.

D) A decline in an asset value may dry up its liquidity.

FRM 一级习题与解析

（下）

融跃教育 FRM 研究院　编著

立信会计出版社
LIXIN ACCOUNTING PUBLISHING HOUSE

目 录
CONTENTS

第一部分

风险管理基础

1. 答案：A
解析：金融风险主要源自金融市场。信用风险是一种金融风险。
2. 答案：C
解析：资金流动性风险(funding liquidity risk)是指机构无法筹集偿还债务所需的现金的风险。
3. 答案：B
解析：当买卖差价(bid-ask spread)扩大时，交易费用会变得越来越高，所以流动性风险可能来自差价的不确定性。
4. 答案：B
解析：流动性风险(Liquidity Risk)是指因难以在短时间内找到市场中的交易对手，从而无法以合理价格平仓而遭受损失的风险。
5. 答案：C
解析：题中讲的是根据主动投资组合(active portfolio) 相对于基准(benchmark)的偏差来衡量风险。答案 A 和 B 不正确，因为他们引用的是绝对风险。答案 D 也是不正确的，因为它指的是由基准引起的风险。
6. 答案：C
解析：结算风险(settlement risk)在 CFA 体系下被分类为非金融风险，流动性风险(liquidity risk)在 FRM 体系下分类为非金融风险。
7. 答案：C
解析：无解释。
8. 答案：C
解析：对于个人而言，风险管理关注的是在承担与个人风险承受水平相一致的风险前提下实现效用最大化。
9. 答案：C
解析：错误设定系数是模型风险(model risk)的例子。
10. 答案：C
解析：风险也可以描述为资产价格或收益的意外波动。
11. 答案：A
解析：竞争对手可能生产更好产品/服务，给本公司带来的风险是商业风险。

12. 答案：B

解析：结算风险(Settlement risk)一般是交易对手未能履行其义务的风险。

13. 答案：D

解析：一个国家不能偿还债务的风险是主权风险(sovereign risk)。

14. 答案：A

解析：董事会在为管理层设定风险管理目标时，必须要有确定的时间范围。

15. 答案：A

解析：VAR 是一种事前(ex-ante)方法。限制头寸(notional limits)的方法有一个缺陷，就是无法把不同类型资产的限制额加总起来。风险敞口限制(exposure limit)不是预测性的(predictive)风险管理措施。在超过累积止损线(cumulative loss threshold)后，止损限制(stop-loss limit)将对头寸进行平仓(liquidate)。

16. 答案：A

解析：VaR 计量的是在一段时间内、在某个置信水平下的最大损失；或者在一段时间内、在某个显著性水平下的最小损失。

17. 答案：A

解析：通常回报率会比风险敞口更难控制。

18. 答案：B

解析：交易所产品(Exchange-traded instruments)仅涵盖某些相关资产，并且非常标准化(例如，到期日、行权价格等)以促进市场中的流动性。场外交易产品(Over-the-counter instruments)在银行和公司等之间进行"私人"交易，因此可以根据公司的风险管理需求进行定制。此外，交易所产品通常不存在任何交易对手的信用风险(例如，违约风险)。

19. 答案：A

解析：通常使用对冲风险敞口的方式来降低公司价值波动性。但是，这样操作可能会因会计收益和现金流量之间的差异，导致公司收益的波动性增加。这是实践中对冲风险敞口的缺点。

20. 答案：B

解析：静态对冲策略是一个简单的过程。相比之下，动态对冲策略是一个更复杂的过程，它考虑到了潜在风险头寸的属性可能随时间而变化的情况，所以动态对冲策略需要更多的监控。Ⅰ和Ⅲ的说法是正确的。

21. 答案：D

解析：应根据和投资者匹配的风险承受能力和回报目标，来定义和衡量风险。

22. 答案：A

解析：风险治理(Risk governance)是自上而下(top-down)的过程，它定义风险承受能力(risk tolerance)，提供风险监督和指导，以使风险与企业目标保持一致。

23. 答案：D

解析：主要管理人员的薪酬是薪酬委员会的职责。

24. 答案：C

解析：董事会的作用包括对以下几个方面进行审查和分析：

- The firm's risk management policies.
- The firm's periodic risk management reports.
- The firm's appetite and its impact on business strategy.
- The firm's internal controls.
- The firm's financial statements and disclosure.
- The firm's related parties and related party transactions.
- Any audit reports from internal or external audits.
- Corporate governance best practices for the industry.
- Risk management practices of competitors and the industry.

25. 答案：A

解析：董事会将代表股东以及其他利益相关者(stakeholders，如债权人debtholders)的利益行事。董事会可能需要考虑管理层的任何决策是否包含极端下行风险。当然，董事会应保持对管理层的独立性。

26. 答案：D

解析：没有要求提供负责人姓名。

27. 答案：B

解析：风险管理委员会是业务层面风险治理结构(risk governance structure)的一部分。因此，它不批准理事机构(governing body)的政策。

28. 答案：A

解析：高级管理层(senior management)批准业务计划和目标，设定风险承受能力，制定政策并确保绩效(performance)。

29. 答案：A

解析：风险承受能力(risk tolerance)定义了风险偏好(risk appetite)，因此必须在接受或减少特定风险之前确定风险承受能力。风险预算(risk budget)确定风险的方式和来源，并通过特定指标量化可容忍的风险。之后，可以测量风险敞口(risk exposure)并将其与可接受的风险进行比较。

30. 答案：B

解析：必须考虑任何业务战略的下行风险(downside risks)。公司的风险偏好(risk appetite)反映了其接受风险的容忍度(tolerance，特别是意愿 willingness)。业务战略(business planning)规划会议需要来自管理团队的风险投入，以确保风险偏好与业务战略之间的一致性。虽然计划活动通常侧重于最大化公司的利润，但由于会超出风险偏好，可能需要取消或修改一些计划活动。

31. 答案：D

解析：风险基础设施(risk infrastructure)是指跟踪风险敞口所需的人员和系统。它执行大部分定量风险分析，以评估组织的风险状况(risk profile)。通常，风险管理基础架构(risk management infrastructure)可识别、测量和监控风险。

32. 答案：C

解析：风险治理(risk governance)是为整个企业建立适当的风险水平。如何处理风险属于风险管理和风险基础架构框架的范畴。

33. 答案：C

解析：确定风险承受能力(risk tolerance)后，风险框架(risk framework)应着眼于衡量、管理和遵守风险承受能力，使风险敞口与风险承受能力保持一致。

34. 答案：D

解析：能够快速适应不利事件，往往可能说明公司有更高的风险承受能力。董事会成员的信念、强大的管理团队和稳定的市场环境可能但不应影响风险承受能力。

35. 答案：A

解析：风险预算(risk budgeting)不包括确定目标回报(target return)和预测风险(predicting risks)。风险预算通过特定指标(specific metrics)量化并分配可容忍的风险。

36. 答案：C

解析：如果将这些风险视为公司面临的总体风险的个别组成部分，投资组合管理提供了公司风险的整体视图。积极的投资组合管理(active portfolio)汇总风险敞口，并允许实施风险分散和对集中度的监控风险。独立管理每项财务风险的公司，需要将这些风险整合到一个全面的企业风险管理流程中，以优化企业风险和回报。

37. 答案：B

解析：风险预算流程会强制公司考虑风险的权衡问题。结果是，公司会选择在单位风险回报率最高的地方进行投资。

38. 答案：A

解析：企业全面风险管理(ERM)被定义为组织内部的对风险的评估(assess)、控制(control)、利用(exploit)、资助(finance)和监控(monitor)。ERM的目的是增加组织对其利益相关者的短期和长期价值。企业风险管理决策是在总体基础上做出的，因此，它对整个组织的决策产生积极影响。ERM对风险管理流程采用了综合的(integrated)方法，这与单独管理组织内的个别风险完全不同。

39. 答案：D

解析：选择自我保险(self-insure)的实体可以设立损失准备金(reserve fund)以弥补损失。

40. 答案：A

解析：企业在风险管理(ERM)实施期间，应该任命适当的企业风险管理负责人；将企业风险管理整合到整个组织的文化中；研究和收集组织中的所有潜在风险；量化运营(operational)和战略风险；确定各种风险之间的相互关系；进行风险转移的选择；持续监测企业风险管理；逐步发展企业风险管理。

41. 答案：B

解析：CRO为企业风险管理(ERM)提供全面的领导、愿景和方向，并制定管理政策框架，包括设定(不是批准)企业的整体风险偏好。CRO是一名高层管理人员，负责整体风险管理，是一个权力集中的角色。向CRO报告的通常是各种风险职能的负责人，包括信贷市场负责人、运营人员和保险风险人员等。创建CRO角色不一定是建立顶级风险监督的最佳解决方案(公司的审计委员会audit committee也可以承担这一角色)。

42. 答案：D

解析：在风险规避（risk avoidance）、风险接受（risk acceptance）、风险转移（risk transfer）和风险转移（risk shifting）的风险修正方法中，并没有哪个有明显的优势。在选择使用方法时，必须根据公司的风险承受能力来衡量收益和成本。

43. 答案：B

解析：策略Ⅰ和Ⅱ都说明，通过风险管理来降低破产成本和避免财务困境，可以为公司带来增值。

44. 答案：B

解析：一般而言，如果一家银行承担的风险太小，可能无法利用足够的盈利机会。风险太小可能会降低银行的价值。

45. 答案：C

解析：尽量避免财务困境（financial distress）可以提高公司价值。财务困境将占用管理时间和精力，并可能导致不利的供应商条款，以及伴随而来的客户流失。

46. 答案：A

解析：银行不应总是获得最高信用评级；获得过高评级可能会导致银行放弃高利润项目；当然评级过低会导致银行流失客户。

47. 答案：B

解析：如果承担 incremental risk 会导致总风险过高和银行价值大幅下降，那么制定风险管理政策以防止银行承担过高风险可以给银行增加价值（add value）。

48. 答案：A

解析：两者都会导致股东价值下降。

49. 答案：D

解析：应该由首席执行官（CEO）来决定此类投资，而非 CRO。CRO 已正确估计有可能损失 10 亿美元或更多。此外，没有关于 VAR 之外的分布的信息。所以，这可能是运气不好。如果 CRO 声明这个概率为零，则可能是由于风险管理失败。

50. 答案：A

解析：只有 Statement Ⅰ是正确的。两项研究检验了风险文化的影响。其中一项研究得出的结论是：如果管理者被认为是诚实和可信赖，那么公司更有利可图并容易获得更高的估值。另一项研究得出结论是：股东治理的改善（shareholder governance improvements）将改变公司的文化，从原来的关注员工诚信（integrity）、客户服务，转变到结果导向。

51. 答案：C

解析：由于利润是假的，这一系列事件并没有导致公司真正的损失（did not result in actual losses）；然而，这些交易引发了对 Kidder Peabody 管理层的信心的丧失。

52. 答案：A

解析：管理层认为 Rusnak 正在进行小额货币套利交易策略，但是，实际实施的策略涉及非常大的金额头寸。Rusnak 为了不引起公司警觉，只是报告了很普通的收益（not substantial fake gains）。

53. 答案：C

解析：为了弥补交易损失，Nick Leeson 放弃了对日经 225 指数的套期保值策略，转而采取极具投机性的策略,以致在市场暴跌时给公司带来巨大风险。他的行为未被发现,因为他控制了交易结算和后台运营,使他可以向管理层报告虚假利润。会计准则要求(financial reporting requirements)、基差风险(basis risk)和期限错配(maturity mismatch)不是相关的因素。

54. 答案:A

解析:巴林银行的倒闭是由于报告制度薄弱、管理监督薄弱以及组织结构不良等严重的问题导致的。Leeson 对交易和结算的双重权责使他能够隐藏交易损失。使用短期工具来对冲长期风险是 Metallgesellschaft 案例中的问题。模型风险(model risk)和杠杆(leverage)是 LTCM 中的问题。

55. 答案:D

解析:Barings 崩溃并非由技术限制造成的。

56. 答案:D

解析:Nick Lesson 在巴林银行做日经指数期货和期权的交易。

57. 答案:B

解析:Leeson 之前在期权上已经遭受了巨大的交易损失,如果披露,将会让他失去工作。为了弥补这些损失,他放弃了对冲策略。他在后台业务中的权限使他能够隐藏他的投机损失并报告虚假利润。高级管理层对 Leeson 的角色缺乏监督和了解,使他的计划没有被发现。巴林银行的倒闭与模型缺陷无关,是一个操作风险控制失败的案例。

58. 答案:C

解析:未能监督其交易员的行为就是操作风险的一个例子。其他选项不涉及操作风险(operational risk)。

59. 答案:C

解析:Metallgesellschaft 在处理流动性危机时同时犯了这两个错误。

60. 答案:C

解析:Metallgesellschaft 的对冲策略产生了中期现金流出,引发了公司的流动性危机,因为石油价格急剧下跌。要求客户定期就固定价格的远期合约进行现金结算,可以带来现金流入,这将缓解现金流的紧张。解决方案是购买看跌期权(Buying puts),因为现货价格下跌,看跌期权可以赚取现金流,以抵消期货上追加保证金要求的影响。卖出看跌期权(Selling puts)将使公司在石油价格下跌时损失更大。卖出看涨期权(Selling calls)只能提供有限的现金流,在引发流动性危机的石油价格大幅下降时作用不大。

61. 答案:B

解析:因素Ⅰ既影响瑞银也影响其竞争对手。因素Ⅱ是影响瑞银独有的因素。

62. 答案:C

解析:长期资本管理公司的模型低估了证券价格在经济危机时期的相关程度(correlations among asset)。这些模型也未能预测到,随着时间的推移,多个经济冲击可能会集中发生(即,正向自相关 autocorrelation)。管理监督不力和财务报告标准不是 LTCM 案例中的问题。

63. 答案:C

解析:长期资本管理公司要求投资者投资 3 年,从而降低(不是增加)融资风险。

64. 答案：D

解析：Bankers Trust 的这个案例说明了充分了解客户需求，并提供相匹配交易的重要性。它还说明了对于可被公开的任何形式的沟通，都要谨慎，因为如果存在不道德的行为，它可能会破坏公司的声誉。

65. 答案：C

解析：模型风险是套期保值或定价模型存在缺陷的风险，在本案例中不相关。大额交易应该需要得到主管的批准，主管需要理解交易员的策略。住友银行的铜交易员拥有太高的自主权，使其在现货市场上可以执行大量高杠杆交易。交易员的权限太大，使他能够操纵损益报告，从而隐藏他的巨大损失。

66. 答案：A

解析：以 Sumitomo 案为例，交易员 Yasuo Hamanaka 试图垄断铜市场。他获得了很大的权限，包括向经纪公司授予授权书，以便在现货市场上为他提供资金。由于管理层监管不力，他能够保留两套交易账并执行大额交易，而无需高级管理层的批准。

67. 答案：A

解析：当期货价格低于现货价格时，叫做期货贴水（backwardation）。当期货价格高于现货价格时，叫做期货升水（Contango）。当市场从贴水转向升水时（shifts from normal backwardation to contango），期货价格上涨幅度超过现货。滚动套保策略涉及卖出相对便宜的短期合约并购买相对昂贵的长期合约，从而增加了套期保值的成本。

68. 答案：C

解析：由于抵押贷款违约率上升和房价下跌导致的金融危机最后导致全球流动性危机，因为：(1)金融机构承担了过多的杠杆；(2)产生了资产和负债之间的大量期限错配（maturity mismatches）；(3)变得过于相互关联。

69. 答案：B

解析：当投资者 A 的资产价值下降 10%，从 100 美元到 90 美元时，投资者 A 已经损失了 10 美元的权益，只剩下 10 美元。为了维持 5 倍杠杆率，投资者 A 将被迫出售价值 40 美元的资产，以使总资产的价值降至 50 美元。当投资者 B 的杠杆率从 5 降至 2 时，投资者 20 美元的权益将支持仅 40 美元的总资产价值，迫使投资者 B 出售价值 60 (100 − 40)美元的资产。

70. 答案：B

解析：贷款标准的下降和廉价的信贷导致银行以低利率和宽松的条件提供贷款。廉价资金和充足的借贷机会导致大量房地产购买行为，从而不断推高房价。外国政府对美国债券的需求的增加会压低利率而不是推高利率。在互联网泡沫破裂后，美联储采取了宽松的利率政策，促进低利率以抵御通货紧缩（deflation）。

71. 答案：D

解析：买卖价差与市场流动性呈反向关系，随着市场流动性增加，买卖价差缩小，选项 D 是正确的。

72. 答案：C

解析：市场流动性（market liquidity）表现为以下形式：(1)买卖价差（bid-ask spread）；(2)市场深度（market depth）；(3)市场回复弹性（market resiliency）。当投资者卖出资

产后立即买回，就会产生买卖价差那么多的损失。价差越大，市场流动性越低，损失越大；反之，亦然。其他选项都是对融资流动性(funding liquidity)的描述。

73. 答案：D

解析：融资流动性(Funding liquidity)与以下内容相关：(1)保证金削减融资风险(margin haircut funding risk)；(2)展期风险(rollover risk)；(3)赎回风险(redemption risk)。展期风险指投资者可能无法用短期债务来融资去购买长期资产的风险。其他选项涉及市场流动性(market liquidity)。

74. 答案：B

解析：资金的减少与保证金的增加具有相同的效果。选项 A 指的是融资流动性而非市场流动性。选项 D，损失螺旋(loss spiral)的严重程度与市场流动性的大小呈反向关系。选择 C 指的是损失螺旋(loss spiral)而非保证金螺旋(margin spiral)。

75. 答案：C

解析：从风险角度来看，权益部分(equity tranche)风险最高，将首先吸收 ABS 资产池中的亏损。

76. 答案：D

解析：为购买资产而筹集资金与融资流动性(Funding liquidity)相关。市场流动性(Market liquidity)衡量出售资产的难易程度。损失螺旋(loss spiral)是指由于资产价值下降，使杠杆投资者强制出售资产，从而维持恒定的杠杆率(maintaining a constant leverage ratio)。保证金螺旋(Margin spiral)指由于保证金增加而被迫出售资产，也就是说，杠杆率会下降。

77. 答案：C

解析：创建 CDO 有三步：(1)形成分散化投资组合；(2)将投资组合切分成多个层级(tranches)；(3)向投资者出售不同风险的层级。优先级(senior tranches)出售给要求高信用评级(比如投资级)的机构，如养老基金。CDO 发行人通常保留权益级(equity tranches)。

78. 答案：D

解析：金融危机的两个主要恐慌时期：(1)2007 年 8 月发生的资产支持商业票据(ABCP)发生挤兑；(2)2008 年 9 月雷曼兄弟申请破产，引发了对货币市场基金的挤兑。

79. 答案：D

解析：证据表明，在雷曼破产之前，稳定银行间市场的最有效的措施是流动性支持(Liquidity support)。雷曼破产之后，资本重组(recapitalization)是最有效的措施。

80. 答案：B

解析：与之前的危机相比，最近的金融危机并不是独一无二的。它们有共同的现象：公共和私人债务的增加，信贷供应的增加，房价大幅上涨。

81. 答案：C

解析：金融危机对公司和经济体的影响是，银团贷款机构的信贷供应减少，向受监管银行的借贷增加。受监管银行和其他金融中介机构(如投资银行、对冲基金、私募股权基金等)减少了信贷供应，因此在危机期间向企业发放的贷款减少。企业利用危机开始前获得的授信额度，向监管银行的借款增加。

82. 答案：A

解析：雷曼破产申请被认为是金融危机的转折点。它削弱了投资者对金融机构的信心并导致货币市场基金的挤兑(run on money market mutual funds)。这种恐慌在市场和国家间蔓延，导致银行更愿意持有现金，从而放大了次级抵押贷款市场的损失。

83. 答案：A

解析：风险管理的目的是让公司的高级管理人员做出最佳的战略决策，以最大化公司价值(firm value)而不是最大化股价。

84. 答案：D

解析：盲目地接受一个假设(比如，AAA 级资产的风险非常低)，会忽略相反的数据。危机期间，各资产间的相关性会增加，也是经常被忽视的一点。

85. 答案：C

解析：当风险管理者不了解单个风险的分布或不了解不同风险之间的相互关系时，就会发生风险误测。对极端事件的估计有一定程度的主观性，这显然具有误测的可能性。

86. 答案：A

解析：发生以下事件，风险管理过程可能会失败：未正确衡量已知风险，未识别某些风险，未向高层管理层传达风险，未充分监控风险，未充分管理风险，未使用适当风险指标。应识别未知风险，但不一定要衡量。

87. 答案：B

解析：风险管理的包括以下任务：(1)评估公司面临的所有风险；(2)将这些风险向决策者汇报；(3)监控和管理这些风险，确保公司只承担必要的风险(only takes the necessary amount of risk)。

88. 答案：C

解析：即使在没有交易的情况下，投资组合风险特征也会发生变化。

89. 答案：B

解析：市场中的大玩家的头寸陷入困境，其他公司试图进一步打压价格以触发其止损，以大玩家的更大损失为代价，使自己的成交价格有利。

90. 答案：B

解析：构建资产组合以分散风险进而降低波动率(volatility)。

91. 答案：B

解析：不同资产之间存在不完全正相关性，可以降低波动率(volatility)。

92. 答案：D

解析：构建资产组合能够降低风险(risk)、增加收益(return)。由于分散化作用，风险降低的程度比收益增加的程度高。

93. 答案：A

解析：组合 1 投资于权益(Equity)和另类资产(Alternative Assets)比重最大，风险最高，适合于风险厌恶程度低(risk aversion)的投资者。

94. 答案：C

解析：持有期收益(holding period return) = $(200\times32-200\times30+105)\div(200\times30)\times$

$100\% = 8.42\%$。

95. 答案：B

解析：持有期收益(holding period return) $= [(1+0.15)(1-0.15)(1-0.01)] - 1 = -0.0323 = -3.23\%$。

96. 答案：A

解析：几何平均收益(geometric mean return) $= [(1+0.20)(1-0.15)(1+0.10)]^{(1/3)} - 1 = 3.91\%$。

97. 答案：B

解析：几何平均收益(geometric mean return)不受投资期间现金流入或者流出的影响。

98. 答案：D

解析：等权重资产组合(equally weighted portfolio)的方差主要取决于资产之间的相关系数或者协方差以及资产的标准差。

99. 答案：C

解析：组合标准差 $= [(0.2\times 20\%)^2 + (0.8\times 15\%)^2 + 2\times 0.2\times 0.8\times 0.5\times 20\%\times 15]^{0.5}\times 100\% = 14.42\%$。

100. 答案：C

解析：组合标准差 $= [(0.2\times 20\%)^2 + (0.8\times 15\%)^2 + 2\times 0.2\times 0.8\times 0.015]^{0.5}\times 100\% = 14.42\%$。

101. 答案：D

解析：组合标准差 $= [(0.2\times 20\%)^2 + (0.8\times 15\%)^2 + 2\times 0.2\times 0.8\times \rho\times 20\%\times 15]^{0.5}\times 100\% = 14.42\%$ 计算得 $\rho = 0.5$。

102. 答案：D

解析：组合标准差 $= [(0.2\times 20\%)^2 + (0.8\times 15\%)^2 + 2\times 0.2\times 0.8\times COV]^{0.5}\times 100\% = 14.42\%$。

计算得 $COV = 0.015$。

103. 答案：C

解析：$(1+0.090)\div(1+0.02) - 1 = 6.9\%$。

104. 答案：A

解析：风险厌恶(Risk aversion)指投资者承担的风险越高，要求的回报率就越高。

105. 答案：D

解析：连接无风险资产和风险资产组合可得到资本配置线(capital allocation line)。

106. 答案：C

解析：投资者持有的资产组合为资本配置线和其无差异曲线的切点，故最优组合落在资本配置线上(CAL)。

107. 答案：B

解析：$w\times 15\% + (1-w)\times 10\% = 12.5\%$，$w = 50\%$。

108. 答案：D

解析：组合标准差 $= [(0.5\times 25\%)^2 + (0.5\times 25\%)^2 + 2\times 0.5\times 0.5\times 0.25\times 0.25\times$

$0.5]^{0.5}\times 100\% = 21.65\%$。

109. 答案：D

解析：组合标准差 $=[(0.5\times 25\%)^2+(0.5\times 25\%)^2]^{0.5}\times 100\% = 17.68\%$。

110. 答案：B

解析：相关性(correlation)越低，分散化作用越强，波动率(volatility)越低；反之，越高。

111. 答案：A

解析：相同风险下，收益最高的资产或者相同收益，风险最低的资产构成了有效边界(efficient frontier)。

112. 答案：A

解析：可行集上方差最小的点代表的组合为全球最低风险组合(the global minimum-variance portfolio)。

113. 答案：C

解析：可行集上位于全球最低风险组合(the global minimum-variance portfolio)以上的组合为有效边界(efficient frontier)。

114. 答案：A

解析：资本市场线(capital market line)连接无风险资产和最优风险资产组合(optimal risky portfolio)。

115. 答案：D

解析：投资者通过借入无风险资产，投资于风险证券，可以获得比最优风险资产组合更高的收益。

116. 答案：D

解析：所有投资者都会持有最优风险资产组合，最优风险资产组合与无风险资产之间的比例取决于投资者的风险偏好(risk preference)。

117. 答案：D

解析：资本配置线(capital allocation line)连接无风险资产和风险资产，其中与有效边界相切的资本配置线为资本市场线(capital market line)。

118. 答案：A

解析：无风险资产收益不变，和风险资产之间的相关性为0。

119. 答案：A

解析：投资者的最优资产组合取决于其无差异曲线(indifference curve)，最优资产组合为资产配置线和投资者最高无差异曲线的切点。

120. 答案：A

解析：风险厌恶(risk aversion)的投资者会投资于无风险资产。

121. 答案：A

解析：资本市场线连接无风险资产和最优风险资产组合，即包括所有风险资产的市场组合(market portfolio)。

122. 答案：D

解析：市场组合包括所有风险资产，不包括无风险资产。

123. 答案：B

解析：不论投资者的风险厌恶程度如何，都会选择最优风险资产组合(the optimal risky portfolio)，即市场组合(market portfolio)，而持有的比例取决于风险厌恶程度。

124. 答案：D

解析：资本市场线以上的点在相同风险下，具有更高的收益，为不可达到的点(unachievable)。

125. 答案：A

解析：投资者借入无风险资产投资于风险资产组合，可以实现比风险资产组合即市场组合(market portfolio)更高的收益。

126. 答案：B

解析：投资者投资无风险资产，即按照无风险收益率借出(lending)资金，同时投资于风险资产组合，可以达到比风险资产组合即市场组合(market portfolio)更低的收益。

127. 答案：B

解析："不要把鸡蛋放在同一个篮子里"说明不同资产之间的分散化作用。其减少的是非系统性风险(Nonsystematic risk)，系统性风险(Systematic risk)无法消除。

128. 答案：B

解析：某一公司 CEO 的离职属于非系统性风险(nonsystematic risk)。

129. 答案：D

解析：根据证券市场线(security market line)，只有系统性风险(systematic risk)才具有风险补偿，非系统性风险(nonsystematic risk)不具有。

130. 答案：C

解析：总风险(total variance)包括系统性风险和非系统性风险。

131. 答案：C

解析：市场模型(market model)中，$R_i = \alpha_i + \beta_i R_m + e_i$，截距是 alpha，斜率是 beta。

132. 答案：B

解析：市场模型(market model)中，$R_i = \alpha_i + \beta_i R_m + e_i$，截距是 alpha，斜率是 beta。

133. 答案：D

解析：市场模型(market model)，$R_i = \alpha_i + \beta_i R_m + e_i$，可用来估计组合的预期收益率。

134. 答案：A

解析：证券 1 的标准差最高为 20。

135. 答案：A

解析：$beta = \rho \times \sigma_i / \sigma_m$，计算得证券 1 的 beta 最大。

136. 答案：B

解析：$beta = \rho \times \sigma_i / \sigma_m$，计算得证券 2 的 beta 最小。

137. 答案：C

解析：市场组合的 beta = 1，即组合中所有资产的加权 beta = 1。

138. 答案：C

解析：证券特征线(security characteristic line)描述的是资产的超额收益和市场组合

的超额收益之间的关系，斜率为资产的 beta。

139. 答案：C

解析：基于资本资产定价模型(capital asset pricing model)的是证券市场线(security market line)。

140. 答案：A

解析：定价准确的资产落于证券市场线(security market line)，定价不准确的证券落于证券市场线以上或者以下。

141. 答案：B

解析：根据资本资产定价模型，资产的收益取决于系统性风险，即 beta。

142. 答案：C

解析：beta 为负，资产的收益小于无风险收益率。

143. 答案：D

解析：市场风险溢价(market risk premium) = 市场组合超额收益(excess market return) = 市场组合收益 - 无风险收益。

144. 答案：D

解析：证券 1 的收益 = $1.2\times6\% + 3\% = 10.2\%$。

145. 答案：B

解析：$12\% = 1.5\times(\text{market return} - 3\%) + 3\%$。Market return = 9%。

146. 答案：B

解析：证券 3 的 beta 最高，预期收益也最高。

147. 答案：B

解析：证券 2 的 beta 最高，受到市场组合影响最大。

148. 答案：B

解析：詹森阿尔法(Jensen's alpha)和 CAPM 模型一致，都是对系统性风险进行调整。

149. 答案：B

解析：特雷诺比率(Treynor Ratio)衡量的是系统风险，适用于完全分散化的投资组合。

150. 答案：A

解析：夏普比率(Sharpe ratio)衡量的是总风险，适用于未完全分散化的投资组合。

151. 答案：A

解析：资产的收益高于 CAPM 估计出的收益，说明资产价格被低估(underpriced)；反之，被高估(overpriced)。

152. 答案：D

解析：同质预期(homogeneity assumption)指的是投资者们对证券收益率的均值(mean)、方差(variance)和协方差(covariance)具有相同的期望值。在同质预期假设下，所有的投资者都会持有最优风险资产组合。

153. 答案：C

解析：同质预期(homogeneity assumption)指的是投资者们对证券收益率的均值(mean)、方差(variance)和协方差(covariance)具有相同的期望值。在同质预期假设下，所有的投资者都会持有最优风险资产组合，即市场组合(market portfolio)。

154. 答案：B

解析：衡量市场组合超额收益和某特定资产组合超额收益的的一元线回归方程中，截距是 alpha，斜率是 beta。

155. 答案：A

解析：詹森阿尔法越大(Jensen's alpha)，资产组合的业绩表现越好。

156. 答案：C

解析：詹森阿尔法越大(Jensen's alpha)，资产组合的业绩表现越好；反之，表现越差。

157. 答案：A

解析：APT 模型包含的因子比 CAPM 模型多，二者都假设非系统性风险可以被分散。根据 CAPM 模型，偏好风险的投资者更多投资于市场组合。

158. 答案：A

解析：预期收益 $=2.5\%+1\times8\%=10.5\%$。

159. 答案：C

解析：因子风险溢价指的是投资者对该因子所要求的风险回报(expected risk premium)，即超出无风险收益部分的补偿。

160. 答案：A

解析：APT 模型假设不存在套利机会(arbitrage opportunities)，APT 模型是多因素模型，非系统性风险可被分散。

161. 答案：D

解析：CAPM 模型包含的因素少于 APT 模型，CAPM 模型假设条件多于 APT 模型，APT 模型更加灵活。CAPM 模型是 APT 模型的一个特例。

162. 答案：C

解析：APT 模型假设不存在套利机会(arbitrage opportunities)。

163. 答案：C

解析：$E(fund_1)=3\%+5\%(0.6)+10\%(0.5)+8\%(1.8)=25.4\%$。

$E(fund_2)=3\%+5\%(0.4)+10\%(1.5)+8\%(0.9)=27.2\%$。

164. 答案：D

解析：CAPM 模型是 APT 模型的一个特例。

165. 答案：C

解析：预期收益 $=2.5\%+(6.0\%)(1.5)+(10.0\%)(1.2)+(5.0\%)(1.0)=28.5\%$。

166. 答案：C

解析：$E(R)=3.0\%+(0.8\times6\%)+(1\times5\%)+(1.5\times10\%)+(1.2\times8\%)=37.4\%$。

167. 答案：D

解析：巴塞尔委员会认为，“风险管理报告应以清晰简洁的方式表述”。报告应易于理解，足够全面，以便帮助做出决策。原则 9(清晰和有用性 Clarity and Usefulness)要求。

(1) 报告应针对最终使用者(例如，董事会、高级管理人员和风险委员会成员)量身定制，并应协助他们进行健全的风险管理和做出决策；（2）报告应包括风险数据（risk data）、风险分析（risk analysis）、风险解释（interpretation of risk）和风险定性解释（qualitative explanations of risks）。

168. 答案：D

解析：巴塞尔委员会关于有效风险数据汇总能力的原则包括准确性（accuracy and integrity）、完整性（completeness）、及时性（timeliness）和适应性（adaptability）。

169. 答案：D

解析：银行可以使用多个数据模型进行数据分类。

170. 答案：D

解析：有效的风险数据整合系统可以带来一些好处。这些好处包括如下几个。

（1）提高预测问题的能力。整合数据使风险管理者能够更全面地了解风险。当风险被视为一个整体而不是孤立时，更容易看到即将出现的问题。

（2）在财务压力大的时候，有效的风险数据整合可以提高银行找到解决财务问题的方法的能力。例如，银行可以更好地找到合适的并购伙伴。

（3）在银行面临财务压力或失败的情况下提高解决问题的能力，监管机构能够获取整合的风险数据，以解决与银行财务状况和银行生存相关的问题。

（4）通过加强银行的风险系统，银行能够更好地做出战略决策，提高效率，减少损失的可能性，并最终提高盈利能力。

171. 答案：C

解析：数据整合和报告决策应独立于银行的实际地理位置和法律结构。

172. 答案：B

解析：GARP会员应充分披露可能会损害其独立性和客观性或干扰其对雇主，客户和潜在客户应尽职责的所有事项。

173. 答案：C

解析：Susan不得与她的慈善基金会讨论有关她的客户和客户意图的任何事情。为客户保密，与这个客户打算在不久的将来向慈善机构捐钱的事，并无直接关系。（准则3.1）

174. 答案：C

解析：从散点图（scattergram）可以直观地看出相关性是正的还是负的。总体回归（population regression）和样本回归（sample regression）的回归系数不完全相等，残差也几乎不可能正好相等。

175. 答案：B

解析：准则2.1和2.2：利益冲突。会员必须在所有情况下公平行事，并且必须向所有相关方充分披露任何潜在的利益冲突。卖方分析师持有所推荐的证券时，应向其客户披露其所有权。

176. 答案：D

解析：准则3.1和3.2涉及保密。遵守这些准则的最简单、最保守和最有效的方法是避免泄露从客户那里得到的任何信息。如果信息涉及非法活动，会员可能有义务向当局报告。

177. 答案：C

解析：根据准则3.1和3.2，会员不得擅自使用机密信息，除非事先征得同意。否则应为雇主和客户(包括现有客户、前客户、潜在客户)的信息保密。

178. 答案：D

解析：ABC都会涉及利益冲突，必须披露。

179. 答案：D

解析：GARP会员应充分披露可能会损害其独立性和客观性的事项，以及会干扰对雇主、客户和潜在客户应尽义务的所有事项。

180. 答案：A

解析：根据准则1.3，会员必须采取合理的预防措施，以确保会员的服务不被用于不正当、欺诈或非法目的。

181. 答案：A

解析：Jack的交易很可能是试图抓住股票和看跌期权之间存在的套利机会。这是一个正当的投资策略，所以他没有操纵市场价格以试图误导市场参与者。她的基金的投资人都知道基金的投资策略，因此Jack即使没有在每一笔交易前披露，也没有违反守则。

182. 答案：A

解析：GARP会员不得提供、索取或接受任何可能会损害自身或他人独立性和客观性的礼物、利益、补偿或安排。John已经拒绝了酒店住宿的提议以及公司私人飞机的使用。但是，John不能接受晚宴的票。由于这是一个正式的上流社会晚宴，入场票很可能是昂贵的。尽管他已经向他的雇主披露了礼物，并且他计划将晚餐作为他公司的营销机会，但礼物本身可能会使John未来的研究结论有利于ElectroCo。因此接受该礼物是违反道德准则的行为。

183. 答案：D

解析：历史增长数据可以被引用为事实。Bob表示，他预期未来盈利会增加，这是他的一个观点，他并未声称这是事实，因此，他没有违反准则5.4。此外，Bob还指出了相关风险因素，包括政治风险和汇率风险，完全遵守标准5.3。

184. 答案：C

解析：根据GARP行为准则，违反准则可能会导致GARP会员资格暂时中止或永久撤销(temporary suspension or permanent removal)。还可能暂时中止或永久性地撤销使用FRM或GARP相关头衔的权利。

第二部分

数量分析

1. 答案：B

解析：函数 x 乘 y 的可能性如下表所示，总和一共是36；由于总概率等于1，所以参数 k 等于1/36，由于 $X+Y>5$ 只有 $X=3$，$Y=3$ 这一种情况，概率 $P=9/36=1/4$。

$X*Y$	$X=1$	$X=2$	$X=3$
$Y=1$	1	2	3
$Y=2$	2	4	6
$Y=3$	3	6	9

2. 答案：B

解析：每次投掷骰子都是独立同分布事件，不管之前滚动掷出点数是多少，骰子掷出3的概率是1/6。

3. 答案：B

解析：当联合概率不等于个体概率的乘积 a 时，即 $P(AB)\neq P(A)P(B)$，是随机变量之间的依赖性结果。如果它们相等，则存在独立的关系。

4. 答案：D

解析：条件期望(Conditional expected) 值取决于某些其他事件的发生，这些事件随着新信息的披露而发生变化。

5. 答案：C

解析：它们是互斥的，所以联合概率是零。

6. 答案：C

解析：掷出正面的概率是1/2，由于这些都是独立事件，因此连续三个正面的概率是：$(1/2)\times(1/2)\times(1/2)=1/8$。

7. 答案：D

解析：注意事件独立意味着他们彼此没有影响。这并不意味着它们是相互排斥的，$P(X\text{或}Y)=P(X)+P(Y)-P(X\text{和}Y)$；根据独立事件的定义 $P(X\mid Y)=P(X)$。

8. 答案：C

解析：假设亚马逊建新仓库为事件 A，建新学校为事件 B；根据公式 $P(AB)=P(A\mid B)\times P(B)$；$P(A\mid B)=P(AB)/P(B)=0.48/0.75=0.64$。

9. 答案：B

解析：通过联合概率的公式：$P(AB) = P(A \mid B) \times P(B)$，因为 $P(B) \leqslant 1$，那么 $P(AB) \leqslant P(A \mid B)$。其他任何选择都不能成立。

10. 答案：C

解析：如果两个事件 A 和 B 是相关的，那么的条件概率 $P(A \mid B)$ 和 $P(B \mid A)$ 将不等于各自无条件概率 P(A)和(B)。

11. 答案：B

解析：既然是独立的事件，概率相乘得到的个体概率。两个学生获得 A 的概率 $= (0.1) \times (0.35) = 0.035$。

12. 答案：B

解析：因为每个债券的违约概率是独立的，第二年3个债券都违约的概率为 $= P(A) \times P(BBB) \times P(CCC) = 0.05 \times 0.11 \times 0.40 = 0.002\,2 = 0.22\%$。

13. 答案：B

解析：如果一个事件的结果不影响另一个事件的结果，那么这个事件是独立的。

14. 答案：C

解析：如果两个事件相互排斥，则两个事件同时发生的概率为零。

15. 答案：A

解析：条件概率是指在一个事件发生的概率的情况下，另外一个事件发生的概率，结果是与随机变量相关联的数字结果，选择完美小部件的概率是 $21/100 = 0.21$ 或 21%。

16. 答案：B

解析：对于此处定义的五个独立事件，指定结果的概率为：$1/2 \times 1/2 \times 1/6 \times 1/6 \times 1/6 = 0.001\,157$。

17. 答案：D

解析：投资组合A是左偏，B是尖峰；所以两个说法都是错误的。

18. 答案：B

解析：相关性是线性相关的度量，独立意味着零关系，但是相关系数为零并不是意味着两个变量没有关系，可能具有非线性关系。

19. 答案：B

解析：根据方差公式 $V(3A + 2B) = V(3A + 2B) = 3^2(A) + 2^2(B) + 2 \times 6 \times \mathrm{COV}(A, B) = 9 + 4 + 12 \times 0.35 = 17.2$。

20. 答案：B

解析：A选项正确，因为对于期望来说 $E(ax) = a \times E(x)$；B选项错误，因为增加常数项不会改变方差的大小；选项C正确，对于 $\mathrm{COV}(ax, by) = a \times b \times \mathrm{COV}(x, y)$；D选项正确，因为 x，y 没有相关关系，协方差为0。

21. 答案：B

解析：根据标准正太分布的性质，偏度 = 0，峰度 = 3，B选项错误。

22. 答案：A

解析：对数正态分布右偏，如果这代表价格的分布，价格最多可以下降到0，但可以增加更多。

23. 答案：D

解析：如果你知道 X 和 Y 是独立的，你可以计算概率为 $0.25\times0.30=0.075$。题目中没有给 X 和 Y 是否相互独立这个条件，所以无法得到答案。

24. 答案：A

解析：预期收益等于情景概率与各阶段收益的乘积之和：$0.35\times0.2+0.2\times0.12+0.45\times0.35=0.2515$。

25. 答案：A

解析：当分布的尾部比正态分布的尾部厚时，我们说分布是尖峰肥尾(leptokurtic)。

26. 答案：A

解析：超额峰度(excess kurtosis)为零表示正太分布；超额峰度大于零表示峰度比正太分布要大。

27. 答案：D

解析：要计算此结果，我们首先需要计算投资组合价值，然后确定每个股票的权重，再计算预期收益。最后，我们再确定 3 年后的复合收益率。

投资组合价值 = 市场价值总和 = 2 500 + 3 500 + 4 000 = 10 000。

组合权重：

$WA = 2\,500\,/10\,000 = 0.25$

$WB = 3\,500/10\,000 = 0.35$

$WC = 4\,000\,/10\,000 = 0.4$

预期收益：

组合的预期收益 $= \sum$[(股票的预期收益)(股票投资中所占权重)]

预期收益(ER) $= (0.25\times18\%)+(0.35\times14\%)+(0.4\times9\%)=13.0\%$

4 年后的预期收益 $= (1+return)^4=(1.13)^4-1=1.6304-1=0.6304$, or 63.04%

28. 答案：A

解析：独立随机变量的协方差为零。因此，两个变量之和的方差等于变量方差的总和。

29. 答案：B

解析：$[(0.40\times(0.25-0.148)^2+0.60\times(0.08-0.148)^2]^{1/2}=8.3285\%$。

30. 答案：B

解析：期望值是随机变量可能结果的概率加权平均值。预期收益为：$[(0.3)\times(0.4)]+[(0.7)\times(-0.1)]=(0.12)+(-0.07)=0.05$。

31. 答案：C

解析：根据给出的数据排序[−18%，−4%，−1%，5%，5%，5%，5%，6%，11%，11%，11%]。我们可以发现众数(mode)为 5%，中位数(median)为 5%，均值(mean)为：[−18%，−4%，−1%，5%，5%，5%，5%，6%，11%，11%，11%]/11 = 3.2727%。

32. 答案：C

解析：ER portfolio（投资组合的预期收益）$= \sum(ER_{stock})W\%$（投资每个股票的权重）。

$ER=(0.4\times22\%)+(0.60\times25\%)=8.8\%+15\%=23.8\%$。

33. 答案：C

解析：协方差是以 Y 和 X 的单位积表示的。协方差的定义是两个变量观测值与其均值的偏差乘积的平均值。相关系数是协方差的标准化版本，范围从 −1 到 +1。

34. 答案：A

解析：$E(R)=(0.40\times20\%)+(0.25\times15\%)+(0.35\times12\%)=15.95\%$。

35. 答案：C

解析：左偏分布是指在分布左侧尾部较长，更多的数据在右侧，所以均值小于中位数小于众数。

36. 答案：D

解析：频率论的方法是根据观察到的事件的发生频率。有一个 5 年的样本，经理每年的表现都高于市场，(e, 5/5 = 100%)。

37. 答案：C

解析：相关性系数等于协方差除以标准差。

38. 答案：D

解析：相关系数在 −1 和 +1 之间有界。

39. 答案：C

解析：独立随机变量之积的特征函数等于特征函数的乘积 $E(XY)=E(X)\times E(Y)$。

40. 答案：C

解析：相关范围从 −1 到 +1，对于 $r=1$ 且 $r=-1$，数据点恰好位于一条线上，但该线的斜率不一定是 +1 到 −1。

41. 答案：C

解析：$\rho_{1,2}=0.048/(0.036^{0.5}\times0.148^{0.5})=0.6576$ 低于原来的 0.79。

42. 答案：D

解析：为了使两个变量之间的相关性为正，协方差必须为正。(标准差总是正的)

43. 答案：D

解析：(预期收益) $ER=0.4\times(-8\%)+(0.5\times18\%)+(0.1\times35\%)=-3.2\%+9\%+3.5\%=9.3\%$。

44. 答案：D

解析：A、B 两个选项都是高峰态，高峰性质高峰肥尾；选项 D 是低峰态，低峰瘦尾；题目问哪一种分布大于极端值概率最小，选项 A、选项 B 肥尾大于极端值概率增加，选项 C 正态分布不变，选项 D 低峰瘦尾大于极端值概率减小。

45. 答案：A

均值是分布的中心，即 a 和 b 的平均值。

46. 答案：B

解析：首先将 32 到 116 这个区间转换为标准正太分布；$Z_1=(32-80)/24=-2$，$Z_2=(116-80)/24=1.5$；题目问不落在 32 到 116 这个区间里面的概率，所以先算出 $P(Z_1<X<Z_2)$ 的概率 91.04%，所以不落在 $P(Z_1<X<X_2)$ 的概率为 $1-91.04\%=8.96\%$。

47. 答案：C

解析：对数正态分布的一个性质：X 服从 $\log N$，$\ln X$ 就服从 N。

48. 答案：C

解析：这里是双尾检验，因此 $\alpha = 1.96$。我们从 \$ 100exp($\mu \pm \alpha \times \sigma$) 中找出上下限。下限为 $100\exp(0.10 - 1.96 \times 0.2) = 100\exp(-0.292) = 74.68$。上限为 $100\exp(0.10 + 1.96 \times 0.2) = 100\exp(0.492) = 163.56$。

49. 答案：C

解析：对数正太分布均值计算公示：$E(X) = \exp[\mu + 1/2\ \sigma^2]$。方差计算公示：$V[X] = \exp[2\mu + 2\sigma^2] - \exp[2\mu + \sigma^2]$；带入数值得 $E(X) = 1.133$，$V(X) = 0.3649$。

50. 答案：C

解析：正态分布和 Student's t 分布具有相同的偏度，但是 Student's t 分布具有更高的峰度；随着自由度的增加 Student's t 收敛于正太分布。

51. 答案：D

解析：试验次数为 $n = 6$，偶然正确猜测的概率是 $p = 1/4 = 0.25$；一次都没猜对的概率是 $\begin{pmatrix} 0 \\ 6 \end{pmatrix} \times 0.25^0 \times 0.75^6 = 0.75^6 = 0.17798$；猜对一次的概率是 $\begin{pmatrix} 1 \\ 6 \end{pmatrix} \times 0.25^1 \times 0.75^5 = 0.35596$；总和为 0.533 94。

52. 答案：C

解析：当 n 即观测次数逐渐增加，泊松的正态近似得到改善（Poisson 分布更接近正太分布）。

53. 答案：C

解析：方法一：计算 Z 值（标准化）$z_1 = (120 - 150/30) = -1$。$z_2 = (210 - 120)/30 = 2$。查表 Z 分布，$P(-1) = (1 - 0.8413) = 0.1587$，$P(2) = 0.9772$，$P(-1 < X < 2) = 0.9772 - 0.1587 = 0.8185$。

方法二：由于平均值在 +/− 1 个标准差内的概率约为 68%，这意味着平均值到 −1 标准差内的面积为 34%。平均值 +/− 2 个标准偏差的概率约为 95%。1.2 亿美元到 1.8 亿美元介于 −1 和 +2 之间，所以概率范围是(95%/ 2) = 47.5%。所以得到区间概率为(47.5% + 34%) = 81.5%的近似概率。

54. 答案：A

解析：Students t-distribution（学生 t 分布）是由一个参数自由度来定义的。

55. 答案：B

解析：对于给定的 N 次伯努力实验，二项随机变量 X 的方差等于 $np(1-p) = npq$，其中 q 代表失败概率。

56. 答案：C

解析：为了解决这个问题，我们首先需要认识到预期的 6 分钟服务客户的数量是 $\lambda = 2 \times 6 = 12$。利用泊松分布，我们知道 $X = 10$，$P\ (X = X) = (\lambda^x \times e^{-\lambda}) / X!$；$P\ (X = 10) = (12^{10} \times e^{-12})\ /10! = 0.104837 = 10.4837\%$。

57. 答案：A

解析：概率一定是等于一个介于 0 至 1 之间的数，但是概率分布不是正态分布。二项分布的概率不是成功就是失败。

58. 答案：C

解析：均值为 12%，标准差为 6%。想知道 6%或更高回报的概率。Z 值等于：$(6\% - 12\%)/6\% = -1$。$P(X > -1) = P(X = 1) = 84.13\%$。

59. 答案：B

解析：这个问题是用已知正态分布的信息来解答；$N(1)$表示从负无穷到 1 的概率为 0.841 3，由于 0.158 7 = 1 − 0.841 3 所以 1 到正无穷的概率就为 0.158 7；又由于正太分布左右对称的，所以负无穷到 1 的概率也为 0.158 7，即 $N(-1) = 0.1587$。

60. 答案：B

解析：样本容量足够大，或者大于等于 30。

61. 答案：C

解析：正态分布可以完全描述它的均值和方差。

62. 答案：D

解析：大于 5%的概率，确定 Z 值：$(5\% - 15\%) \div 10\% = -1$，$P(X > -1) = 1 - N(-1) = 0.8413$；大于 25%的概率，确定 Z 值：$(25\% - 15\%) \div 10\% = 1$，$P(X > 1) = 1 - 0.8413 = 0.1587$；介于 15%至 35%之间的概率为 $P(15\% - 15\% \div 10\% < x < 35\% - 15\% \div 10\%) = P(0 < x < 2) = 0.4772$；小于 25%的概率，确定 Z 值：$(25\% - 15\%) \div 10 = 1$，$N(1) = 0.8413$。

63. 答案：D

解析：$E(X) = np = 8 \times 0.55 = 4.4$，$Var(X) = np(1 - p) = 8 \times 0.55 \times 0.45 = 1.98$。

64. 答案：D

解析：假设用 S 表示成功，U 表示不成功和 W 表示良好的报告；我们有 $P(S) = 0.40$，$P(U) = 0.60$，$P(W \mid S) = 0.80$，和 $P(W \mid U) = 0.25$。利用贝叶斯定理，在给出有利报告的情况下，新品牌成功的概率为：

$$P(S \mid W) = \frac{P(S)P(W \mid S)}{P(S)P(W \mid S) + P(U)P(W \mid U)}$$

$$= \frac{0.40(0.80)}{0.40(0.80) + (0.60)(0.25)} = 0.680851$$

65. 答案：C

解析：根据贝叶斯公式：$P(A/\text{not default}) = P(\text{not default and } A)/P(\text{not default})$。

$P(\text{not default and } A) = P(\text{not default}/A) \times P(A) = 0.85 \times 0.40 = 0.34$。

$P(\text{not default and } BBB) = P(\text{not default}/BBB) \times P(BBB) = 0.75 \times 0.60 = 0.45$。

$P(\text{not default}) = P(\text{not default and } A) + P(\text{not default and } BBB) = 0.79$。

$P(A/\text{not default}) = P(\text{not default and } A)/P(\text{default}) = 0.34/0.79 = 0.43038$。

66. 答案：C

解析：使用加法规则，被谷歌或者苹果录取的概率 = $P(\text{apple}) + P(\text{google}) - P(\text{apple and google}) = 0.3 + 0.52 - 0.056 = 0.764$ 或 76.4%。

67. 答案：A

解析：$P(AB)=P(A\mid B)\times P(B)$ 先确定事件；假设：A，新开KFC；B，新开7－11便利店。所以 $P(A\mid B)$ 就表示在新开7－11便利店的情况下，新开KFC；所以 $P(AB)=0.9\times 0.7=0.63$。

68. 答案：C

解析：假设 I 代表证券种类为债券，B 代表发行方为国企的证券；要求的概率就是 I 和 B 的联合概率，$P(B\cup A)=P(B)+P(A)-P(B\cap A)$，$P(I)$ 的概率就为10/20；$P(B)$ 的概率为13/20；$P(B\cap A)$ 的概率为6/20；$P(B\cup A)=10/20+13/20-6/20=17/20$。

69. 答案：C

解析：概率加法规则用于确定两个或多个事件中至少发生一个事件的概率。将每个事件的概率相加，并减去联合概率(如果事件不是互斥的)以得到解决。

方法一：P(专业摄像头或环保电池)＝P(专业摄像头)＋P(环保电池)－P(专业摄像头和环保电池)＝105/225＋135/225－70/225＝75.6%。

方法二：1－P(没有专业摄像头和没有环保电池)＝1－55/225＝75.6%。

70. 答案：C

解析：显著性是指第一类错误或拒绝正确的概率，也叫 P(reject H_0 | H_0 is true)；相比之下，第二类错误是指接受错误的概率。

71. 答案：A

解析：显著性是指第一类错误或拒绝正确模型的概率，当显著性水平下降第一类错误也减小，选项B，C错误；当第一类错误减小了，会导致第二类错误上升，即接受错误的概率上升，选项D错误。

72. 答案：C

解析：根据公式：$\sigma/\sqrt{T}=\dfrac{100}{\text{sqrt }1\,600}=\dfrac{100}{40}=2.5$。

73. 答案：A

解析：我们可以从方差分解中找到 X 的波动率，公式：$V(X)=[V(Y)-V(e)]/\beta^2=(0.067\,6-0.01)/1.44=0.04$；所以 $SD(X)=0.2$。

$$\rho=\beta*\left(\frac{SD(X)}{SD(Y)}\right)=1.2\times\frac{0.2}{0.26}=0.923。$$

74. 答案：B

解析：使用双尾 t 检验；根据 t 检验的决定规则，先计算出 t 值，自由度为15，$\alpha/2=0.005$。

$$t_{15}=\frac{\bar{x}-\mu_0}{s/\sqrt{n}}=\frac{55-50}{6/\sqrt{16}}=3.33$$

查表知在 $df=15$，$\alpha/2=0.005$ 时的关键值等于2.947；由于3.33＞2.947，所以拒绝原假设。

75. 答案：B

解析：卡方检验用于检验单个方差的假设检验，所以卡方检验是单尾检验，如果 $X^2>\alpha=0.05$，$df=15$ 时的卡方关键值，则判定是拒绝 H_0。

$$x_{n-1}^2=\frac{(n-1)S^2}{\sigma_0^2}=\frac{15\times 36}{25}=22.5$$

右尾临界卡方值为 24.995 8，由于 $X^2=22.5<24.995\ 8$，H_0 不能被拒绝。

76. 答案：C

解析：由于总体方差未知，用单侧 t 检验。先计算出 t 值：

$$t_{24}=\frac{\bar{x}-\mu_0}{s/\sqrt{n}}=\frac{58-56}{8/\sqrt{25}}=1.25$$

根据查表在 $df=24$，$\alpha=0.1$ 的关键值等于 1.318；由于 1.318>1.25，所以不能拒绝原假设。

77. 答案：B

解析：如果估计量的抽样分布的方差小于所关注参数的其他估计量，估计量就是有效的。

78. 答案：C

解析：F-distributed 计算值的关键值公式，F，s_1^2/s_2^2；方差相等，$F=1$。

79. 答案：D

解析：根据样本方差计算公式 $S^2=\frac{\sum(X_i-\bar{x})^2}{n-1}=\frac{\sum(X_i-6)^2}{4}=32.5$ 所以 $S=5.700\ 9$。

80. 答案：A

解析：中心极限定理指出，人口平均 μ 和有限方差 σ^2，所有可能的样本均值的抽样分布的样本大小为 n 将近似为一个正态分布均值等于 μ 和方差等于 σ^2/n；样本的标准偏差等于：$\sigma(X)/\sqrt{n}$. 这种标准偏差测量被称为标准误差。

81. 答案：B(此题了解即可，考试不会遇到这么难的)

解析：使用假设检验的过程。

Step 1：建立假设检验，35%的奖金 H_0：$m\leqslant 40\%$，H_a：$m>40\%$（由于 40%与平均营业收入 24.2%相差过大，检验与否没有必要了）；20%的奖金 H_0：$m\leqslant 25\%$，H_a：$m>25\%$（H_0 与 H_a 交换原则，H_0 假设时遵循以下原则：①将主观上怀疑或者认为可能被拒绝的一方设为原假设；②如果假设检验时作出错误决策代价与成本很高，那么应该使做出错误决策概率较低，以此为原则设立原假设）20%的奖金假设检验变为 H_0：$m\geqslant 25\%$ H_a：$m<25\%$（通俗说就是老板避免发错钱的错误，所以原假设大于等于 25%）。

Step 2：选择合适的统计量，这里已知方差（标准差是方差的平方根）的正态分布总体和一个较大的样本容量（大于 30）所以，我们将使用 z 统计量。

Step 3：明确显著性水平 $\alpha=0.10$。

Step 4：拒绝法则，在显著性水平 $\alpha=0.10$ 的情况下对应的关键值 -1.28。

Step 5：计算统计量关键值，Z (for 20% bonus) $=(24.2-25)/(16/\sqrt{100})=-0.5$。

Step 6：做决定，同理 Z (for 20% bonus) $=-0.5>-1.28$ 统计量大于临界值，不能拒绝原假设，所以应该发 20%奖金。

82. 答案：B

解析：第一类错误发生在拒绝原假设，而原假设是真的时候；第二类错误发生在没有拒绝原假设，而原假设是假的时候。

83. 答案：D

解析：第一类错误发生在拒绝原假设，而原假设是真的时候；第二类错误发生在没有拒绝原假设，而原假设是假的时候。

84. 答案：A

解析：$Z_{\frac{\alpha}{2}} = Z_{0.025}$；所以置信区间为：$0.15 \pm 1.96 \times \frac{0.04}{8} = [14.02\%, 15.98\%]$。

85. 答案：C

解析：样本数量大于(30)使用 z 统计量。根据 Z 统计量计算公式 $= (X - \mu)/[\sigma/n^{(1/2)}] = (66\,000 - 60\,000)/[5\,500/145^{(1/2)}] = 13.136\,2$。

86. 答案：C

解析：研究者首先需要建立假设检验；更重要的是，在选择合适的检验统计量之前，有必要建立假设检验。

87. 答案：B

解析：总体标准差是方差的平方根（$\sqrt{0.36} = 0.6$）。因为我们知道总体标准差，我们用 z 统计量。95%置信区间的 z 统计可靠性因子是 1.96。置信区间是 $0.9 \pm 1.96 \times (0.6/\sqrt{49})$，计算出结果为[0.792, 1.068]。

88. 答案：C

解析：Z 统计量计算公式，the test statistic = (sample mean − hypothesized mean)/(population standard deviation/(sample size)$^{1/2}$

$$\frac{X - \mu}{\frac{\sigma}{\sqrt{N}}} = \frac{7.5 - 6}{\frac{4}{\sqrt{25}}} = 1.875$$

89. 答案：A

解析：备择假设一般是研究者所相信的。研究人员指定 $NF \leqslant JF$ 作为原假设；他希望拒绝原假假设（支持另一种选择）；注意，通常我们都把我们需要验证的理论放在备择假设里。

90. 答案：C

解析：根据置信区间的计算公式：$\bar{X} \pm Z_{\frac{\alpha}{2}} \times \frac{\sigma}{\sqrt{n}} = 9 \pm 1.96(1)$。注意：在95%置信水平下的置信因子是 1.96。

91. 答案：D

解析：F 检验用于检验两个样本之间方差的差异。

92. 答案：B

解析：均值为标准误 $= s/\sqrt{n} = 24\%/\sqrt{36} = 4\%$；由于总体方差未知用 t 分布构造统计量；$df(n-1)$ 对应的临界值为 2.030 1。这就得到了一个近似的置信区间：$9\% \pm 2.030\,1 \times (4\%)$ 得到[0.879 6%, 17.120 4%]。

如果你使用 z 统计量，置信区间为 $9\% \pm 1.96 \times (4\%) = [1.16, 16.84\%]$ 这是最接近正

确的选择。

93. 答案：D

解析：注意这里的样本大小是年：样本均值的标准误(standard error of the sample mean) = $16\%/\sqrt{38} = 2.595\%$。

94. 答案：D

解析：两个股票收益的均值：

$(0.06+0.05+0.02+0.13)/4=0.065$ 和 $(0.02+0.09+0.02+0.04)/4=0.0425$。

两个股票标准差为：$\sigma_1 = \dfrac{\sqrt{\Sigma(x-\bar{x})^2}}{n-1} = 0.0465 \quad \sigma_2 = \dfrac{\sqrt{\Sigma(x-\bar{x})^2}}{n-1} = 0.03304$。

协方差是：$\text{cov}(1,2) = \rho \times \sigma_1 \times \sigma_2 = 0.56 \times 0.0465 \times 0.03304 = 0.000645$。

95. 答案：B

解析：根据样本均值的标准误(standard error of the sample mea)计算公式：$18\% \div \sqrt{360} = 0.948\%$。

96. 答案：C

解析：置信区间等于 $28.5 \pm 2.56X$，这里 X 就是标准误；现在我们知道区间上下界，所以我们可以求出标准误：$28.5 +/- 2.56x = 20$，or $2.56x = 8.5$；$x = 3.32$。

97. 答案：D

解析：$\dfrac{X-\mu}{\sigma/\sqrt{N}} = \dfrac{2.5\%-0}{3\%/\sqrt{16}} = 3.33$。

98. 答案：A

解析：在99%的置信水平下，Z 统计量关键值2.56；根据决定法则，$2.8>2.56$，所以我们拒绝原假设，得到总体均值与1不显著的结论。

99. 答案：D

解析：H_o：$\mu=11$；H_a：$\mu \neq 11$. 不能拒绝原假设 $|t|=1.39<1.96$ (critical value)。

100. 答案：C

解析：备择假设一般是研究者想要支持的假设，所以小于(less than)应该放在备择假设。

101. 答案：B

解析：两个样本方差相等的 F 检验的检验统计量是两个样本方差的比率。

$$F = \frac{S_1^2}{S_2^2}$$

102. 答案：D

解析：自变量与残差(或扰动项)不相关。其他选项是对的。扰动项是同方差的，因为它具有恒定的方差；它是独立分布的，因为一个观测值的残差与另一个观测值的残差不相关。

103. 答案：C

解析：这是一个第二类错误。原假设是被告是无辜的，这一假设应该被拒绝但是却没有被拒绝。

104. 答案：D

解析：在 5%的显著性水平双尾检验的关键 z 统计量是 1.96；原假设 H_0：$x = 12\%$。备择假设 H_a：$x \neq 10\%$。由于计算的 z 统计量大于临界 z 统计量（1.4＜1.96），因此我们不能拒绝原假设，并得出大盘收益接近 12%的结论。

105. 答案：B

解析：H_o：$\mu = 5$ hours。

106. 答案：B

解析：这是一个双边测试。我们想要测试如果平均 5 小时（即"不同"。H_a：$\mu \neq 5$ 小时）。

107. 答案：B

解析：$\dfrac{X-\mu}{\sigma/\sqrt{N}} = \dfrac{5-4.5}{2.5/\sqrt{36}} = -1.2$。

108. 答案：A

解析：在 $\alpha/2 = 0.005$，Z 关键值等于：$= \pm 2.56$。

109. 答案：B

解析：拒绝法则：拒绝 H_0；如果计算出的 Z 值＜－2.56，或计算出的 Z 值＞＋1.96。由于－1.20＞－2.56，接受 H_0。

110. 答案：B

解析：关键值（1－95%，23－2 df.）＝2.08

截距的置信区间＝269.67 ＋/－ StandardError（截距的标准误）×2.08

斜率的置信区间＝0.52 ＋/－ StandardError（斜率的标准误）×2.08

111. 答案：C

解析：ESS/TSS＝947.906÷1 072＝0.884 241。

112. 答案：B

解析：检验统计量 $t = (1.5-0)/0.55 = 2.727$。28 个自由度的关键是 2.763＞2.727 因此，不能拒绝原假设，斜率显著等于 0。

113. 答案：C

解析：样本回归函数有一个残差而不是一个误差项；虽然残差项和误差项在它们各自的方程中具有相似的目的，但也有区别。

114. 答案：C

解析：自由度为 $n-k-1$，k 是自变量的数量。$df = 24-1-1 = 22$。在 t 分布中查找 22 个自由度，得到 95%置信水平，双尾部检验的临界值是 2.074。置信区间是 1.22±2.074×（0.45）得到｛$0.286\,7 < b_1 < 2.153\,3$｝。

115. 答案：B

解析：Y = 截距项（intercept）+ 斜率（slope）×（X）

小盘股收益（small Stock returns）= 1.68 + 1.42 × 12 = 18.72%。

116. 答案：C

解析：Y 的预测值为：$Y = 6.0 - [1.3 \times 10] = 6 - 13 = -7$。

117. 答案：C

解析：拟合优度、确定系数和 R^2 是同一概念的不同名称；变异系数不是回归模型的直接部分。

118. 答案：A

解析：R^2，或确定系数，是相关系数(r)的平方，相关系数描述了 X 和 Y 变量之间线性关系的强度；在 B 选项中“由因变量的可变性解释的自变量的可变性百分比”，变量的定义是相反的。

119. 答案：D

解析：斜率表示自变量一单位变化导致因变量会变动多少；如果 X 的值为零，则 Y 的值将等于截距，在这种情况下为 0.88。

120. 答案：C

解析：如果相关性为 1.0，那么 y 变量与 x 变量值正比例相关；这些点位于从西南到东北的直线上。

121. 答案：D

解析：截距项等于因变量，当自变量的值都为零的时候。

122. 答案：B

解析：预测销售额为：销售额 = 2.85 + [1.5×(5)] = 10.35 million。

123. 答案：B

解析：线性回归(不是线性函数)，要求系数是线性的，对变量是否是线性没有要求；也就是说变量可以是线性的，也可以是非线性的。Joy 的描述中 $B1^2$ 不是线性的，所以这个不是线性回归。

124. 答案：A

解析：自变量是预测变量，因变量是被预测变量。

125. 答案：C

解析：完全相关意味着观察值落在回归线。斜率为正表示直线向上，斜率为负表示直线向下；R^2 为 100% 表示完全相关。当没有相关性时，回归线是平的，残差标准差等于 Y 的标准差。

126. 答案：B

解析：这个问题需要建立一个回归模型，根据题目给出的 $R(A) = 2\% + 0.9 \times (10\%/10\%) \times [R(B) - 2\%] + \epsilon$；带入 $R(B) = 3\%$ 得到 $R(A) = 2.9\%$。

127. 答案：D

解析：由于样本协方差的范围可以从负到正无穷取决于两个变量的规模，它是最常用来计算一个更有用统计量相关系数。

128. 答案：C

解析：决定系数，$R^2 = ESS/TSS = 1.728/4.442 = 0.3890$；这个题目中相关系数，$r = \text{sqrt}(R^2) = \text{sqrt}(0.3890) = 62.37\%$。

129. 答案：A

解析：由于 $R^2 = 1 - SSR/TSS$，$SSR = (1 - R^2) \times TSS$。在这个题目中，$SSR = (1 - 0.18) \times 3.23 = 2.6486\ dollars^2$. $SER = \text{sqrt}[SSR/(n - k - 1)]$，由于 $n - k - 1$，$k = 1$，因此 $SER = \text{sqrt}(2.6486/34) = 0.279$。

130. 答案：B

解析：根据 beta (stock，index) = covariance(stock，index)/variance(index) = correlation(stock，index) × volatility(stock)/volatility(index)，推导出
correlation(stock，index) = beta (stock，index) × volatility(index)/volatility(stock)；所以 correlation(stock，index) = 1.050 × 20% ÷ 30% = 0.70，R^2 = correlation^2 = $0.70^2 = 0.49$。

由于 $R^2 = ESS/TSS$，$ESS = R^2 \times TSS$。所以我们可以计算出 $ESS = 0.49 \times 0.30 = 0.1470$

131. 答案：C

解析：由于 $SER = Sqrt[SSR/(n-k-1)]$，$SSR = SER^2 \times (n-k-1)$。本题中，(again，2 coefficients = 2 df)：$SSR = 1.20^2 \times (60-2) = 83.52$；

$R^2 = ESS/TSS = 1 - SSR/TSS = 1 - 83.52/90.625 = 0.07840$；

$correlation = SQRT(0.07840) = 0.280$。

132. 答案：B

解析：根据决定系数的计算公式：$\beta^2 \times \left(\frac{\sigma_M^2}{\sigma_P^2}\right) = 0.977^2 \times \left(\frac{0.156^2}{0.167^2}\right) = 0.83$。

133. 答案：D

解析：相关性是 $\sqrt{0.66} = 0.81$，所以Ⅰ是不正确的。接下来，66%的 Y 变化是由基准(benchmark)解释的，所以Ⅱ是不正确的。投资组合收益是因变量 Y，所以Ⅲ的说法是正确的；最后，为了求出 95%双尾置信区间，我们使用正态分布中的 Z 值(1.9695%的置信区间)，由于 1.96 接近 2.0；区间为 $[y - 2SD(e);\ y + 2SD(e)]$，得到(7.16；16.84) 所以Ⅳ说法正确，即Ⅲ和Ⅳ正确。

134. 答案：D

解析：年龄和经验可能高度相关；当系数的标准误差很大时，即使 R^2 很高，多重共线性也会表现出来。

135. 答案：B

解析：当残差的方差不是常数时会出现异方差，因此 A 选项是正确的；条件异方差会影响假设检验，但是不影响估计结果，B 选项错误。

136. 答案：D

解析：如果回归包含了三个变量并且 Z 同时对 X、Y 都产生影响，则误差项将不会有条件地独立于 X，这违反了 OLS 模型的假设之一。这会人为地增加回归的解释力。变量 X 只是因为与 Z 相关而更多地解释了 Y 的变化。

137. 答案：C

解析：观测数量变为原来的 4 倍，置信区间的范围将减少一半；之所以出现这种改进，是因为区间是由标准差除以观测数量的平方根确定的。

138. 答案：D

解析：自变量与残差不相关。

139. 答案：C

解析：相关系数是 R^2 的平方根，$r = 0.87$。

计算协方差将相关系数乘以两个变量的标准差的乘积：COV = $0.87 \times \sqrt{5} \times \sqrt{8}$ =

5.5。

140. 答案：B

解析：误差项体现了模型中省略的变量的影响。

141. 答案：A

解析：如果存在相关性时就存在自相关，这样会导致残差项不是正态分布的；这与线性回归不一致。

142. 答案：D

解析：假设检验细分有 7 个步骤：

1. 建立假设检验；
2. 计算测试统计量及其概率分布；
3. 指定显著性级别；
4. 说明决策规则；
5. 收集数据并执行计算；
6. 做出统计决策；
7. 做出经济或投资决策。

假设检验不需要对结果进行分析。

143. 答案：B

解析：添加回归变量对调整的 R^2 的影响不能够确定是变小。

144. 答案：C

解析：计算出 $SER=3.43$，Adjusted $R^2=0.22$。

$SER=SQRT[SSR\div(n-k-1)]=SQRT[106\div(12-2-1)]=3.43$。

Adjusted $R^2=1-SSR/TSS\times[(n-1)\div(n-k-1)]=1-106\div166\times(11/9)=0.22$。

145. 答案：A

解析：由于 $SER=SQRT\ [RSS/n-k-1]$ 时，df 的增加会使 SER 减小；B，这是正确的：$R^2=1-RSS/TSS$。当 $RSS=0$ 意味着 $R^2=1.0$；C 是正确的，因为 $SER=SQRT\ [RSS/n-k-1]$ 推导出 $RSS=SER^2\times n-k-1$；D 是正确的，SER 和 R^2 都可以有效地估计回归的拟合优度。

146. 答案：D

解析：由于 sample variance(样本方差) $=\sum(Y(i)-Y)^2/(n-1)$，所以可以推导出 $\sum(Y(i)-Y)^2=$ sample variance $\times(n-1)$，(注意 $\sum(Y(i)-Y)^2$) 代表 TSS)，$TSS=66.67\times9=600.03$；$R^2=ESS/TSS=238/600.03=0.396\,646\,83$；$\rho=\sqrt{(R^2)}=0.629\,79$。

147. 答案：D

解析：对数线性模型最适合于以相对恒定的增长率增长的时间序列。

148. 答案：B

解析：自由度惩罚因子最大的最一致选择准则是 Schwarz 信息准则(SIC)。虽然 SIC 被认为是最一致的标准，但 AIC 仍然是一个有用的衡量标准。如果我们考虑到真实的模型可能比想象中的模型要复杂得多,那么就应该检查 AIC 度量。

149. 答案:C

解析:Schwarz 信息准则(*SIC*)具有最高的惩罚因子;均方误差(*MSE*)不会基于增加的参数 k 来惩罚回归模型;$s2$,*AIC* 和 *SIC* 的惩罚因子分别是$(T/T-k)$,$e^{(2k/T)}$和 $T(k/T)$;所以,*SIC* 具有最大的惩罚因子。

150. 答案:B

解析:关于 *SIC*,惩罚因子计算为 $T^{(k/T)}$;罚因子等于 $450^{(36/450)} = 450^{0.08} = 1.63$。

151. 答案:A

解析:在 *MSE* 统计量中将残差平方和乘以 $1/T$ 不会改变基于残差平方的模型的排名;排名不会改变。

152. 答案:B

解析:$MSE = SSR/T = 1\,435/100 = 14.35$;

修正后的 $MSE = SSR/(T-k-1) = 1\,435/(100-8-1) = 15.769$;

SER = sqrt(修正的 MSE) = sqrt$[SSR/(T-k-1)]$ = sqrt$[1\,435/(100-8-1)]$ = 3.97。

153. 答案:C

解析:*MSE*,S^2,*AIC*,*SIC* 四个判断指标只有 *SIC* 满足一致性(Consistent)。

154. 答案:D

解析:$A(t) = \beta(0) \times \exp[\beta(1) \times TIME(t)]$ 描述以 $\beta(1)$的连续速率增长的指数趋势;在这种情况下,$\beta(0)$是 \$100.00 的初始值,$\beta(1)$是 9.0%的增长率。然后我们也可以得到两边的自然对数并观察到 $LN[A(t)]$是时间的线性函数:$LN[A(t)] = \ln(\beta(0) \times \exp[\beta(1) \times TIME(t)]) = LN[\beta(0)] + \ln(\exp[\beta(1) \times TIME(t)]) = \ln[\beta(0)] + \beta(1) \times TIME(t)$。

155. 答案:D

解析:利用二元一次方程知识,图像开口朝上,二次项系数为正数排除 B, C;对称轴在 Y 轴右侧,所以一次项系数为负。

156. 答案:D

解析:相关图表上显示的波段通常是零或 $2/\sqrt{T}$ 的两个标准误差。

157. 答案:A

解析:预测经季节性调整的公司收益时间序列是不合适的:在这种业务情况下,我们希望预测时间序列中的所有变化,而不仅仅是非季节性部分。通过消除季节变化然后建模和预测季节性调整的时间序列来完成季节性调整,这种类型的调整通常在宏观经济预测中进行,其目标是仅测量变量的非季节性波动。

158. 答案:C

解析:每当我们想要在包含截距的模型中区分 s 个季度时,我们必须使用 $s-1$ 虚拟变量;一年有四个季度数据,$s=4$,那么我们将包括 $s-1=3$ 个季节性虚拟变量。

159. 答案:D

解析:截距项表示第四季度每股收益的平均值。每个虚拟变量的斜率系数估计了每个季度(即,第一、二或三季度)和遗漏的季度(第四季度)的差额。

160. 答案：B

解析：就业率受到每年毕业季影响；每年 6 月大学毕业都会有大部分学生参加就业；大部分企业春招和秋招都会有大批应届生就业；所以就业率最有可能包含季节性。

161. 答案：C

解析：如果模型已经包含一个截距，那么只需要 $(s-1)$ 虚拟变量。

162. 答案：C

解析：2010 年 Q1 发生在 20×4 = 80 季度，在 95%的置信区间 $y(t)=0.510+2.30\times 80\pm \text{sqrt}(16)\times 1.96$；算出结果在[177，192]这个范围。

163. 答案：D

解析：理论上，时间序列的长度可以是无限的，但协方差仍然是平稳的；要使协方差平稳，时间序列必须有一个稳定的均值、一个稳定的协方差结构（自协方差只依赖于位移，不依赖于时间）和一个有限的方差。

164. 答案：B

解析：如果白噪声过程是高斯的（正太分布）则该过程是独立的白噪声；但是事实并非如此；可以有独立的非正态分布的白噪声过程。C 选项错误。只有那些均值为零、方差为常数的序列不相关的过程才是白噪声。

165. 答案：D

解析：一致性表示指标需要满足的两个特征。

166. 答案：A

解析：季节性时间序列不是协方差平稳的。

167. 答案：C

解析：因为 $y(T+23)=0.30\times 23+20.10+0.9\times 1=27.90$，2018 年 10 月住房开工数为 $27.9\times 1\,000=27\,900$。

168. 答案：C

解析：虽然许多模型不是协方差平稳的，但是经常可以使用对非平稳部分进行特殊处理的模型，如趋势和季节性，这样剩下的周期性的部分可能是协方差静止的。我们将通常采用这种方法。

169. 答案：D

解析：协方差平稳需要满足的三个条件：①均值有限且为常数，即 $E(y_t)=\mu$；②方差有限且为常数，即 $VaR(y_t)=\sigma^2$；③协方差只与滞后阶数 π 有关，与时期 t 无关，即 $\text{Cov}(y_t,\ y_{t-1})=\gamma(\pi)$。

170. 答案：A

解析：首先，零均值白噪声可能是不相关的，但不一定是串联独立的（相关性和独立性之间的差异）。其次，白噪声（也就是零均值白噪声）不一定是正态分布的。

171. 答案：B

解析：白噪声（又名弱白噪声，零均值白噪声）不一定要正态分布；（弱）白噪声要求不相关，零均值的平稳观测。

172. 答案：B

解析：如果预测者在自相关系数逐渐衰减的过程中注意到周期性的峰值，这表明数据中可能存在季节性效应。

173. 答案：D

解析：移动平均（*MA*）表示与自回归（*AR*）过程的关键区别在于，*MA* 过程显示自相关截止；而 *AR* 过程显示自相关的逐渐衰减。

174. 答案：D

解析：使用更多的独立变量的目的在 q^{th} 移动平均过程获取更好的估计因变量。滞后算子越多，估计的稳健性越强。

175. 答案：D

解析：自相关是 $y(t)$ 和 $y(t-\pi)$ 之间的相关关系，偏自相关是在控制 $y(t-1)\cdots y(t-\pi+1)$ 不变的情况下，测量 $y(t)$ 和 $y(t-\pi)$ 之间的关联。

176. 答案：C

解析：任何纯粹的非确定性协方差平稳过程都是白噪声过程的滞后值的线性组合。

177. 答案：D

解析：*ARMA*(1，1)在条件下是协方差平稳的；*ARMA* 过程具有固定的无条件均值和随时间变化的条件均值。

178. 答案：A

解析：在 95%的置信区间下，CHISQ.INV(0.95，24) = 36.41，两个统计量均小于临界值；即；落入卡方分布的接受区间，即接受这个白噪声。

179. 答案：B

解析：Ljung-Box Q 统计量与 Box-Pierce Q 统计量有效相似，不同之处在于它适用于小样本。

180. 答案：A

解析：GARCH 方程的格式 $\sigma^2 n = \omega + \alpha\mu_{n-1}^2 + \beta\sigma_{n-1}^2$，$(\alpha+\beta)$ = 持久性。要使模型随时间保持稳定，持久性必须小于 1。持久性为 1 意味着不存在均值回归，持久性越高（假设它小于 1），波动性在发生重大震荡或波动后恢复到长期均值水平所需的时间就越长。股票 2 的持久性为 0.99(0.04 + 0.95)，小于 1，表示存在均值回归。股票 2 的持久性高于股票 1，意味着股票 2 的均值回归时间更长，也就是股票 1 的均值回归时间更快。因为方程 1 的持久性小于 1，所以方程 1 是一个平稳模型。方程 3 的持久性大于 1，这意味着模型没有均值回归。只有表述Ⅰ是正确的。

181. 答案：D

解析：假设随机游走，我们可以使用时间平方根法则。每周波动率 = 34 34% × $1/\sqrt{52}$ = 4.71%。

182. 答案：A

解析：随着均值回归，波动率的增长速度比时间的平方根要慢。

183. 答案：D

解析：根据计算投资组合方差的公式：$\sigma_P^2 = (0.4)^2 \times 25 + (0.6)^2 \times 121 + 2 \times 0.4 \times 0.6 \times 0.3\sqrt{25 \times 121} = 55.48$，所以波动率为 7.45。

184. 答案：B

解析：由于 $(\alpha+\beta)$ 代表持久性，*A*，*B*，*C*，*D* 值分别为 0.94，0.98，0.97 和 0.96；

具有最高持久性的模型将花费最长的时间来恢复到平均值。

185. 答案：D

解析：如果初始波动率等于长期波动率，则可以使用时间平方根规则计算 T 日 VAR，假设正态分布。如果起始波动率较高，那么 T 日 VAR 应小于$\sqrt{T}$乘以一天 VAR。相反，如果起始波动率较低，那么 T 日 VAR 应该大于长期值。但是，问题并不表明起点。因此回答 D。是正确的。

186. 答案：B

解析：长期均值方差为 $b = \alpha_0 \div (1 - \alpha_1 - \beta) = 5 \times 10^{-7} \div (1 - 0.04 - 0.94) 0.0025$，取平方根，得到每日波动率为 0.005，乘以$\sqrt{252}$得到年化波动率为 7.937%。

187. 答案：D

解析：GARCH 模型在条件波动率中具有均值回归，因此 A 和 B 是正确的；当 σ_t 低于长期平均值时，波动率将会上升；较高的持久性 $\alpha + \beta$ 意味着平均回归较慢，因此声明 C 也是正确的。

188. 答案：A

解析：收益率为 $\ln(18/20) = -10.54\%$。预测的方差 $b = 0.90 \times (1.5\%)^2 + (1 - 0.90) \times (-10.54\%)^2 = 0.001313$，取平方根得到 3.62%。

189. 答案：B

解析：最后一天的权重为 $(1 - 0.95) = 0.050$；前一天是 0.05×0.95，四天前的权重是 $0.05 \times 0.95^3 = 0.04287$。

190. 答案：B

解析：该模型假设固定收益市场中只有一个风险来源，这是一个单因素期限结构模型。

191. 答案：D

解析：$V_l = \dfrac{\omega}{1 - \alpha - \beta} = \dfrac{0.05}{1 - 0.4 - 0.32} = 0.178$。

192. 答案：B

解析：收益率 $u_i = \ln \dfrac{S_i}{S_{i-1}} = \ln \dfrac{29.5}{28} = 5.22\%$。

$\sigma_n^2 = 0.92 \times 0.025^2 + (1 - 0.92) \times 0.0522^2 = 0.000793$ 开根号得 2.82%。

193. 答案：D

解析：$\sigma_n^2 = 0.85 \times 0.025^2 + (1 - 0.85) \times 0.007^2 = 0.000538$ 开根号得 2.32%。

194. 答案：A

解析：根据 n 天前收益率权重推导公式：

$\lambda^{n-1} \times (1 - \lambda) = 0.93^6 \times (1 - 0.93) = 0.045289$。

195. 答案：D

解析：随机游走意味着有效市场，有效市场一词意味着未来回报的分配不依赖于过去的回报，回报不相关；但可能会发生回报分布是独立的，偶然情况下，两个连续的回报相也可能相等。

196. 答案：D

解析：EWMA 模型在最新观测值上的权重为 0.06，高于 60 天等权重（1/60）= 0.016 7 和 250 天（1/250）= 0.04 的权重。

197. 答案：D

解析：协方差（X，Y）= $E(X \times Y) - E(X) \times E(Y)$ = 5.20 − 1.50 × 3.40 = 0.10。标准差（X）= 0.50；标准差（Y）= sqrt(0.240) = 0.489 89，所以可以求出 X 和 Y 的相关系数 = Covariance(X，Y) ÷ [Standard deviation(X) × Standard deviation(Y)] = 0.10/[0.50 * sqrt(0.240)] = 0.408 248。

198. 答案：B

解析：A 与 B 的协方差 Covariance(A，B) = $\beta(A) \times \beta(B) \times \sigma(M)^2$ = 0.80 × 1.40 × 0.20^2 = 0.044 80；相关系数为 correlation(A，B) = 0.044 80/(0.32 × 0.40) = 0.350。

199. 答案：B

解析：0.70 × 0.12 = 0.084 0。

200. 答案：C

解析：Covariance($n-1$) = 0.50 × 2.0% × 3.0% = 0.000 30；

Covariance(n) = 0.85 × 0.000 30 + (1 − 0.85) × (− 2.0%) × (− 5.0%) = 0.000 405 0；

Updated variance(A) = $\sigma^2(A)$ = 0.85 × $2.0\%^2$ + (1 − 0.85) × (− $2.0\%^2$) = 0.000 400；

Updated variance(B) = $\sigma^2(B)$ = 0.85 × $3.0\%^2$ + (1 − 0.85) × (− $5.0\%^2$) = 0.001 140；

Update correlation, $\rho(A, B)$, = 0.000 405 0/[sqrt(0.000 400) * sqrt(0.001 140)] = 0.599 75。

201. 答案：D

解析：Covariance($n-1$) = 0.30 × 3.0% × 5.0% = 0.000 45；

Covariance(n) = 0.8 × 0.000 45 + (1 − 0.8) × ln(11/10) × ln(21/20) = 0.001 29；

Updated variance(A) = $\sigma^2(A)$ = 0.8 × $3.0\%^2$ + (1 − 0.8) × $[\ln(11/10)]^2$ = 0.001 816 81，$\sigma(A)$ = 0.002 537；

Updated variance(B) = $\sigma^2(B)$ = 0.8 × $5.0\%^2$ + (1 − 0.8) × $[\ln(21/20)]^2$ = 0.002 476 06，$\sigma(B)$ = 0.050 36；

Update correlation, $\rho(A, B)$ = 0.001 29/(0.042 624 × 0.049 768) = 0.514 8。

202. 答案：C

解析：Covariance($n-1$) = 0.50 × 3.0% × 6.0% = 0.000 9；

Covariance(n) = 0.001 544；

Updated $\sigma(A)$ = 0.034 82；

Updated $\sigma(B)$ = 0.068 68；

Update correlation, $\rho(A, B)$ = 0.001 542 ÷ (0.002 537 × 0.050 36) = 0.645 6。

203. 答案：D

解析：相关系数 (correlation coefficient) = $a(1) \times a(2)$ = 0.650 × 0.480 = 0.312 0。

204. 答案：B

解析：连接函数(Copula)可用于定义两个以上变量之间的相关结构。

205. 答案：D

解析：略。

206. 答案：D

解析：股票价格的过程的波动率 $\sigma\sqrt{\Delta T}=0.14\times\sqrt{0.01}=0.014$；因此第一步是 $S_1=S_0(1+0.014\times0.263)=100.37$；第二步是 $S_2=S_1[1+0.014\times(-0.475)]=99.70$。

207. 答案：B

解析：dS/S 和 $d\ln(S)$ 都是正态分布；S 是对数正态分布，所以唯一不正确的答案是Ⅰ。

208. 答案：A

解析：A 选项太绝对了。预期价格高于今天的价格，但肯定不是所有的价格都高于今天的价格。

209. 答案：A

解析：这是期限结构的无套利模型，为单因素模型或双因素模型。

210. 答案：B

解析：Vasicek 和 CIR 模型都是具有均值回归的单因素均衡模型；Hull-White 模型是一种具有均值回归的无套利模型；Ho-Lee 模型是一种早期无套利模型，没有均值回归。

211. 答案：B

解析：蒙特卡罗模拟能解释期权；第一步是模拟风险因素的过程，第二步为期权定价，所以 *MC* 能解释非线性。

212. 答案：D

解析：空头期权头寸有很长的左尾，这使精确估计左尾分位数变得更加困难，准确性随着 k 的平方根的增加而增加；所以增加重复次数会缩小标准误差，所以答案 D 是正确的。

213. 答案：B

解析：观察次数的减少和置信度的提高，导致抽样变异（或不精确）增加；所以，样本均值的精度与数据点个数的平方根呈反比；同样的，更高的置信水平意味着在左尾尾部有更少的观测值(即更少的 exception)。

214. 答案：A

解析：变量 ε 应具有标准正态分布(具有平均零和单位标准偏差)；答案 B 是不正确的，因为 ε 随后被转换为所需的均值和标准差；此处不应用 Cholesky 分解，因为随机变量序列没有序列相关性。

第三部分

金融市场和产品

1. 答案：C

解析：经济资本指的是银行通过自己内部评估、模型测算等方式估计出来的资本类型，一般来说，经济资本通常低于监管要求的需要，维持最低资本充足率的资本数额。

2. 答案：B

解析：银行建立防火墙是一种内控方式，目的在于防止商业银行、投资银行相互进行信息共享来获取非法利益。

3. 答案：A

解析：收取风险费率制保费是一种应对银行道德风险的方式，这种做法是保险公司在承担更高风险的一种补偿方式。

4. 答案：D

解析：在包销模式下，投行会先将拟发行证券全额买进然后再通过一级市场高价卖给公众，但是在定向增发或者代销模式下，投行仅仅赚取服务费收入而非买卖证券价差，而A选项的荷兰式拍卖模式指的是证券的定价方式而不涉及投行参与买卖证券。

5. 答案：D

解析：在代销 best effort basis 协议下，投行仅仅是中间代理销售证券而非自己先全额购买(包销)，如果没有完全卖掉，投行是不需要对未销售的部分承担责任的。

6. 答案：D

解析：在银行的资产证券化模式下，将贷款打包出售发行资产支持证券获取资金可以用再贷款，某种程度上是可以扩大借贷水平的，但是这会降低银行的借贷标准；降低了贷款标准可能会提升银行的风险。

7. 答案：A

解析：由于经济资本通常是低于监管资本的，所以银行必须要维持监管资本的最低要求，经济资本是银行自身结合实际情况和模型测算估计出的资本数额，而监管资本是监管者要求的银行最低资本数额，根据监管要求，权益资本被划分为一级资本，次级长期债被划分为二级资本。

8. 答案：B

解析：银行的交易账户指的是跟银行的交易活动相关的资产和负债，而银行账户指的是跟存贷款相关的资产和负债，对于银行账户中的不良贷款是缺乏流动性的，所以是不可以用市场价格模型来计量的，选项D错误。

9. 答案：C

解析：责任险公司最容易面临长尾风险，即在保险期过后可能会出现的法律责任。例如，在一个致癌险合同中，保险期内病患癌症状并未出现，但是在很多年后出现了症状。

10. 答案：B

解析：经营比率等于承保损失率加上费用率加上股利支付率减去投资收益率 = loss ratio (74%) + expense ratio (23%) + dividends (2%) − investment income (5%) = 94%。而合并比率 = 承保损失率加上费用率 = loss ratio (74%) + expense ratio (23%) = 97%。

分红后合并比率等于承保损失率加上费用率加上股利支付率 = loss ratio (74%) + expense ratio (23%) + dividends (2%) = 99%。

11. 答案：A

解析：逆向选择是指的当保险公司无法辨别被保险人或者财产的好坏的时候，尤其是在寿险合同中，对保单持有人收取相同的保费(忽略了被保险人健康状况)，这样的话保险公司可能面临被保险人健康状况下降的风险，为了规避逆向选择，寿险公司会要求在签单之前被保险人提供体检证明。

12. 答案：A

解析：当存款人过少的关注银行自身的财务状况时，存款保险制度更加容易引发道德风险，而非过多，所以 A 错误

13. 答案：C

解析：预期一年期赔付金额的期望 = 0.005 038 × $250 000 = $1 259.50，所以假设年中赔付事件发生的话，那么，贴现到当前时点上的保费金额 = $1 259.50 ÷ 1.02 = $1 234.80，所以盈亏平衡点上的保费金额是 1 234.8。

14. 答案：D

解析：DB plan 不涉及个人账户，个人养老金的计算仅仅基于养老金基金的账户，B 不对。相反，DB plan 为所有雇员提供一个集合账户，所以养老金的缴纳和支付都来自该账户，DB plan 会明确承诺雇员在退休后每期会受到的养老金的数额。

15. 答案：D

解析：长寿风险对于年金支付保险来说是坏事但是对于生命险来说是好事，因为生命险可以比预期中更晚来支付给被保险人由于死亡的保险金赔付，而对于死亡风险来说刚好相反。

16. 答案：B

解析：对于财险公司来说，经营比率等于分红后合并比率减去投资收益，由于现金流流入流出期限的错配可以使得保险公司进行投资获取投资收益。

17. 答案：B

解析：保险公司通常投资于固定收益证券，而这类证券一般都是长期债券。如果违约增加，保险公司将会遭受损失，投资分散化可以有效减小这种损失。

18. 答案：C

解析：开放式基金由于是定期公布净资产价值使得其价格透明度比较低，所以一般都是在收盘之后才会公布价格，而盘中很难计算，因此对于开放式基金的买卖只能以市场

指令报价，而封闭式基金可以在二级市场交易所以可以执行止损指令或者限价指令，对于特殊的比如 ETF 基金，可以卖空。

19. 答案：B

解析：共同基金接受实时赎回，这是 *SEC* 的要求，但是对冲基金必须要有通知期和锁定期，是不可以实时赎回的。

20. 答案：A

解析：该对冲基金的预期收益率为，当盈利的时候收取 2%的固定费率加上超出的 53%的盈利的 20%，等于 12.6%，而当亏损的时候收取 2%的固定费率，所以按照各自的概率算出期望 $=(0.35\times 12.6\%)+(0.65\times 2\%)=5.71\%$。

21. 答案：B

解析：多空期股权投资基金是可以是市场中性的，该基金是通过做多做空股票头寸对冲进行获利，也可以是因素中性的，因素中性基金则是针对特殊的经济因素进行对冲，而非行业，比如针对石油价格和利率等因素进行对冲。

22. 答案：C

解析：该基金的净资产价值 $=\dfrac{450+100+25-10.5}{18.55}=30.43$。

23. 答案：A

解析：有管理的期货对冲基金试图通过技术分析或者基本面分析去预测现货价格未来的波动，技术分析主要通过过去的价格数据来总结规律作为预测依据，当技术分析被使用的时候，基金经理将利用历史数据回测他们的交易规则。

24. 答案：D

解析：有若干共同基金监管要求不适用对冲基金，比如投资者并不可以随时赎回基金份额，对冲基金也不用披露每日基金净值和投资策略。对冲基金和共同基金都提供专业化管理和，共同基金对所有市场投资者开放，而对冲基金仅仅对高净值和有投资经验的投资者开放，共同基金不可以加杠杆而对冲基金可以。

25. 答案：A

解析：对冲基金设置 2 加 20 的费率结构相对于硬门槛提成来说使得基金可以多赚取管理费，对投资者是不利的，而硬门槛提成，高水位提成以及回拨条款都是有利于保护投资者利益。

26. 答案：B

解析：看跌期权持有方的收益是 $(0, X-ST)$ 的孰高值，看涨期权的持有方的收益是 $(0, ST-X)$ 的最高值。

27. 答案：B

解析：看涨期权给予期权持有者以约定价格从卖方手里买进标的资产的权利。

28. 答案：D

解析：OTC 场外市场规模比交易所市场要大，并且不设置严格的期限，灵活磋商，记录期权交易。

29. 答案：B

解析：套利交易者试图通过发现证券的错误定价来获取无风险利润。

30. 答案：A

解析：看涨期权持有者的收益是行权价小于股价的差额 70－62＝8,看涨期权持有者的利润是行权价小于股价的差额再减去期权的权利金,8－3.25＝4.75。

31. 答案：C

解析：用于确定股票指数的无套利远期价格的套利模型不使用通货膨胀率,尽管它是无风险利率的一部分。

32. 答案：B

解析：买入报价是一个交易商愿意购买一个证券的最高报价。

33. 答案：B

解析：$Profit = St - S_0 + max\ (0,\ X - St) - P_0$

$= 541 - 575 + (575 - 541) - 3.70$

$= -3.70$

该空头交易(买入看跌期权)可以在股价下跌的时候保护投资者的利益,而唯一的成本就是期权权利金,通过该交易的获利是[(575－541)－3.70],而股票多头的获利是(541－575),所以总获利是＝541－575＋(575－541)－3.70＝－3.70。

34. 答案：A

解析：期货合约的初始投资包括初始保证金,而期权的初始买入的时候才是需要期权费(权利金)的。

35. 答案：C

解析：套利是指的针对同一资产在不同时刻价格不一样所面临的潜在获利机会,套利者需要快速的采取行动获取无风险利润,因为价格偏差会在短时间内快速修正,并且套利不需要资本,因为套利同时会做一笔反向交易。

36. 答案：C

解析：期货合约的盯市的方式结算,这降低了交易的信用风险。

37. 答案：C

解析：更替(Novation)涉及交易对手的替代,清算所使用此流程在买家和卖家之间进行干涉；这需要所有各方的同意。

38. 答案：B

解析：保证金支付确保所有的利润和损失是每一天的,并以现金/证券的方式来扣除损失。这大大降低了任何一方违约造成信用损失的可能性。

39. 答案：B

解析：该交易商必须在开始时提供 4 500 美元的保证金,如果保证金价值跌至 3 750 美元,就会接到追加保证金通知。假设价格将降至 P,交易员将收到维持保证金通知,(4 500－3 750)÷5 000＝0.15；所以价格只要下到 2.9 就会吃追加保证金通知。

40. 答案：B

解析：第一天价格下降 5,所以保证金账户损失＝5×250＝1 250；保证金账户还在维持保证金额之上,所以变动保证金为 0。

41. 答案：C

解析：逐日盯市机制是根据每日合约价值的变化每天计算需要追加或者可以提取的保

证金数额的每日结算制度。

42. 答案：D

解析：期货合约第一天收于 985 点，初始保证金 = 12 500 × 20 = 250 000 美元；维持保证金为 20 万美元，由于该头寸的价值在第一天损失了了 75 000 美元，因此保证金账户现在价值 175 000 美元（低于 20 万美元的维持保证金），需要 75 000 美元的变动保证金才能使该头寸恢复到最初的保证金。仅仅将头寸拉回维持保证金是不够的。

43. 答案：D

解析：June 1 期货价格上升 4.3，margin account 余额 = 2 000 + 100 × 4.3 = 2 430，June 2 价格相比 June 1 下跌 1.2，margin account 余额 = 2 430 − 1.2 × 100 = 2 310。

44. 答案：B

解析：期货合约是标准化合约，所以必须遵从交易所设置的合约条款，并且期货合约的交易所结算制度确保对手方不存在违约风险。

45. 答案：B

解析：投机者可以通过发现套利机会并交易来平滑价格波动性并提供市场流动性，但是当银行提高保证金比率的话会使其面临资金流动性的问题。

46. 答案：C

解析：将伦敦交易所的股价 52.03 英镑换算成美元：52.03 GBP × 1.557 \$ / GBP = 81 美元，所以可以在伦敦交易所卖出股票获得 81 美元，然后再在纳斯达克交易所以 76 美元购进，价格差额即套利所得。

47. 答案：A

解析：套利机会存在于当两种证券在未来将会产生确定的收益，并且该收益大于无风险利润的时候，所以可以以无风险利率借贷并购买可以产生确定的大于无风险利率的收益的资产。

48. 答案：C

解析：对于不同月份或合约的多头和空头头寸，主要面临基差风险。头寸Ⅱ是同一合约的两倍，因此没有基差风险（但存方向风险）。

49. 答案：C

解析：两个资产有一致的收益且不受其他事件的影响，我们认为会产生套利机会，套利使价格推向均衡，即买进低估资产同时卖出高价资产，在获利的同时又不会产生未来负债，而一价定律是套利遵循的基本原理而非过程。

50. 答案：A

解析：因为投资者做空，价格下跌这个头寸创造了利润；所以投资者的保证金账变动为 0。

51. 答案：D

解析：D 选项错误，如果保证金账户余额低于维持保证金（非零），将发出追加保证金通知。

52. 答案：D

解析：最优套期保值比率 = 相关性 × 现货标准差 ÷ 期货标准差 = 0.80 × \$3.20 ÷ \$5.10 = 0.502。

最优合约数量 = 最优套期保值比率 × 持有头寸金额 ÷ 合约价值 × 合约乘数 = 0.502 × 1 000 000 ÷ 10 × 250 = 200 份合约(近似)。

53. 答案：B

解析：$HR = \rho_{s,f}\dfrac{\sigma_s}{\sigma_f}$；可以反推出相关系数 $\rho_{s,f} = HR \times \dfrac{\sigma_f}{\sigma_s} = 0.86 \times \left(\dfrac{0.3}{0.6}\right) = 0.43$

54. 答案：D

解析：The number of hedge = beta × (portfolio value ÷ futures contract value)

$N = 1.5 \times [\$55 \text{ million} \div (250 \times 1\,320)] = 250$，所以需要卖空 250 份期货合约。

55. 答案：C

解析：根据对冲公式:(目标 beta − 投资组合 beta) × 投资组合价值 ÷ 期货合约价值，在这种情况下，$(1.0 - 0.30) \times \$10\ MM \div (250 \times 1\,380) = 20.29$，所以我们需要增加 20 份期货合约来把投资组合 beta 调整成 1。

56. 答案：D

解析：根据对冲公式:合约数量 = 投资组合 beta × 投资组合价值 ÷ 期货合约价值

$N = 1.14 \times [3\,500\,000 \div (1\,343 \times 250)] = 11.88$。

57. 答案：D

解析：$HR = \rho_{s,f}\dfrac{\sigma_s}{\sigma_f} = 0.90 \times 1.0 = 0.90$。

期货合约份数 = 对冲比率 × 现货合约的价值 ÷ 期货合约价值

带入数值得：$N = 0.90 \times (1.2 \text{ miilion} \times \$106) \div$ (每份合约 1 000 桶 × \$102) $\cong$ 1 122 份合同

58. 答案：A

解析：根据 EAR 的定义：$FV/PV = (1 + EAR)^t$，所以 $EAR = (FV/PV)^{12} - 1$；$T = 1/12$,所以 $EAR = 17\%$。

59. 答案：D

解析：最初投资的美元将增长至：

$$(1 + EAR) = \left(1 + \frac{R_n}{n}\right)^n \rightarrow EAR = \left(1 + \frac{R_n}{n}\right)^n - 1$$

$(CD_1) \times (1 + 7.82\%/12)^{12} = 1.081\,07$

$(CD_2) \times (1 + 8.00\%/4)^4 = 1.082\,43$

$(CD_3) \times (1 + 8.05\%/2)^2 = 1.082\,12$

$(CD_4) \times \exp(7.95\%) = 1.082\,75$

因此，CD_4 给出了最高的最终金额和 EAR。

60. 答案：C

解析：根据 $PV \times (1 + 8\%)^t = FV$，等式变换 $FV/PV = 2 = (1 + 8\%)^T$ 取两侧的对数，得到 $T = \ln(2) \div \ln(1.08) = 9.006$。

61. 答案：B

解析：由于票息率大于收益率，债券必须以溢价或价格高于面值的当前价格出售。如果收益率不变，债券价格将收敛于面值，所以它必须减小。

62. 答案：A

解析：债券没有任何的付息，麦考林久期等于 10 年因为这是零息债券期限；按年复利，修正久期为 $D^{*}=10\div(1+10\%)$，接近 9 年。

63. 答案：B

解析：如果收益率低(<6%)，则久期小的债券有利；

如果收益率很高(> 6%)，则久期大的债券有利。

64. 答案：B

解析：选项将两个具有相同期限的投资组合做比较。杠铃型投资组合由短期债券和长期债券组成。子弹型投资组合只有中期债券。因为凸性是付息时间的二次函数，长期债券在杠铃型投资组合中产生了巨大的凸性，比子弹型投资组合的凸性大。

65. 答案：A

解析：根据久期变化公式：$\Delta P=-D^{*}\times P\times\Delta y$，当利率上升的时候，债券价格下降。这个时候投资者通过 10 年期的互换来付固定利率收浮动利率，利率上升的时候这个互换(swap)赚钱，就对冲了投资者在债券价格下跌的损失。

66. 答案：C

解析：价格变化：

$$
\begin{aligned}
\Delta p &= -(D^{*}\times p)\times\Delta y+\frac{1}{2}\times[C\times P]\times\Delta y^{2}\\
&= -[8\times100](0.0025)+0.5[150\times100](0.0025)^{2}\\
&= -1.953125
\end{aligned}
$$

67. 答案：C

解析：根据有效久期公式：

$$
D^{E}=\frac{[P_{-}-P_{+}]}{(2P_{0\Delta y})}=\frac{[127.723-122.164]}{(125.482\times0.6\%)}=7.38。
$$

68. 答案：A

解析：我们列出现金流，发现第一年的权重等于 0.083 8，第二年的权重等于 0.079 8，第三年权重等于 0.836。所以算出久期等于 2.75，修正久期等于 2.62。

Period t	Payment C_t	Yield y	$PV_t=C_t/(1+y)^t$	tPV_t
1	100	5.00	95.24	95.24
2	100	5.00	90.71	181.41
3	1 100	5.00	950.22	2 850.66
Sum:			1 136.16	3 127.31

69. 答案：B

解析：对于支付息票的债券，麦考利久期肯定要小于债券的到期日，即 1.5 年，因此 B 比较符合。

70. 答案：C

解析：期限是无限债券久期公式：$D=\dfrac{(1+y)}{y}$，我们可以看到，它不依赖于票息率，只与收益率有关；因此，A 和 B 的久期肯定是相等的。

71. 答案:C

解析:久期与票息率和付息频率呈反比;也就是说票息率越高,付息频率越大,久期越小;同时久期与债券期限(t)呈正比,与收益率($yield$)呈反比,期限越长久期越大,收益率越小久期越大;所以Ⅲ和Ⅳ说法正确。

72. 答案:B

解析:固定利率债券,到期时间上升,久期收敛于 $D=\dfrac{(1+y)}{y}$。所以 B 选项正确。

73. 答案:A

解析:9 年期债券 5 的期限较短,因为在可比债券中,期限最短,为 9 年。接下来,我们要在债券 1 和债券 2 之间做出选择,这两种债券只在付息频率上有所不同,半年期债券 2 在 6 个月内有第一次支付,期限比一年期债券短;接下来我们再在债券 1 和债券 4 之间做出选择,这两种债券的收益率不同。收益率越低,未来现金流占的权重越大,所以债券 4 的久期大。最后,零息债券的久期最大。顺序是 5-2-1-4-3。

74. 答案:C

解析:6 个月的零息利率 $=\ln(100/98)\times 2=4.0405\%$。

现在我们反推一年的利率:$97=1\times \exp(-4.0405\%\times 0.5)+101\times \exp(-R\times 1.0)$,

所以 $R=-\ln\{[97-\exp(-4.0405\%\times 0.5)]\div 101\}=5.0564\%$。

75. 答案:B

解析:$1\times \exp(-1.0\%\times 0.5)+1\times \exp(-1.6\%\times 1.0)+1\times \exp(-1.9\%\times 1.5)+101\times \exp(-2.5\%\times 2.0)=\$99.03$。

76. 答案:B

解析:$A=\exp(-0.02\times 0.5)+\exp(-0.03\times 1.0)+\exp(-0.04\times 1.5)+\exp(-0.05\times 2.0)=3.80710$。

平价收益 (Par yield) $=[1-1\times \exp(-0.05\times 2.0)]\times 2\div 3.80710=4.99922\%$;

连续复利下的平价收益率 (Par Yield) $=2\times \ln(1+4.99922\%\div 2)=4.94\%$

77. 答案:D

解析:根据远期利率公式 $R_{1,2}=\dfrac{R_2\times T_2-R_1\times T_1}{T_2-T_1}$

所以 $r(1.0, 2.0)=(3\%\times 2-2.4\%\times 1)\div(2-1)=3.6\%$

检查计算是否正确:

2-year spot $=\exp(3\%\times 2)=1.0618365=$

1-year spot × 1-year forward $=\exp(2.4\%)\times \exp(3.6\%)=1.0618365$

78. 答案:D

解析:方法一:$\ln(88/82)\times 100\%=7.06\%$。

方法二:$r(0, 4)=\ln(100/88)\div 4\times 100\%=3.20\%$

$r(0, 5)=\ln(100/82)\div 5\times 100\%=3.97\%$

$r(4, 5)=(3.97\%\times 5-3.2\%\times 4)\div(5-4)\times 100\%=7.05\%$

选最接近的选项 7.06%(最优选项原则)。

79. 答案:C

解析：连续付息下半年的即期利率（spot rate）= ln(100/97) ÷ 0.5 = 6.091 8%；
连续付息下一年的即期利率（spot rate）= ln(100/94) ÷ 1.0 = 6.187 5%。
我们需要推导 1.5 年的即期汇率：
2 coupon × exp(− 6.091 8% × 0.5) + 2 coupon × exp(− 6.187 5% × 1.0) + 102 × exp(− rate × 1.5) = 95.00
1.5 spot rate = − ln{[95.00 − 2 × exp(− 6.091 8% × 0.5) − 2 × exp(− 6.187 5% × 1.0)] ÷ 102} ÷ 1.5 = 7.476%
Forward rate(1.0，1.5) = (7.476% × 1.5 − 6.187 5% × 1) ÷ (1.5 − 1) = 10.052%

80. 答案：B

解析：根据远期利率定价公式：$S \times \left(\frac{1 + R_{jpy}}{1 + R_{usd}}\right)^t = F$，通过远期汇率的定价公式反求日本本国利率：

$112.5 \times \left(\frac{1 + R_{jpy}}{1 + 4\%}\right)^1 = 110.5$，解得：$R_{jpy} = 2.15\%$。

81. 答案：C

解析：远期价格是现货价格、利率和股息收益率的函数。

82. 答案：D

解析：根据远期定价公式：$s \times e^{(r-q)t} = F$，远期价格收股票收到股票市场影响，A 选项正确；股票分红增加（假设分红按照连续复利）股票分红增加远期价格降低（反比关系），B 选项正确；到期时间 t 增加远期价格增加（正比关系），C 选项正确；远期价格与利率呈正比，D 选项错误。

83. 答案：C

解析：按照期货合约公允价值的定价公式：$F = s \times e^{(r-q)t} = 990 \times e^{(4\%-2\%)\times\frac{3}{12}} = 994.96$，所以实际的期货价格要高 5.04（1 000 − 994.96）。

84. 答案：A

解析：根据 $F = s \times e^{(r-q)t}$ 推导出 $S = F \times e^{-(r-q)t} = 552.3 \times e^{-(7.5\%-4.2\%)\times 0.5} = 543.26$。

85. 答案：B

解析：根据远期定价的平价公式：$F = s \times e^{(r-q)t} = 750 \times e^{(3.5\%-2\%)\times 0.5} = 755.65$，
市场上实际交易价格为 757，因此以低价买进，以远期价格卖出，利润为 1.35 美元。

86. 答案：C

解析：由于凸性与时间 t 的平方呈正比，付息债券现金流权重分散于不同的付息时间，而零息债券集中于到期时间 t，答案Ⅰ是正确的；因为付息债券久期等于 10，所以付息债券到期时间 t 一定大于 10，答案Ⅱ是错误的，因为持续 10 年的 6% 债券必须在未来 30 年内有更多的现金流，这将产生更大的凸性。答案Ⅲ是错的，因为凸性随时间的平方而增长。答案四是错误的，因为某些债券，如 MBS 或可赎回债券，可能具有负凸性。答案Ⅴ是正确的，因为对于支付息票的债券，凸度必须是正的。

87. 答案：A

解析：投资组合的美元久期是 $D \times P = \sum x_i D_i \times P_i = +8 \times 2.5 \times \$90\,000 - 6 \times 3.0 \times \$110\,000 + 12 \times 3.3 \times \$120\,000 = \$4\,572\,000$。投资组合价值的变化是 −（$D \times$

$P)(\Delta y) = -\$4\ 572\ 000 \times 0.002\ 5 = -\$11\ 430$。

88. 答案：C

解析：每张债券的市场价格是通过票面金额乘以市场价格再除以 100 得到的，最终算出 DV01 是 8 584 美元。

Bond	Price	Par	Market Value	D*	DD
A	101.43	3	3.043	2.36	7.181
B	84.89	5	4.245	4.13	15.530
C	121.87	8	9.750	6.27	61.130
Sum					85.841

89. 答案：A

解析：这两种合约的标的资产都是短期存款，其价值与利率呈强烈的负相关关系。由于期货合约的日盯市特性，可比较合约的远期和期货价格并不完全相等，而且价差随着合约期限的延长而增大。

90. 答案：A

解析：$R - d = 5.5\% - 1.5\% = 4\%$。

91. 答案：A

解析：$F = s \times e^{(r-q)t} = 1\ 025 \times e^{(2.75\% - 1.2\%) \times 0.25} = 1\ 028.98$。

92. 答案：B

解析：便利收益率代表拥有现货资产有利或便利。这通常意味着相关资产的现货价格将高于期货价格（现货溢价）。便利收益率有助于降低期货定价关系中的成本。

93. 答案：B

解析：根据无套利定价公式：$F = s \times e^{(r-q)t} = 800 \times e^{(2.5\% - 3\%) \times 0.5} = 798$，由于期货合约的市场价格低于该价格，存在套利机会，以低价买进高价卖出套利收益：$798 - 758 = 40$。

94. 答案：C

解析：$S \times e^{-qt} - K \times e^{-rt} = 1\ 100 \times e^{-0.02 \times 0.25} - 1\ 080 e^{-0.04 \times 0.25} = 25.26$

95. 答案：A

解析：现货价格中间汇率是 1.022 3 美元。使用年度（非连续）复利，远期价格为 $F = S(1 + r) \div (1 + r^*) = 1.022\ 3 \times [(1.027\ 5) \div (1.042\ 5)] = 1.007\ 6$。

96. 答案：C

解析：3 月，收到 $16 \times 10\ 000 = 160\ 000$

4 月，支付股息 $0.06 \times 10\ 000 = -600$。短期必须向经纪人支付股息，以便可以转移为长期。

6 月，支付 $12 \times 10\ 000 = -120\ 000$。

6 月，收到短期回扣利息 $= 0.375\% \times 160\ 000 = 600$。

净额为 40 000。

97. 答案：A

解析：短期挤压是指当空头头寸（已借入头寸）被施压关闭其头寸（回购股票）时，空头就会出现短缺。这种购买压力进一步推高了价格。因此，短期挤压的出现条件是短期利率和资产价格的上升(空头损失)。

98. 答案：D

解析：交易对手风险是期货合约和远期合约的另一个关键区别，当期货和远期的标的资产和利率为正相关时，期货价格高于远期。

99. 答案：A

解析：$F[0, 0.5] = 7.00 \times \exp[(4\% + 2\%) \times 0.5] = 7.2132$。

折现利率 (The discount rate) $= 4\% + (9\% - 4\%) \times 0.4 = 6.0\%$。

$E[S(0.5)] = F[0, 0.5] \div \exp[(4\% - 6\%) \times 0.5] = 7.2857$。

远期多头的预期收益 $E[S(0.5)] - F[0, 0.5]$。

空头头寸的预期收益 $F[0, 0.5] - E[S(0.5)]$。

所以在这个例子中答案为：$7.2123 - 7.2857 = -0.072$。

100. 答案：B

解析：远期价格曲线，我们可以知道 $F(X) = S(0) \times \exp(r + u)$，即升水(Contango)；对于远期的现货价格，正的系统风险意味着现货溢价，$F(x) < E[S(x)]$，即贴水(Backwardation)。

101. 答案：C

解析：凸性调整方程表明，期货利率大于远期利率。

102. 答案：B

解析：结算风险是指衍生品交易的交易对手之一在合约到期时无法履行的风险。*FRAs* 是一种场外交易工具，因此比欧洲美元期货合约具有更大的结算风险。

103. 答案：A

解析：利率上限涉及多种期权，即一个上限。第一个在 3 个月后，它锁定了最大值 $[R(t+3) - 4\%;\ 0]$ 的函数，支付发生在 6 个月内；第二个是 $\text{Max}[R(t+6) - 4\%;\ 0]$ 的函数。第三个是 $\text{Max}[R(t+9) - 4\%;\ 0]$ 的函数，支付发生在 12 个月，然后就停止了因为上限的期限只有 12 个月。因此有 3 个 caplet。

104. 答案：D

解析：欧洲美元期货合约具有高流动性，在交易所交易的短期利率合约具有标准化的合约规模和条款。FRAs 是场外交易。

105. 答案：D

解析：CTD 最赚钱的即最大化(收入 − 成本)：

空头头寸债券的收入 − 购买债券的成本 =(结算价格 × 转化因子 $CF + AI$) − (报价债券价格 + AI)；AI:应计利息。 两式(AI)抵销时，我们不需要 AI。

最大化:结算价格 × CF − 报价债券价格；或者等效地，最小化:报价债券价格 − 结算价格 × CF。

106. 答案：C

解析：债券 B 是 CTD，因为交割债券 A 的每份合约的成本为 545 美元：$98.50 \times 0.96 - 97 = -2.44$(每份合约 2 440 美元)。

债券 B 成本:$98.50 \times 1.03 - 102 = -0.545$(− 每份合约 545 美元)。

107. 答案：B

解析：我们可以通过对债券定价来估算 CF，假设市场利率为 6%。

债券价格 $A = -PV(I/Y=5/2, N=30, PMT=2.5, FV=100) = 90.20$ 美元，因此 CF 约为 \$90.20 ÷ 100 = 0.90

债券价格 $B = -PV(I/Y=6.5/2, N=40, PMT=3.25, FV=100) = 105.78$ 美元，因此 CF 约为 \$105.78 ÷ 100 = 1.057 8

债券价格 $C = -PV(I/Y=6/2, N=50, PMT=3, FV=100) = 100$ 美元，因此 CF 约为 \$100 ÷ 100 = 1

债券价格 $D = -PV(I/Y=5.5/2, N=60, PMT=2.75, FV=100) = 94.22$ 美元，因此 CF 约为 \$94.22 ÷ 100 = 0.942 2

108. 答案：C

解析：合同价格 $=10\,000\times[100-0.25\times(100-Q)]$。在这种情况下，$10\,000\times[100-0.25\times(100-95.940)]=989\,850$ 美元。

109. 答案：B

解析：公司 A 在两个市场货币都拥有绝对优势，但有一个比较优势在 2%（6% − 4%）英镑和 1%（3% − 2%）的日元之间；相对于公司 A 去借日元，A 公司借英镑更具有优势。

110. 答案：D

解析：投资者现在想把手里的浮动利率资产转化为固定利率资产，做一个支付浮动利率收固定利率的互换，这样浮动利率资产和付浮动利率就抵销了。

111. 答案：A

解析：公司可以发行浮动利率债券并使用利率互换协议将其转换为固定利率债券。

112. 答案：D

解析：互换的初始值始终为零，随着利率的变动和支付的发生，互换的价值将随发生变化。

113. 答案：A

解析：这种互换类似于欧元计价债券的多头头寸和日元的计价债券空头头寸。因此，欧元利率的下降对持有多头头寸有利。同样地，日元价值的下降使日元计价债券的价值降低（这对空头债券有利）。

114. 答案：C

解析：步骤 1，计算固定债券价值 $A = 25\,000\,000\times 8.29\% \div 2 = 1\,036\,250$ 美元。

步骤 2，计算浮动债券价值 B 方 $= 25\,000\,000\times 7.65\%/2 = 956\,250$ 美元。

步骤 3，互换（swap）价值为：$1\,036\,250 - 956\,250 = 80\,000$。

115. 答案：B

解析：固定利率支付者支付 6%利率且半年付息一次，因此利率为 $6\%\div 2=3\%$。

浮动利率支付者在期初支付 $LIBOR$ 利率 + 0.50%，即 $5\% + 0.50\% = 5.5\%$。因此浮动利率支付：$0.055\div 2\times 100\% = 2.75\%$。

固定利率付款人支付 $25\,000[10\times(3\% - 2.75\%)]$ 美元的净付款。

116. 答案：C

解析：$B_{fix} = \left(2\,000\,000 \times \frac{7\%}{2}\right) e^{-6.5\% \times 0.5} + \left(2\,000\,000 \times \frac{7\%}{2}\right) e^{-6.8\% \times 1} + \left(2\,000\,000 + 2\,000\,000 \times \frac{7\%}{2}\right) e^{-7.5\% \times 1.5} = 1\,982\,906$

$B_{float} = 2\,000\,000$（在付息时间点浮动利率债券面值等于现值）

$V_{swap} = 2\,000\,000 - 1\,982\,906 = 17\,093$

117. 答案：C

解析：算出固定端现值和浮动端现值再计算互换(swap)的价值。

$V_{SWAP}(USD) = B_{USD} - (Spotrate \times B_{CAD})$

$B(CAD) = 14\,438\,805$

$B(USD) = 9\,631\,182$

$V_{SWAP}(USD) = 9\,631\,182 - \left(\frac{1}{1.52} \times 14\,438\,805\right) = 131\,967$

118. 答案：C

解析：步骤 1，该机构支付美元并收日元，因此该互换的价值将等于当前汇率乘以日元部分的价值减去美元部分的价值。

步骤 2，互换日元部分 $= 70\ e^{(-0.005)} + 3\,570\ e^{(-0.005 \times 2)} =$ JPY 3 604.13m。

步骤 3，互换美元部分 $= 5.4\ ^{e(-0.03)} + 125.4^{(-0.03 \times 2)} =$ USD 123.34m。

步骤 4，$V(swap) = 3\,604.13/120 - 123.34 = -$ USD 93.3m。

119. 答案：D

解析：日元计价债券的面值：JPY $= 40e^{(-2\% \times 1)} + 104e^{(-2.5\% \times 2)} = 1\,028.487$。

美元计价债券的价值：USD $= 0.6e^{(-4.5\% \times 1)} + 10.6e^{(-4.75\% \times 2)} = 10.213$。

互换价值：$BY \div 115 - BD = 1\,028.487 \div 115 - 10.213 = -1.270$。

120. 答案：D

解析：由于每份合约的金额为 1 000 000 美元，而借款人希望对冲 LIBOR 的增加，公司应该签订三份空头合约头寸。利率(R)的增加意味着报价($100 - R$)的下降，使空头头寸在利率上升时增长收益。

由于每份合约按设计收益或损失每基点 25 美元，100 个基点的增加意味着每份合约 2 500 美元，或 3 份合约 7 500 美元。

121. 答案：B

解析：银行同业拆借利率(LIBOR)从 2.00%(100 − 98)上升至 2.80%(100 − 97.2)。由于合约价格从 98.00 下跌至 97.20，多头头寸在此处下跌；多头头寸损失为每基点 25 美元；在这种情况下，−80 bps×25 = 损失 2 000 美元。

122. 答案：D

解析：收到一个固定利率互换头寸等于持有一个固定利率债券或者看空一个远期利率互换(FRA)；也可以等于卖一个利率顶策略(cap)和买一个利率底策略(floor)具有相同的行权价格。

123. 答案：A

解析：远期互换利率应当从期权取消的第五年开始，到期日应该与剩余期限相等

2年。

124. 答案：B

解析：互换给了借款人更好的灵活性来锁定利率。

125. 答案：D

解析：题目给出了固定利率7.5%，所以我们可以知道在第一年结束后每年的现金流，250×7.5%＝18.75(第一年现金流)；250＋18.75(第二年现金流)。

净现值 (*NPV*) ＝ 18.75exp(－1×8%)＋(250＋18.75)exp(－2×8.5%)＝244 million；又由于再重置日期(Just after the payment)，所以浮动端现值就等于250 million。

银行是收浮动付固定，所以互换(swap)价值＝250－244＝6 million。

126. 答案：D

解析：浮动利率债券的(Macaulay)期限大约到下一个付息时间。

127. 答案：B

解析：100万美元是合同到期结算时参考的名义金额，多头实际上并没有借入100万美元。

128. 答案：C

解析：根据凸性调整公式 convexity adjustment ＝ 0.5 × volatilty^2 × T(1) × T(1＋0.25)。

代数值计算，convexity adjustment ＝ 0.5 × 4%^{2} × 5 × 5.25 ＝ 2.10%。

129. 答案：A

解析：凸性调整 (convexity adjustment) ＝ 0.5 × 1%^{2} × 4.0 × 4.25 ＝ 0.0850%。

期货利率为每年3.0%(100% － 97%)，根据ACT/360和季度复利等效连续利率(The equivalent continuous rate) ＝ ln(1＋3%/4)^{360}/90 ＝ 2.98881%，所以远期利率＝ 2.98881% － 0.0850% ＝ 2.904%。

130. 答案：D

解析：欧洲美元期货利率高于远期利率(每 *FRA*)，因为：(1)期货合约每天结算；(2) *FRA* 可能在 T＋0.25年结算。由于：远期利率＝期货利率－凸性调整时，期货利率更大。此外，请注意，远期利率合约在合约到期日结算。时间(T)时，报价以当时的3个月伦敦银行同业拆息(LIBOR)为基础，但远期利率合约并不等待在 T＋0.25时结算。

131. 答案：C

解析：期权合约不会指定市场价格或市场衍生变量(例如，隐含波动率)。

132. 答案：C

解析：期货(远期)合约比期权提供好的保险作用；此外，期权需要预付保费。二元期权提供固定收益的条件是达到行权价格。

133. 答案：B

解析：如果有10.0%的股票股息，期权合约将成为卖出110股[100×(1＋10%)]，行权价格＝50美元÷(1＋10%)＝45.45美元。

134. 答案：C

解析：香草期权与业绩表现并不完全一致；公司业绩表现好，期权收益可以是一个很好的薪酬奖励工具；公司业绩表现差，不承担损失的风险。

135. 答案：D

解析：a)没有影响；b)下降；c)没有影响；d)看涨期权价格上涨。

136. 答案：C

解析：收益：$(83-63)\times100=2\,000$。

利润：$2\,000-510.25=1\,489.75$。

137. 答案：C

解析：上限是 $S=50$。下限是 $c\geqslant S-Ke-r\times T=50-45\exp(-0.03\times2)=50-42.38=7.62$。因此，上限与下限差是 42.38。

138. 答案：D

解析：为了保持看跌期权平价关系，看涨期权和看跌期权的价值必须同等变化。由于看涨期权和看跌期权价值与标的股票价格波动率正相关，因此两种期权的价值都会增加。看待这种情况时注意欧式看涨的 vega 和欧式看跌的 vega 是相等的。

139. 答案：D

解析：美式看跌对非股息支付的期权定价的下界：$P\geqslant\max(X-S)$，所以下限是 $P\geqslant(110-106)=4$。

140. 答案：A

解析：美式期权必须具备以下关系：$S-K\leqslant C-P\leqslant S-K\times e^{-rt}$。

141. 答案：C

解析：欧式看跌期权的下限由公式给出：

$$X\times e^{-rt}-S\times e^{-rf*t}=0.688\,0\times\exp\left(-0.01\times\frac{5}{12}\right)-0.665\,0\times\exp\left(-0.045\times\frac{5}{12}\right)=0.032\,5。$$

142. 答案：D

解析：美式期权可以提早行权。因此，其价值不一定等于欧式期权的价值。请注意，非支付股息的美式看涨期权不会提前行权，因此其价值等于欧式看涨期权。美式期权提前行权的特征使看跌期权平价公式不适合它。

143. 答案：B

解析：非支付股息（或没有收入的资产）的美式看涨期权不应提前行权。如果资产支付股息，可能会发生提前行权，并且提前行权概率随着收入的增加而增加。

144. 答案：B

解析：非支付股息的美式看涨期权不应提前行权，而美式的非支付股息的看跌期权可以提前行权。

145. 答案：B

解析：美式看涨期权价格的下限是 $PV(S)-X$；到期前行权的收益是 $S-X$，小于价格的下限（假设无风险利率为正）。因此，美式对非支付股息的期权来说，提前行权并不是最佳选择。

146. 答案：A

解析：如果股票不支付股息，则美式看涨期权的价值总是高于提前行权的价值（主要是因为没有收到股息）。因此，美式看涨不会提前行权。美式看跌期权提前行权是合理的，因为 $X \times \exp(-rt) - S$。提前行权收益更大。

147. 答案：D

解析：到期时间（T）增加与欧式看涨/看跌期权（付息股票）之间不是增加函数关系。到期时间与美式看涨/看跌期权（对支付股息或非股息支付股票）和欧式看涨/看跌期权（非股息支付的股票）之间是增加函数关系。

148. 答案：A

解析：无风险利率的增加肯定会降低欧式无派息股票看跌期权价值的下限：下限 = $K \times \exp(-rt) - S(0)$。

149. 答案：C

解析：如果股价下跌，那么买入看跌期权会产生收益，这类似于在股票下跌前卖出股票。从好的方面来看，损失的上限是买看跌期权费。

根据利率平价公式：$P + S = C + X \times e^{-rt}$，等式移项得：$P = C + X \times e^{-rt} - S$。

150. 答案：B

解析：历史波动性是回测的，并不一定对应平价/价内/价外期权的隐含波动率。

151. 答案：C

解析：根据利率平价公式：$C = P + S - X \times e^{-rt} = 3.19 + 23 - 25 \times e^{-0.05\times 1} = 2.409$，注意波动率没有使用。

152. 答案：C

解析：答案a和b的收益，具体取决于股票价格，因此不能创造套利利润。看跌期权平价表示 $c - p = 3 - 2 = 1$ 应等于 $S - X \times e^{-rt} = 42 - 44 \times 0.9048 = \$2.19$。看涨期权很便宜，可以通过买低卖高进行套利。

153. 答案：C

解析：通过期权平价公式，$C - P = S \times e^{-dt} - X \times e^{-rt}$

因此，$S \times e^{-dt} = C + X \times e^{-rt} - P = 10 - 15 + 90\exp(-0.05 \times 5) = 65.09$

股息收益率则为 $y = -(1/T)\ln(65.09/85) = 5.337\%$。

154. 答案：B

解析：购买看跌期权可以防止欧元下跌，而支付的价格为 0.022 × 10 million = 220 000。

155. 答案：C

解析：如果看涨期权目前的交易价为5美元且其内在价值为5美元，则看涨期权的时间价值为0美元，因此6个月的利率必须为零。

156. 答案：A

解析：随着股票上涨，看跌期权价值会下降，美式看跌期权的价值随 t 增加而增加。

157. 答案：C

解析：无风险利率、股价和波动率的增加，都会引起欧式看涨期权价值增加，而到期时间的增加对欧式期权的影响是不确定的。

158. 答案：D

解析：买入看涨期权的收益与出售短期债券、买入股票和买入看跌期权的收益相同。你可以通过使用 put-call parity 来看到：

$P + S = C + X \times e^{-rt} \rightarrow C = S - X \times e^{-rt} + P$

159. 答案：C

解析：$P + S = C + X \times e^{-rt} \rightarrow P = C + X \times e^{-rt} - S$。

160. 答案：B

解析：$P + S = C + X \times e^{-rt} \rightarrow - P = - C - X \times e^{-rt} + S$。

161. 答案：D

解析：使用平公式求欧式看跌期权的价值。

$P = C + X \times e^{-rt} - S = 30 + 120 \times \exp(-0.05 \times 0.5) - 100 = 47.04$

162. 答案：C

解析：使用平公式求欧式看跌期权的价值。

$P = C + X \times e^{-rt} - S = 2.25 + 50 \times \exp(-0.1 \times 0.25) - 48 = 3.02$

163. 答案：D

解析：$P = C + X \times e^{-rt} - Se^{-qt}$

$= 50 + 140 \times \exp(-0.05 \times 2) - 100\exp(-0.02 \times 2) = 80.6$

164. 答案：D

解析：每年 6%的利率(单利)大约相当于连续复利的 5.826 9%利率(四舍五入到小数点后四位)。ln(1 + 0.06) = 5.826 9%，使用看跌期权平价公式：

$P = C + X \times e^{-rt} - S = 4.1 + 27.5 \times \exp(-0.058\,269) - 25 = 5.04$

165. 答案：C

解析：我们可以在这里使用看跌期权利率平价公式来解出持续的股息收益率；我们有：$C + X \times e^{-rt} = P + S \times e^{-qt}$；$85 \times xp(-q \times 5) = 10 + 90 \times \exp(-5\% \times 5) - 15$；解得 $q = 5.34\%$。

166. 答案：C

解析：看跌期权利率平价公式是 $C + X \times e^{-rt} = P + S$

$P + S = 2 + 42 = 44$；$C + X \times e^{-rt} = 3 + 44 \times \exp(-0.1 \times 1) = 42.81$。

因此，通过持有多头头寸并购买无风险债券，做空股票和看跌期权，存在套利机会。

167. 答案：C

解析：由于正在考虑的美式看涨期权在不支付股息的情况下，其价值等于具有相同参数的欧式看涨期权。因此，我们可以应用看跌期权平价来确定利率。

$C + X \times e^{-rt} = P + S$　$2.25 + 22 = 0.46 + 24 \times \exp(-r \times 0.25)$，算出 $r = 3.52\%$。

168. 答案：D

解析：欧式看涨期权的最小值：$\text{Min}[0, 86 - 80 \times \exp(-0.03 \times 3/12)] = 6.59$

美式看涨期权必须至少与欧式看涨期权一样具有相同的最小值。

169. 答案：B

解析：下限是股票价格与行权价格现值之间的差额：$S - K \times \exp(-rt) = 90 - 80 \times \exp(-0.05) = 13.9$。

170. 答案：A

解析：下界等于 $= 100 - 102 \times \exp(-0.0725 \times 9/12) = 100 - 96.6 = 3.4$。

171. 答案：B

解析：当标的资产价格下跌时，看跌期权具有内在价值。买入看跌期权的收益与标的资产的空头头寸和看涨期权的多头头寸的收益相同。当相关资产的价格下降时，这种合成策略具有价值。当标的资产的价格上涨时，看涨期权买方将行权，并且看涨期权卖方需要清算资产中的多头头寸。

172. 答案：B

解析：考虑一个投资组合，卖一个欧式看跌期权行权价为 X_1，并且买一个欧式看跌期权行权价为 X_2，其中 $X_2 > X_1$。到期时该投资组合的最大收益为 $X_2 - X_1$（即两个期权之间的行权价格差异）。当标的股票价格低于 X_1 时，发生最大的费用是 $P_2 - P_1$（两个期权之间的价格差异）。理性投资者为投资组合支付的价格不能高于投资组合的最大收益，这意味着价格差异不能超过行权价格的差异。因此选项 B 是错误的。

173. 答案：B

解析：有保障的看涨策略是股票中的多头头寸和看涨期权的空头头寸。股票头寸的收益等于卖空头寸，其中两者抵销，消除了上行潜力，但仍有下行风险。

174. 答案：A

解析：牛市价差涉及买入低行权价的看跌期权、卖出高行权价的另一个看跌期权或买入低行权价的看涨期权并卖出高行权价的另一个看涨期权。

175. 答案：A

解析：

看涨期权的净利润，执行价格为 30，最大利润为 9。

看涨期权的净利润，执行价格为 40，最大利润为 -0.5。

总净利润：$9 - 0.5 = 8.5$。

176. 答案：A

解析：在同一股票上买入一个执行价格较低的看涨期权和卖出一个执行价格较高的看涨期权就是牛市价差策略。

177. 答案：C

解析：预计短期内通胀水平将温和上涨，市场波动预期仍将维持低位，股价将温和上涨，因此选择牛市价差。

178. 答案：D

解析：这是一种牛市价差策略。股票价格为 45 或以上的话的最大利润为 3，股票价格为 40 或以下的最大利润为 -2，因此，最大损失为 2 美元，最大利润为 3 美元。

179. 答案：A

解析：熊市价差策略是指期权交易者买入行权价较高的看涨期权和卖出行权价较低的看涨期权。

180. 答案：A

解析：虽然移动的方向很不确定，但移动的幅度很可能很大；我们应该采取跨式交易。

买一个看涨期权和一个买看跌期权，这个策略叫做跨式。

181. 答案：C

解析：看跌期权多头和股票多头头寸可能只会限制下跌风险。看跌期权的空头头寸加上股票的空头头寸可能只会限制上行风险。对具有特定执行价格的股票买入看涨期权并在具有更高执行价格和相同到期日期的同一股票上卖出看涨期权可能会限制上行风险和下行风险。以相同的执行价格和到期日期购买看涨期权只会限制下行风险。

182. 答案：A

解析：以较低的行权价购买一个看涨期权，再以较高的行使价购买另一个看涨期权，在高价和低价之间的行权价卖出两个中间价的看涨期权称为蝶式价差策略。

183. 答案：B

解析：该策略是一个蝶式价差策略，根据蝶式价差策略的图像我们可以知道上行和下跌的空间的最大值(也就是盈利在一个范围内浮动)。

184. 答案：D

解析：最简单的方法是找出每个头寸的净利润或损失，然后将它们加在一起。

43 美元行权价格的看跌期权净利润：$43-19=24$。

37 美元行权价格的看跌期权净利润：$37-19=16$。

32 美元行权价格的看跌期权净利润：$32-19=13$。

由于投资者买入一份 43 美和 32 美元行权价的看跌期权，卖出两份 37 美元行权价的看跌期权，总净利润为：$24+13-32+8-7=6$。所以每一份赚：$6\div 3=2$(美元)。

185. 答案：D

解析：日历价差策略是由两个具有不同到期时间的期权组合而成的，两个期权都具有相同的执行价格。该策略下只有当股票仍然处于窄幅区间时，投资者才会获利，但损失是有限的。总体而言，收益与蝶式差价最相似。

186. 答案：C

解析：通过卖一个看涨期权来减小买看跌期权的费用，这最符合衣领策略，换句话说衣领策略给资产价值变动限定了一个上下界。

187. 答案：B

解析：异价跨式组合(Strangle)由买入的不同行权价的看涨期权和看跌期权构成。以相同的价格购买看涨期权和看跌期权是跨式组合(Straddle)；买入牛市价差涉及买一个行权价较低的看涨期权和卖一个行权价较高的看涨期权。而卖出牛市价差则相反，涉及卖出一个行权价较低的看涨期权并且买入一个行权价较高的看涨期权。垂直价差对应于不同的执行价格，而不是到期日。通过买入两个不同行权价的两个期权和卖出两个执行价格相同的期权，形成了买入蝶式价差策略。

188. 答案：D

解析：strap 是由两份看涨和一份看跌期权组成(相同行权价格)，它在股票价格上行行情中获得更多回报；短期内股票是牛市所以 strap 收益更大。

189. 答案：A

解析：利率底策略是一种看跌期权，当参考利率低于执行率时，利率底策略是价内的。

190. 答案：A

解析：衣领策略的结构由买入一个利率顶策略和卖出一个利率底策略构成。

191. 答案：C

解析：期权中买看跌期权最高损失期权费，因此 B 是错的；价差策略在期权中涉及多头和空头头寸，下行损失有限，因此 A 是错的。无保护的卖出期权方面临巨大损失；在购买看跌期权的情况下，如果资产价格变为零，则最严重的损失是执行价格 K；然而，在购买看涨期权的情况下，最坏的损失在理论上是无限的，因为股票价格上涨幅度不确定；在 D 和 C 之间，C 是更好的答案。

192. 答案：A

解析：coveredcall 可以通过限制损失的方式降低风险，具体方法是卖出看涨期权获取权利金，但是如果股价上行将会产生损失，使获利数额被限制，所以该策略的获利数额也是有限的。

保护性卖权策略需要购买一个看跌期权，该策略的最大损失等于期初的头寸的价格，即最初的股票价格(购买成本)与行权价的价格差的加上购买期权的权利金。所以 Joe Bob 说的最大损失是错误的。

193. 答案：D

解析：由于是由两个看涨期权组成，所以是牛市价差；最严重的损失发生在 $K_1 = 40$ 美元 以下，当时没有任何期权被行权且净损失溢价为 2(5 − 3) 美元。最大利润在 $K_2 = 45$ 美元时，赚了一个期权费 3 美元。

194. 答案：B

解析：由于最终价格低于 3 个执行价格中的最低价格，因此所有看跌期权都将被执行。最终的回报 = (50 − 33) − 2(42 − 33) + (37 − 33) = 3 美元。扣除前期成本，即 −7 + 2 × 4 − 2 = −1。总利润 = 3 − 1 = 2 美元。

195. 答案：D

解析：其中最好的策略是蝶式策略，如果价格保持在当前水平，将会获得收益；A 是一个跨式组合，因为如果现货价格不变，将会赔钱；B 是一个牛市价差策略，因为它假设现货价格会上涨才会有收益；C 是持有实物资产的空头，当汇率下跌时获利，汇率上涨时亏损。

196. 答案：A

解析：亚洲期权的收益取决于持有期内股票价格的平均值，因此是有路径依赖的。

197. 答案：B

解析：回望期权中的浮动回望期权执行价是浮动极值，固定回望期权使用存续期内标的资产价格的极值代替标的资产的最终价格，所以回望期权的收益总大于普通的欧式期权。选择期权涉及期权期限内的额外选择，因此比常规期权更有价值。直到亚洲期权涉及期间资产价格的平均值，其期权收益的波动性小于普通欧式期权，所以比普通欧式期权更便宜。障碍期权，对于投资者来说使期权有效需要达到一定条件，对投资者不利；因此障碍期权价值要小于普通期权。

198. 答案：B

解析：下跌敲入期权，当价格到达一个低点时候这个期权就有效，所以价格的增加使它远离障碍。这是不利的，所以 B 是正确的答案。

199. 答案：D

解析：$N(d_2)$是行权概率。

200. 答案：C

解析：假设资产没有收入，给出 $c = S \times N(d_1) - K\ \exp(-rT) \times N(d_2) = 100 \times 0.457\,185 - 110\exp(-0.1 \times 0.5) \times 0.374\,163 = \$6.568$。

201. 答案：B

解析：A 正确，因为障碍往往会降低成本，因为障碍期权的成本必须低于普通期权；B 错误，障碍期权带来的不连续和波动性的突然跳跃，这使障碍期权不适合静态对冲；C 正确，与等效的非障碍期权相比，降低了成本，也赌了合约在某个方向上成立；D 正确，只有在严重的下行（肥尾）情况下，下跌敲入期权才会降低看跌期权的成本。

202. 答案：D

解析：根据公式：$Q \times EXP(-rt) \times N(d_2)$

直觉上，这只是一个概率加权平均值，$Q \times EXP(-rT)$ 是未来现金支付的折现 PV，$N(d_2)$是期权到期执行价内（ITM）的概率；由于 $N(d_2)$是执行的概率，二元看涨期权价值 = PV（现金支付）× $Prob$［现金支付概率］。

203. 答案：A

解析：持有 asset-or-nothing 看涨期权。

204. 答案：C

解析：这是浮动回望期权的缺点，但不是固定回望期权的。例如，一个回望看涨期权可以有一个很高的执行价格，并且在期权有效期内资产价格可能永远不会超过执行价格。

205. 答案：A

解析：喊价期权，在赚钱的时候可以先锁定一个价格防止期权变成价外期权（OTM）。

206. 答案：C

解析：Vanilla call＜Shout＜Lookback。

普通期权的价值肯定要小于喊价期权的价值；因为喊价期权包含了投资者“喊”（shot）的一个权力；回望期权是以之前标的物出现过最好的价格来计算，所以肯定比喊价期权（shutoption）值钱。

207. 答案：C

解析：虽然在几何平均值下定价更容易，但大多数实际市场选择使用算术平均值。

208. 答案：D

解析：CCP 通常会降低交易对手风险，但如果失败则可能成为系统性风险的来源。

209. 答案：C

解析：并非所有的交易所成员都可以从加入清算环中受益，只和单个交易对手发生交易的会员不会在清算环中收益。

210. 答案：A

解析：由于场外交易市场缺乏可替代性、合同的替换（即更换合同）等问题，换句话说，由于合同之间缺乏替代性，合同通常不容易被平仓；交易所交易的衍生品是具有流动性、活跃性和受监管市场的标准化合约，通常在短期内交易，并在几天内结算；场外交易的衍生品是私有谈判的双边合约，在市场上交易很少或没有监管。

211. 答案：A

解析：清算所服务有三个主要功能：产品标准化、交易场所和报告服务。关于交易场所，交易所可以是物理位置或电子平台，提供交易的中心位置，交易所的实体交易必须接受交易所的规则和条件。

212. 答案：A

解析：通过变动保证金调整合约价格（通常每日结算）来应对标的资产的市场价值或参考利率、货币的变化。CCP 将初始保证金作为成员违约情形中潜在损失的第一道防线。因此，初始保证金可作为针对会员违约的第一个缓冲，并能降低交易对手风险。虽然初始保证金并非中央清算衍生工具所独有，但与双边交易相比，初始保证金不能再被抵押或重新用作其他交易的保证金。

213. 答案：D

解析：单一险种保险公司（Monoline）是通过信用互换这种工具来为客户提供信用保证服务的，信用衍生品公司（CDPC）集中于信用违约互换类产品，和单一险种保险公司（Monoline）商业模式类似。

214. 答案：D

解析：与交易所交易衍生品相比，*OTC* 衍生品的一个缺点是缺乏可替代性。

215. 答案：C

解析：*SPV* 在制度上可以实现风险隔离，即使母公司发生破产，也不至于影响到 *SPV* 的资产，更不会损害 *SPV* 的支付能力。

216. 答案：B

解析：*SPV* 在实践中往往会产生法律风险，部分国家的法律并不认可 *SPV* 的偿付顺序；如果法律不认可 *SPV* 的偿付顺序，很有可能在母公司破产时，*SPV* 被直接清算。

217. 答案：A

解析：衍生品产品公司，其作用就是为了管理对手方风险，这类型的公司往往有 AAA 的高信用评级，一般由银行设立。

218. 答案：A

解析：*DPC* 作为与设立者彼此破产隔离的机构而存在，解决了 *SPV* 在法律上难以被认定为独立子公司的问题，实现了法律范畴内的优先偿付。

219. 答案：C

解析：损失共同化意味着由所有的成员共同承担损失，从而减小损失的影响，降低成本，并最小化市场影响和系统性风险；虽然损失互惠是中央清算过程的一个优势，但它可能导致潜在的问题，包括道德风险和逆向选择。

220. 答案：D

解析：对于初始保证金，通常不考虑成员的信用质量，因此具有不同信用风险的成员可能会提交相同数额的初始保证金。

221. 答案：C

解析：在这种情况下，通过 CCP 的多边净额结算将导致交易对手 Y 向 CCP 支付 45，交易对手 Z 向 CCP 支付 60，以及 CCP 对手 X 支付 105(245－140)。

222. 答案：B

解析：当 CCP 被纳入清算过程时，金融市场的系统性风险会降低，但可以和每个卖方的买方一起降低交易和参与者的相互关联性，并降低违约或拖欠付款的风险。交易对手。同时，该过程改善了交易流动性和透明度。

223. 答案：B

解析：从业务流程的角度看，清算位于交易执行之后、结算之前。

224. 答案：B

解析：由于 CCP 处于市场买家和卖家之间，CCP 有一个“匹配账簿(matched book)”，不承担任何净市场风险，而这一风险仍由每笔交易的原始方承担。但是，CCP 确实承担了交易对手风险，这种风险集中在 CCP 的结构中。也就是 CCP 存在“有条件的市场风险”，因为一旦某个成员违约，它将不再拥有匹配的账簿。为了达到交易之间匹配，CCP 将使用各种方法，如拍卖违约成员的头寸。CCP 还通过要求其成员提供财务资源来减轻交易对手风险，这些都是在弥补其中一个或多个交易方违约时的潜在损失。

225. 答案：A

解析：CCP 的主要缺点有：道德风险(Moral hazard)、逆向选择(Adverse selection)、分岔(Bifurcations)、Procyclicality(顺周期性)。

226. 答案：A

解析：要集中清算，以下条件通常很重要。

标准化：法律和经济上必须是标准的，因为清算涉及现金流的合同责任。

复杂性：只有香草(或非奇异)交易才能被清算，因为清算需要及时相对容易和稳健的估值，以支持变动保证金计算。

流动性：产品的流动性很重要，因此可以进行风险评估，以确定应该收取多少初始保证金和违约基金。此外，如果清算会员违约，非流动性产品可能难以在拍卖中更换。

227. 答案：B

解析：与清算会员不同，非会员不需要向违约基金交钱，因此，非会员不会因 CCP 失败而遭受损失。

228. 答案：A

解析：FICO 是一种美国信用评分系统，用于评估向抵押贷款客户贷款时的风险。660 以上的分数被认为是次级(低风险)，低于 660 分数被认为是次级抵押贷款(风险较高)。

229. 答案：C

解析：CCP 会产生金融风险，因为它们代表了交易对手风险集中的市场体系中的一点。CCP 失败会在市场上造成系统性风险，这是通过 CCP 进行中央清算的一个缺点。

230. 答案：A

解析：在 CCP 之间进行交叉保证金安排(抵消对冲头寸)可以避免由于各种 CCP 的对冲活动导致的流动性问题。

231. 答案：D

解析：当 CCP 被纳入清算过程时，金融市场的系统性风险会降低，但可以同时增加。成员在市场波动加剧期间发布较高初始保证金的潜在要求可能会增加系统性风险。

232. 答案：C

解析：集中度风险是指风险头寸过多地集中于某些成员或同一地理区域内的成员手中。这些会员一旦违约，将引发连锁反应。

233. 答案：C

解析：CCP 是有可能发生失败的，一旦发生失败会造成严重的市场风险（例如，1987 年美国股市崩盘，使全球股市大跌）。

234. 答案：C

解析：在五大类场外衍生品中，利率衍生品占据了整个市场的一大部分，市场占比接近 84%。

235. 答案：D

解析：交易对手风险现在通常通过信用价值调整（CVA）反映在交易中。

236. 答案：B

解析：CCP 可能最容易通过其初始保证金水平暴露于模型风险之下，因为对于初始保证金的测算，如果对波动率、相关性、尾部风险估计出现偏差都会造成初始保证金估算不准确无法覆盖平仓损失。

237. 答案：B

解析：CCP 所面临的风险：违约风险（连锁反应，拍卖失败，会员退出，名誉影响），非违约损失事件，模型风险，流动性风险，操作风险于法律风险，其他方面的风险。

238. 答案：C

解析：CCP 需要外部流动性，因为缺乏流动性会造成违约，在金融危机时大规模的违约时，外部银行或央行注资对维护市场正常运作有很大帮助；依赖于外部流动性不是造成逆向选择的主要原因。

239. 答案：D

解析：玉米是生产具有季节性而需求不断的商品，玉米是在每年秋生产的，但年都在消费。

240. 答案：C

解析：电具有的特征：难储存，拥有固定的最大供应量，具有高度季节性的需求。

241. 答案：B

解析：电的远期价格也可以用这个表达式表达：$F(0)=E[S(t)]\times\exp[(r-a)T]$。

242. 答案：D

解析：$F(0,1)=E[S(1)]\times[\exp(r-k)T]$。其中($k$)是贴现率。

$E[S(1)]=F(0,1)\div[\exp(r-k)T]=47\div\exp(3\%-8\%)=\$49.41$。

243. 答案：D

解析：租赁费率 = 贴现率 − 增长率。

244. 答案：B

解析：The forward rate is calculated as follow：

$F = 22e^{(008-005)\times 2} = \$23.36$。

245. 答案：D

解析：交叉对冲的例子：(1)用原油对冲航空燃料；(2)公用事业公司使用天气衍生品来对冲能源购买成本。

246. 答案：B

解析：反向市场期货价格低于现货价格；投机者是净多头头寸，所以必须以低于现货价格的价格卖出它们，承担一定损失；期货价格在合约期限内上涨，这可以弥补投机者多头头寸的损失。

247. 答案：A

解析：连续租赁率 = 无风险 − 1 ÷ $T \times \ln(F/S)$ = 2% − 1 ÷ 0.5 × ln(1 830/1 822) = 1.123 8%。

年租赁率 =(1 + 无风险) ÷ $[F/S]^{(1/T)}$] − 1 = 1.02 ÷ [1 830/1 822 $^{(1/0.5)}$] − 1 = 1.110%

248. 答案：C

解析：通过购买与债务的每个月的到期日和数量相匹配的期货合约来创建条形对冲。通过基于未来债务的现值购买具有单一到期日的期货合约来创建堆栈对冲。一对一对冲(strip hedge)通过买与未来每个月相同到期时间的期货来对冲；滚动对冲(stack hedge)是通过对冲最近的一个单一到期日期货合约进行对冲。

249. 答案：C

解析：在反向市场下，现货价格高于期货价格。

根据远期价格定价公式：Forward = Spot × exp[+ riskfree rate + storage cost − dividend − lease/convenience]。

低无风险利率，高租赁利率，底储存成本，高便利利率会导致这种情况发生。

250. 答案：A

解析：Ⅱ是错的，虽然在定价模型中两者方向相似，但租赁率不是直接获取的，不像持有股票会产生股息，租赁利率只有在商品被借出时才能获得。

251. 答案：C

解析：根据公式：$S(T) = [S(T) - F(0, T)] + F(0, T)$ = 远期合约收益 + 债券收益，这样：合成头寸 = 持有远期 + 持有现金，多头头寸现值 = $F(0, 1) \times \exp(-rT)$ = \$8.00 × exp(− 4% × 1) = 7.69 美元 / bushels。

252. 答案：B

解析：A 这是一个裂解价差交易：做多原油期货加上做空汽油和热油期货；C 这是一个挤压差价交易：做多豆期货加做空豆粕（豆粕）和豆油（豆油）；D 这是一个牛饲价差交易：做多期饲养牛和玉米期货加上做空期活牛期货。

253. 答案：C

解析：(2 × \$270) + (1 × \$280) − (3 × 100) ÷ 3 = 173。

254. 答案：D

解析：一对一对冲(strip hedge)是完美对冲，因为它与合同到期时的时间相匹配，但在以下两种情况下，stackandroll 更有利：①远期合约中一个较高的交易成本（较低的流动性）可能有利于滚动对冲；②远期价格曲线由陡峭变的平滑，远期价格降低。

255. 答案：B

解析：四种大宗商品现货市场风险分别为：价格风险，运输风险，交割风险，关系到所交付商品的质量。信用风险，一直存在到交易最终完成。

256. 答案：D

解析：对于这种情况，不能使用金融工具对冲。唯一的解决办法是有一个非常定制的合理的交割机制或与供应者有长期稳定供应关系。

257. 答案：A

解析：根据公式：

$$\text{variance}(S-F)=\text{variance}(S)+\text{variance}(F)-2\times\text{volatility}(S)\times\text{volatility}(F)\times\text{correlation}(S,F)$$

带入数值计算 variance $(S-F)=20\%^2+30\%^2-2\times20\%\times30\%\times0.7=0.046$。

258. 答案：A

解析：天然气的储存成本很高，美国的需求在冬季的高使用期间达到峰值。此外，由于国际运输成本高，各地区的天然气价格也不同。

259. 答案：C

解析：一些商品具有可影响其远期价格的独特属性。如果库存较低，将可能增加便利性收益，因为在短缺时持有实物资产更有价值。便利收益率是非套利定价公式中的成本调整，用于确定远期价格。

260. 答案：A

解析：由于电力不可存储，相比金融期货，电力每日价格波动较高，并且不存在套利机会。

261. 答案：C

解析：净风险 =（100－70）+（50－60）= 20 亿英镑；该银行的净头寸是英镑，面临英镑贬值的风险；如果增加 20 亿英镑负债，银行净头寸为 0，减低了银行风险。

262. 答案：D

解析：由于银行净投资卢布计价的资产，银行看涨俄罗斯卢布。由于俄罗斯的通货膨胀应导致俄罗斯卢布贬值，这将导致多头货币头寸的损失。

263. 答案：D

解析：方法一：

在年初，美元兑换成欧元 = 500 000 ÷ 1.111 1 = 450 004.50 欧元。

在年底，欧元兑换成美元 = 450 004.50 × 1.224 0 = 550 805.51。

有效年回报 = 550 805.51 ÷ 500 000 − 1 = 10.161 1%。

方法二：

10.161 1% = 1.224 0 ÷ 1.111 1 − 1

264. 答案：B

解析：（125 000 − 78 000）+（27 000 − 5 000）= 69 000，银行净额头寸是巴西雷亚尔的多头头寸。如果巴西雷亚尔贬值，那么这个多头头寸的价值将会减小，贬值 3.0%，意味着 2 070（3.0% × 69 000）雷亚尔损失，2 070 ÷ 3.497 = 591.94 美元。

265. 答案：C

解析：资金成本＝0.035×2 亿＝700 万美元。

美国贷款利息＝0.04×1 亿美元＝400 万美元。

投资巴西债券＝1 亿×3.500 0＝3.5 亿美元。

投资巴西债券一年后兑换成美元：3.5×1.05/3＝1.225 亿美元。

投资巴西债券和巴西货币升值收益：1.225－1＝22.50 万美元。

净回报＝(4.0＋22.5－7.0)÷200.0＝9.75%。

266. 答案：D

解析：6 个月利息加本金支出＝1 000 000×(1＋0.025÷2)＝1 012 500 美元。

瑞典债券本金＝1 000 000 美元÷0.114 0＝8 771 929.82 克朗。

6 个月利息加本金支出＝kr 8 771 929.82 ×(1＋0.035÷2)＝kr 8 925 438.60。

6 个月再兑换成美元：8 925 438.60×0.121 0＝1 079 978.07 美元。

投资半年的利差＝(1 079 978.07－1 012 500.00)÷1 000 000＝0.067 48。

每年利差为：0.067 48×2＝0.134 956 或 13.495 6%。

267. 答案：C

解析：利用利率平价公式：$\text{forward rate} = \frac{1 + 9\%}{1 + 1\%} \times 3.5 = 3.777\,2$

268. 答案：A

解析：根据购买力平价，相对于美国商品价格上涨 2.0%，欧元区商品价格上涨 5.0% 导致欧元贬值 3.0%(5.0% － 2.0%)。新的欧元兑美元即期价格＝0.970×1.130 0＝1.096 10 美元。

269. 答案：A

解析：必须强调的是，受托人是由债券发行者支付的，只能按照契约的规定行事。

270. 答案：C

解析：购买时债券价格：$N = 14$，$I/Y = 1.5$，$PMT = 0$，$FV = 100$ 和 $CPT\ PV = 81.185$。

利率上涨后，债券价格：$I/Y = 1.7$，$N = 13$，$PMT = 0$，$Fv = 100$ $PV = 80.320\,7$。

半年复利的年回报率等于 $2 \times (80.320\,7 \div 81.185 - 1) = -0.021\,29 = -2.129\%$。

271. 答案：D

解析：固定价差收购要约消除了要约收购窗口期间债券持有人和发行人面临的利率风险。

272. 答案：D

解析：零息债券久期大，所以利率风险更高。由于在投资风险的问题债券到期收益率不太可能等于债券收益率。零息债券到期前没有利息不存在再投资风险。

273. 答案：C

解析：向优质资产的转移是出售企业债和购买美国国债。

274. 答案：B

解析：根据公式：hazard rate＝spread/(1－recovery rate)＝spread /LGD，

推导出 LGD＝spread/hazard rate。

275. 答案：A

解析："BBB－"是标准普尔投资评级最低的评级；BB＋是最高的投机级别(又名，高收益率，垃圾级)

276. 答案：B

解析：Bondindenture 是无担保债券，不是公司债。

277. 答案：C

解析：利息拆分债券和本金拆分债券都表现出更大的价格波动性，这是因为利息拆分债券和本金拆分债券是负相关的。

278. 答案：A

解析：在 2015 年 4 月 1 日，($I/Y=4/2$，$N=2.5\times2$，$PMT=100\times0.09\div2$，$FV=\$100$)。

债券的价格 $PV=111.783\,65$。

作为美国公司债券，它按照 30/360 天一个月计息，自上次付息以来有 150 天。此债券在结算日的含息价格 (dirty price) $=111.783\,65\times1.02^{(150/180)}=113.643\,63$。债券的净价 (clean price) $=113.643\,63-(4.50\times150\div80=109.893\,63$。

279. 答案：C

解析：设备信托凭证中由信托人持有的设备是可直接用于生产的，产生现金流的能力相对稳定，所以利率最低。

280. 答案：D

解析：留置权是一种安全功能，它是房主抵押贷款(和 MBS)典型的嵌入式预付(看涨)期权。但是在公司债券中，嵌入期权特征的存在不一定会产生负凸性。

281. 答案：D

解析：当有选举权普通股包含在抵押品中时，只要债券没有违约，契约就允许发行人投票，这对于此类债券的发行人来说非常重要，发行人依赖行使表决权来控制公司。

282. 答案：A

解析：债券是无抵押债券，即没有通过特定的指定财产抵押担保。

283. 答案：B

解析：担保债券的安全性取决于担保人的财务能力和发行人的财务能力。

284. 答案：D

解析：根据公式 $DV01=P\times D\div10\,000$，价格(P)是增加，但是久期(D)是减小的，所以影响不确定。

285. 答案：A

解析：根据 SMM 定义公式：$\frac{X}{250\,000-80}=0.55\%$，解得 $X=1\,374.56$。

286. 答案：A

解析：利息支付随着贷款期限内的本金支付的上升而下降，而不是相反。

287. 答案：D

解析：房屋抵押贷款(MBS)可以通过两种方式创建。首先，符合政府机构要求的贷款由机构收取保险费(担保费)，然后证券化。不符合要求的贷款或通过代理机构、成本过高的贷款在非机构或自有品牌交易中进行证券化。虽然这些证券本身没有代理担保,但有私人担保或分层的形式保险(高级阶层得到最大程度的保护)。在一系列抵押贷款证券化后,它作为投资出售给投资者。

288. 答案:A

解析:基于蒙特卡罗的模拟计划的各个供应商之间的主要区别在于假定的利率波动水平。假设关键再融资利率差价(再融资利率与每个模拟路径的1个月利率之间的利差)保持不变。必须对蒙特卡罗模型进行校准,以便模型中路径产生的平均价格等于运行中的基准20年的市场价格。

289. 答案:B

解析:通过担保,相关抵押贷款池获得的利息和本金支付按比例分配给债券持有人。这意味着每个持有者都会收到相同数量的利息和相同数量的本金。剥离抵押贷款支持证券的不同之处在于本金和利息不按比例分配。

290. 答案:D

解析:预付款或缩减将减少贷方在贷款期限内获得的利息金额。

291. 答案:D

解析:抵押贷款利率下降时,预计付款将增加。因此,只有本金剥离的投资者可以更快地获得付款的价值。

292. 答案:B

解析:抵押通过证券代表对一个抵押贷款池的收益索取凭证。可以使用任意数量的抵押贷款来形成池,并且池中包括的任何抵押贷款都被称为证券化抵押。

293. 答案:D

解析:蒙特卡罗模拟利用利率模型来生成沿着一组模拟利率路径中的每一个的每个月的抵押再融资利率。然后将这些再融资利率以及抵押贷款特征值输入预付款模型,该模型估算每条路径上每个月的预付费率。通过这些预付费率预测,可以估算每月现金流量。

294. 答案:A

解析:当利率下降时,许多借款人会进行再融资(即偿还贷款并将其转移给新的贷方)。一旦他们这样操作,他们就会陷入新的交易;无法再次再融资然而利率不断下降——称为再融资倦怠。

295. 答案:A

解析:利息拆分债券现金流量开始的时候较大,随着时间的推移逐渐变小。

296. 答案:C

解析:抵押贷款是一种贷款,由特定的不动产(住宅或商业)抵押。

297. 答案:B

解析:本金拆分的债券在低利率下表现出一些负凸性,本金拆分的债券相当于折价出售。

298. 答案:A

解析:根据公式:本金$\times[1-(1-\text{SMM})^{12}]=\$10.0$ million$\times[1-(1-0.01)^{12}]=\$10.0$ million$\times0.113\,615\,128=1\,136\,151$。

299. 答案:A

解析:按计算器步骤

$N = 15 \times 12 = 180$

$PV = -100\ 000$

$PMT = 740$

$FV = 0$（最后房贷欠款为 0）

$CPT\ I/Y = 0.333\ 9 \times 12 = 4.006\ 2\%$

300. 答案：C

解析：方法一：

$i = 6\% \div 12 = 0.5\%$ 每月

$T = 30 \times 12 = 360$ 月

每月支付金额 $= \$200\ 000 \times [0.5\% \times (1+0.5\%)^{360}] \div [(1+0.5\%)^{360} - 1] = \$1\ 199.10$

方法二：

$N = 360 \quad I/Y = 0.5 \quad PV = -200\ 000 \quad FV = 0$，$CPT\ I/Y = \$1\ 199.10$

301. 答案：D

解析：对于本金拆分的债券投资者不会获得利息只能获得本金，因此，投资者越早收到本金，回报越高。

302. 答案：C

解析：大的 OAS 表明风险调整范围更广，相对价格更低。期权成本衡量预付风险；最高的 OAS 和最低的期权成本最具吸引力。Tranche C 拥有最高的 OAS 和最低的期权成本。

303. 答案：B

解析：本金拆分的债券以一个比票面价格有相当大的折扣的价格出售。

304. 答案：D

解析：MBS/CMO 意味着证券化，在二级市场向投资者发行打包产品，但一级市场需要发起人。

305. 答案：B

解析：抵押贷款是由不动产担保(抵押)的贷款。

306. 答案：A

解析：pass-through 的基本特征就是按比例分配现金流。

307. 答案：A

解析：根据公式 $CPR = 1-(1-p)^{12}$，代入数值得 $CPR = 1-(1-0.40\%)^{12} = 4.70\%$

308. 答案：C

解析：100% PSA levels off at 6% CPR for months 31 to maturity. 200% PSA implies 12% CPR after 30 months.

Therefore, $SMM = 1-(1-CPR)^{(1/12)} = 1-(1-12\%)^{(1/12)} = 1.06\%$

在 31 个月至到期之间，100% PSA 水平为 6% CPR。200% PSA 意味着 30 个月后 CPR 为 12%。

因此，$SMM = 1-(1-CPR)^{(1/12)} = 1-(1-12\%)^{(1/12)} = 1.06\%$

第四部分

估值和风险模型

1. 答案：C

   解析：如果投资组合的每日 90%置信水平风险价值(VaR)估计为 5 000 美元，则可以预期 90%的时间(10 个中的 9 个)，投资组合的损失将少于 5 000 美元；相当于，10%的时间(10 个中的 1 个)投资组合将损失 5 000 美元或更多。

2. 答案：C

   解析：方差 $V(2\text{-day}) = V(1\text{-day})[2+2b]$，在险价值 $VAR(2\text{-day}) = VAR(1\text{-day}) \times \sqrt{2+2b} = \$1 \times \sqrt{2+0.2} = \$1\,483$。

3. 答案：B

   解析：VaR(Value at Risk)按字面解释就是“在险价值”，其含义指：在市场正常波动下，某一金融资产或证券组合的最大可能损失。更为确切的是，在一定概率水平(置信度)下，某一金融资产或证券组合价值在未来特定时期内的最大可能损失。

4. 答案：A

   解析：在发生亏损后，止损限额(stop loss limits)会削减头寸，这在趋势市场中很有用。风险敞口限制(Exposure limits)不允许在不同头寸间使用分散化，因为不考虑相关性。VAR 限制(VAR limits)可以套利，特别是较弱的 VAR 模型。最后，因为止损(stop loss limits)是在损失后实施的，所以不能防止所有的损失。陈述Ⅰ和Ⅱ是正确的。

5. 答案：A

   解析：$VAR = [E(R) - z_\sigma] \times \text{portfolio value} = -27\,125\ [= 10\,000 - 1.65(22\,500)]$。

6. 答案：B

   解析：VAR 是一定置信度下的最大损失，因此本题中有 95%可能性为损失不太严重。或者，损失将有 5%的可能性会更糟糕。所以 B 是正确的。

7. 答案：D

   解析：$VAR = [E(R) - z_\sigma] \times \text{portfolio value}$

   $VAR = \$200M \times [0.12 - 2.326 \times 0.08] = -\$13.216M$

8. 答案：B

   解析：$VaR = 1\ \text{million} \times 1.65 \times 0.008 \times \text{sqrt}(5) = \$29\,516.1$。

9. 答案：D

   解析：假设随机游走，我们可以使用时间平方根规则。

   那么，周波动性 $= 34\% \times 1 / \sqrt{52} = 4.71\%$。

10. 答案：B

解析：VAR = 市场价值 × 波动率 × Z = ($8 219 271) × (0.8%) × (1.65) = $10 849.4。

11. 答案：D

解析：蒙特卡罗 VaR(Monte Carlo VaR)使用模拟出来的收益率数据计算 VaR。

12. 答案：D

解析：显著性水平(significancelevel)越低，置信区间越大，VaR 越大。

13. 答案：B

解析：基金 1 权重 $W_A = 0.40$，股票权重 $W_B = 0.60$

组合的期望收益 $E(R_p) = 0.4 \times 8\% + 0.6 \times 12\% = 10.4\%$

组合的标准差

$$\sigma_p = [(W_A)^2(\sigma_A)^2 + (W_B)^2(\sigma_B)^2 + 2(W_A)(W_B)r_{AB}\sigma_A\sigma_B]^{0.5}$$
$$= [(0.4)^2(0.16)^2 + (0.6)^2(0.24)^2 + 2(0.4)(0.6)(0.16)(0.24)(-0.30)]^{0.5}$$
$$= 13.89\%$$

组合的 VAR = 组合的价值 × (期望收益 − 波动率 × Z)

= Portfolio value × $[E(R) - z_\sigma]$

= 500 000[0.104 − (1.65)(0.138 9)] = − $62 592.5

14. 答案：C

解析：债券权重 $W_A = 0.20$，股票权重 $W_B = 0.80$

组合的期望收益 $E(R_p) = 0.2 \times 6\% + 0.8 \times 10\% = 9.2\%$

组合的标准差

$$\sigma_p = [(W_A)^2(\sigma_A)^2 + (W_B)^2(\sigma_B)^2 + 2(W_A)(W_B)r_{AB}\sigma_A\sigma_B]^{0.5}$$
$$= [(0.2)^2(0.10)^2 + (0.8)^2(0.15)^2 + 2(0.2)(0.8)(0.10)(0.15)(0.30)]^{0.5}$$
$$= 12.74\%$$

组合的 VAR = 组合的价值 × (期望收益 − 波动率 × Z)

= Portfolio value × $[E(R) - z_\sigma]$

= 1 000 000[0.092 − (2.33)(0.127 4)] = − $204 842

15. 答案：C

解析：美国债券权重 $W_A = 0.60$，日本债券权重 $W_B = 0.40$

组合的期望收益 $E(R_p) = 0.6 \times 10\% + 0.4 \times 15\% = 12\%$

组合的标准差

$$\sigma_p = [(W_A)^2(\sigma_A)^2 + (W_B)^2(\sigma_B)^2 + 2(W_A)(W_B)r_{AB}\sigma_A\sigma_B]^{0.5}$$
$$= [(0.6)^2(0.10)^2 + (0.4)^2(0.20)^2 + 2(0.6)(0.4)(0.2)(0.10)(0.20)]^{0.5}$$
$$= 10.92\%$$

组合的 VAR = 组合的价值 × (期望收益 − 波动率 × Z)

= Portfolio value × $[E(R) - z_\sigma]$

= 1 000 000[0.12 − (1.65)(0.109 2)] = − $60 180

16. 答案：D

解析：90% 的置信水平内，最大损失为 $1 000。10% 的显著性水平内，最低损失为

$1 000；损失超过 $1 000 的概率为 10%。

17. 答案：B
解析：组合的 $VaR = 120 \times 50\,000 = 6\,000\,000$。

18. 答案：C
解析：肥尾分布(fat-tailed distributions)在尾部的概率比正态分布大。形成肥尾的原因主要是分布的方差是随着时间而变化的(time-varying)。

19. 答案：D
解析：实际损失可能会超过 VaR。

20. 答案：A
解析：根据平方根法则(square root rule)，$VAR = \$10\,849.4 \times \sqrt{9} = \$325\,483.1$。

21. 答案：B
解析：我们需要使用 $141 398($100 000 × 2.326 ÷ 1.645) 将 VAR 扩展到 99%的水平。乘以 sqrt(10)，得到 447 140 美元。

22. 答案：C
解析：极端值出现的概率大，即肥尾，会使用正太分布估计方差偏低。

23. 答案：B
解析：$VAR = \text{Portfolio Value}[E(R) - z_\sigma] - 1\,200\,000$

$= 7\,000\,000[0.0625 - (1.65)(X)] - 1\,200\,000$

$= 437\,500 - 11\,550\,000(X)$

$X = 14.18\%$，注意 VAR 一般为正值。

24. 答案：D
解析：根据巴塞尔协议，general market risk charge(general MRC)是 99%，10 天 VAR 的 3 倍，所以：$3 \times VAR_{99\%,\text{daily}} \times \text{sqrt}(10) = 3 \times \$1\,000\,000 \times (2.33/1.65) \times \text{sqrt}(10) = \$13\,396\,000$。

25. 答案：D
解析：资产组合的方差：$\sigma_p^2 = (0.4)^2 25 + (0.6)^2\ 121 + 2(0.4)(0.6)0.3\sqrt{25 \times 121} = 55.48$. 所以波动率是 7.45。

26. 答案：D
解析：随机游走(random walk)一词意味着未来回报的分配不依赖于过去。因此，不同时间的回报不相关；回报分布是独立的；但偶然情况下，两个连续的回报也可能相等。

27. 答案：D
解析：这些陈述都不正确。历史方法(historical approach)使用过去危机事件的历史数据，预期情景条件方法(scenario conditional approach)包括风险因素之间的相关性，因子推动方法(factor push method)是一种前瞻性方法而非历史方法。

28. 答案：A
解析：对"肥尾"最可能的解释是，该时间序列是二阶非稳态的，即是波动率随时间变化的条件分布。

29. 答案：C
解析：RiskMetrics 方法使用修改后的 delta-normal 方法，使用价格比率的对数，而不是回报率。

30. 答案：B

解析：不是 the probability of default，而是 the probability of significant。

31. 答案：A

解析：我们通过将每个 VAR 除以时间的平方根来计算每日 VAR。例如，10 天：316 ÷ sqrt(10) = 100，同理可以根据 15 天、20 天和 25 天来获得每日 VAR。最后会发现 A 选项与众不同。

VAR(10-day) = 316 ； *VAR*(1-day) = 316/sqrt(10) = 100

VAR(15-day) = 465 ； *VAR*(1-day) = 465/sqrt(15) = 120

VAR(20-day) = 537 ； *VAR*(1-day) = 537/sqrt(20) = 120

VAR(25-day) = 600； *VAR*(1-day) = 600/sqrt(25) = 120

32. 答案：B

解析：风险管理最简单的方法是盯市(Mark to Market Analysis)；Parametric VaR 理论上也是比较干脆的；SimulationVaR 需要一些直觉判断；Stress/Scenario analysis 可以识别和模拟 VaR 的假设。

33. 答案：A

解析：Delta-gamma 方法包含了衍生品价格相对于基础资产价格的一阶和二阶变化。对于普通期权而言，这构成了影响期权价格的主要因素。

34. 答案：B

解析：混合方法(hybrid approach)结合了两种估计 VaR 的方法，历史模拟(historical simulation)和指数平滑方法(即 EWMA 方法)。与历史模拟方法类似，混合方法直接估计收益的百分位数，但它使用与指数加权移动平均相同的方法来重新估计过去数据的权重。

35. 答案：A

解析：会低估真实的 VaR，因为分配尾部的损失概率更高。

36. 答案：C

解析：Delta-normal 可用于固定收益产品(除非它包含许多 MBS)。对于期权产品，至少应考虑二阶导数；所以，需要 delta-gamma 方法。

37. 答案：A

解析：RiskMetrics 方法是一种 delta-normal 模型，要求回报近似正态分布；历史模拟模型不需要严格的假设；与大的投资组合相比，只包含少量证券的投资组合的回报率不太可能正常分布；新兴市场指数的正态分布可能性不如成熟市场指数。因此，对于具有少量新兴市场证券的投资组合，历史模拟方法很可能比 RiskMetrics 提供更好的 VaR 估计。

38. 答案：D

解析：VaR 的主要缺点是不满足次可加性，(资产正态分布时，VaR 是满足次可加性的)

39. 答案：B

解析：一般来说，较少的观察数和较高的置信水平，会使样本波动率增加。我们可以参考样本均值波动率的公式，该公式与数据量的平方根呈反比。较高的置信水平涉及左尾部的较少观察数，从而 VaR 增加。

40. 答案：A

解析：下面的公式用于计算线性导数的 VAR：$VAR_p = \Delta VAR_f$。公式中的 delta 是一个敏感度因子，它反映了衍生品合约价值相对于底层资产价值的变化。对相关资产的 VAR 的 delta 调整说明了底层证券和衍生证券之间价值的相对变化可能不是一比一的，但至少仍然是线性的。当然，期权是非线性的，只能在小范围内看成时线性的。

41. 答案：C

解析：Daily standard deviation = sqrt(0.000 20) = 0.014 14. Annual VaR

$= 6\,247\,000 \times 2\,500^{0.5} \times 0.014\,14 \times 1.645$

$= 2\,297\,507$

42. 答案：A

解析：均值回归情况下，波动率的增长速度比时间的平方根慢。

43. 答案：D

解析：时间平方根规则：如果随机过程中从一个周期到下一个周期的波动是独立的，则波动率随着时间单位的平方根而增加。当波动率是均值回归时，则效果取决于我们目前是高于/低于长期方差。如果初始波动率较高，那么 T-day VAR 应该小于 $\sqrt{T}\times$ one-day VAR。相反，如果初始波动率是较低，那么 T-day VAR 应该大于长期值。然而，问题并没说初始波动率是高是低，所以选择 D。

44. 答案：B

解析：The persistence（$\alpha+\beta$）分别是 0.94，0.98，0.97 和 0.96，最高的 persistence 所需的回归时间最长。

45. 答案：B

解析：长期均方差 The long-run mean variance $V_L = \omega/(1-\alpha-\beta) = 0.005/(1-0.04-0.94) = 0.25$。取平方根，得到每日波动率为 0.5。乘以根号下 252，我们的年化波动率为 7.937%。

46. 答案：D

解析：GARCH 模型在条件波动率中引入均值回归，因此 A 和 B 是正确的。当 σ_t 低于长期平均值时，波动率会逐步上升。更高的 persistence $\alpha+\beta$ 意味着均值回归的过程更慢，所以 C 是正确的。

47. 答案：A

解析：回报率 ln(18/20) = −10.54%。方差预计值 $\sigma^2 = 0.90\times(1.5^2)+(1-0.90)\times 10.54^2 = 0.001\,313$，取平方根，得到 3.62%。

48. 答案：B

解析：最后一天的权重是 0.050(1 − 0.95)。对于前一天，权重为 0.05×0.95，4 天前为 $0.05\times0.95^3 = 0.042\,87$。

49. 答案：B

解析：EWMA 模型在最新观测值上的权重为 0.06，高于 60 天 MA 的权重 0.016 7(1/60) 和 250 天 MA 的权重 0.004(1 ÷ 250)。

50. 答案：A

解析：GARCH 模型具有有限的无条件方差，因此 C 是正确的。相反，由于 $\alpha+\beta$ 为 1，EWMA 模型的长期均值方差并不存在。在两种模型中，权重均随时间呈指数式下降。

51. 答案：A

解析：The daily delta-normal VAR 的计算公式：$[R_p-(z)(\sigma)]$(value of portfolio)。R_p 表示资产预期回报率，z 表示相应置信度下的 z-value，σ 是标准差。

Annual VaR = $[0.1-(2.33\times0.15)]\times10\,000\,000=-€\,2\,495\,000$。为了把 annual VaR 转成 daily VaR，就要使用平方根法则（250 天）$VaR=\{0.1/250-[(2.33\times0.15)/250^{(1/2)}\}\}\times10\,000\,000=-€\,217\,043$。

52. 答案：B

解析：组合的 VAR = 组合的价值 ×（期望收益 − 波动率 × Z）

$$= \text{Portfolio value}\times[E(R)-z_\sigma]$$

$$=2\,000\,000[0.08-(1.65)(0.15)]=-\$\,335\,000$$

53. 答案：B

解析：组合的标准差 $=[0.35^2(0.02^2)+0.65^2(0.05^2)+2(0.35)(0.65)(0.02)(0.05)(0.2)]^{0.5}=3.46\%$

VAR：$z_{2.5\%}\times\sigma=1.96(3.46\%)=6.78\%$

54. 答案：D

解析：与正态分布相比，肥尾分布(Fat-taileddistributions)在正负一个标准差内，概率质量更低(lower probability mass)。从建模的角度来看，肥尾分布就是针对那些罕见事件，虽然发生的概率低，但也必须要考虑。虽然我们常常用正态分布对很多事件进行建模，但当一个事件的本质是肥尾分布而我们误用了正态分布或指数分布时，就存在着对“小概率事件真的发生”这种危险的低估。

55. 答案：C

解析：参数方法需要假定概率分布，只估计少量参数。其他方法不需要知道数据的概率分布。

56. 答案：C

解析：真正的 VAR 将低于计算值。止损限额(Loss limits)会在遭受巨大损失时直接减少头寸。这类似于期权中的多头头寸，其中 delta 随着价格上涨而增加；反之，亦然。期权多头头寸左尾较短，因此比未受保护的头寸风险更小。

57. 答案：A

解析：基于 100 个交易日，95%的 VaR 为 −8%。

58. 答案：D

解析：方差 − 协方差方法需要假定风险因子服从正态分布。

59. 答案：D

解析：非参数法对于收益率的分布不做假设；参数法使用数据更有效；参数法中，肥尾、偏度会影响波动率的估计；多变量密度估计(MDE)法依据数据和当前的市场状况的相关程度进行赋权。

60. 答案：D

解析：EWMA 模型：$\sigma_n^2 = (1-\lambda)u_{n-1}^2 + \lambda\sigma_{n-1}^2$，$\lambda$ 越大，波动率受到前一日回报率的影响越小，对新数据反应越慢。

61. 答案：B

解析：VAR 可以看作是持有期和置信度的函数，持有期越长，置信度越大，VAR 也就越大。

62. 答案：A

解析：10%的损失尾部包括 5%的无损失（即 90%至 95%的 CDF）和 5%的损失事件。因此，该 10%尾部的平均值由下式给出：$50\% \times 0 + 50\% \times [E(\text{损失事件})] = 50\% \times [20\% \times 10 + 50\% \times 18 + 30\% \times 25] = 925$ 万美元。

63. 答案：B

解析：截止点在 10%的位置，是第三低的观测值，即 $VAR = 10$。ES 是尾部观测的平均值，即 15。

64. 答案：A

解析：VAR 测量在给定时间段内在给定置信水平内可预期损失的预期资本量。VAR 的一个问题是它没有提供有关 VAR 之外的预期损失大小的信息。VAR 的问题通常由 Expected Shortfall 来弥补，ES 是在超过 VAR 的损失的条件下来衡量预期损失。请注意，由于 ES 基于 VAR，因此更改置信水平（confidence level）可能会改变这两个指标。这两项指标之间的主要区别在于，VAR 不满足次可加性，这意味着两个基金分开的风险可能低于两个基金合并后作为投资组合的风险。违反次可加性是 VAR 的一个问题。而 ES 不存在这个问题。

65. 答案：D

解析：CVAR 的损失平均值比 VAR 差，所以选项 A 不正确。VAR 低于 CVAR，因此 VAR 是“最乐观的损失”。

66. 答案：B

解析：蒙特卡罗法（Monte Carlo VaR）和历史模拟法（Monte Carlo VaR）都是非参数法。

67. 答案：A

解析：$(1-\lambda)\lambda^t = (1-0.96)(0.96)^0 = 0.04$；$1/K = 0.04$，$K = 25$

68. 答案：A

解析：蒙特卡罗法将所求解的问题同一定的概率模型相联系，用计算机实现统计模拟或抽样，以获得问题的近似解。

69. 答案：C

解析：正态分布是对称分布，参数稳定，偏度（skewness）为 0，峰度（kurtosis）为 3。

70. 答案：C

解析：隐含波动率（implied-volatility）法基于当前市场价格求波动率。

71. 答案：A

解析：$p \times 97 + (1-p) \times 93 = 95 \times 1.01$，$p = 73.75\%$。

72. 答案：B

解析：$\{[p \times 98.45] + [(1-p) \times 96.00]\} \div [1 + (0.025/2)] = 97.00$，$p = 0.9$，$(1-$

$p)=0.1$

73. 答案：D

解析：$50\times\exp(0.05)=55p+45\times(1-p),p=75.6\%$

或者代入公式，$p=(e^{r\Delta t}-d)\div(u-d)=(e^{0.1\times0.5}-0.9)\div(1.1-0.9)=0.756$

74. 答案：A

解析：$p=(e^{(r-y)\Delta t}-d)\div(u-d)=(e^{(0.06-0.04)\times1}-1\div1.05)\div(1.05-1\div1.05)=0.69$，其中 $u=1/d$

75. 答案：D

解析：$u=12\div10=1.2$，$d=8\div10=0.8$

$p=(e^{r\Delta t}-d)\div(u-d)=(e^{0.04\times0.5}-0.8)\div(1.2-0.8)=0.55$

$c=(2\times0.55+0\times0.45)\times e^{-0.04\times0.5}=1.0792$

76. 答案：B

解析：$u=e^{\sigma\sqrt{\Delta t}}=e^{0.09531\times1}=1.1$，$d=e^{-\sigma\sqrt{\Delta t}}=e^{-0.09531\times1}=1/1.1$

$s_{uuu}=10\times1.1\times1.1\times1.1=13.31$

$s_{uud}=10\times1.1\times1.1\div1.1=11$

$s_{udd}=10\times1.1\div1.1\div1.1=9.090909$

$s_{ddd}=10\div1.1\div1.1\div1.1=7.513148$

$c=(13.31-11)\times0.4\times0.4\times0.4\times e^{-0.04\times3}=0.1311$

77. 答案：C

解析：$p=(e^{r\Delta t}-d)\div(u-d)=(e^{0.08\times0.25}-0.85)\div(1.15-0.85)=0.5673$

78. 答案：C

解析：$p=(e^{r\Delta t}-d)\div(u-d)=(e^{0.12\times0.25}-0.9)\div(1.1-0.9)=0.65227$

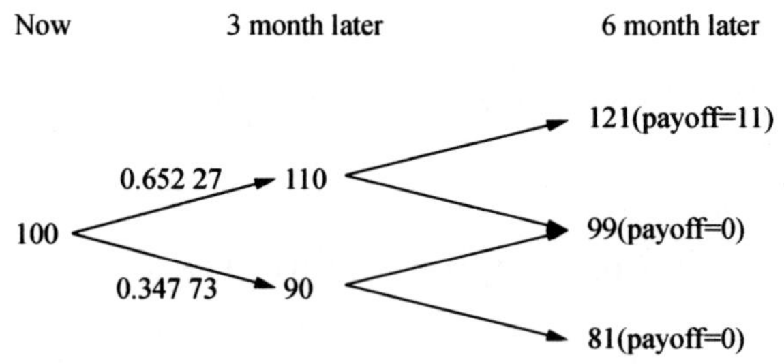

$s_{uu}=100\times1.1\times1.1=121$

$s_{ud}=100\times1.1\times0.9=99$

$s_{dd}=100\times0.9\times0.9=81$

$c=(121-110)\times0.65227^2\times e^{-0.12\times0.5}=4.4075$

79. 答案：C

解析：$p=(e^{r\Delta t}-d)\div(u-d)=(e^{0.08\times0.25}-0.94)\div(1.06-0.94)=0.6683445$

$s_{uu}=48\times1.06^2=53.9328$

$s_{ud}=48\times1.06\times0.94=47.8272$

$s_{dd}=48\times0.94^2=42.4128$

$c = (53.9328 - 50) \times e^{-0.08\times0.5} \times 0.6683445^2 = 1.6878$

80. 答案：D

解析：股票价格上涨的风险中性概率是 57.61%。

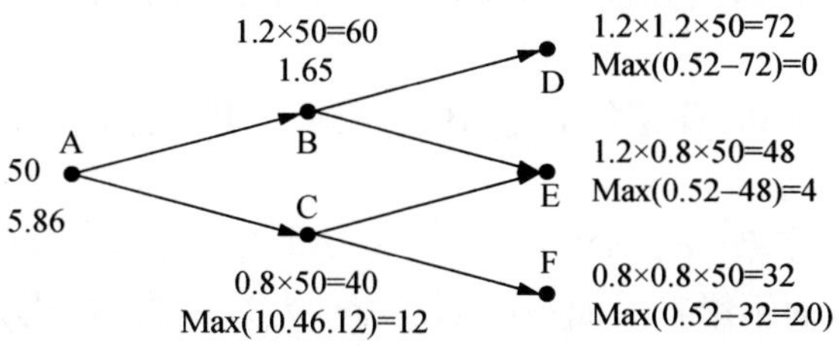

这个图展示了股票价格在各个节点上的期权价值，最终的节点的价值是 max (0, $K-S$)。

节点 B：$(0.5761 \times 0 + 0.4239 \times 4) \times e^{-0.12\times3/12} = 1.65$，大于这个点的内在价值 max(0, 52 − 60) = 0，所以期权不应该在这时行权。

节点 C：$(0.5761 \times 4 + 0.4239 \times 20) \times e^{-0.12\times3/12} = 10.46$，低于这一点的内在价值 max(0, 52 − 40) = 12，所以期权应该在节点 C 行权，节点 C 的价值是 12。

节点 A：$(0.5761 \times 1.65 + 0.4239 \times 12) \times \exp^{-0.12\times3/12} = 5.86$，高于这一点的内在价值 max(0, 52 − 50) = 2，所以期权不应该在这时行权。

81. 答案：C

解析：$u = 120 \div 100 = 1.2$，$d = 80 \div 100 = 0.8$

$p = (e^{r\Delta t} - d) \div (u - d) = (e^{0.06\times0.5} - 0.8) \div (1.2 - 0.8) = 0.5761363349$

如果初始时刻行权，$payoff = 0$

如果 6 个月后行权，$s_u = 120$，$s_d = 80$

$payoff = (120 - 110) \times 0.5761363349 \times e^{-0.06\times0.5}$

82. 答案：A

解析：美式期权可以用蒙特卡罗模拟的方法定价。

83. 答案：C

解析：对于美式看涨期权，如果标的股票不支付股利，一般不提前行权。对于美式看跌期权，如果标的股票跌得足够低，则应该提前行权。

84. 答案：D

解析：股票收益率的均值是零，波动率是 $\sigma\sqrt{\Delta T} = 0.14\sqrt{0.01} = 0.014$，所以第一步是 $S_1 = S_0(1 + 0.014 \times 0.263) = 100.37$；第二步是 $S_2 = S_1[1 + 0.014 \times -(0.475)] = 99.70$。

85. 答案：B

解析：dS/S 和 $d\ln(S)$ 都是正态分布，S 是对数正态分布，只有 I 是错的。

86. 答案：A

解析：只有 A 是错的，A 说得过于绝对。期望价格更高不代表未来价格就一定比现在高。

87. 答案：B

解析：BSM 模型假定：标的资产价格的变化是连续的。利率未知且恒定。收益率的方差恒定。流动性很好,无交易摩擦。

88. 答案：A

解析：BCD 都是 BSM 模型的假定,BSM 模型中用到的利率是无风险利率,看涨期权的价格是利率的增函数,看跌期权的价格是利率的减函数,A 错误。

89. 答案：C

解析：ABD 都是 BSM 模型的假定,BSM 模型中利率是恒定不变的,C 错误。

90. 答案：D

解析：根据 BSM 模型，$c = SN(d_1) - Ke^{-rt}N(d_2)$，公司宣布发放股利这件事只影响前面一项 $SN(d_1)$,而不影响后面一项 $Ke^{-rt}N(d_2)$,因为 $N(d_2)$没有变化,所以期权价格的变化等于 $SN(d_1)$的变化。

宣布前，$SN(d_1) = 40 \times 0.233\,78 = 9.351\,2$

宣布后，$SN(d_1) = (40 - 0.5e^{-0.05/12}) \times 0.298\,76 = 11.652\,882\,24$

$c = 1.65 + 11.652\,882\,24 - 9.351\,2 = 3.95$

91. 答案：B

解析：根据 BSM 模型，$c = (S - I)N(d_1) - Ke^{-rT}N(d_2)$，$I$ 表示股利的贴现值,I 的系数$N(d_1)$越大,(也就是 delta 越大)发放股利就对期权价格的影响越大,而实值期权的 delta＞平值期权＞虚值期权,所以实值期权的价格受到股利的影响更大。

92. 答案：D

解析：$p = Ke^{-rT}N(-d_2) - SN(-d_1) = 30 \times e^{-0.04\times0.5} \times (1 - 0.851\,7) - 35 \times (1 - 0.897\,6) = 0.776\,9$。

93. 答案：C

解析：$d_1 = \ln(S_0/K) + (r + \sigma^2/2)T/(\sigma\sqrt{T}) = 0.15$

$d_2 = d_1 - \sigma\sqrt{T} = 0.05$

$$p = Ke^{-rT}N(-d_2) - SN(-d_1) = 60e^{-0.04\times0.25} \times N(-0.05) - 60 \times N(-0.15) = 2.090\,5$$

94. 答案：C

解析：假定标的资产不会带来收入，$c = SN(d_1) - Ke^{-rT}N(d_2) = 100 \times 0.457\,185 - 110\,e^{-0.1\times0.5} \times 0.374\,163 = \$6.568$。

95. 答案：B

解析：$c = SN(d_1) - Ke^{-rT}N(d_2) = 30 \times 0.954\,6 - 26 \times e^{-0.05\times0.25} \times 0.927\,9 = 4.81$

96. 答案：A

解析：根据 BSM 模型,欧式看涨期权的价格为：

$$c = SN(d_1) - Ke^{-rT}N(d_2) = 50 \times 0.541\,7 - 60 \times e^{-0.08\times1} \times 0.486\,2 = 0.155\,85$$

相同条件下,美式看涨期权的价格应高于欧式看涨期权,故排除 BD。

而美式看跌期权的价格应大于它的内在价值（$K - S = 10$ USD)，故排除 CD,选 A。

97. 答案：D

解析：$N(d_2)$是行权概率。

98. 答案：C

解析：欧式看涨期权的价值是 $S \times N(d_1) - Ke^{-rT} \times N(d_2)$，$S$ 股票的当前价格。由于股利的存在，S 应减去股利的现值。股利的宣告会影响 S，d_1 和 d_2。但题目告诉我们 d_2 不变，期权价格变化取决于 $S \times N(d_1)$ 的变化。

一开始 $S \times N(d_1) = 40 \times 0.291\,23 = 11.649\,2$

后来 $S \times N(d_1) = (40 - 0.5 \times e^{-3\%/12}) \times 0.299\,28 = 11.821\,9$

变化 $= 11.821\,9 - 11.649\,2 = 0.172\,7$

所以新的看涨期权价格应该在原来的价格上增加 0.172 7，即 1.952 7。

99. 答案：A

解析：远期合约多头的 delta 是 $e^{-rT} = e^{-0.10 \times 0.5} = 0.95$。

100. 答案：A

解析：如果股票不支付股息，美式看涨期权的价值总是高于提前行权的价值(因为没有股息可获取)。因此，提前执行看涨期权是不划算的。而提前执行美式看跌期权可能是合理的，因为利率为正时，现在接受执行价格比将来更好。

101. 答案：C

解析：虚值(out of money)看涨期权对股利不敏感，A 错误。实值(in the money)期权受股利变化影响最明显。

102. 答案：D

解析：根据 BSM 模型，$c = (S - I)N(d_1) - Ke^{-rT}N(d_2)$，其中 I 表示股利的贴现值。所以 $N(d_1)$越大(也就是 delta 越大)，期权价格 c 就受股利影响越大。根据 delta 和 S 的图像关系，期权在深度实值时，delta 最大(接近 1 或 -1)。所以深度实值的期权的价格受股利影响最大，深度虚值的期权价格受股利影响最小。

103. 答案：B

解析：$7.04 \times N/(N + M) = 5.87$。

104. 答案：C

解析：看涨期权的 delta 是正的，等于 $e^{-qt} \times N(d_1) = e^{-0.01 \times 2} \times 0.64 = 0.63$。

105. 答案：D

解析：A 错误，当看涨期权深度实值，看跌期权深度虚值时，delta 对标的资产的变化不敏感。B 错误，当看涨和看跌期权都深度实值时，delta 对标的资产的变化不敏感。C 错误，当看涨和看跌期权都深度虚值时，delta 对标的资产的变化不敏感。D 正确，当看涨看跌期权都平值时，delta 对标的资产的变化最敏感(平值期权的 gamma 最大)。

106. 答案：B

解析：现货价格接近执行价格，所以这是一个平值看跌期权，delta 接近 -0.5。

107. 答案：D

delta 衡量期权价格对标的资产价格的变化率。期限短并且内在价值高的期权的 delta 接近 1，gamma，rho，vega 都接近零。

108. 答案：D

解析：平值期权的 delta 接近 0.5。指数变化 1 会导致看涨期权价格变化：$0.5 \times EUR\ 10 = EUR\ 5$。因此 percent delta(又称 local delta)定义为 $\%D = (5 \div 350) \div (1 \div 2\,200) = 31.4$。

所以看涨期权的 99% VaR = %D × VaR(99% of index) = %D × call price × alpha (99%) × 1-day volatility = 31.4 × EUR 350 × 2.33 × 2.05% = EUR 525。 alpha (99%) 表示标准正态分布 99%的分位数，等于 2.33。

109. 答案：B

解析：线性 VAR 是由指数往不利的方向变动算出的。$VAR = \alpha \times S \times \sigma \times \text{sqrt}(T)$ = 1.645 × 3 000 × (24% ÷ sqrt(260)) × sqrt(10) = 232.3，再乘以 delta(0.6)得到 139。

110. 答案：C

解析：delta 必须在 0.5 左右，说明线性的 VAR = \$100 000 × 10.4% × 0.5 = \$5 200。 该头寸是一个期权多头并且 gamma 为正，二次的 VAR 小于 \$5 200。

111. 答案：A

解析：深度实值(deep in the money)的看涨期权的 delta 接近 1。深度虚值(deep out of money)的看跌期权的 delta 接近零。同时满足这两个条件的是 A 选项。

112. 答案：C

解析：为了对冲卖空看涨期权的风险，应选择持有标的资产多头。

delta = 0.5 的含义是，标的资产的价格每变动 \$1，看涨期权的价格就变动 \$0.5，所以每一单位的看涨期权要用 0.5 单位的标的资产去对冲，选 C。

113. 答案：C

解析：gamma 定义为期权的 delta 对标的资产价格的变化率，即期权价格对标的资产价格的二阶导数。所以期限越短的平值期权的 gamma 越大，因为这样的期权对标的资产价格变化更敏感。正确选项是期限较短的平值看涨期权。

114. 答案：B

解析：对于深度实值的看涨期权，delta 接近 1(小于 1)，标的资产每下跌一个单位，期权下跌接近一个单位，排除 CD。

对于深度虚值的看跌期权，delta 接近 0(小于 0)，标的资产每下跌一个单位，期权几乎不怎么上涨，排除 AC，选 B。

115. 答案：A

解析：交易员的目的是用期权做 delta hedge，对于 at the money call，delta = 0.5，交易员希望期权的 delta 能够稳定在 0.5 左右。但期权的 delta 会随着标的资产价格的改变而改变，一旦标的资产价格产生大幅波动，期权的 delta 也会大幅变化，则原先构建的头寸不能很好地对冲标的资产的价格变化。所以交易员希望标的资产的价格在原来的价位(strike price 的位置)左右小幅度震荡，这样期权的 delta 不会发生明显变化，从而始终保持对冲的效果。

116. 答案：B

解析：根据 BSM 模型，$c = Se^{-qT}N(d_1) - Ke^{-rT}N(d_2)$

看涨期权的 delta 就是 S 的系数，即 $e^{-qT}N(d_1) = e^{-0.01\times4} \times 0.6 = 0.576\,5$

117. 答案：C

解析：远期合约的价值 $= Se^{-qT} - Ke^{-rT}$

远期合约的 delta 就是 S 的系数，即 $e^{-qT} = e^{-0.05\times0.5} = 0.975\,3$

118. 答案：B

解析：这道题问的是：什么样的欧式期权的 delta 最不稳定（受到标的资产价格的影响最严重）。我们知道 delta 关于 S 的图像是一个正态分布的累积分布函数的图形，在图形的对称中心（$S=K$ 的位置，也就是 at the money 的时候）delta 对 S 的导数最大，即此时 delta 最不稳定，最容易受到 S 的影响。

119. 答案：A

解析：因为 gamma 为负，所以要买看涨期权让投资组合的 gamma 回到零。买的数量应该是 400（600 ÷ 1.5）份看涨期权。但这会使 delta 从零增加到 300（400 × 0.75）。所以还需卖空 300 份股票。

120. 答案：C

解析：原先 200 份期权的总 delta = 200 × 0.687 3 = 137.46，此时用 13 746 份股票对冲后来 200 份期权的总 delta = 200 × 0.983 1 = 196.62，不难看出，此时应该用 19 662 份股票对冲。所以应再购买 6 216 份（19 962 − 13 746）股票。

121. 答案：C

解析：由 Delta 可以算出当欧元汇率上升 \$0.01，银行的头寸上涨 \$300（0.01 × 30 000）。由 gamma 可以算出当欧元汇率上涨 \$0.01，投资组合的 delta 下跌 800（0.01 × 80 000）。为了构建 delta 中性的投资组合，要卖空 30 000 欧元。当汇率上升至 0.93，我们期望投资组合的 delta 下降 2 400[(0.93 − 0.90) × 80 000]。为了维持 delta 中性，应卖空 27 600 欧元。如果一个投资组合的 delta 为零，但 gamma 为负，标的资产价格较大的变动会导致损失。所以该银行很有可能会亏钱。

122. 答案：A

解析：深度实值的期权的 delta 较大（接近 1），因此需要用更多的股票头寸去对冲，所以持有成本更大。

深度虚值的期权的 delta 较小（接近 0），因此只需要较少的股票头寸去对冲，所以持有成本较小。

123. 答案：B

解析：$\Delta c = \text{delta} \times \Delta S + 1/2 \times \text{gamma} \times (\Delta S)^2$，当 delta = 0，gamma > 0 时，无论 S 上涨还是下跌，Δc 始终大于零，即 c 始终是上涨的，所以风险最小。

124. 答案：B

解析：要构造一个 delta-neutral 并且 gamma-neutral 的组合，要先用期权对冲 gamma，再用股票对冲 delta。

对冲 gamma 需要 100（150 ÷ 1.5）份期权，此时会产生 40（100 × 0.4）的 delta，因此还需 40 份股票空头对冲多余的 delta。

125. 答案：A

解析：平值期权的 delta 是 0.5。银行卖空了起权，所以要通过买股票的方式对冲 delta。delta 是 0.54，所以需要买将近 50 000 份股票。A 正确。其他条件是多余的。

126. 答案：B

解析：当波动率增大时，期限长的期权价格比期限短的期权上涨得多。交易员看涨波动率，但又不想持有暴露的头寸，所以应该买期限长的期权，同时卖空期限短的期权。

127. 答案：B

解析：为了让原来的投资组合同时满足 delta neutral 和 gamma neutral，应该先用期权对冲 gamma，再用股票对冲 delta。

方法一：卖看涨期权对冲正的 gamma，此时会产生负的 delta，再买股票对冲 delta

方法二：卖看跌期权对冲正的 gamma，此时会产生正的 delta，再卖股票对冲 delta

128. 答案：C

解析：用股票对冲期权的风险(或者用期权对冲股票的风险)，即使做到了 delta neutral，也只是在股票和期权价格小幅波动的条件下可以有效对冲，若价格大幅波动，必须动态调整头寸，C 错误。

129. 答案：C

解析：方法一：先卖空看涨期权对冲 gamma，这时会产生负的 delta，然后买股票对冲 delta。

方法二：先卖空看跌期权对冲 gamma，这时会产生正的 delta，然后卖空股票对冲 delta。C 正确。

130. 答案：B

解析：深度实值的看涨期权的 delta = 1，买入 2 000 份看涨期权让 delta 变成 2 000，应卖出 2 000 份股票以保持 delta neutral。

131. 答案：C

解析：平值期权多头的 theta 为负，A 错误。实值期权的 gamma 较小，B 错误。实值看跌期权的 delta 趋向 −1，D 错误。

132. 答案：C

解析：实值期权比虚值期权对利率变化更敏感(rho 更大)。

133. 答案：D

解析：平值的欧式期权的 vega 最大，所以 A 正确。Delta 为负并且随着 S 上升趋向零，B 正确。平值期权临近到期日时 gamma 上升，C 正确。短期平值期权的 theta 较大，D 错误。

134. 答案：A

解析：股价和执行价格非常接近，所以 delta≈0.5，并不是最高的(最高是 1)，该期权只距离到期只有 20 分钟的时间，theta 也不是影响期权价格的关键因素根据 gamma 和 S 的图像，当股票价格 S 在执行价格 K 附近时，gamma 达到最大值，因此 gamma 最容易影响期权价格，即对期权产生的风险最大。

135. 答案：D

解析：根据 gamma 和股价 S 的图像，当 S 等于执行价格 K 时，gamma 达到最大。根据 gamma 和期限 T 的图像，在 at the money 的条件下，T 越短，gamma 越大。

136. 答案：B

解析：根据 gamma 和股价 S 的图像，S 和执行价格 K 的差距越小，gamma 越大。根据 gamma 和期限 T 的图像，在近似 at the money(S 和 K 相差不多)的条件下，期限 T 越短，gamma 越大。

137. 答案：A

解析：先用 1 000(3 000 ÷ 3)份期权多头对冲 gamma，此时会产生 800(1 000 × 0.8)的

delta，再用 800 份股票空头对冲 delta。

138. 答案：C

解析：C 的说法是毫无根据的，up and call 是一种奇异期权，不能用欧式期权的 Greeks 衡量。

139. 答案：B

解析：组合的 delta：$-1\,000\times0.50-500\times0.80-2\,000\times(-0.40)-500\times0.70=-450$

组合的 gamma：$-1\,000\times2.2-500\times0.6-2\,000\times1.3-500\times1.8=-6\,000$

组合的 vega：$-1\,000\times1.8-500\times0.2-2\,000\times0.7-500\times1.4=-4\,000$

买入 4 000 个期权即可将组合做成 gamma 中性投资组合，因为 gamma 为：$4\,000\times1.5=6\,000$。此时整个投资组合 delta 为：$4\,000\times0.6-450=1\,950$。因此，除了买入 4 000 个交易期权外，还需要卖出 1 950 份的股票，以使投资组合既满足 gamma 中性要求也满足 delta 中性要求。

140. 答案：C

解析：期限越长，gamma 越小，vega 越大，所以只有买短卖长的策略才能构造正 gamma 负 vega 的组合。

141. 答案：B

解析：期权临近到期日时，rho，gamma，vega 都接近零，而深度实值的期权的 delta = 1，所以期权价格直接受标的资产的影响，delta 比其他三项更明显地反映了期权的风险。

142. 答案：A

解析：平值期权的 theta 比实值和虚值期权负的更多，所以随到期日的临近，期权价格下降得更快。

143. 答案：C

解析：期限越长，gamma 越小，vega 越大，所以只有买短卖长的策略才能构造正 gamma 负 vega 的组合。

144. 答案：A

解析：vega 是期权价格对波动率 σ 的导数，反映了期权价格对波动率的敏感程度，其他条件相同的情况下，标的资产的价格 S 越接近执行价格 K，vega 越大，所以平值期权对波动率变化更灵敏。

145. 答案：D

解析：深度实值的看跌期权的 delta 接近 -1，A 错误。

在其他条件一样的情况下，平值期权的 gamma 比实值/虚值期权都大，B 错误。

期权的 Theta 一般是负的，C 错误。

146. 答案：A

解析：vega 的定义是期权价格对波动率的导数，对冲 vega 也就是对冲波动率变化给期权带来的影响。

147. 答案：C

解析：一般情况下，期权的 theta 都是负的，但有例外，如实值欧式看跌期权，或者利率较高时的实值欧式看涨期权。Ⅰ错误。

随着到期日的来临,期权的 rho 会缩减为零,这对看涨期权和看跌期权都是成立的。Ⅱ错误。

148. 答案:A

解析:分别参考 theta 关于期限 T, vega 关于 T, gamma 关于 T 的图像,对于平值期权,T 越大,theta 负的越少,vega 越小,gamma 越小,综合分析下来,只有买短期卖长期才能符合要求。

149. 答案:D

解析:期权空头会产生负的 gamma 和负的 vega, Ⅰ正确。

根据 gamma 和股价 S 的图像以及 vega 和股价 S 的图像,当 S 远离执行价格 K 时,gamma 和 vega 都逐渐缩小为零,Ⅱ正确。

150. 答案:C

解析:对于看涨和看跌期权而言,gamma 和 vaga 是一样的。

151. 答案:C

解析:平值期权的时间价值最大,因为它的 theta 最大。

152. 答案:D

解析:平值期权的时间价值最高。

153. 答案:D

解析:时间的流逝是可以预见到的,不算 unexpected loss,所以 theta 不反映风险。

154. 答案:A

解析:别的条件一样的情况下,平值期权比实值期权和虚值期权的时间价值都高。

155. 答案:A

解析:分别参考 theta 关于期限 T, vega 关于 T, gamma 关于 T 的图像,对于平值期权,T 越大,theta 负的越少,vega 越小,gamma 越小,综合分析下来,只有买短期卖长期才能符合要求。

156. 答案:B

解析:期权的 theta 一般是负的,平值期权负的最多,其次是实值期权,再次是虚值期权,D 错误。

157. 答案:A

解析:vega 在 $S=K$ 处达到最大,Ⅰ正确。

远期合约的价值是 S 的线性函数,不能用来对冲 gamma, Ⅱ正确。

Rho 是 S 的增函数,对于看跌期权,实值期权的 S 更低,rho 更小,Ⅲ正确。

Theta 是期权价格对期限 T 求导,Ⅳ错误。

158. 答案:C

解析:这个 portfolio 有两个要求,一是 vega 为零,二是和利率正相关。

根据 vega 和股价 S 的图像,S 越接近执行价格 K, vega 较高,S 远离 K 时,vega 趋于零,所以应该选深度实值或深度虚值的期权。

Portfolio 和利率正相关,说明应选看涨多头或看跌空头,结合以上两点,选 C。

159. 答案:B

解析:根据 theta 和期限 T 的图像,平值期权的 theta 负得最多,其次是实值期权,再次虚值期权。A 错误。

Vega 是期权价格对波动率的导数，vega = 10 表示波动率每增长一个单位，期权价格增长 10 个单位。B 正确。

看涨期权的 delta 取值范围是 0 到 1。C 错误。

160. 答案：D

解析：做多 gamma 意味着投资组合是由 gamma 较高的期权多头（比如，短期平值期权）构成的。做空 vega 意味着投资组合卖空了 vega 较高的期权（比如，长期平值期权）。

161. 答案：A

解析：期权多头有正的 gamma 和 vega。临近到期日时，gamma 会上升，vega 会下降。所以为了得到正 gamma 和负 vega，应该买短期期权，卖长期期权。

162. 答案：A

解析：这样的投资组合是卖空 vega（波动率）和 theta（时间）。要通过买卖不同期限的期权是投资组合达到 delta 中性。短期限的期权多头有较小的正 vega 和较高的负 theta。可以通过卖空短期限的期权，买长期限的期权来对冲。

163. 答案：A

解析：$FV = 100$，$I/Y = 6$，$N = 6$，$PMT = 5$，$CPT\ PV = -95.08$

164. 答案：A

解析：$FV = 100$，$I/Y = 2$，$N = 14$，$PMT = 3$，$CPT\ PV = -112.10$

165. 答案：A

解析：$FV = 100$，$I/Y = 4.5$，$N = 30$，$PMT = 0$，$CPT\ PV = -26.7$

166. 答案：A

解析：$FV = 100$，$I/Y = 4$，$N = 2$，$PMT = 10$，$CPT\ PV = -111.32$

$FV = 100$，$I/Y = 4$，$N = 2$，$PMT = 6$，$CPT\ PV = -103.77$

167. 答案：A

解析：A 溢价发行，$YTM < 5\%$；B 平价发行，$YTM = 6\%$；C 折价发行，$YTM > 5\%$。

168. 答案：B

解析：债券期限越短，coupon rate 越高，价格相对 basis point 变动越小。

169. 答案：A

解析：年化收益率 EAR 的公式是：$FV/PV = (1 + EAR)^T$，所以 $EAR = (FV/PV)^{1/T} - 1$. 本题中 $T = 1/12$，所以 $EAR = (1\,000/987)^{12} - 1 = 17.0\%$。

170. 答案：D

解析：最初投资的 1 美元将增长至：

(CD1) $(1 + 7.82\%/12)^{12} = 1.081\,07$

(CD2) $(1 + 8.00\%/4)^4 = 1.082\,43$

(CD3) $(1 + 8.05\%/2)^2 = 1.082\,12$

(CD4) $e^{7.95\% \times 1} = 1.082\,75$

CD4 最终金额最高，所以 EAR 也最大。

171. 答案：C

解析：$FV/PV = 2 = (1+8\%)^T$， $T = \ln(2)/\ln(1.08) = 9.006$。

172. 答案：B

解析：coupon rate 越低，价格相对 basispoint 变动百分比越大。

173. 答案：A

解析：债券期限越长，couponrate 越小，价格相对 basispoint 变动百分比越大。

174. 答案：A

解析：在下面的等式中，债券 A 的价格相当于其六个月的到期现金流，这是本金加上每半年 3.00 美元的息票。

$101.182 = 103.00 \times d(0.5)$

$d(0.5) = 0.9823$

接下来使用 Bond B 的价格和现金流来计算 $d(1.0)$ 折现因子。六个月的现金流是每半年 6.00 美元的息票，折现因子为 $d(0.5)$。一年到期的现金流是本金加上每半年 6.00 美元的息票。

$102.341 = 6.00 \times d(0.5) + 106.00 \times d(1.0)$

$102.341 = 6.00 \times 0.9823 + 106.00 \times d(1.0)$

$d(1.0) = 0.9099$

175. 答案：A

解析：$PV = 6 \div (1+2\%) + 106 \div (1+4\%)^2$。

176. 答案：B

解析：债券价格是 $50 \div (1+6\%) + 50 \div (1+7\%)^2 + 1\,050 \div (1+8\%)^3 = 924.36$。

177. 答案：A

解析：$PV = 10 \div 1.08 + 10 \div 1.09^2 + 110 \div 1.10^3$。

178. 答案：B

解析：债券价格接近 95.28。计算此债券价格的公式为：

$PV = 8 \div (1+0.08)^1 + 8 \div (1+0.09)^2 + (8+100) \div (1+0.10)^3$

$PV = 7.41 + 6.73 + 81.14 = 95.28$

179. 答案：C

解析：债券价格接近 92.76。计算此债券价格的公式为：

$PV = 7 \div (1+0.08)^1 + 7 \div (1+0.09)^2 + (7+100) \div (1+0.10)^3$

$PV = 6.48 + 5.89 + 80.39 = 92.76$

180. 答案：B

解析：计算 Bond Z 价格的公式为：

$PV = 6 \div (1+0.08)^1 + 6 \div (1+0.09)^2 + (6+100) \div (1+0.10)^3$

$PV = 5.56 + 5.05 + 79.64 = 90.25$

使用此价格，债券的到期收益率可以计算为：

$90.25 = 6 \div (1+r)^1 + 6 \div (1+r)^2 + (6+100) \div (1+r)^3$

$r = 9.92\%$

181. 答案：D

解析：随着无风险利率的上升，公司债券的收益率将会增加。同样，随着违约概率的增加（无论是公司业务风险的增加还是杠杆率的增加都会发生），该公司债券的收益率会增加。

182. 答案：A

解析：$PV = 9 \div 1.08 + 9 \div 1.09^2 + 109 \div 1.10^3$

183. 答案：A

解析：由于剥离/重组 STRIPS 所涉及的成本，投资者通常会为 STRIPS 支付溢价。短期 C-STRIPS 倾向于以溢价交易，而长期 C-STRIPS 倾向于以折价交易。没有证据表明 STRIPS 存在非流动性的重大风险；但是，它们可能是流动性相对差一些。

184. 答案：D

解析：$PV = 7 \div 1.08 + 7 \div 1.09^2 + 107 \div 1.10^3$。

185. 答案：B

解析：$\$10\,000[1 - 0.068 \times (91/360)] = \$9\,828.11$。

186. 答案：D

解析：$PV = 6 \div 1.08 + 6 \div 1.09^2 + 106 \div 1.10^3 = 90.25$

$PV = -90.25$，$N = 3$，$PMT = 6$，$FV = 100$，$CPT\ I/Y = 9.92$

187. 答案：C

解析：债券交易商使用债券净价报价。应计利息是债券自上一次付息后累计未付的利息。在债券买卖时，债券卖出的结算价格应是债券的市场价格加上应计利息，即买主应向卖主支付债券市场价格加应计利息。

188. 答案：B

解析：当 yield-to-maturity ＜coupon 时，债券以溢价出售。随着时间流逝。债券价格将走向平价。因此价格会下降。

189. 答案：A

解析：距离债券到期日共计两年半时间，$N = 5$，$I/Y = 2$，$PMT = 2.5$，$FV = 100$，$CPT\ PV = 102.36$。

2018 年 4 月 10 号到 6 月 14 号按 30/360 计算共计 64 天，$102.36 \times 1.02^{64/180} = 103.08$。

190. 答案：A

解析：2018 年 4 月 10 号到 6 月 14 号按 30/360 计算共计 64 天，应计利息 $= 64 \div 180 \times 5\%/2 \times 100 = 0.89$。

191. 答案：A

解析：债券净价需要扣除应计利息。

距离债券到期日共计两年半时间，$N = 5$，$I/Y = 2$，$PMT = 2.5$，$FV = 100$，$CPT\ PV = 102.36$。

2018 年 4 月 10 号到 6 月 14 号按 30/360 计算共计 64 天，债券全价 $= 102.36 \times 1.02^{64/180} = 103.08$。

应计利息 $= 64/180 \times 5\%/2 \times 100 = 0.89$

债券净价 $= 103.08 - 0.89 = 102.19$

192. 答案：A

解析：Matrix pricing 的目的共有两个，一是给交易不活跃债券和暂未发行债券定价；二是承销债券时预估 spread。具体参考具有相似到期时间、息票利率和信贷质量的债券进行定价。

193. 答案：C

解析：Matrix pricing 的目的共有两个，一是给交易不活跃债券和暂未发行债券定价；二是承销债券时预估 spread。

194. 答案：B

解析：$N=40$，$PV=-111$，$PMT=3$，$FV=100$，$CPT\ I/Y=2.56$

年化到期收益率 $=2.56\times 2=5.12$

195. 答案：A

解析：$N=48$，$PV=-80$，$FV=100$，$PMT=0$，$CPT\ I/Y=0.466$，$0.466\times 12=5.59$

196. 答案：A

解析：可以算出，按月计复利的到期收益率约为 3.87%。将年化收益率从一个计息周期转换为另一个计息周期的公式如下：

$(1+APR_m/m)^m=(1+APR_n/n)^n$

$(1+0.038\,97/2)^2=(1+APR_{12}/12)^{12}$

$APR_{12}=0.003\,22\times 12=0.038\,65$，约 3.87%。

197. 答案：D

解析：$N=10$，$PMT=4$，$FV=100$，$PV=-101$，$CPT\ I/Y=3.877\%$。

$YTM=3.877\%\times 2=7.75\%$。

198. 答案：D

解析：$N=6$，$PMT=4$，$FV=102$，$PV=-101$，$CPT\ I/Y=4.1$。

$YTM=4.1\times 2=8.2$。

199. 答案：C

解析：$N=8$，$PMT=4$，$FV=101$，$PV=-101$，$CPT\ I/Y=3.96$。

$YTM=3.96\times 2=7.92$。

200. 答案：C

解析：

Yield to first call：$N=6$，$PMT=4$，$FV=102$，$PV=-101$，$CPT\ I/Y=4.1$，$YTM=4.1\times 2=8.2$。

Yield to second call：$N=8$，$PMT=4$，$FV=101$，$PV=-101$，$CPT\ I/Y=3.96$，$YTM=3.96\times 2=7.92$。

Yield to maturity：$N=10$，$PMT=4$，$FV=100$，$PV=-101$，$CPT\ I/Y=3.88$，$YTM=3.88\times 2=7.75$。

201. 答案：A

解析：浮动利率债券 A 报价差额 0.41＞贴现差额 0.32，溢价发行。

202. 答案：D

解析：$PV = 95$，$BEY = 365 \div 320 \times (100 - PV)/PV \times 100\% = 6\%$

203. 答案：D

解析：$PV = 100 \times (1 - 180/360 \times 0.052) = 97.4$

$BEY = 365 \div 180 \times (100 - PV)/PV \times 100\% = 5.4\%$

PV 按 360 天/年，BEY 按 365 天/年计算。

204. 答案：A

解析：平价收益率曲线(par yield curve)：债券的息票率等于其收益率时相应的收益率曲线。此时，债券的价格将等于它的票面值。

205. 答案：C

解析：题意可知 $m = 2$，$d = e^{-0.07\times2} = 0.8694$，并且有：

$A = e^{-0.05\times0.5} + e^{-0.06\times1.0} + e^{-0.065\times1.5} + e^{-0.07\times2} = 3.6935$

根据 par yield 的公式反推，可得平均收益率为 $(100 - 100 \times 0.8694) \times 2 \div 3.6935 = 7.072$。

为证明结论的正确性，可以得息票率为 7.072%（即半年支付 3.5365）的债券的价值，即：

$3.536e^{-0.05\times0.5} + 3.536e^{-0.06\times1.0} + 3.536e^{-0.065\times1.5} + 103.536e^{-0.07\times2.0} = 100$

即说明 7.072%为平价收益率。

206. 答案：A

解析：Spot curve 根据 Zero Coupon Bond 所得到的不同期 Yield 绘制而成。

207. 答案：A

解析：forward curve 作为 spotcurve 的副产品，其直观意义是短期 spot rate 未来变动路径。

208. 答案：D

解析：远期利率可以由此推导：$P_4 = P_3 \div (1 + F_{3,4})$，or $(1 + R_4)^4 = (1 + R_3)^3(1 + F_{3,4})$，解方程，得 $F_{3,4} = (85.16 \div 79.81) - 1 = 0.067$。

209. 答案：A

解析：息票收益率曲线是即期利率曲线的平均，因此当它向上倾斜时，它必须位于即期利率曲线的下方。远期利率曲线可以解释为即期利率曲线加上它的斜率。如果即期利率曲线向上倾斜，则远期利率曲线必然在它上方。

210. 答案：D

解析：$1.009 \times 1.0113 \times 1.0395 = (1 + Z)^3$。

211. 答案：D

解析：$3.6 \div 1.0081 + 103.6 \div 1.0081 \times 1.0113 = 105.19$。

212. 答案：A

解析：宏观经济因素如通货膨胀影响 benchmark yield。

213. 答案：A

解析：见下表。

名称	含义	无风险利率标杆	无风险利率类别
国债息差 spread-to-Treasury	信用债券收益率减标杆国债收益率	标杆国债的收益率	国债
插值国债息差 Interpolated Spread-to-Treasury	信用债券收益率减国债收益率曲线内插值	国债收益率曲线在期限匹配点的内插值	国债
I—息差 *I*—Spread	信用债券收益率减利率互换曲线内插值	利率互换曲线在期限匹配点的内插值	Libor
资产互换息差 Asset Swap Spread	借助利率互换将信用债券固息现金流置换为浮息现金流(Libor + 息差)时，浮息现金流相对于 Libor 的息差	利率互换曲线	Libor
Z-息差 Z-Spread	相对于 Libor 即期收益率曲线的收益率溢价	利率互换曲线	Libor

214. 答案：D

解析：对于 $T=3$，$(1+3.50\%)^3=1.10872$。对于 $T=5$，$(1+4.50\%)^5=1.24618$。构建方程 $1.24618=(1+F_{3,5})^2\times1.10872$。解方程，得 6.018%。或者也可以做近似运算 $5R_5=3R_3+2F_{3,5}$，$F_{3,5}=R_5+(3/2)(R_5-R_3)=4.50\%+1.5(4.50\%-3.50\%)=6\%$。

215. 答案：D

解析：在管理国内债券组合时，外汇风险无关紧要。

216. 答案：C

解析：$PV=-100.65$，$N=3$，$PMT=5$，$FV=100$，$CPT\ I/Y=476$ bps

$PV=-100.25$，$N=3$，$PMT=4$，$FV=100$，$CPT\ I/Y=392$ bps

$476-392=84$ bps

217. 答案：D

解析：$5/(1+4.86\%+1\%)+5/(1+4.95\%+1\%)^2+105/(1+5.65\%+1\%)^3$

218. 答案：C

解析：Z-spread − OAS = option cost in percent。

219. 答案：C

解析：对于一个持有至到期的债券，在到期前投资者不会考虑卖给其他人，不存在资本收益。

220. 答案：D

解析：再投资风险是指中间的支付的利息按不同于初始利率的利率再投资。利率保持不变时，或者零息债券，没有在投资风险。可赎回债券可以提前赎回，这产生了更多的再投资风险。

221. 答案：D

解析：债券的收益来源通常有三种，capital gain, coupon and principal payment,

Reinvestment income from coupon。对于一个持有至到期的债券，在到期前投资者不会考虑卖给其他人，因此没有 capital gain/loss。在到期前，债券投资者会收到 coupon payment，这部分收到的钱可以拿来再投资，受到利率风险影响。在到期时，债券投资者会收到承诺的本金，不受利率风险影响。

222. 答案：A

解析：资本收益相对于 carrying value 进行计算，即价格轨迹(trajectory)。如果债券以高于(低于)其恒定收益率价格轨迹的价格出售，则会产生资本收益(损失)。轨迹上的一个点代表当时债券的账面价值。也就是说，资本收益/损失是根据债券的账面价值，即恒定收益率价格轨迹上的点而非原始购买价格来衡量的。如果债券以低于票面价的价格购买，则账面价值为原始购买价格加上折价的摊余金额(amortized amount)。如果以高于面值的价格购买债券，则账面价值为原始购买价格减去(不加)溢价的摊余金额。每年的摊销金额是轨道上两点之间价格的变化。

223. 答案：B

解析：由于息票率大于收益率，所以债券以溢价卖出，即价格大于面值。如果利率不变，债券价格将收敛于面值。鉴于一开始是溢价，所以价格会逐渐降低。

224. 答案：C

解析：$PV=0$，$N=5$，$I/Y=9$，$PMT=7$，$CPT\ FV=41.89$

225. 答案：D

解析：$N=4$，$PMT=7$，$I/Y=9$，$FV=100$，$CPT\ PV=-93.52$，

Capital gain/loss $=93.52-100=-6.48$

226. 答案：C

解析：当 $YTM=10.45\%$ ($I/Y=5.225$) 时，$PMT=40$，$N=24$，$FV=1\,000$，$PV=\$834.61$。当 $YTM=10.07\%$ ($I/Y=5.035$) 时，$PV=\$857.67$，增加了 $\$23.06$。

227. 答案：A

解析：债券的近似修正久期接近 2.78。修正久期的计算如下：

$$\text{ApproxModDur}=\frac{PV_{-}-PV_{+}}{2\times\Delta\text{Yield}\times PV_0}$$

Lower yield-to-maturity by 5 bps to 2.95%

$$PV_{-}=5/(1+0.029\,5)^1+5/(1+0.029\,5)^2+(5+100)/(1+0.029\,5)^3$$
$$=105.804\,232$$

Increase yield-to-maturity by 5bps to 3.05%

$$PV_{-}=5/(1+0.030\,5)^1+5/(1+0.030\,5)^2+(5+100)/(1+0.030\,5)^3$$
$$=105.510\,494$$

$PV_0=105.657\,223$，$\Delta\text{Yield}=0.000\,5$

$$\text{ApproxModDur}=\frac{105.804\,232-105.510\,494}{2\times0.000\,5\times105.657\,223}=2.78$$

228. 答案：A

解析：无需计算，麦考利久期为 10 年，因为这是零息债券。如果按年计复利，修正久期 modified duration 为 $D^*=10/(1+10\%)$，接近 9 年。

229. 答案：A

解析：先列表列出现金流，再进行计算。

Period t	Payment C_t	Yield y	$PV_t = C_t/(1+y)^t$	tPV_t
1	100	5.00	95.24	95.24
2	100	5.00	90.71	181.41
3	1 100	5.00	950.22	2 850.66
Sum:			1 136.16	3 127.31

得到麦考利久期是2.75，修正久期是2.62。

230. 答案：B

解析：对于支付息票的债券，Macaulay久期略低于到期时间的1.5年。因此，B选项将是一个很好的猜测。当然我们也可以通过计算来得到精确结果。

231. 答案：C

解析：修正久期＝麦考利久期/(1＋市场利率)，即ModDur＝MacDur/(1＋r)

232. 答案：C

解析：有效久期(effective duration) $= \dfrac{PV_{-} - PV_{+}}{2 \times \Delta\text{Yield} \times PV_0} = \dfrac{(127.723 - 122.164)}{2 \times 0.3\% \times 125.482} =$ 7.38.

233. 答案：C

解析：久期最接近2.83。麦考利久期(MacDur)是收到现金流量的加权平均值。权重是与每期利息和本金现值相对应于全价的比重。

Period	Cash Flow	Present Value	Weight	Period×Weight
1	6	5.555 556	0.058 575	0.058 575
2	6	5.144 033	0.054 236	0.108 472
3	106	84.146 218	0.887 190	2.661 570
	求和	94.845 806	1.000 000	2.828 617

因此，债券的麦考利久期(MacDur)为2.83。

234. 答案：A

解析：资产价值的变化将减少：$500 000 000×7×0.005＝$17 500 000，而负债价值的变化将减少：$400 000 000×5×0.005＝$10 000 000。所以股权价值下降750万美元。

235. 答案：A

解析：投资组合的美元久期是：$D^* P = \sum x_i D_i^* P_i = +8 \times 2.5 \times \$90\,000 - 6 \times 3.0 \times \$110\,000 + 12 \times 3.3 \times \$120\,000 = \$4\,572\,000$。投资组合价值的变化是 $-(D^* P)(\Delta y) = -\$4\,572\,000 \times 0.0025 = -\$11\,430$。

236. 答案：B

解析：有效久期 Effective duration (ED) = $\frac{PV_{-} - PV_{+}}{2 \times \Delta \text{Yield} \times PV_0}$

无论对于有没有内嵌期权 embeddedoptions 的债券都适用，比如可赎回债券(callable bonds)或可回售债券(putable bonds)。

237. 答案：D

解析：假设收益率曲线是平行移动的，则预期的价格变化是：$\Delta P = -P \times \Delta y \times D$。其中，$P$ 是当前价格或净现值，Δy 是产量变化，D 是久期。在其他条件相同的情况下，收益率曲线向下变动对债券价值绝对值变化的影响更大(价格增长更高)。收益率曲线向上平行运动使债券更便宜，但价格变化会稍小一些。

238. 答案：D

解析：当利息不固定时，债券久期与到期日无关。在下一个重置日时，FRN 的利率按当时的市场利率设定。那时，票据的市场价值将等于票面价值。久期和价格波动风险仅与下一次重置日的时间有关。

239. 答案：B

解析：对于收益率曲线的非平行移动，可以使用 key rate duration 关键利率久期进行衡量，债券在每一个年限都有一个 key rate duration。

240. 答案：C

解析：永久债券的久期不取决于息票率，而只取决于收益率(注：永续债券的麦考利久期 = $(1 + y)/y$)。因此，A 和 B 的久期必然相同。当然，债券 A 的价格只是债券 B 的一半。

241. 答案：C

解析：较高的久期一般与现金流延迟支付的倾向相关联。例如，期限较长，较低的息票率和较少的付息次数，以及较低的市场收益率，因为这些都会增加未来支付的相对权重。

242. 答案：B

解析：对于固定息票率的债券，即使期限不断增加，久期也不会是无限的，而是逐步接近于永续债的久期。

243. 答案：A

解析：9 年期债券(5 号)的期限较短，因为到期日为最短的 9 年。1 和 2 的差别是支付利息的频率，半年付息的债券比一年付息的久期短。1 和 4 的差别是收益率。收益率越低，未来现金流权重越大，4 的久期更长。零息债券的久期最长。

所以，顺序是 5-2-1-4-3。

244. 答案：C

解析：10 年期收益率的 10 个基点变化到 20 年期收益率线性下降至 0，因此。每年减少 1 个基点，并导致 14 年收益率增加 6 个基点。

245. 答案：B

解析：Effective Duration = (520 - 370) ÷ (2 × 0.01 × 450) = 16.67。

246. 答案：C

解析：零息债券的价格永远低于票面金额，看涨期权不会被执行，所以久期是 10 年。

247. 答案：C

解析：麦考利久期与债券到期收益率负相关。

248. 答案：A

解析：基准利率上升，看跌期权价值上升，行权的结果是以平价卖出债券，从而降低了债券价格相对于基准利率变化的敏感度，即有效久期下降。

249. 答案：D

解析：资产组合的修正久期是各个债券修正久期基于市场价格的加权平均。

100 000 + 200 000 + 300 000 = 600 000

$6.42 \times 1 \div 6 + 9.44 \times 2 \div 6 + 11.38 \times 3 \div 6 = 9.91$

250. 答案：A

解析：资产组合的久期，需要假设组合中的所有债券同时同向移动，比如同时移动 100 个基准点 basis point(即收益率曲线 yield curve 的一个平行移动)。很多时候因为不同的债券有不同的到期日，信用风险以及含权情况不同，收益率曲线并不是平行移动的。在这样的情况下，portfolio duration 不适用。

251. 答案：A

解析：向上倾斜的利率期限结构说明远期利率高于即期利率，或者短期利率将会上升。短期利率比长期利率增长得快，说明收益率曲线比较平。

252. 答案：D

解析：Money Duration = AnnModDur × PVFull = 5.22 × 95.00 = 495.90。

253. 答案：B

解析：$PVBP$ 接近 0.064 8。price value of a basis point 的公式为：$PVBP = [(PV_-) - (PV_+)] \div 2$

将到期收益率降低一个基点至 4.99%会导致债券价格为 85.849 134：

$PV_- = 3 \div (1 + 0.0499)^1 + \cdots + (3 + 100) \div (1 + 0.0499)^9 = 85.849134$

将到期收益率提高一个基点至 5.01%会导致债券价格为 85.719 638：

$PV_+ = 3 \div (1 + 0.0501)^1 + \cdots + (3 + 100) \div (1 + 0.0501)^9 = 85.719638$

所以 $PVBP = [(85.849134) - (85.719638)] \div 2 = 0.06475$

254. 答案：B

解析：由于存在 convexity effect，discount rate 下降导致的债券价格上升大于 discount rate 上涨导致的债券价格下降。

255. 答案：C

解析：凸度指债券到期收益率发生变动而引起的债券价格变动幅度的变动程度。凸度是债券价格对收益率的二阶导数，用于衡量债券久期对利率的敏感性。在价格—收益率出现大幅度变动时，它们的波动幅度呈非线性关系，由久期作出的预测将有所偏离，凸度就是对这个偏离的修正。

256. 答案：B

解析：effective convexity 公式：

$$\text{convexity} = \frac{BV_- + BV_+ - 2 \times BV_0}{BV_0 \times \Delta y^2}$$

$=(100+97-2\times 98)\div(98\times 0.012)=102$

257. 答案：C

解析：预期百分比价格变动接近 1.78%。在给定到期收益率变化的情况下，债券的凸度调整百分比价格变化通过以下方式估算：

$\Delta PV \approx (-D\times\Delta y)+[0.5\times C\times(\Delta y)^2]$

$\approx[-7.020\times(-0.0025)]+[0.5\times 65.180\times(-0.0025)^2]$

$=0.017754$, or 1.78%

258. 答案：B

解析：预期百分比价格变化接近 −3.49%。在给定到期收益率变化的情况下，债券凸度调整后的百分比价格变化通过以下方式估算：

$\Delta PV \approx (-D\times\Delta y)+[0.5\times C\times(\Delta y)^2]$

$\approx(-7.140\times 0.005)+[0.5\times 66.200\times(0.005)^2]$

$=-0.034873$, or -3.49%

259. 答案：D

解析：收益率波动的期限结构向下倾斜，说明短期收益率波动大于长期收益率波动，因此长期收益率波动更稳定。

260. 答案：D

解析：价格风险(price risk)指市场利率波动，在投资期限结束时，未到期债券的出售价格可能低于预期的价值甚至低于面值，因而形成价差损失的可能性。

再投资风险(Reinvestment risk)指在投资期间，债息或偿还本金因市场利率波动后，不能以原先的目标收益率进行再投资，因而产生的利差损失的可能性。

债券免疫策略通过设计投资组合，使得组合中的资产面临的价格风险与再投资风险能冲抵，维持投资组合的期末价值不低于预期的资产价值，具体方法为设定投资组合的 Macaulay 久期与设定的投资计划期间维持相等。

261. 答案：C

解析：麦考利久期减去投资期限得出 Duration Gap。

一个正的 Duration Gap 意味着市场价格风险占据主要地位，

一个负的 Duration Gap 意味着再投资风险占主要地位。

262. 答案：A

解析：Macaulay Duration = modified duration × (1 + YTM) = 12.5 × 1.08 = 13.5

Duration gap = Macaulay duration − investment horizon = 13.5 − 8 = 5.5

263. 答案：A

解析：久期反映债券价格相对于利率变动的敏感程度。

264. 答案：B

解析：$I/Y=8/2=4$；$FV=100$；$N=24$；$PMT=0.05/2\times 100=2.50$；$PV=V_0=77.13$

$I/Y=7/2=3.50$；$FV=100$；$N=24$；$PMT=0.05/2\times 100=2.50$；$PV=V_-=83.94$

$I/Y=9/2=4.50$；$FV=100$；$N=24$；$PMT=0.05/2\times 100=2.50$；$PV=$

$V_+ = 71.01$

$D = \text{effective duration} = (V_- - V_+)/[2V_0(\Delta y)]$

$= (83.94 - 71)/(2 \times 77.13 \times 0.01)$

$= 8.38 \text{ years}$

265. 答案：B

解析：杠铃投资组合(Barbell portfolios)通常包含较大的凸度，可用于对冲较大凸度的负债。

266. 答案：A

解析：选项 B 正确，因为可赎回债券空头等价于普通债券空头和看涨期权多头的组合。选项 C 正确，因为看跌期权有利于投资者，所以它的收益率低。选项 D 正确，因为反浮动利率债券的久期更长。

267. 答案：B

解析：选项将两个具有相同期限的投资组合做比较。杠铃型投资组合由短期债券和长期债券组成。子弹型投资组合只有中期债券。因为凸性是付息时间的二次函数，长期债券在杠铃型投资组合中产生了巨大的凸性，比子弹型投资组合的凸性大。

268. 答案：D

解析：有效久期 Effective duration $(ED) = \dfrac{PV_- - PV_+}{2 \times \Delta Yield \times PV_0}$

$= (935 - 875)/2 \times 905 \times 0.005 = 6.63$

269. 答案：C

解析：隐含期权债券存在负凸度，当利率上升，债券发行发倾向于行权并赎回债券，形成债券价格上限，因此债券价格上升速度降低。

270. 答案：B

解析：可赎回债券是一个期权空头，会产生负的凸性。选项 C、选项 D 中涉及的普通债券，以及 puttable bond 都有正的凸性。

271. 答案：D

解析：不可提前赎回债券具备正凸度，含权债券具备负凸度。

272. 答案：A

解析：有效久期 Effective duration $(\text{ED}) = \dfrac{PV_- - PV_+}{2 \times \Delta Yield \times PV_0}$

适用于内嵌期权 embeddedoptions 的债券，如可赎回债券(callable bonds)或可回售债券(putable bonds)。

273. 答案：B

解析：coupon 越高，convexity 越低。

274. 答案：B

解析：可赎回债券的价值等于普通债券的多头减去债券看涨期权，可回售债券的价值等于普通债券的多头加上债券看跌期权，可赎回债券(callable bond)给了发行人一个权力，所以价格低，收益率就会比较高；可售回(puttable bond)给了投资者一个权力，价格高，收益率就会比较低。

275. 答案：C

解析：资产组合的久期是各个债券久期基于市场价格的加权平均。

276. 答案：C

解析：每张债券的市场价格是通过票面金额乘以市场价格除以 100 得到的。市场价格乘以久期得到美元久期 8 584.1 万美元。最终算出 DV01 是 8 584 美元。

Bond	Price	Par	Market Value	D*	DD
A	101.43	3	3.043	2.36	7.181
B	84.89	5	4.245	4.13	17.530
C	121.87	8	9.750	6.27	61.130
Sum					85.841

277. 答案：B

解析：For the 6% bond，$N=20\times2=40$；$I/Y=6\div2=3$；$PMT=5\div2=2.5$；$FV=100$；$CPT\rightarrow PV=88.4426$. For the 6.01% bond，$N=20\times2=40$；$I/Y=6.01\div2=3.005$；$PMT=5\div2=2.5$；$FV=100$；$CPT\rightarrow PV=88.3365$. $P_0-P_1=88.4426-88.3365=0.1061$. 注意：本题假设收益率上升 1 bp。如果假设收益率下降 1 bp，则 DV_{01} 为 0.106 3。

278. 答案：A

解析：投资组合的美元久期为：$1\times10+9\times10=100$ 美元。乘以 0.01 和 1.65，得到 1.65 美元。

279. 答案：C

解析：收益率下降，债券价格上升；距离到期日时间越长，价格波动性越大。

280. 答案：A

解析：固定收益投资工具直接受到利率风险影响，其他市场间接受到利率风险影响。

281. 答案：C

解析：由于凸性与付息时间的平方呈正比，债券的凸性主要由流入未来的现金流决定。Ⅰ是正确的，因为 10 年零息债的现金流只有一个，而付息债券会降低凸性。Ⅱ是错误的，因为这个债券在未来 10 年都有现金流，导致久期更大，凸性更大。Ⅲ是错误的，因为凸度和时间的平方成正比。Ⅳ是错误的，因为有些债券，如 MBS 或可赎回债券，具有负凸性。Ⅴ正确，因为付息债券的凸性一定为正。

282. 答案：A

解析：投资组合的 DVBP 是 \$1 100，期货价值是 \$25，所以比率是 1 100/25 = 44。

283. 答案：B

解析：卖空的合约数是 $N^*=-\dfrac{(D_S^*S)}{(D_F^*F)}=-(7.8\times10\,000\,000)/[8.4\times(95.0625)\times1\,000]=-97.7$，或者 98 份合约。CTD 和久期相关，别的数字和本题无关。

284. 答案：A

解析：首先算出资产和负债的美元久期，以百万为单位，分别是 33 016(4 000 ×

8.254) 和 34 125(5 000 × 6.825)。负债的美元久期超过资产，利率下降会导致赤字恶化。Albert 应该买利率期货对冲风险。合约数应该 = (34 125 − 33 016) ÷ (68 336 × 2.146 8/1 000 000) = 7 559。

285. **答案：A**

解析：收益率与债券价格负相关，较大收益率波动引起较大价格波动幅度，它们的波动幅度呈非线性关系，由久期作出的预测将有所偏离，凸性就是对这个偏离的修正。

286. **答案：A**

解析：不含权债券具有正凸度。即利率下降时，债券价格以加速度上升，利率上升时，债券价格以减速度下降。

287. **答案：C**

解析：Since the bond is selling at par, its yield = coupon rate = 8%, $V_0 = Par = 100$, $I/Y = 7.00$; $FV = 100$; $N = 12$; $PMT = 0.08 \times 100 = 8$; $PV = V = 107.94$。

Since the call price is 102 which is lower than 107.94, we use $V_- = 102$,

$I/Y = 9.00$; $FV = 100$; $N = 12$; $PMT = 0.08 \times 100 = 8$; $PV = V_+ = 92.84$。

$$\begin{aligned}\text{Duration} &= (V_- - V_+)/2V_0(\Delta y)\\ &= (102 - 92.84)/(200 \times 0.01)\\ &= 4.58\end{aligned}$$

288. **答案：C**

解析：不含权债券具有正凸度。即利率下降时，债券价格以加速度上升，利率上升时，债券价格以减速度下降。

289. **答案：B**

解析：当利率下降时，具有负凸性的债券价值将会以递减的速度增加。利率风险是指只能以低于当前水平的利率再投资的风险。抵押贷款支持证券(MBS)可能具有负凸性，因为当利率下降时，抵押贷款所有者将为较低利率再融资。从而提前偿还本金并增加 MBS 投资者可能产生的利率风险。可赎回债券(Callable bonds)与 MBS 类似，因为如果利率下降，则债券可能被提前赎回(本金可能会比预期更快地返还给投资者)，从而导致更高水平的利率风险。高收益债券(high-yield bond)可能表现出负凸性，因为它们是低信用债券，息票率往往很高；因此当利率下降时导致较大利率风险(因为投资者必须以较低的利率再投资，这类似于 MBS 和可赎回债券)。随着利率下降，高收益债券发行人更倾向于再融资债务，降低融资成本。

290. **答案：A**

解析：在价格—收益率出现大幅度变动时，它们的波动幅度呈非线性关系，由久期作出的预测将有所偏离，凸性就是对这个偏离的修正。

291. **答案：C**

解析：
$$\begin{aligned}\Delta P &= -[D^* \times P](\Delta y) + 0.5\,[C \times P](\Delta y)^2\\ &= -[8 \times 100](0.0025) + 0.5[150 \times 100](0.0025)^2\\ &= -2.000000 + 0.046875\\ &= -1.953125。\end{aligned}$$

292. **答案：A**

解析：低利率条件下，发行人倾向于对隐含期权的债券行权，以更低成本重新融资，从而形成债券价格上限，因此价格－收益率关系为 concave。

293. 答案：A

解析：PVBP = initial price − price（利率变化一个基点）

Initial price：	Price with change：
$FV = 1\,000$	$FV = 1\,000$
$PMT = 80$	$PMT = 80$
$N = 18$	$N = 18$
$I/Y = 9\%$	$I/Y = 9.01$
$CPT\ PV = 912.443\,75$	$CPT\ PV = 911.627\,1$

$PVBP = 912.443\,75 - 911.627\,1 = 0.82$（$PVBP$ 一般都用正数表示）

294. 答案：B

解析：凸度是价格相对于收益率的二次导数，与 maturity 平方呈正比，与 coupon 反向相关，与收益率变化负相关。

295. 答案：A

解析：久期就是债券价格相对于债券收益率的敏感性，用来衡量债券的利率风险的。

296. 答案：A

解析：对于没有隐含期权的债券来说，存在正凸度，即利率下降时，债券价格以加速度上升，利率上升时，债券价格以减速度下降。

297. 答案：B

解析：美国国债不可提前赎回，具有正凸度。

298. 答案：B

解析：久期(Duration)反映了债券价格与收益率之间的线性关系。因为真实关系不是线性的，所以要进行凸度调整。当凸度较高时，在预测给定利率变化的债券价格时，仅使用久期将不太准确。期限短的债券通常凸性也较低。

299. 答案：A

解析：PVBP 的含义是相对于初始价格，如果市场收益率上下波动一个基点时，债券价格的变动值，两者负相关。因为 PVBP 就是 DV01。

300. 答案：A

解析：effective convexity 公式：

$$convexity = \frac{BV_{-} + BV_{+} - 2 \times BV_0}{BV_0 \times \Delta y^2}$$

以 100 bps 为例，$BV_0 = 100$

$I/Y = 7.00$；$FV = 100$；$N = 10$；$PMT = 0.08 \times 100 = 8$；$PV = V_{-} = 107.02$

$I/Y = 9.00$；$FV = 100$；$N = 10$；$PMT = 0.08 \times 100 = 8$；$PV = V_{+} = 93.58$

convexity = $(107.02 + 93.58 - 200)/(100 \times 0.01^2) = 60$

301. 答案：B

解析：对于没有隐含期权的债券来说，存在正凸度，即利率下降时，债券价格以加速度上升，利率上升时，债券价格以减速度下降。选项 A 错的原因，在于利率上升时，高凸性的债券的敏感性下降。

302. 答案：A

解析：对于没有隐含期权的债券来说，存在正凸度，即利率下降时，债券价格以加速度上升，利率上升时，债券价格以减速度下降。

303. 答案：A

解析：对于没有隐含期权的债券来说，存在正凸度，即利率下降时，债券价格以加速度上升，利率上升时，债券价格以减速度下降。

304. 答案：B

解析：$N=20$；$I/Y=4.45\div 2$；$PMT=500\div 2$；$FV=10\,000$；$CPT\ PV=10\,440.05=V_-$。

$N=20$；$I/Y=4.55/2$；$PMT=500/2$；$FV=10\,000$；$CPT\ FV=10\,358.33=V_+$；

$N=20$；$I/Y=4.50/2$；$PMT=500/2$；$FV=10\,000$；$CPT\ PV=10\,399.09=V_0$。

$$\text{Duration}=\frac{PV_- - PV_+}{2\times\Delta Yield\times PV_0}=\frac{10\,440.05-10\,358.33}{2\times 0.000\,5\times 10\,399.09}$$

305. 答案：C

解析：凸度的计算：

$$\text{convexity}=\frac{BV_- + BV_+ - 2\times BV_0}{BV_0\times\Delta y^2}$$

$$=\frac{10\,440.05+10\,358.33-2\times 10\,399.09}{10\,399.09\times 0.000\,5^2}$$

$$=76.93$$

306. 答案：C

解析：Percentage price change $=[-\text{duration}\times\Delta y\times 100]+[(1/2)\times\text{convexity}\times\Delta y^2\times 100]=-7.86(0.002)100+(0.5)76.93(0.002)^2(100)=-1.556\,6$

307. 答案：B

解析：向上倾斜的利率曲线可以用对短期收益的偏好来解释，长期利率必须比短期利率更大才行，不选选项 A。向上倾斜的收益率曲线也可以由人们预期未来更高的利率或更高的通货膨胀来解释，不选选项 D。改善信贷条件将减少违约率，使利率期限结构更平，不选 C。只有预期的利率下降不会导致收益率曲线向上倾斜。

308. 答案：B

解析：假定是：收益率曲线的小幅平行移动。选项 A、选项 C 都忽略了移动的幅度，选项 D 应该把 highly 改成 perfect，并加上小幅移动。

309. 答案：A

解析：对于没有隐含期权的债券来说，存在正凸度，即利率下降时，债券价格以加速度上升，利率上升时，债券价格以减速度下降。

310. 答案：D

解析：有效久期 Effective duration (ED) $=\dfrac{PV_- - PV_+}{2\times\Delta Yield\times PV_0}$

$$=(118-114)/(2\times 0.01\times 116)=1.7$$

311. 答案：C

解析：key rate duration 假设只有几个关键期限的 spot rate 发生改变。

312. 答案：C

解析：7 年期收益率相对于 20 年期收益率线性下降到 0，因此 20 bp 变动相当于每年下降 20/13 bp。$20\ \text{bp} - (10 - 7) \times 20/13 = 15.4\ \text{bp}$。

313. 答案：A

解析：$2.78/1.67 \times 100 = 166$

314. 答案：D

解析：债券收益受到邻近的 Keyrate 影响，周围利率受关键利率的影响。

315. 答案：B

解析：bucket shift approach 假定收益率曲线平行移动。

316. 答案：A

解析：Forward-bucket 01s 首先对不同期限结构的 forward rate 进行移动，然后计算新的 bucket 的 PV 和原来 PV 之间的差额。

317. 答案：A

解析：key rate duration 假设只有几个关键期限的 spot rate 发生改变，而 bucket shift 则假设每一个不同期限的 forward rate 都发生改变，更适合于 swap 资产组合。

318. 答案：A

解析：关键利率久期反应资产组合对于利率变动的敏感情况，可以近似用关键期限的价值变动代表整个资产组合的价值变动。

319. 答案：B

解析：bucket shift approach 假定收益率曲线在每个 bucket 内部是平行移动的。

320. 答案：A

解析：bucket shift approach 假定收益率曲线在每个 bucket 内部是平行移动的。

321. 答案：A

解析：邻近的 Key rate 会影响 3 年期债券收益。

322. 答案：C

解析：在过去 50 年中，拉丁美洲每年至少占外汇违约的 60%。事实上，在过去的 200 年里，拉丁美洲一直处于主权违约的中心。

323. 答案：D

解析：2001 年，阿根廷在本国货币债务和美元债务同时违约。A 是错误的，因为分散化的投资组合不可能亏损这么多。B 错误，因为这些基金以 80%的价格投资于以美元计价的资产。C 错误，因为即使当地货币部分全部亏损也无法解释投资组合高达 40%的损失。如果基金购买了信用保险，就不会损失这么多。D 正确，基金有以阿根廷为对手方的信用风险。

324. 答案：B

解析：人们不仅要考虑国家对外国银行和投资者的债务，还要考虑国家在评估违约风险时欠其本国公民的金额。养老金承诺和医疗保健承诺较高的国家违约风险较高。税收越大，一个国家偿还债务的能力就越强。经济多元化的国家更有可能获得稳定的税收收入。

325. 答案：A

解析：关于政治风险，政治风险的一个组成部分是风险与不连续风险的连续性。偏民主国家的风险是连续的，但通常很低。相比之下，偏独裁国家的风险是不连续的（即政策变化不那么频繁，但往往更严重）。关于经济增长生命周期，成熟的市场和公司风险更低。关于法律风险，产权保护和争议解决的速度会影响违约风险。关于经济结构，对经济中单一商品或服务的过度依赖会增加一个国家的风险敞口。

326. 答案：C

解析：主权违约后往往发生急剧的货币贬值，主权违约之后，GDP会下降0.5%～2.0%，主要的下降发生在违约之后的一年内，主权违约之后会发生贸易战，C选项，违约的国家的信用评级会下降1个评级或2个评级。

327. 答案：C

解析：Market-based spreads比评级更灵活。随着债券交易的发生，债券收益率会上升和下降，违约风险利差（default risk spread）也会发生变化，反映了市场对风险的看法。而计算违约风险利差，必须有无风险利率。违约风险利差是不稳定的，利差的变化可能会受到与主权债务违约风险无关的变量的影响。地方债的利率中有可能反映了对不同货币膨胀的预期，并不代表无风险利率，所以不能进行比较。

328. 答案：B

解析：At-the-point approach就是在商业周期的低谷，银行降低债券或公司评级，但这样会限制公司信贷，对恢复增长造成不利影响。相反，在商业周期顶峰，银行将升级债券或公司评级，造成过多风险。

329. 答案：B

解析：评级变化对股票价格的影响可能会有所不同，具体取决于变化的原因和方向。通常，降级会导致股价下跌。鉴于公司倾向于比坏消息更容易发布好消息，股票价格通常预期升级，信用评级下降会导致债券价格下降。

330. 答案：D

解析：Moody's评级中用的1，2，和3对应S&P评级中用的+和－。其中，1代表+；3代表－。

331. 答案：C

解析：内部评级的一个问题是银行在更新和改变评级方面往往滞后。

332. 答案：C

解析：债券升级可能会引起价格上涨，YTM下降。流动性风险也会降低，因为债券现在将被归类为投资级债券，养老金计划和共同基金可以投资。如果评级升级是由于公司的财务状况改善，则可能会增加赎回风险（如果是可赎回债券），但不能完全确定。

333. 答案：C

解析：评级为Baa3及以上的债券被视为投资级别，评级为Ba1及以下的债券为非投资级别。

334. 答案：D

解析：穆迪（Moody）和标准普尔（Standard and Poor）等评级机构指定债券评级。技术性违约通常是指发行人违反了债券契约中的其他条款，例如债务比率，而不是未支付利息或本金。如果违约，持有人（贷方）可通过法律诉讼或谈判收回部分或全部投资。回收的百分比称为回收率。市场通过更高或更低的市场收益来反映这些评级。市场通常会要求降级债券的收益率更高（风险溢价增加），因此价格可能会下跌。

335. 答案：B

解析：债券价格更受评级变动的影响。对股票价格的影响是混合的（例如，降级有时也可能会导致更高的股票价格）。

336. 答案：C

解析：在穆迪的评级方案中，Aaa，Aa，A 和 Baa 是投资级评级。最高的投机等级评级为 Ba。

337. 答案：C

解析：穆迪对 Baa 或以上的评级被视为投资级别。

338. 答案：D

解析：任何低于 BBB 的投资都被认为是投机性的。因此，标准普尔指定的最高（风险最低）投机评级为 BB。Ba 是穆迪指定的风险投机评级最低的评级。

339. 答案：A

解析：AAA，AA，A 和 BBB 的评级被视为标准普尔信用评级方案的投资级别。

340. 答案：B

解析：像S&P和 Moody 这样的评级机构在评级表明债券和公司的相对违约率方面有相当好的记录。

341. 答案：A

解析：at-the-point approach 这种方法更可能是顺周期性的。例如，如果出现经济衰退，由此导致的降级可能会进一步降低经济活动。此外，评级和贷款政策的变化可能会滞后于经济周期，因此，当经济陷入低谷并即将开始扩张时，银行可能限制企业所需的信贷渠道。

342. 答案：B

解析：At-the-point approach 适用相对较短的时间内进行信用评级，而 Through-the-cycleapproach 则侧重于更长的时间范围。

343. 答案：A

解析：Through-the-cycle 方法的目的是让更长的时间来平均化商业周期所造成的影响。

344. 答案：C

解析：经济资本（Economic capital）代表银行预留的资本，以弥补非预期损失（Unexpected Loss）。一般来说，经济资本将合理地设定在非预期损失水平之上。例如，两个标准偏差以上。

345. 答案：C

解析：BBB 及 BBa 以上的评级被称为投资级。

346. 答案：B

解析：企业信用评级上升，信用差价风险下降，违约风险降低，债券价格上升。

347. 答案：D

解析：B 级债券的第一期违约概率为 2%。在第二期，违约概率是第 1 期存活的概率和第 2 期的违约概率之积。第 2 期违约概率 = (0.03 × 0.00) + (0.90 × 0.02) + (0.05 × 0.14) = 2.5%。因此，两期累计违约概率 = 2% + 2.5% = 4.5%。

348. 答案：A

解析：$EL = AE \times EDF \times LGD$ = ($ 150 000.000) × (0.02) × (0.80) = $ 240 000。

349. 答案：D

解析：非预期损失是实际损失远大于预期的部分。

350. 答案：B

解析：Expected Loss = Exposure × Loss given default × Probability of default

Loss given default = 1 − recovery rate

351. 答案：A

解析：预期损失计算如下：$EL = AE \times LGD \times EDF$。因此，增加 LGD 直接增加预期损失。默认使用率(UGD)计算为提款(draw down)百分比。因此，增加提款将增加 UGD。由此可见，预期损失也将增加。

352. 答案：A

解析：降低回收率(recovery rate)会增加违约损失率，根据 UL 的计算公式，UL 会增加；$UL = EA \times \mathrm{sqrt}(PD \times \sigma_{LR}^2 + LR^2 \times \sigma_{PD}^2)$。

353. 答案：C

解析：$ 200 000 = $ 5 000 000 × (1 − RR) × 5%，所以 the recovery rate = 20%，loss given default = 80%。

354. 答案：B

解析：$UL = (15\,000\,000) \times \sqrt{0.02 \times 0.03^2 + 0.8^2 \times 0.05^2} = 603\,366$

355. 答案：D

解析：两年后 Expected value = (10)(1 − 0.03)(1 − 0.03) ($ 1 000 000) = $ 9 409 000，所以两年的累计损失为 $ 10 000 000 − $ 9 409 000 = $ 591 000。

356. 答案：B

解析：随着同等加权投资组合中资产数量的增加，每个资产的方差(或标准差)对投资组合的波动性的贡献会减少。以下等权重投资组合方差的等式说明了这些要点：

$$\sigma_p^2 = \frac{\bar{\sigma}^2}{N} + \frac{N-1}{N}\overline{\mathrm{COV}} = \frac{\bar{\sigma}^2}{N} + \frac{N-1}{N}\bar{\rho}\,\bar{\sigma}^2$$

357. 答案：C

解析：随着同等加权投资组合中资产数量的增加，资产之间的相关性增加(即协方差和相关性)。以下等权重投资组合方差的等式说明了这些要点：

$$\sigma_p^2 = \frac{\bar{\sigma}^2}{N} + \frac{N-1}{N}\overline{\mathrm{COV}} = \frac{\bar{\sigma}^2}{N} + \frac{N-1}{N}\bar{\rho}\,\bar{\sigma}^2$$

358. 答案：C

解析：非预期损失(Unexpected loss)定义为预期或平均损失水平的标准差。

359. 答案：C

解析：银行必须持有资本储备(即 economic capital)以缓冲非预期损失并继续经营。

360. 答案：C

解析：提高回收率(recovery rate)和降低违约概率(probability of default)将减少预期损失。降低/提高回收率和降低/增加违约概率是模糊的。降低回收率和增加违约概率肯定会增加预期损失。

361. 答案：C

解析：降低回收率(recovery rate)和增加违约概率(probability of default)将增加预期损失;提高回收率和降低违约概率可能会增加或减少预期损失,具体取决于因素的相对变化。

362. 答案：A

解析：Expected loss 用以下公式计算：$EL = AE \times LGD \times EDF$,所以增加 LGD 会增加预期损失。

363. 答案：A

解析：自上而下(top-down)的操作风险测量技术可能适用于确定公司的整体经济水平,但是不太适用于在特定环节中通过设计业务流程来降低公司操作风险。也就是说,他们没有对实施操作风险控制进行任何调整,也不能帮助管理层找到业务过程中的具体弱点。另外,自上而下的技术也是事后的(backward looking)的,难以及时反映可能影响运营损失分布的风险环境因素变化。

364. 答案：C

解析：如果管理层开始关注某一类特定损失,则未来可能不太可能在将来重复这类特定的损失。

365. 答案：D

解析：专属保险公司(Captive insurers)经常是为避税目的的离岸的全资子公司,用于在收入中扣除所有未来预期损失的现值(这些损失可能源于今后几年的索赔)。这允许自我保险公司(self-insurers)在损失实际发生之前扣除损失。通过增加管理和控制操作风险的成本,原则上结果与自我保险相同。或有信用额度也是一种自我保险形式,在发生损失时提供流动性,而不是在预期亏损的情况下建立现金储备(cash reserves)。

366. 答案：B

解析：RCSA 不提供风险测量(risk measurement)和识别(identification)的独立验证(independent verification)。

367. 答案：A

解析：通常使用泊松分布描述损失发生的频率。

368. 答案：D

解析：Ⅰ是模型问题，Ⅱ是内控问题,两者都属于操作风险。

369. 答案：D

解析：对于标准化方法,CBI 必须对特定业务线应用不同的 beta 因子。这些金额乘以过去 3 年期间的年平均总收入。零售银行业务(retail banking),商业银行业务(commercial banking)和投资银行业务(investment banking)的 beta 因素分别为

12%，15%和 18%

零售银行业务的年均总收入：(380 + 344 + 326)/3 = 350 million

商业银行的年均总收入：(712 + 645 + 599) /3 = 652 million

投资银行业务的年均总收入：(846 + 777 + 687)/3 = 770 million

操作风险资本要求：0. 12(350) + 0. 15(652) + 0. 18(770) = 278. 4 million

370. 答案：A

解析：操作损失不易映射到风险因素。Operational VaR 可以通过严重程度和频率分布来计算。蒙特卡罗技术可用于除正态分布之外的其他分布。

371. 答案：C

解析：记分卡数据(scorecard data)的使用通常可以帮助获得比使用历史损失数据更低的资本金需求。

372. 答案：D

解析：记分卡数据(scorecard data)是通过调研机构的业务经理开发的。

373. 答案：A

解析：压力测试可以覆盖个人，整个机构或机构内各种子级别的范围。压力测试结果可能会排除重要因素。例如，投资组合，负债和风险敞口等。压力测试应该包含各种风险和风险之间的关系，并检测可能对机构产生负面影响的风险集中度和风险原因。压力测试可适用于短期和长期。

374. 答案：B

解析：高级管理层对董事会负责，并在董事会授权下实施压力测试。这需要建立健全的政策和程序，以确保遵守这些活动，审查和协调压力测试活动，并纠正任何问题。其余选项都是董事会的职责。

375. 答案：D

解析：适当的治理和控制对于压力测试尤其重要，因为压力测试需要大量的假设或正确估计极端事件和条件的不确定性。

376. 答案：D

解析：模型验证的主要问题可以通过专家判断，灵敏度分析，模拟技术，强调稳健的压力测试，以及对内部或外部模型进行基准测试来解决。应仔细选择基准(benchmark)，以确保可以恰当地反映机构的风险和敞口。

377. 答案：B

解析：审计师应具有足够的知识和技术专长，以发表意见，不能依赖于其他部门。

378. 答案：C

解析：除Ⅳ之外，所有其他说法都是正确的，因为假设太多的情景反而会使得了解相关资产得风险敞口变得更加困难。

379. 答案：D

解析：压力测试使用从历史数据中观察到的极值或从蒙特卡罗模拟中生成的极值。峰度为 3 和偏度为 0 实际是正态分布，即使是 99% confidence level 下的 VaR 这样的假设也不太满足压力测试的要求。

380. 答案：B

解析：VAR 的一个主要缺点是它无法描述极端市场事件可能发生的损失。VAR 的这个缺点需要由压力测试来补充。VAR 是一种前瞻性(forward-looking)措施，而不是一种后瞻性(backward-looking)措施。

381. 答案：D

解析：预测行业、机构或产品的结构性转变并非是一线业务经理的擅长。最近的历史数据无法提供足够完整的历史记录来识别关键变量的极端变动。如果是多维压力测试(multi-factor stress test)，则往往会考虑因素之间的相关性。

382. 答案：D

解析：股指一天下跌 2%不算极端事件。

383. 答案：B

解析：压力测试不能用于消除所有风险。

384. 答案：A

解析：压力测试用于评估极端事件的影响。Ⅱ说得是回溯测试，而不是压力测试。

385. 答案：C

解析：压力测试的主要目的是模拟非常规事件的影响，而非常规事件。这些影响可能不会反映在典型的 VAR 计算中。然而，压力测试容易受到分析师的有意和无意的影响，经常会忽略一个因素的变化如何影响另一个因素的价值，有时也不考虑风险因素的同时不利变动的情况。

386. 答案：B

解析：stress-testing 一般会假设风险因子的较大变化，所以局部估值法不太合适，而要使用全局估值方法。

387. 答案：D

解析：压力事件可能会重复发生；Stressanalysis 是 Scenarioanalysis 的特例；Stressanalysis 的假设并非 unpractical。

388. 答案：A

解析：先求日波动率 $25\%/\sqrt{252}=1.57\%$，然后再求变化 $150\times1.57\%\times4=\$9.45$。

389. 答案：D

解析：在次贷危机之前，压力测试方法常常假设风险是由已知和非随机过程产生的。基差是现金和期货市场之间价格(或利率)的差异，基准风险是基差变化的不确定性。或有风险一般是指可能因特定事件而产生的风险。

390. 答案：D

解析：计算风险市场价值(VaR)并不是压力测试的必须部分。其他选项都是压力测试的一部分。

391. 答案：D

解析：银行声誉的好坏很显然会影响银行的流动性；市场剧烈变化可能会降低银行买卖资产的能力，从而对其流动性产生不利影响；如果证券化市场状况恶化，银行的资产可能无法证券化；当市场流动性发生问题时，基差可能会发生重大变化，那么对冲可能会失效，导致重大损失。

392. 答案：C

解析：巴塞尔委员会曾表示：对于金融危机中表现相较好的银行，他们的高级管理层对压力测试的开发和运作往往保持一个积极的态度……但大多数银行的压力测试并没有进行足够的内部辩论或质疑以前的假设。因此，巴塞尔委员会建议对压力测试中曾经使用的假设进行挑战，以确保压力测试能够更好地捕捉当前市场条件下极端情景的可能性。

393. 答案：B

解析：监管者有必要质疑压力测试的使用，防止这些压力测试产生不切实际的结果或与银行的风险偏好不一致。

394. 答案：D

解析：如果对冲工具和资产不一致或相关性不为 1 的话，就会出现基差风险（basis risks）。如果对冲工具到期时间和资产套期保值时间不一致，也会存在基差风险。

395. 答案：B

解析：reverse stress testing 的三个阶段是：outcome，events and hedging。

396. 答案：A

解析：风险敞口加大同时违约概率也会增加，这属于错向风险（Wrong-way risk）；公司发行（write）自己股票的看跌期权属于错向风险；期货头寸开盘和平仓之间基差的变化称为基差风险（basis risk）；由于资产价值（或类别）下降而导致流动性枯竭的情况成为资金流动性风险（funding liquidity risk）。